MEDIEVAL PHILOSOPHY:

From St. Augustine to Nicholas of Cusa

READINGS IN THE HISTORY OF PHILOSOPHY

SERIES EDITORS:

PAUL EDWARDS, The City University of New York, Brooklyn College

RICHARD H. POPKIN, University of California, San Diego

The Volumes and Their Editors:

GREEK PHILOSOPHY: THALES TO ARISTOTLE
Reginald E. Allen

GREEK AND ROMAN PHILOSOPHY AFTER ARISTOTLE
Jason L. Saunders

MEDIEVAL PHILOSOPHY: FROM ST. AUGUSTINE TO NICHOLAS OF CUSA
John F. Wippel and Allan B. Wolter, O.F.M.

THE PHILOSOPHY OF THE SIXTEENTH AND SEVENTEENTH CENTURIES
Richard H. Popkin

EIGHTEENTH-CENTURY PHILOSOPHY
Lewis White Beck

NINETEENTH-CENTURY PHILOSOPHY
Patrick L. Gardiner

TWENTIETH-CENTURY PHILOSOPHY: THE ANALYTIC TRADITION
Morris Weitz

In Preparation:

TWENTIETH-CENTURY PHILOSOPHY: THE SPECULATIVE TRADITION

Medieval Philosophy:

From St. Augustine to Nicholas of Cusa

Edited by
John F. Wippel
Allan B. Wolter, O.F.M.
The Catholic University of America

THE FREE PRESS
A Division of Macmillan Publishing Co., Inc.
NEW YORK
Collier Macmillan Publishers
LONDON

PHILOSOPHERS DEPICTED ON THE COVER ARE:
UPPER LEFT, ROGER BACON; UPPER RIGHT, MOSES MAIMONIDES;
LOWER LEFT, ST. THOMAS AQUINAS; LOWER RIGHT, ST. AUGUSTINE.

THE FREE PRESS
A Division of Macmillan Publishing Co., Inc.
866 Third Avenue, New York, New York 10022

Collier Macmillan Canada, Ltd.

Library of Congress Catalog Card Number: 69-10043

Printed in the United States of America

Printing number
12 13 14 15 16 17 18 19 20

PREFACE

In this series of readings in the history of philosophy, the present volume is unique in that it attempts to span some twelve centuries of human thought, a time period fully half as long as that covered by the remaining seven books conjointly. Some norms for narrowing down this vast field were obviously needed, and the very meaning of *medieval* or *Middle Ages* suggested to the editors one such limitation. For these terms originally referred to the civilization that gradually evolved in Western Europe after the barbarian invasions and Moslem conquests had isolated it from Byzantium and Eastern culture. Yet this only partially facilitated the editors' task, because even in the Latin West the twilight of learning was neither so long nor so complete as the Renaissance thinkers who coined these pejorative labels would have us believe. With the scores of new translations following in the wake of a wealth of new primary source material on this period, it was no small chore to select suitable samples for a volume of this size. In the main, we sought to avoid duplicating material found in other collections or anthologies and even to include a fair number of items as yet unavailable in English translation. Where duplication seemed warranted in virtue of the importance of the material, we tried to provide a more readable translation.

Whether or not we succeeded in achieving our aims, we are deeply grateful to all those who assisted us in any way. Particular thanks are due to Father Ignatius Brady for making available unedited manuscript material on Odo Rigaud; to Fathers J. A. Arnold, Owen Blum, and Hermigild Dressler and to Professor Richard Frank for undertaking special translations for this work; to Professor George F. Hourani for his helpful suggestions as well as for the items he permitted us to reprint; to Monsignor John K. Ryan for his kind advice and encouragement; to Librarians Carolyn T. Lee and David J. Gilson for their gracious providing of information; to Mary Linda Clarke for typing the manuscript; and to Mary R. Homan for assisting with the Index.

WASHINGTON, D.C.

JOHN F. WIPPEL
ALLAN B. WOLTER, O.F.M.

CONTENTS

INTRODUCTION

In any discussion of the philosophy of the Middle Ages the question inevitably arises as to when to begin and end. Difficult though it is to assign any fixed dates, certain periods and/or figures stand out as turning points. Thus the closing of the Athenian Academy by the Emperor Justinian in 529 is often cited as the official ending of the period of pagan philosophizing. However, one particular aspect that sets medieval Western philosophy apart from its Greco-Roman antecedents is the fact that the various thinkers of medieval Christendom believed in a definite divine revelation. Found in Scripture and tradition, this revealed message was accepted on faith and regarded as an unquestioned source of truth. As Christian scholars began to philosophize and to reflect on the content of their religious belief, questions as to the proper relationship between faith and reason were bound to be raised.

If one accepts this as a distinguishing feature of Western medieval philosophy, a case might be made for carrying its history all the way back to the first apologists and fathers of the Church. However, practical considerations suggest that we set the limits of this volume somewhat more narrowly. Nevertheless, one mighty figure towers above all others in the patristic age in terms of his influence on subsequent philosophy and theology. No apology need be offered for beginning this set of readings with St. Augustine, in the light of his own thought and his commanding influence throughout the medieval period.

When we turn to the close of our period the same difficulty appears again. One might conclude with the decline of scholasticism and the rise of nominalism in the fourteenth century. But if we have found it good to begin with one pivotal figure who was not himself a "scholastic," it seems advisable to conclude with another who was also not a scholastic. Nicholas of Cusa was turned against scholasticism by the sterile school disputes of its declining years. He is another personality who seems to mark the end of one period and the beginning of another and who might therefore be included either in a volume on Renaissance philosophy or in this set of readings in medieval philosophy.

Period of Transition

ST. AUGUSTINE

Augustine was born in 354 in North Africa of a Christian mother and a pagan father and was thoroughly trained in rhetoric. He died as Bishop of Hippo in 430. His thought is profoundly personal and reflects his own search for wisdom. His early acceptance of the Manichean position, his flirtation with the skepticism of the New Academy, his subsequent contact with Neoplatonism, and his conversion to Christianity—all of these factors are reflected in the problems he subsequently considered and, as regards Neoplatonism and Christianity, in many of the solutions he embraced. Neoplatonism enabled him to account for evil as an absence of good rather than to persist in the dualistic solution offered by the Manicheans. It also freed him from Manichean materialism by suggesting to him the spiritual nature of the divine. After his conversion to Christianity his pursuit of wisdom became a pursuit of Christian wisdom. Because of this there can be no real separation between his philosophy and his religious thought. Together they form one great whole. He is not interested in constructing a philosophical system but rather seeks a deep understanding of the soul and of God. Granted this, however, one can at least single out certain elements in his thought of paramount importance to the history of philosophy.

His period of skepticism had left him highly concerned about man's capacity to know anything with certainty. Not surprisingly, then, one finds a detailed critique of the skeptical position in his writings. It is sometimes objected that the senses are unreliable. Nevertheless, replies Augustine, the fact that things perceived *appear* to us cannot itself be denied. Error may occur when one attempts to distinguish between reality and distorted images of reality and, because of this, one may wish to limit sense knowledge to the level of opinion. But absolute doubt proves to be completely self-defeating when one turns inward toward oneself. At the very least we are certain that we exist and that we know that we exist. Someone may suggest that we are deceived even here. Augustine replies:

"But if I am deceived, I exist!" His refutation of skepticism is interesting from another point of view, in that it reveals the inwardness of his thinking. It implies that the mind enjoys direct and immediate knowledge of at least one spiritual reality: itself. Further, in turning within, the mind discovers certain truths such as those of mathematics and other "eternal verities," which are necessarily and unchangeably true. Finding that he cannot account for their necessary and immutable character either by appealing to the world of sense or to the soul itself, since all such things are subject to change, Augustine concludes to some kind of contact with eternal and unchanging truth by any mind in possession of such truths. Thus, in knowing ourselves and in knowing that we can know truth we are led to affirm the existence of God.

The above procedure illustrates his primary concern with the soul and God. At the same time it raises questions as to the nature of the soul's contact with God as the source of all truth. Although commentators on Augustine disagree as to the meaning of his theory of divine illumination, there seems to be some consensus on the following points. Divine illumination is not to be equated with mystical experience. At least in his mature writings, Augustine rejects any theory of learning by recollection or by means of innate ideas. He does not maintain that the human intellect directly contemplates eternal truths in the divine essence. Illumination cannot be reduced to or equated with the action of an Aristotelian agent intellect. Because of a certain lack of clarity and fuller development in Augustine's writings, positive description of divine illumination is more difficult. However, he seems to mean that in some way the eternal truths found in the divine mind are the source of truth in our minds without thereby implying that we enjoy any direct vision of the divine ideas.

Augustine's theory of *rationes seminales* further emphasizes the creature's dependence on God. All things were created by God in the beginning. Many, however, were not created in perfect and completed form, but rather remain latent ("in seed") until their time comes to emerge into fully formed beings. The implication is that no second cause can really bring new forms into being. It can only aid a form already existing in its seminal principle to emerge. As in the theory of divine illumination, the role of the created agent is minimized so as to emphasize divine omnipotence.

Augustine's concentration on the soul raises certain problems as to its mode of union with the body. He knows that the body is also part of human nature, but he frequently describes man as a soul using a body. The soul is not related to the body as form is to matter. The union is rather one of "vital attention." The soul watches over the body and is present as a whole in all parts of the body. Since the lower cannot act on the higher, the body cannot act on the soul. To account for sensation he suggests that because of this "vital attention," the soul is aware of any changes that the body or bodily senses undergo. It is not the body, however, but the soul that senses. He also strongly stresses the will and its power of choice. Love is viewed as the power that moves the will in its act of choice. To choose rightly one must love rightly. To love rightly is to love God above all else. For this Augustine insists upon the need for divine grace. Love is also the driving force of society. Two loves lead to his well-known distinction between two societies or two cities. Those who love God are united in the City of God. Those who love the world and self rather than God are united in the City of the World.

BOETHIUS

Boethius (480-524/25) appeared at a critical moment in the history of Western philosophy, when the classical age was coming to an end and the very survival of learning was soon to rest in the hands of the emerging "barbarian" nations. At this time translation and preservation of the learning of the past became critically important. Boethius was the ideal figure to exercise the choice necessary for this situation. Trained in Greek philosophy and in the Greek language, he proposed to translate Plato and Aristotle into Latin and to establish their fundamental harmony. Although an untimely death prevented completion of this ambitious project, his translations and commentaries on Aristotle's logical works and on Porphyry exercised considerable influence during the early Middle Ages. In addition, his widely read *Consolation of Philosophy* and a series of short theological treatises were to have their effect for many centuries to come. His own thought betrays both Aristotelian and Platonic-Neoplatonic influences, but his first loyalty seems to be the latter tradition.

In his second commentary on Porphyry's *Isagoge,* he repeats Porphyry's three questions about the nature of universals and thus passes on this problem to subsequent philosophy. As regards genera and species (universals), Porphyry had refused to attempt to answer these questions: (1) Do they subsist or are they found only in the understanding? (2) If they do subsist, are they corporeal or incorporeal? (3) If they are incorporeal, do they subsist in sensible things or apart from them? Boethius then proposes an answer along Aristotelian lines in accord with the commentator Alexander of Aphrodisias. But after contrasting this solution with Plato's view he declines to decide between them. This refusal to accept the Aristotelian theory as his own is not surprising in the light of the basically Platonic theory of knowledge in his *Consolation of Philosophy*. In addition to the influence of his translations and commentaries and independent writings, Boethius is also known as the "first of the scholastics" for another reason. In his theological treatises he expressly states his intention to subject the content of revealed truth to rational investigation insofar as such is possible. This explicit effort at harmonious conjunction of faith and reason was to become one of the distinguishing marks of scholasticism.

If we must wait some three centuries after the death of Boethius for the appearance of another outstanding philosophical personality, nevertheless, the dark ages notwithstanding, the medievals did not have to begin from an absolute vacuum. Although the greater part of the philosophical literature of the ancient world was lost to them until the great translation movement of the twelfth and thirteenth centuries, a considerable amount of Neoplatonism was preserved through the writings of Augustine, Boethius, and Pseudo-Dionysius, and some knowledge of Aristotelian logic through the translations and commentaries of Boethius. ("Pseudo-Dionysius" and "Pseudo-Denis" are standard ways of referring to the unknown author of a number of letters and treatises on theology that exercised considerable influence on medieval philosophy. Because of the author's reference to himself as a disciple of St. Paul these writings were mistakenly attributed to Dionysius the Areopagite, mentioned in the *Acts of the Apostles*. As a consequence they enjoyed immeasurable prestige during the medieval period. In fact they seem to have been written *ca.* 500 in Syria by a Christian heavily influenced by the earlier Christian Platonism of men such as Gregory of Nyssa, Clement of Alexandria, and Origen, as well as by Neoplatonism in general and by Proclus in particular.)

The Carolingian Renaissance

During the years following the death of Boethius, troubled political circumstances made it impossible for philosophy to flourish in the West. The monasteries became the major centers for preserving something of the cultural heritage of the past. However, a revival of learning was inaugurated under Charlemagne (768-814). He gathered together a number of scholars at his court and, under the guidance of Alcuin of York, a palace school was organized there. Legislation was enacted to implement a reform of learning on a much broader scale throughout the kingdom. Although this movement was primarily devoted to the dissemination of knowledge rather than to original thinking, two figures of philosophical interest were associated with the Carolingian revival. Fridugis (Fredegisus), formerly a student of Alcuin at York, eventually joined him as a teacher in the palace school. While there he composed his rather curious letter *On Nothing and Darkness,* wherein he defends the reality both of nothingness and of darkness.

JOHN SCOTUS ERIUGENA

Both the trace of Platonism and the feeble effort at originality found in Fridugis became more marked in the case of John Scotus Eriugena, head of the palace school of Charles the Bald in the mid-ninth century. Skilled to some degree in the Greek language, Eriugena's reading of certain Christian Neoplatonist theologians and his translations of Pseudo-Dionysius left their mark on his thought. His *De divisione naturae* stands out as perhaps the most original work of the period from Augustine to Anselm. Far from being an effort at "pure philosophy," this work might rather be regarded as another example of "Christian wisdom." It draws heavily upon Neoplatonic philosophical themes in its search for insights into the content of revelation, and results in a powerful synthesis of philosophical and theological speculation.

The term "Nature" in its title applies to the whole of reality, including God. Nature falls into four subdivisions: (1) nature which creates but is not created, (2) nature which creates and is created, (3) nature which is created and does not create, (4) nature which neither creates nor is created. The first and fourth divisions both refer to one and the same God, regarded in the first instance as creating and in the fourth as the end to whom creatures return. Considered in the first way, the eternal and inaccessible perfection of God is stressed to such an extent that he is said to be incomprehensible not only to us but even to himself. In order to save God from such a lack of self-knowledge the second division of nature becomes necessary, i.e., the region of the divine Ideas (nature which creates and is created). Because the Ideas are eternal manifestations of the divine and exist in the Word they enable God to know himself. At the same time they serve as exemplars or archetypes for all created things. Yet they are not fully coeternal with God because they are created by him. This description of the divine Ideas as created raises its own problems but at least seems to provide a defense for Eriugena against the charge of pantheism. If he distinguishes between God and his Ideas, then he can hardly be suspected of having failed to distinguish between God and the creatures that derive from these Ideas.

The created universe (nature which is created and does not create) is a further instance of the process whereby the many derive from the one. As we have seen, Ideas are produced by God (the Father) in the Word. All things are already implicitly contained in the Ideas as in their universal prototypes. The more general Ideas divide into genera, the genera into subgenera, and the subgenera into species. From the species result the individuals of our universe. These give some hint as to the perfection and beauty of the creator and thus likewise constitute imperfect theophanies. In the most fundamental sense, man is the Idea of man in the divine mind. All individual men are contained therein. The division of the sexes and the present division of the material world into countless individuals resulted from original sin. When man eventually returns to God (nature which neither creates nor is created) the material universe will also recover the unity it lost through the sin of man. For all things visible will be transformed into things intelligible, and the intelligibles into God, but not "by a confusion of their essences or substances."

The Eleventh Century

ST. PETER DAMIAN

After another period of cultural "darkness" almost approaching the period prior to the Carolingian Renaissance, conditions improved again in the late tenth and eleventh centuries. Interest in dialectics began to develop in the early eleventh century and soon the stage would be set for the controversy concerning universals and the interventions of Abelard. However, this newly awakened interest in dialectics encountered opposition on the part of some, such as St. Peter Damian (1007-72), one of the leading reformers of his time. Apparently disturbed by the excesses of certain Christian writers who had raised reason and dialectic above the revealed mysteries, Peter used his own rhetorical skills to argue against secular learning and philosophy with a vehemence that reminds one of Tertullian.

ST. ANSELM

More balanced in his attitude towards the use of human reason is Anselm of Canterbury (1033-1109). Heavily influenced by Augustine, Anselm recognizes two sources of knowledge in faith and reason. Against the rationalistic excesses of certain dialecticians he makes faith his point of departure: "I believe in order that I may understand." Unlike Peter Damian, however, he then seeks to understand the content of faith with the aid of human reason, insofar as such is possible. In this effort he exhibits surprising confidence in the mind's ability to provide necessary reasons even for mysteries such as the Trinity and the Incarnation.

Anselm is best known to the history of philosophy for his arguments for the existence of God, in particular for his so-called ontological argument. However, it should not be forgotten that before developing this particular argument in his *Proslogion,* he had already presented some more-or-less Platonic proofs in his *Monologion.* In brief, they are based on our observation of varying degrees of perfection in the things about us and on the Platonic principle that wherever one finds different things sharing in the same perfection to a greater or lesser degree, it can only be because they participate in a source which is that perfection itself. The argument in the *Proslogion* is presented as the result of his search for a less complicated formulation. Its point of departure is the believer's description of God as that than which no greater can be conceived. Even one who says that there is no God will understand the meaning of these words. Even he must admit that there is in his intellect something than which no greater can be conceived. But if it is such that no greater can be conceived, it cannot exist solely in the mind. To exist in reality would be greater. Hence, to say that that than which no greater can be conceived exists only in the mind is to maintain both that it is and yet is not that than which no greater can be conceived. To avoid such a contradiction one must admit that it also exists in reality.

As the subject of more-or-less continuous controversy in the subsequent history of philosophy, the argument's validity was questioned by one of Anselm's own contemporaries, the monk Gaunilon. His objections and Anselm's replies throw further light on the latter's understanding of the argument.

The Twelfth Century

Reference has already been made to the great interest in dialectics in the eleventh and early twelfth centuries. This is not surprising when one recalls that in reading Aristotle, Latin thinkers of the time were restricted to his logical works. With the exception of a partial translation of Plato's *Timaeus,* the great Platonic and Aristotelian works on physics, metaphysics, psychology, ethics, and politics remained unavailable. If there was a revival of Platonism early in the twelfth century (cf. the School of Chartres), it derived primarily from secondary sources. During the twelfth century itself Plato's *Meno* and *Phaedo* were also translated. As regards Aristotle's logical works, only those included in the "old logic" *(Categories* and *Peri Hermeneias)* were used until early in the twelfth century, when the "new logic" *(Prior* and *Posterior Analytics, Topics, Sophistic Refutations)* also became available. Other major philosophical sources of the time included some commentaries on Aristotle's logical works by Porphyry and Boethius, and writers such as Seneca, Cicero, Macrobius, Chalcidius, Pseudo-Dionysius, Nemesius *(De natura hominis),* Augustine, Boethius, John Scotus Eriugena, and Anselm.

Because of the absence of the "physical" works of Aristotle, even the scientific world view of antiquity had been forgotten. A rather naive conception of the physical makeup of the universe had won wide acceptance and is carefully described for us by Honorius of Autun in his *De imagine mundi,* written *ca.* 1122.

PETER ABELARD

The great interest in dialectics in the early twelfth century is clearly reflected in the controversy concerning universals and in the career of Peter Abelard (1079-1142). Abelard is important to subsequent moral philosophy for having emphasized the role of intention in determining the moral value of an act. His theological work *Sic et non* contributed to the development of the scholastic method, with its citation of authorities for and against a given question before his own discussion of the same. But Abelard was first and foremost a logician. As regards the theory of universals, his teachers had included Roscelin (a leading nominalist) and William of Champeaux (an outstanding realist). Roscelin seems to have represented one extreme by asserting that universals are nothing but vocal utterances *(flatus vocis)* i.e., nothing but the sounds we make in uttering them. William at first defended an extreme kind of realism according to which universals are substances or essences common to all individual members of a class or species. If authoritative historians of medieval philosophy today apply labels ranging from nominalism to conceptualism to moderate realism in assessing Abelard's own solution to the problem, this may result in part from the fact that he rejects both the nominalism of Roscelin and the realism of William. At the same time, due undoubtedly in large measure to the lack of Aristotle's works on psychology and metaphysics, his solution also suffers from the absence of any well-grounded metaphysics or psychology to serve as its support.

PETER LOMBARD

Peter Lombard's *Book of Sentences* was completed in 1157 or 1158. It is primarily a theological work, in large measure a compilation with extensive citations from the fathers and contemporary writers brought to bear on particular questions. In apparent reaction against the extreme usage of dialectics by some in theology, the work deliberately avoids extensive philosophical speculation. Nonetheless, it is also heavily influenced by the more systematic approach recently introduced into theology by Peter Abelard, by the method of the latter's *Sic et non,* and by certain rules he had developed there for reconciling differences between authorities. Lecturing on the *Sentences* was to become a regular part of the formation of Masters of Theology at the University of Paris in the thirteenth century, thus contributing to its widespread usage throughout the medieval period.

RICHARD OF ST. VICTOR

In the twelfth century, the Augustinian Abbey of St. Victor, outside the walls of Paris, became a center of intensive intellectual activity, above all for the study of theology and the contemplative life. Its outstanding representatives were Hugh of St. Victor (d. 1141) and Richard of St. Victor (d. 1173). Richard's theology is centered on a loving contemplation of the divine reality. At the same time he shows a great desire to provide "necessary reasons" for many of the things he holds on faith. Here he continues the Anselmian tradition of "faith seeking understanding." In his *De Trinitate* he notes that authority frequently tells us that there is one God, that he is eternal, uncreated, immense, and almighty, that he is both one and three. Yet Richard cannot recall reading how these points are proved. Consequently, he offers rational argumentation not only to establish the existence and unity of God and to derive the divine attributes, but also to prove the eternal necessity of the Trinity. However, Richard's arguments for the existence of God are of greater philosophical interest than his trinitarian speculations. A first argument starts from the contingency of the objects of our experience, a second from their varying degrees of perfection, and a third from the idea of possibility and the need for a ground of that possibility.

The New Philosophical Literature

Approximately midway through the twelfth century, an intensive translation activity began which introduced to the Latin West a wealth of hitherto unknown scientific and philosophical material. Two channels should be distinguished in this process, the one consisting of Latin translations of Greek originals directly from the Greek, the other of Latin translations of both Greek and Arabic originals from the Arabic. Due to the presence of Greek texts and the Greek cultural heritage in lands conquered by the Arabs during the early period of Islam, many of the scientific and philosophical texts of Greek antiquity had been translated either directly from the Greek or from Syriac translations of Greek originals into Arabic. Thus almost all of the Aristotelian corpus known to us today had been preserved in the Arabic-speaking world together with influential pseudo-Aristotelian treatises such as the *Theology of Aristotle* (part of the *Enneads* of Plotinus) and the *Liber de causis* (based on Proclus). As a consequence, the Aristotle known by Arabic philosophy was highly Neoplatonized. Leading centers for translation from Arabic to Latin developed in Sicily and Spain. A major part of the Aristotelian corpus was translated from Arabic into Latin in the twelfth and early thirteenth centuries along with the *Liber de causis* and a number of important philosophical works originally written in Arabic by men such as al-Kindī, al-Fārābī, Avicenna, and Averroës. If the Arabic-Latin translation activity was heavier at first, in the thirteenth century direct Greek-Latin translation gradually gained the ascendancy. During the twelfth and thirteenth centuries Plato's *Phaedo* and *Meno,* the *Elementatio physica* and *Elementatio theologica* of Proclus, various Greek commentaries on Aristotle, and new and revised texts of Aristotle himself were translated from the Greek.

The discovery of this vast body of philosophical literature was to have an enormous impact on the West. In the case of Aristotle, Christian scholars were now faced with a powerful metaphysical, psychological, and ethical system that treated of ultimates concerning man and the universe and the "divine" without any possible concern for the demands of Judeo-Christian orthodoxy. Aristotelian views on the eternity of the world, divine knowledge, and divine providence, and difficulties in the Aristotelian text concerning the nature of the human soul would almost certainly lead to tension and controversy. With Avicenna, Averroës, and Maimonides, however, one finds philosophies developed within religious cultures based on a divine revelation. To this extent their situations more closely paralleled that of the Christian philosophers in the West.

The two outstanding philosophers of medieval Islam were Avicenna (d. 1037) and Averroës (d. 1198). In Avicenna one finds a fusion of Aristotle and Neoplatonism. The latter clearly appears in his theory of the necessary creation or emanation of lower reality from God, the One. From the One only one can come. Hence, the first creature, the first Intelligence, is necessarily and eternally produced by God. In knowing God it produces a second Intelligence. In knowing itself as necessarily produced by God it produces the soul of the first heavenly sphere. In knowing itself as a possible being it produces the matter or body of that same sphere. This same process is repeated by the second Intelligence, resulting in the production of a third Intelligence and of a second heavenly sphere, and so on, until one arrives at the ninth Intelligence and the ninth sphere. The Intelligence governing this last sphere creates a tenth Intelligence, the agent intellect. The agent intellect is the cause of the various forms found in matter in our universe *(Dator formarum)*, and at the same time illumines our individual "possible" intellects, thereby enabling us to grasp intelligible forms or essences. Avicenna's metaphysics exercised great influence on Latin scholasticism throughout the thirteenth century. His protests of Muslim orthodoxy notwithstanding, various features of his system caused alarm among Islamic theologians and among Christian thinkers of the West. Thus he defends an eternally and necessarily created universe. Realities below the level of the first Intelligence derive only mediately rather than immediately from God. God knows himself and in so doing knows all possible things, but only in a general or universal way. Divine knowledge of individual creatures as they exist in themselves seems to be severely threatened and, along with it, divine providence.

Averroës is justly famed for his commentaries on Aristotle and it was through these that he became known to the thirteenth-century scholastics. In other less technical works such as the *Incoherence of the Incoherence* and the *Decisive Treatise* he had defended philosophy against charges that it is opposed to the teachings of the Koran. In his commentaries he prides himself on following Aristotle as closely as possible. Consequently, he is far less subject to Neoplatonic influences than Avicenna and more closely approaches an authentic Aristotelianism. His theories, such as the eternity of the universe, and certain difficulties inherent in his efforts to account for divine knowledge of singulars were to alarm theologians of the 1260s and 1270s at Paris, and his views on the intellect would be even more sharply controverted. Avicenna had defended the unicity and the separated character of the agent intellect but had safeguarded human immortality by ascribing to individual men their own possible intellects, which were also spiritual powers. The thirteenth-century scholastics concluded from reading Averroës' commentary on Aristotle's *De anima* that he rejected the reality of both an individual agent and an individual possible intellect in the human soul. Finding no individual spiritual principle in man according to this theory, the scholastics concluded that it involved a denial of personal immortality. In the light of Averroës' defense of the resurrection of the body in another context, certain recent interpreters have suggested that this judgment may be unfair. A completely satisfying reconciliation of all texts on the point has yet to be presented.

Originally written in Arabic and then translated into Hebrew, Moses Maimonides' *Guide of the Perplexed* was also translated into Latin before 1240. It was directed to learned Jews who were troubled by apparent conflict between Greek philosophical science and their own religious beliefs, and the treatise clearly shows that, as in Christendom and in Islam, tensions also arose when Judaism was confronted with Greek and Arabic philosophy. In attempting to resolve such conflicts Maimonides displays a fine knowledge of Aristotle and the "philosophers." In cases of clearcut conflict between philosophical conclusions and the obvious meaning of a scriptural passage, one must determine whether or not the philosophical argument is demonstrative. If so, Maimonides would then allow for reinterpretation of the scriptural text in accord with proper exegetical methods. However, frequently enough the supposed philosophical conclusions have not been demonstrated. Thus many philosophers defend the eternity of the world. The obvious meaning of Genesis points to a temporal beginning for the cosmos. Upon examining the arguments offered by the philosophers, Maimonides finds that they are not demonstrative and that they were not so regarded by Aristotle himself. On the other hand, efforts by certain Muslim theologians to demonstrate the temporal origin of the universe have likewise remained inconclusive. Hence, in this case there is no reason not to follow the obvious meaning of Scripture. His position seems to anticipate that of Aquinas as regards philosophical efforts to demonstrate either the eternity or temporal origin of the universe, and one also finds strong foreshadowings of some of the "five ways" in Maimonides' arguments for the existence of God.

The Thirteenth Century

By the year 1200, Christian scholars in the West had already been confronted with a sizable portion of the ever-increasing wave of newly translated non-Christian philosophical literature. A series of decrees prohibiting members of the arts faculty at Paris from lecturing on Aristotle's books on natural philosophy and metaphysics *(libri naturales)* suggests that the process of absorbing and evaluating the new data was not always smooth. By 1240 or thereabouts, however, the prohibitions seem to have lost their practical effect. Thus one finds Roger Bacon lecturing on these books as a member of the arts faculty at Paris at about this time (*ca.* 1241-47). Nevertheless, although private consultation of these works was not prohibited, the bans do account for the surprising emphasis on Aristotle's logic and ethics to the neglect of his metaphysics and natural philosophy in the arts faculty until that time. During the same period, however, unencumbered by such restrictions, various members of the theology faculty at Paris made increasing use of Aristotle in their theological speculations.

More or less paralleling the entry of Aristotle and the other "philosophers" into Western circles was the rise of the universities. The oldest were Paris (*ca.* 1200), Bologna (*ca.* 1200), Oxford (*ca.* 1214), and Naples (1224), with Paris quickly becoming the leading philosophical and theological center. The arts faculty at Paris was an outgrowth of the older schools of liberal arts and served as a kind of preparatory school for the higher faculties, placing heavy emphasis on grammar and logic. During the course of the century, however, the purely propaedeutic character of its program seems to have changed and with the eventual acceptance of all of Aristotle's known works, it became more and more a faculty of philosophy. Early in the century the theology faculty was highly conservative in outlook, reacting against the use of dialectics in theology and preferring to concentrate on patristic and biblical studies. Fairly soon, however, considerable interest in speculative theology developed among many of its members, thereby making it an extremely important center for philosophical speculation, as well.

ROGER BACON

Reference has already been made to Roger Bacon's lectures on Aristotle's *libri naturales* at Paris in the 1240s. His relative youth notwithstanding, these early writings reveal penetrating insights into Aristotle's physical and metaphysical theory. Avicenna, Averroës, and Boethius are cited most frequently after Aristotle, with some rather harsh remarks at times reserved for Averroës. While commenting on Aristotle, however, Bacon was also heavily influenced by Neoplatonism as found in Avicenna, Avicebron (Solomon Ibn Gabirol, a Jewish philosopher of eleventh-century Spain and author of the influential *Fons vitae*), and the Pseudo-Aristotelian *Secret of Secrets* (mistakenly thought to be instructions by Aristotle for Alexander the Great). One finds him defending plurality of substantial forms and universal hylemorphism. According to this latter theory, even pure spirits and human souls are composed of form and a spiritual matter. Although Bacon had lectured on Aristotle at Paris, he became disenchanted with the rising scholasticism there and upon his return to Oxford, devoted himself for some years to the pursuit of experimental science and the study of languages. He was highly critical of certain developments in theology at Paris, in particular of the recently introduced custom of lecturing on the *Sentences* of Peter Lombard. He called for a return to the study of the Scriptures and a mastery of the biblical languages.

Bacon seems to have accepted Augustine's ideal of an all-embracing Christian wisdom, and he thus viewed philosophy as simply one step in its pursuit. This perfect wisdom is found in the Scriptures and "is to be unfolded by canon law and philosophy." Philosophy comes to us through a kind of divine revelation. God is the separated agent intellect for men and thus, as illuminating principle for particular human intellects, is the source of philosophical truth as well.

His *Opus Maius* concludes with a discussion of moral philosophy. In accord with the practical bent of his mind he subordinates all other human knowledge and all of speculative philosophy to it. However, he is perhaps best known for having extolled the values of experimental knowledge, to which a major portion of this work is devoted. Experience is either external (grounded on sense perception) or internal (a higher kind grounded on inner illumination according to its various stages). Although not a great experimental scientist, he devoted considerable attention to the possibilities of penetrating the secrets of nature by means of the experimental method. In addition to original contributions to optics, some of his insights as to future applications of science to nature are truly remarkable. Although he is far in advance of his times in these respects, his notions of theology link him to a bygone age. He seems to have been completely bypassed by efforts of contemporaries such as Odo Rigaud to construct a scientific theology. There is some debate among contemporary historians as to whether his philosophy should better be described as Augustinian or as Neoplatonic-Aristotelian. If Neoplatonic and Aristotelian influences abound, Augustinian elements are also present. His thought is fundamentally eclectic and thus reflects the formative stage of the philosophical efforts of the period.

ST. BONAVENTURE

With St. Bonaventure the early Franciscan school reaches its peak. One of the truly great theologians of all time, his thought manifests a richness and unity hitherto unknown in the scholastic era. Because he was first and foremost a theologian, because of the unity of his own theological synthesis, and because of his view of philosophy as a stage in man's pursuit of a unified Christian wisdom, it is difficult to discuss his philosophy apart from his theology. Although he clearly distinguished between the two, he refused to separate them in practice. His philosophy must be gleaned from his theological writings, where it appears insofar as it is of service to his overall religious purpose. The issue is further complicated by the fact that he never joined these various elements into a complete philosophical synthesis, as distinguished from his highly unified theology. Even in his earliest writings he indicates certain shortcomings of any pure or separated philosophy. Later, in the series of conferences delivered in 1267, 1268, and 1273 during the crisis provoked by Siger of Brabant and others in the arts faculty at Paris, his attitude towards Aristotelianism becomes considerably more severe.

Bonaventure tells us that his metaphysics is centered around three elements: emanation, exemplarism, and consummation. Emanation has to do with the procession of creatures from the Creator. As a Christian and a theologian, he defends the free creation by God of all lower reality as opposed to any Neoplatonic or Avicennian theory of necessary emanation. Moreover, he holds that a created universe cannot be eternal, differing from Aquinas on this point.

Exemplarism is the very heart of his metaphysics. The philosopher of nature may view things as originated by God. The moralist will be concerned with God as man's last end. Only the metaphysician considers God as exemplar cause of all creatures by noting that divine ideas serve as models or exemplar causes in his creative activity. Because Aristotle rejected Plato's ideas and any theory of exemplarism, he cannot be counted as a metaphysician, granted his preeminence in natural philosophy. Although Plato's theory of ideas was imperfect, Augustine was able to correct it by drawing upon St. John's Gospel and placing the divine exemplar ideas in the eternal Word of God. Once divine ideas are recognized, every creature may be viewed as bearing some degree of likeness to God, whether as shadow or as image or as similitude. Pursuing this Augustinian theme, Bonaventure also finds traces of the Trinity throughout creation. Here again, however, reason must be completed by faith. For if the philosopher can reason to the existence of a supreme spiritual reality, faith is needed for fallen man to recognize the various manifestations of the Trinity in creation.

Consummation means that creation not only comes forth from God and reflects him but that it fulfills its destiny by returning to him. Lower creation effects this return through man in his praise of and in his return to God. Man returns by leading an upright life grounded in faith and love. Knowledge is also involved in man's return. If natural reason begins by reflecting on traces of God in the external world and then turns inward to reflect on the soul, it is perfected by divine illumination.

Illumination introduces another distinctive aspect of Bonaventure's thought, his theory of knowledge, which combines Aristotelian and Augustinian themes. His view that the content of sensation derives from without is fundamentally Aristotelian. However, for the mind to pass any kind of judgment upon a sensible object, divine illumination is required, to provide a standard for judging. Agent and possible intellects enable one to grasp material things by the process of abstraction. However, they differ only as distinctive functions of one and the same intellect. The mind also may turn inward to discover the soul without depending on sense experience. But for it to arrive at certain knowledge, whether gained from within or from without, illumination is always necessary. Although we do not directly contemplate the divine Ideas, in some mysterious way our minds are illumined so as to enable us to judge in accord with them concerning the object in question.

Augustine's influence also appears in Bonaventure's theory of seminal reasons. Aristotle's matter-form theory undergoes modifications in that Bonaventure defends plurality of substantial forms, universal hylemorphism (including matter-form composition even of created spiritual realities), and a version of the "light metaphysics" originally developed by Robert Grosseteste (*ca.* 1168-1253) and the Oxford school, in which light becomes the most general and most basic of bodily substantial forms. There has been considerable discussion in recent times as to whether Bonaventure's philosophy is basically Aristotelian or Augustinian. His theology and his concept of Christian wisdom are surely in the Augustinian tradition. In his philosophy one finds Aristotelian and Augustinian and

Arabic-Neoplatonic elements joined together. All are placed at the service of theology in his pursuit of Christian wisdom.

ST. THOMAS AQUINAS

In the philosophical and theological thought of Thomas Aquinas one meets, perhaps, the most successful integration of Aristotelian philosophy and Christian thought of all time. In pursuing his vocation as a theologian, Aquinas judged it necessary to develop a coherent philosophical synthesis. His philosophy is to be found in a number of smaller philosophical treatises, in his detailed commentaries on Aristotle, and in his many theological writings. Quite aware of the distinction between philosophy and theology, he was also convinced of their ultimate harmony because of their common derivation from one divine source of truth. Hence, in addition to revealed mysteries and matters of purely scientific and philosophical interest, he also found other truths that are both contained in revelation and discoverable by human reason. If Aristotle is Thomas' greatest single philosophical source, it would be a gross oversimplification to reduce his philosophy to that of the Stagirite. In fact, one finds a major rethinking of Aristotle together with powerful Neoplatonic influences coming through such varied channels as Augustine, Boethius, the *Liber de causis* and Proclus himself, Pseudo-Dionysius, Avicenna, and Avicebron. Moses Maimonides and Averroës must also be kept in mind. His ability to unite so many seemingly disparate elements from such diverse sources into a highly unified and coherent whole is perhaps his greatest mark of genius.

The vast range of his thought precludes any adequate summary here. However, the following characteristics should be noted. His position on universals may be described as moderate realism. His theory of knowledge falls within the Aristotelian tradition. Intellectual knowledge arises by abstraction of intelligible content from data provided by sensation. Once this content has been abstracted by the agent intellect, it is impressed on a distinct power, the possible intellect. While it is the agent intellect that abstracts, it is the possible intellect that knows. Against the Augustinian tradition, then, Aquinas rejects any special illumination to account for human intellection apart from the abstracting action of the agent intellect itself. Against the "Averroistic" interpretation circulating among members of the arts faculty at Paris in the 1260s and

1270s, he insists that both agent and possible intellects are distinct powers found in the soul of every individual man, rather than being some kind of separated intellect for all humanity.

His philosophy of nature is basically Aristotelian. In fact it marks a return to a purer kind of Aristotelianism in that Neoplatonic and Stoic accretions such as plurality of forms, spiritual matter, and *rationes seminales* are rejected. He accepts the Aristotelian theory of matter-form composition of all corporeal reality and insists on the purely potential character of prime matter. Matter is related to form as potency is to act.

In his metaphysics one finds his most original insights. Having as its subject neither being-as-material nor being-as-quantified, but instead being-in-general *(ens commune)*, the metaphysics of Aquinas stresses the importance of *esse* (sometimes translated as existence), the act of being or that in virtue of which something is said to be. Here Thomas extends the Aristotelian theory of act and potency and applies it to *esse* itself. Regarded as the "act of all acts and the perfection of all perfections," *esse* is not self-limiting. It is unlimited of itself and thus finds its fullest realization in God, the self-subsistent being *(esse subsistens)* and pure act. To distinguish all created reality from God (and thus also to provide an answer for the ancient problem of "the One and the Many") Aquinas posits a radical composition of two distinct principles in all beings other than God, the composition of *esse* (existence) and essence which receives and limits *esse*. *Esse* is related to essence as act to potency. The degree of *esse* (and hence the perfection) of any finite being will be measured in accord with its correlative limiting and receiving principle, essence. Thus the essence-existence composition also serves as a foundation from the side of creation for Thomas' theories of a hierarchically structured universe and the dependence of all derived reality upon God by way of causal participation. The origin and dependence upon God is expressed in terms of efficient and exemplary causality. Creation's return to him is formulated through two descriptions of final causality: finality by assimilation, whereby creatures fulfill themselves by imitating him in the orders of being and action; finality by intellectual possession and love of God, which is immediately available to intellectual creatures and achieved by nonintelligent creation through intellectual beings.

Were one to stop here he might conclude that this metaphysics is basically Platonic and Neoplatonic. However, at almost every level Aristotelian principles are neatly joined with these non-Aristotelian themes. Thus the Aristotelian theory of act and potency is now generalized to find application in three great metaphysical compositions: essence-existence, matter-form, and substance-accident. The Aristotelian theory of the causes is expanded so as to be applied analogically to the creative action of God. The Aristotelian rudiments of analogy of being are raised from the level of substance-accident predication so as to admit of application to infinite being as well. Needless to say, the position of God is central in such a view of reality. Thus we find Aquinas proposing a number of arguments for his existence, the best-known formulation being the "five ways" found in the *Summa theologiae*. Not surprisingly, the relationship between creature and creator in the orders of being and action is also carefully investigated, as in his *Disputed Questions on the Power of God*.

In his philosophy of man there is a further combination of Aristotelian and Neoplatonic elements. Not content to divide man into two more-or-less independent entities, Thomas insists that soul is related to body as form is to matter, resulting in their substantial union. As in the rest of his natural philosophy, he also defends unicity of substantial form in man. Not content to sacrifice the spiritual nature of individual men, he insists on the spirituality of the human soul. Thus it is both the form of the body and a spiritual principle that survives destruction of the body.

SIGER OF BRABANT AND BOETIUS OF DACIA

In the middle 1260s Siger of Brabant and other members of the arts Faculty at Paris began to develop a radical form of Aristotelianism. Philosophers rather than theologians by profession, they regarded Aristotle as their model and frequently turned to Averroës and various Neoplatonic sources in interpreting him. Their movement is sometimes known as Latin Averroism and sometimes as Radical or Heterodox Aristotelianism. Siger's expressly stated aim was to determine what the philosophers had said about any problem he might be considering. Even while teaching a number of points in direct conflict with religious orthodoxy, he insisted on the firmness of his faith. Rather than reject his religious beliefs he maintained that while such conclusions necessarily resulted from human reasoning, the teachings of the Church were to be regarded as true in case of conflict. Neither he nor Boetius of Dacia defended the theory of double truth, sometimes ascribed to them, according to which something taught by faith and something contradicting this but established by human reason might both be regarded as true. Siger's heterodox views center around divine creative causality and the production of the universe with only the First Intelligence immediately created by God; eternity of the universe; unicity of the intellective soul for the human species resulting in the denial of both a personal agent and personal possible intellect and hence, of any personal spiritual principle in man; and, finally, the consequent rejection of personal immortality and of moral sanctions in the life to come. In December, 1270, the Bishop of Paris condemned thirteen propositions drawn from the teaching of members of the arts faculty. Thomas Aquinas reacted sharply to Siger in his *On the Unity of the Intellect against the Averroists.* In Siger's subsequent *De anima intellectiva* some commentators detect modifications of his earlier views on the human intellect in a more orthodox direction. Others find no such shift in the text.

Best known after Siger in this movement is Boetius of Dacia. His attitude toward philosophy and religious belief is well expressed in his *De summo bono.* Philosophical wisdom is extolled as the highest form of human life and reaches its summit in knowledge and love of God. His highly laudatory description of the philosophical life has led some to conclude that he was a sheer naturalist and rationalist. Yet, in the same treatise he refers to a higher happiness in the life to come, which we await through faith. He was cited by one manuscript as the principal defender of the propositions condemned in 1277; his name is also closely linked by other documents with that of Siger in the heterodox Aristotelian movement. Some of the condemned propositions appear to be taken literally from his writings. However, the possibility of giving them an orthodox reading in the light of their original context is defended by some today. In writings known and analyzed to date he appears to be less radical than Siger. But his unqualified praise of the life of philosophy must have offended many theologians at the time.

The condemnation of 1270 did not halt this movement of Radical Aristotelianism at Paris. In 1277 Pope John XXI asked the Bishop of Paris, Stephen Tempier, to investigate the situation. Apparently going beyond his mandate, Stephen assembled a commission of sixteen theologians who hastily drew up a haphazard list of 219 propositions. These were condemned on March 7, 1277. Directed in large measure against Siger, Boetius, and their party, they also extend to Aristotelianism in other forms and include some perfectly orthodox Thomistic theses. The prohibition was a local reaction on the part of certain churchmen and theologians against the autonomous concept of philosophizing fostered by Siger and his group and also marked the triumph of a Neo-Augustinian movement inspired by Bonaventure and founded by John Peckham (d. 1292). Although primarily directed against heterodox Aristotelianism, it also symbolizes a growing opposition to the balanced synthesis so recently worked out by Thomas Aquinas. Thomistic theses were also included in prohibitions at Oxford in 1277, 1284, and 1286.

That interest in the problem of the intellect and its relationship to the human soul continued is indicated by an anonymous work entitled "Beatitude and the Agent Intellect" and included in this volume. Written early in the fourteenth century, it not only reflects its author's interest in and familiarity with the earlier history of the problem, but also shows that thinkers in the decades following 1277, such as Henry of Ghent (d. 1293), Godfrey of Fontaines (d. *ca.* 1306), Durandus (d. 1334), and Dietrich of Freiberg (d. shortly after 1310), concerned themselves with it. In Henry of Ghent one meets a leading secular theologian with a broad command of philosophy who is an outstanding representative of the Neo-Augustinian reaction of the time. His influence on Duns Scotus is considerable.

Late Medieval Thinkers

JOHN DUNS SCOTUS

One of the greatest Franciscan thinkers of all time, John Duns Scotus (d. 1308) was a theologian by profession rather than a philosopher. Formed in the Augustinian-Franciscan tradition at Oxford and Paris and heavily influenced by Aristotle and Avicenna, his thought is too personal and too original to be reduced to any earlier tradition. In pursuing his vocation as a theologian he developed a highly sophisticated philosophy, in which he was much concerned with what human reason can determine about God and the soul. Granted that his ethics and natural philosophy are not without interest, he was first and foremost a metaphysician. With Avicenna he holds that metaphysics is the science of being and its transcendental attributes. Rather than restrict the transcendentals to those properties that are coextensive with being, Scotus distinguishes at least four classes: (1) being itself; (2) the three attributes coextensive with being, viz., one, true, and good; (3) a series of disjunctive attributes such as finite-or-infinite, contingent-or-necessary that are coextensive with being only when taken disjunctively; (4) pure perfections whose formal notion contains no imperfection. (The latter include those found in classes one and two, the higher member of each disjunction in class three, and attributes that may be predicated of God.)

Investigation of these transcendentals and their interrelationships eventually leads the metaphysician to consider the existence of that one being in which all pure perfection is found. Here Scotus seems to wish to unite the strongest points of earlier efforts in working out his detailed proof for God's existence. His discussion and rejection of an infinite series of essentially ordered causes and his effort to ground the argument on necessary premises are noteworthy. Rather than start from the actual existence of any contingent reality, he prefers to concentrate on that which is necessary about such an entity, its very *possibility*. The possibility of produced being eventually leads him to admit the possibility of an uncaused cause. For such a being to be possible, however, it must actually exist. It could not remain uncaused and still be possible if it did not exist. If this procedure leads to a first efficient cause it may also be used to establish a first in the order of ends and a first in the order of eminence. After showing that these three are one and the same, he concludes to the infinity of the first being. Discussion of God's existence introduces another central theme of his metaphysics. Scotus insists that the concept of being as applied to God and creatures is univocal rather than analogical. When applied to God or to creatures, being must be determined by some mode such as finite or infinite, created or uncreated. Underlying such predication and making it possible is a neutral notion of being which abstracts from all such modes and is found in every application of being. Denial of this sameness or common element of the concept of being, that is to say, denial of its univocal character, would render knowledge of God impossible.

Scotus is well known for defending the "formal distinction." Other thinkers had seen the need for some intermediate type between the real distinction and the purely logical or conceptual distinction. Scotus develops this intermediate distinction in his own way, however, arguing that if one and the same thing can produce different concepts of itself in the mind, this can only be so because of the actual presence of different "formalities" in the thing prior to the mind's consideration. (By "formality" he means an intelligible feature of a thing that is less than its total intelligible content.) This distinction obtains widely as, for instance, between the divine attributes, between the powers of the soul, and between the transcendentals, unity, truth, and goodness. For Scotus, all of these distinctions are less than real but more than logical.

Unlike most of the earlier Franciscans, Scotus rejects universal hylemorphism. Neither angels nor human souls are composed of matter and form. Against the Aristotelians, however, he does not regard prime matter as pure potentiality, but assigns some actuality to it. The human soul is the form of the body. But before receiving a spiritual form, matter must be informed by a "form of corporeity." To this extent Scotus is in agreement with earlier defenders of plurality of forms in man. The principle of individuation is not matter as quantified but rather is a formality known as "thisness," which renders particular and individualized the "common nature" found in the various members of a class. This common nature accounts for their resemblance to one another and of itself is neither universal nor individual. It is made universal by the mind and individual by "thisness."

Basically Aristotelian in his theory of knowledge, Scotus rejects Augustinian illumination and defends abstraction of universal concepts from sense experience. However, his description of the respective roles of agent and possible intellects in the knowing process differs from classical Aristotelianism. Against Aquinas he also allows for a direct intellectual intuition of the singular, although he may have wished to limit this to our awareness of our own acts of mind, will, and so on, reserving for the afterlife direct intellectual intuition of other objects.

Finally, mention should be made of his great stress on divine freedom and his highly original analysis of human liberty. He is sometimes regarded primarily as a forerunner of Ockham because of his critical attitude toward certain arguments regarded as probative by earlier thinkers. Scotus' ability as a speculative thinker merits for him a place among the greatest philosophical synthesizers of the thirteenth century.

Nonetheless, his keen powers of logical analysis, his critical skills, and his rigorous standards for demonstration also link him with Ockham and other thinkers of the fourteenth century.

WILLIAM OCKHAM

William Ockham (d. 1347) never developed a finished philosophical system. A theologian by training and interest, much of his philosophy is to be found in theological writings. He is not the builder of great metaphysical syntheses, as were Scotus and Aquinas. However, he is perhaps without parallel in the Middle Ages as a logician. His notion of scientific or demonstrative knowledge is extremely exacting, being understood in the strict sense as evident knowledge of a conclusion caused by evident knowledge of its necessary premises and the syllogistic process from which it follows. Although one may have evidence for and certitude about many other statements, they are not scientifically demonstrated unless they meet this test.

Central to his thinking is the conviction that all that exists outside the mind is singular and individual. If our knowledge of the external world begins with sense perception, intellectual cognition may be either intuitive or abstractive. Intellectual intuition of something enables the mind to judge that it exists or does not exist, has or does not have a given quality. Intuition also extends to our inner acts of thinking, willing, and so forth. Abstractive cognition abstracts from the existence or nonexistence of the object. If Ockham at first distinguishes between abstracting and universalizing, in a later treatment of the point he suggests that they occur together. In line with his view that all that exists outside the mind is singular, Ockham rejects the presence of any kind of common or universal nature in things, even if it is said to be universal only potentially or incompletely. Here he takes to task earlier forms of realism, including those of Scotus and Aquinas. Universal concepts will apply to different individuals for the simple reason that the individuals themselves are similar. In attempting to determine what kind of being the universal has in the mind, he considers different possibilities. The universal might be regarded as a mere thought-object made by the mind to represent the thing known and enjoying no real being. It might be regarded as a real quality existing in the soul and distinct from the act of knowing. Or it might be regarded as identical with the act of knowing the individuals of which it is the concept.

Ockham eventually adopts this final view. Often called a nominalist, a number of current writers suggest that he should rather be described as a conceptualist.

Ockham distinguishes between "real science" and logic. A real science is about terms that stand for things. Logic is about terms or mental contents that stand for other terms or mental contents. His discussion of the supposition of terms is highly interesting. In metaphysics he is perhaps best known for his criticisms of earlier views. Metaphysics is regarded as a real science. If there is no such thing as "being as such" but there are only individual beings outside the mind, there is one concept that can be predicated of all that exists or can exist: the univocal concept of being. Denial of univocity would eliminate the possibility of philosophical knowledge of God. There is no real distinction between essence and existence in creatures. Ockham is critical of earlier attempts to demonstrate God's existence but finds more promise in arguments based on efficient causality. Even here the argument from production should be shifted to an argument based on conservation of creatures. In this way difficulties concerning an infinite regress of caused causes can be overcome. In the case of conserving causes, an infinite regress would entail an actual infinite multitude of caused causes, something that Ockham regards as impossible. However, for certitude regarding divine unicity, divine omnipotence, divine freedom, and many other attributes, one must rely on faith.

Prime matter enjoys some actuality in itself. Ockham inclines toward plurality of forms in man in accord with the general Franciscan tradition. Demonstrative argumentation cannot be offered to prove that an immaterial and incorruptible form such as the intellective soul either exists in man or is joined to the body as its form. Again, one must have recourse to the teachings of the Church. There is neither a real nor a formal distinction between the soul and its faculties. Intuition rather than demonstration assures us of our freedom. Divine freedom and divine omnipotence are religious truths frequently employed by Ockham in his philosophy. His stress on the freedom and liberality of God and the radical contingency of the created order is well known. A human act is good or moral simply because it is commanded by the divine will, not because it conforms to eternal law. Central to his methodology is his famed "razor": what can be explained by assuming fewer things should not be explained by assuming more. Further application of this may be seen in his elimination of sensible and intelligible species and his rejection of the distinction between agent and possible intellects.

Certain critical, empiricist, and even skeptical tendencies latent in Ockham were carried further by others in the fourteenth century in what came to be known as the modern way *(via moderna)*. Sometimes known as nominalists or as terminists, these Ockhamists were more or less united in their common opposition to the realism of the old way *(via antiqua)*, which lived on in various schools, most notably among the followers of Thomas and Scotus. At the same time, Ockham's severe restrictions on the possibilities of metaphysical demonstration had limited positive contribution by philosophy to theology, thus contributing to the dissolution of the philosophical-theological syntheses of the thirteenth century. Unfortunately, during the fourteenth and fifteenth centuries scholasticism tended more and more to harden into schools, such as Thomism, Scotism, the followers of the *via moderna*, a revived Latin Averroism, and Albertism (followers of the influential teacher of Thomas Aquinas, Albert the Great).

NICOLAS OF CUSA

Deeply interested in synthesis and the reconciliation of differences, Nicholas of Cusa (1401-64) found little hope for this in Aristotelian dialectics and in the school debates of his time. Much more to his liking was the Christian Neoplatonism developed by Pseudo-Dionysius, John Scotus Eriugena, the School of Chartres, and Meister Eckhart (d. 1327), with its great debt to Proclus. Nicholas was convinced that man is wise only to the degree that he is aware of his limits in knowing truth (learned ignorance). On the level of discursive reason, man approximates but never fully possesses absolute truth. This becomes particularly evident in his search for God. Rational inquiry rests on relating and comparing. Since there is no proportion or relation between the finite and the infinite, such procedure falls short in seeking the infinite. Knowledge is really conjecture. True as far as it goes, its point of view is always partial and incomplete. But in the Neoplatonists Nicholas finds a higher power in man, superior to discursive reason and known as intellect *(intellectus)*. This power enables one to rise above the principle of noncontradiction, the basic principle on the level of discursive reason, and grasp the "coincidence of opposites" in reality. Because normal language is better suited to discursive reason, symbols and analogies drawn from mathematics are used to express the insights of intellect. In God one meets the absolute maximum, the fullness of being, and the coincidence of opposites. (Note, however, that in his *De coniecturis* Nicholas elevates God above the coincidence of opposites.) If God is the maximum he is also the minimum in that all opposition is reconciled in him in perfect unity. As the fullness of perfection and absolute maximum God may be said to "contain" all other things. To that extent he is their "enfolding" *(complicatio)*. But insofar as they come forth from him as partial manifestations of his perfection he is said to be their "unfolding" *(explicatio)*. If the universe is to reflect God then it, too, must be a maximum, but a relative maximum. Although not positively infinite, it is bounded neither by time nor by space. The universe is a "contraction" of the infinite while individual creatures are "contractions" of the universe. If all creation reflects God, man is the perfect microcosm where matter, organic life, animal life, and the spiritual combine. Hence human nature is well suited for union with the absolute maximum, a union best expressed through the meeting of the divine and human in Christ.

At the beginning of this Introduction it was suggested that one distinguishing feature of medieval philosophy in the Latin West was the acceptance of divine revelation as an unquestioned source of truth. Some have regarded the religious and theological commitments of medieval Christian writers as an unmitigated disaster for philosophy. Others have maintained that the dominating influence of Christianity provided ideal conditions for philosophizing. In fact, favorable and unfavorable aspects for philosophical development can be detected in this Christian influence. The view that all creation derives from and reflects the divine was a standing invitation for Christian philosophers to seek to know more of man and the universe, since both were regarded as reflections of God. The successful employment of philosophy by theologians in seeking deeper insights into revelation demanded a highly sophisticated philosophy to serve as theology's instrument. Various themes contained in Christian revelation suggested new areas for philosophical investigation. On the other hand, excessive ecclesiastical reactions such as the condemnation of 1277 dampened the spirit of free philosophical inquiry for a time. The great stress on theological research attracted many who might otherwise have given themselves more completely to philosophy. Finally, the conclusions of the Christian philosopher were subject to some control in that positions directly contradicting articles of faith had to be reexamined. Insofar as he recognized in revelation an unquestioned source of truth, the believer might well be grateful for this negative kind of guidance. The unbeliever might rather regard it as an unwarranted limitation of the philosopher's freedom. However, these and other plus and minus factors deriving from religious influences are better weighed in the light of the evidence, the philosophy found in the writings of the medieval thinkers themselves.

J. F. W.

1

ST. AUGUSTINE

Aurelius Augustinus was born November 13, 354 at Tagaste in the Roman Province of Numidia (modern Souk-Ahras, Algeria) to a pagan father and a Christian mother. He studied and taught rhetoric at Carthage (370-383). "At the age of nineteen," he wrote, "on reading in the school of rhetoric Cicero's *Hortensius,* I was inflamed by such a love of philosophy that I considered devoting myself to it at once." This quest for wisdom turned him away from Christianity, which he considered too naive and anthropomorphic in its conception of God and lacking a solution to the problem of evil. He joined the Manichean sect, with its belief in rival gods as the source of good and evil. Its claim of providing rational solutions to all life's problems together with its esoteric doctrine of salvation appealed to his pride, while its pseudoscientific explanation of "sin as inevitably determined by the celestial bodies" flattered his vices. From Carthage he went to Rome (383) and then to Milan (384), where the Roman emperor resided and St. Ambrose was bishop. Disillusioned with Mani's doctrines and unable to find peace in the pursuit of material pleasures, he turned briefly to the skepticism of Cicero and the New Academy. But at Milan Augustine underwent a twofold conversion, one intellectual, the other spiritual. The first came from reading such Neoplatonic works as Plotinus' *Enneads,* newly translated into Latin by the Christian convert Marius Victorinus. Abandoning his materialistic beliefs, Augustine began to search for truth, goodness, and happiness as things spiritual and incorporeal. From St. Ambrose he learned to look for the spiritual meaning behind the letter of the Scriptures and undertook to reexamine Christian beliefs in the light of Neoplatonic philosophy. The end result was his dramatic spiritual conversion to Christianity, described so graphically in his *Confessions*. He retired to Cassiciacum near Milan for a year of prayer and study after which he was baptized by St. Ambrose (387). On his return to Africa, Augustine sold his property and set up a monastic community at Tagaste. He was persuaded to help the ailing bishop at the nearby seaport of Hippo Regius, and he was ordained priest in 391. In 395 he was consecrated coadjutor and the following year became Bishop of Hippo. The three decades spent in the ministry were marked by intense activity as a thinker, writer, and spiritual leader. He died on August 28, 430, as the Vandals were laying siege to his episcopal city.

Probably no medieval thinker had a greater influence than St. Augustine on Christian thought in the Latin West. Equal in bulk to the contents of a modern encyclopedia, his writings cover a wide variety of subjects of interest not only to the scriptural scholar or professional theologian, but to the philosopher and humanist as well. His *Confessions* and *The City of God* are still read among the great books of Western literature. Even such professedly theological works as his fifteen books *On the Trinity* contain chapters with profound philosophical insights. Philosophers with as little general interest in the history of philosophy as Wittgenstein have found profit and enjoyment in reading him.

Most of the items in the first selection are excerpts from an early dialogue *Against the Skeptics (Contra Academicos)* based on a stenographic report of a long discussion Augustine held with his companions at the country villa of Cassiciacum before his baptism. In the interest of brevity, we have selected only some of the more concentrated passages together with two chapters taken from his later works, *The City of God* and *On the Trinity*. Here he still had occasion to rebuke the skepticism of the academy in a famous passage reminiscent of Descartes' later reasoning.

The other two selections are from dialogues in which Evodius, one of Augustine's closest friends, is the interlocutor. The first of these, *On the Greatness of the Soul (De quantitate animae)*, written shortly after Augustine's conversion, reflects his new-found belief in the incorporeality of the soul and his repudiation of Manichean materialism. Only his answers to the first two questions have been included. The other dialogue, *On Free Choice of the Will (De libero arbitrio)*, was begun shortly after the first (*ca.* 387-88); but the second book, from which the proof of God's existence is taken, was completed only around 395. The translations were made by A. B. Wolter especially for this volume.

A Critique of Skepticism

1. [THE DOCTRINE OF THE NEW ACADEMY][1]

The members of the [New Platonic] Academy maintained: (1) where matters of philosophy are concerned—and Carneades disowned interest in anything else—man can know nothing for certain. Despite this, he can be wise and the total task of a wise man is to search for truth. From this it follows: (2) a wise man will not assent to anything. If he did, he would inevitably fall into error, which is something wicked in a wise man.

And they were not content to merely propose these points but backed them with a plethora of arguments based on the dissension among philosophers, the errors of the senses, delirium and dream states, sophistries and sorites. . . .

Since it would seem to follow that one who assents to nothing will do nothing, the position of the academicians provoked considerable animosity. . . . Consequently, they proposed their theory of the "probable" or "truth-like," as they called it, insisting that the wise man does not desert his duties at all since he has some norm to follow. Truth as such, however, remains hidden either because it is shrouded or obfuscated by a kind of opacity of nature or because of its indistinguishable resemblance to falsity. Actually, they insist, it is a great achievement for the wise man to withold his assent, or to suspend judgment as it were. . . .

2. [CRITIQUE OF CARNEADES][2]

You say [Carneades] that in philosophy nothing can be perceived for certain. And to gain widespread acceptance of your assertion you poke fun at the dissension and disagreements of philosophers, thinking these provide you with weapons against them. How shall we settle the dispute between Democritus and the earlier philosophers of nature as to whether there are innumerable worlds or only one, when we cannot find agreement even between him and his heir Epicurus. For this seeker of pleasure delighted to embrace in the dark, like little handmaids, these tiny bodies or atoms, but in permitting them to move freely to other quarters, he let his whole patrimony slip away through litigation. All this of course is no affair of mine, but if there is something about such matters that pertains to wisdom, it should not be hidden from a wise man. But if there is nothing of this sort, then the wise man would know this and would put little value on such matters. But even I, who am far from being anything near wise, know something about these questions of natural philosophy. For I am sure there is either only one world or more than one. I am also certain that if there is more than one, the number of worlds is either finite or infinite. Carneades would teach that this at most only appears to be the case. Another point I know for certain is that the arrangement of our present world stems either from the nature of bodies or is something due to providence. I am also sure it always was and will be, or it had a beginning but will never end, or it never began but will come to an end, or it had a beginning and will eventually cease to be. There are countless other items I know in this fashion about the philosophy of nature. For such statements are true in disjunction and no one can confuse them with anything having a semblance to what is false.

"But," he asks, "how do you know the world exists if the senses are deceptive?" Well your objections will never so prevail over sense experience as to convince us we see nothing at all. Even you do not dare go so far. Rather you expend your efforts persuading us that things can be other than they seem. But note that what I call "world" is this totality, whatever it be, that surrounds and sustains us. I am talking only about what appears to my eyes and seems to contain heaven and earth, or at least what looks like heaven and earth. If you insist that what I see is nonexistent, I still would not be wrong. For only he errs who rashly accepts appearances as facts. Even you do not claim it is pure nothingness, but rather something false, that is seen by those endowed with senses. Indeed the whole basis for this dispute you so wish to win dissolves if it is not merely that we don't know anything, but that nothing even appears to us. But if you deny that it is the world that appears to me, you make an issue of words, for I have stated that this is precisely what I mean by "world."

"But," you persist, "is this the same world you see if you are asleep?" I've already admitted that I call "world" whatever appears as such to me. But if you wish to restrict the name to what appears to men awake and of sound mind, then maintain, if you can, that it is not in the world that sleepers or the insane are asleep or demented. All that I am saying is that this entire mass or framework of bodies in which we exist, be we sane or mad, awake or asleep, is either one or not one. Tell me how this statement can be false? For if I am asleep, I may have uttered nothing at all, or if these words did fall from my lips in sleep as sometimes happens, it may be that I did not say them here, or to this audience, or while sitting so. But the statement itself cannot be false. I don't claim to have perceived the world the way I would if I were awake, for you might say that it could also appear so to me in sleep and therefore could bear some resemblance to what is false. But if the number of worlds be six plus one, it is clear that there are seven worlds no matter how I am disposed. And without being brazen I affirm that I know this. Show me then how sleep or insanity or sense deception make this addition incorrect or the aforesaid disjunctions false. If I remember it when I awake, I'll admit I've been bested. For I believe it abundantly clear that what appears false by reason of sleep or insanity pertains to the bodily senses. If the whole human race were snoring away, however, it would still be necessarily true that three times three are nine and that this is the square of a number one can comprehend. There is also a great deal more that can be said for the senses that I find unrefuted by the academicians. I don't believe the senses should be blamed because the deranged suffer delusions or what we see in dreams is not the case. For if the senses report things correctly to such as are sane and awake, what does it matter what the mind of the sleeper or madman may fancy to itself?

The question remains whether the senses in reporting, report the truth. What if an Epicurean were to say: "I've no complaint to make about the senses. It would be unfair to expect more of them than they are equipped to do." Do they see an oar in water truly? Of course. For there is a reason it looks that way. If it appeared straight when dipped in water, I would protest that my eyes gave a false report. But why multiply instances? The same can be said of the apparent motion of towers, the changing hues in the plumage of birds, or countless other examples.

"But," someone counters, "I am deceived if I give assent." Restrict your assent to appearances, then, and there will be no deception. I see no way the academician can refute one who says: "I know this looks white to me. I know I like what I hear and enjoy what I smell. I know this tastes sweet to me and that feels cold to me." "Tell me instead," says he, "whether the leaves of the wild olive that the goat likes so well are bitter as such." You rogue! Is the goat that unreasonable? I know not how they taste to cattle, but I find them bitter. What more do you want? Some perhaps may not find them so. Must you go out of your way to be obnoxious? Have I claimed that all find them bitter? I merely affirmed they taste so to me—and that not even at all times. Why, for various reasons, should not something be bitter at one time and sweet at another? All I claim is that when a man tastes something, he can swear in good faith that he knows that something does or does not taste sweet to his palate. No Greek sophistry can deprive him of that knowledge. Who would be so brazen as to say when I smack my lips with delight, "Perhaps you are not really tasting, since it may be only a dream"? Would I protest? Why I would relish this even in a dream. Hence there is no semblance to falsity to cast doubt on what I've said I know.

Perhaps an Epicurean or the Cyrenaics would have even more to say for the senses that the academicians have not contradicted to my knowedge. But this is not my concern. If they want to and are able, the academicians may refute such claims with my blessing. The point is the arguments they adduce against the senses are not valid against all philosophers. For there are some [i.e. the Platonists] who maintain that what the mind can grasp by way of the bodily senses is opinion, not knowledge. Knowledge is found in intelligence. It abides in a mind far removed from the senses. Among them, perhaps, the wise man we seek is to be found. But we shall speak of this at another time.

3. [MORAL MATTERS][3]

Does the bodily sense help or hinder ethical inquiry? If the dove's neck, the dubious voice, the burden that is heavy for man but light for a camel, or fifty dozen other such puzzles do not prevent men who regard pleasure as man's supreme good from asserting they know they find pleasure in what pleases them (and I see no way to refute them), should they bother him who places the ultimate good in the mind?

Which of these views do you choose? If you ask me, I think man's supreme good is in the mind. But we are concerned with knowledge at present. Inquire of the wise man, then, who must know wisdom. But in the meantime even I, stupid and slow of mind though I be, can know this much about this good in which life's happiness abides. Either it is to be found in the mind or the body or both or there is no such thing. Convince me, if you can, that I don't know this. And if you cannot, because you find no semblance to falsity there, shall I hesitate to infer that, since even I know so many things to be true in philosophy, what seems to me to be correct is that the wise man knows whatever is true in philosophy.

But perhaps the wise man fears he will select his supreme good while asleep. Well, there's no danger in that. If it pleases him when awake, he will keep it, whereas if it displeases him, he will disown it. . . .

4. [IS THE "PROBABLE" AN ADEQUATE NORM OF ACTION?][4]

Here in this country villa I have long and leisurely pondered how [the Academy's theory of] "the probable" or "truth-like" could rule out error in regard to actions. At first their position seemed beautifully protected and fortified, as it also looked to me when I taught such matters for money. But a more careful examination revealed one opening where error might break through their security. For I believe a man errs by failing to follow the right path and not merely by following one that is false.

Picture two men en route to the same place, one skeptical, the other credulous. At a fork in the road, the credulous says to the shepherd or farmer standing there, "Hello, my good man. Please show me the right road to this place." "If you take this road," is the reply, "you will not go wrong." Turning to his companion, he says: "He speaks the truth. Let us go this way." The cautious man laughs, and ridicules his credulous companion for assenting so readily. While the latter departs, he remains at the junction. He is beginning to feel foolish standing there, when, behold, a neatly dressed urbanite comes riding up the second road on horseback. The traveler rejoices. He greets the new arrival, tells him where he is headed and inquires about the way. Esteeming the newcomer more than the shepherd, he even explains the reason for his delay, hoping to win the other's favor. But the latter turns out to be one of those [professional pranksters] commonly called "Samardacs." The rogue follows his usual practice and that without charge. "Go this way," he says, "I've just come from there." And having tricked the traveler, he moves on.

But has he tricked the traveler? "I don't accept his information as something true," he insists, "but only as truth-like. But since it is neither becoming nor helpful to remain standing here, I shall take the second road." In the meantime, the man who erred by too readily accepting the shepherd's words as true, has reached his destination and is already refreshing himself. But the man who avoided error by following the probable is wandering about in God-knows-what woods. He has still to find someone who knows where he wants to go.

Truly, I tell you, I could not suppress a smile in thinking of the situation. By the academicians' own words, the man who follows the right road by chance is in error, whereas the person led by probability over pathless mountains, who never finds the place he set out for, does not seem to have made a mistake. To express my disapproval of rash assent, I should admit both erred, rather than that the second avoided it.

More wary of their teaching then, I began to consider the actions and mores of men. Then so many capital arguments against the academicians came to mind that I could no longer laugh. It was rather a revolting and tragic situation that such learned and intelligent men should have fallen for anything so criminal or shameful.

It may well be that not everyone who errs, sins. But everyone grants that whoever sins, errs or does something worse. Now suppose some young man hears them say: "To err is shameful, hence we ought not assent to anything. But when one follows what seems probable to him, he neither sins nor errs." Hearing this, he plans to seduce another's wife.

Now I ask you Marcus Tullius—yes, you—for advice. We are dealing with the morals and lives of the young toward whose education and training all your writings are directed. What can you say but that it seems improbable to you that the young man will do this? But to him it is probable that he will. Now if we are to regulate our lives according to what seems probable to someone else, then you should not have taken it upon yourself to serve the republic, for Epicurus did not regard this as something one should do. Consequently, our young man will commit adultery with another's wife. And if he is caught, where will he find you to defend him? And even if he should find you, what will you say? Will you deny the whole thing happened? But what if the case is so clear, it is futile to deny it? You will try to persuade the court, as you might your students at Cumae or Naples, that he did not sin, indeed, he did not even make a mistake. For he did not consider "I ought to commit adultery" as true. But it occurred to him he probably ought to and so he did. Or maybe he didn't really do it, but it only seemed to him that he did. But the stupid husband is stirring up all this litigation to defend the honor of his wife with whom he is now sleeping perhaps, but doesn't know it. Now if the judges can make any sense of all this, they will either ignore the academicians and punish this as a real crime or they will capitulate to them and, acting in accord with what seems probable and truth-like, they will condemn the man so that his defense attorney will be at a loss what to do. He will have no cause to be angry with anyone, for all will claim they gave no consent but merely did what seemed the probable thing to do. The role of advocate then will be laid aside in favor of that of a sympathetic philosopher. He will easily persuade the young man—who already has advanced far in the Academy—to believe it is only in a dream he is sentenced.

Perhaps you think I am jesting, but I swear by all that is sacred I don't see how anyone commits sin by doing what seems probable to him—unless perhaps they claim to err is one thing, to sin another, and that they have set up their precepts to keep us from erring, whereas they consider sin of no great importance.

I won't mention homicide, parricide, sacrileges and all the deviltry or crimes that can be imagined or committed, all of which are justified by a few words, and worse still, defended before the wisest of judges. "I gave no assent, consequently I did not err. How could I avoid doing what seemed probable to me?" Whoever thinks these points cannot be argued persuasively on probable grounds, let him read Catiline's oration commending parricide of one's country, wherein all crimes are embodied.

The academicians themselves claim they follow only the

probable in acting. Still they go to great pains to seek the truth, although they think it probable that truth cannot be found. Who would not laugh at this? What amazing absurdity! But let's skip that; it doesn't concern us or affect our lives or fortunes. But the other point is of capital importance, fraught with formidable consequences, and must provoke dismay in every upright person. For if this reasoning of the academicians is probable, then one may perpetrate any crime if it appears probable he ought to, so long as he assents to nothing as true. It will not be charged to him as a sin or even a mistake. What about this? Did the academicians not see this? Indeed they saw it, for they were clever and cautious. I surely would not be so arrogant as to maintain I have come near to Marcus Tullius in industry, alertness, genius, or learning. And still, when he claimed man cannot know anything, he would not be able to refute one who answered: "But I know that it seems so to me."

5. [I KNOW FOR CERTAIN I EXIST!][5]

We (1) *exist* and (2) *know* that we do, and this existing and knowing is something we (3) *love*. No fear of falsity disguised as truth troubles us where these three items I have mentioned are concerned. For unlike the things outside us, they are not grasped by any of the body's senses the way we do colors by seeing, sounds by hearing, odors by smelling, flavors by tasting, and what is hard and soft by touching. By forming mental pictures of such sensible things we turn them over in our minds, store them in our memories, and keep our desire for them alive. But with no image of things fancied or apparent to deceive me, I know most certainly that I exist and know and love. About such truths I fear no arguments from the Academy's skeptics. "What if you are deceived?" they protest. If I am deceived, I exist! For one who does not exist, cannot be deceived. Consequently I exist if I am deceived. But if it follows that I exist if I am deceived, how can I be mistaken about existing when it is certain I exist if I am deceived? Since it would be I who exist as deceived, even if I were deceived, it would certainly not be in the matter of knowing I exist. Neither am I in error then in knowing that I know. For just as I know that I am, so too do I know that I know.

And when I take delight in these two facts, I add a third and equally important item to what I know, the fact that I love. Nor am I mistaken that I love when I am not deceived about the things that I love. And even were these false, it would still be true that I love what is false. Were it not so, why would it be right to reprehend me or right to forbid me to love the false, if it were not true that I loved such? But since what I love is true and known with certainty to be the case, who will question that when I love such things my love itself is something true and known with certainty to be the case?

6. [I KNOW I AM ALIVE][6]

By an inner knowledge we know too that we are alive. Here not even an academician can object: "What if you are asleep and don't know it, for who is not aware that things seen in sleep are similar to what we see when awake?" One who is sure he is alive, however, does not claim in virtue of such knowledge "I know I am awake," but "I know I am alive." For whether he be asleep or awake, he is alive. He cannot be deceived about this just because of dreams, since to sleep and to see in dreams pertains to the living. Irrelevant also is the academician's protest: "But perhaps you are insane and don't know it, since what the mad see resembles what is seen by the sane." For the insane man is still alive. The retort to the academician then is not "I know I am not insane," but "I know that I am alive." He can never be deceived or lie, then, who declares he knows that he lives. Parade a thousand optical illusions before one who claims "I know I'm alive" and they will not disturb him, for even one deceived still lives.

If human knowledge comprised only such things, it would be meager indeed, unless each type were to be multiplied to where the items known are no longer few, but infinite in number. For one who says "I know I live" knows one thing. If he were to add "I know that I know I live," he knows two things. To recognize they are two is to know a third point. In this way he can add a fourth, a fifth, and countless other items until he has enough. But since a countless number cannot be grasped in terms of adding individuals or counting aloud indefinitely, he recognizes and asserts with the greatest certainty that it is true that the number of such items is so beyond the possibilities of counting that the total number is truly infinite and cannot be comprehended or stated.

We notice the situation is similar where the will is involved. For who would not regard it as brazen to retort to one who says: "I want to be happy!" "Maybe you are mistaken"? Now if the speaker were to continue: "I know I want this" and "I know I know this fact," then to these two items he could also add a third, viz., that he knows these two, and a fourth also, viz., that he knows that he knows these two, and so on indefinitely. Also if someone were to say: "I do not wish to err," will it not be true that whether or not he falls into error, he does not wish to do so? Would it not be extremely impertinent to argue: "Perhaps you are deceived"? For no matter what he is mistaken about, he is surely not in error about not wanting to be deceived. And if he adds that he knows this fact, he can add any number of known items he wishes and perceives such possibilities to be infinite in number. For he who says "I don't want to be deceived" and "I know that I don't want to" and "I know that I know this" is now able to point to an infinite number, however awkward it may be to state it. And there are many other things that can be used to refute the academicians who claim man can know nothing for certain. . . .

There are two types of things one can know; one comprises what the mind perceives with the aid of the bodily senses, the other what it perceives on its own. While the babblings of these philosophers have some relevancy in regard to the former, they are completely powerless to cast doubt on what the mind on its own perceives to be most certainly true, such as the aforementioned "I know that I live."

Far be it from us, however, to cast doubt on what we have learned through the bodily senses. For by their aid we have come to learn of the heavens and earth and all that we know them to contain, to the extent at least that he who created both them and us wished us to have knowledge of them. Far be it also from us to deny what we have learned from the testimony of others, for otherwise we would not be aware of the existence of the ocean, or that those famous countries and cities exist that we so often hear of. Neither would we know there were such men and deeds as we have discovered from reading history, or the daily news that comes to us from far and wide and is confirmed by consistent and convincing evidence.

How Great Is the Soul?[7]

CHAPTER 1

EVODIUS: Since you seem to have time on your hands, I beg you to answer some questions troubling me that I believe are neither foolish nor inopportune. Often before when I plagued you with questions, you would put me off with what Greek proverb I know not as to how we ought not be curious about things beyond our comprehension. Now I do not regard ourselves as such a subject. So when I inquire about the soul, I don't deserve the answer: Why bother about things beyond us? but you ought to tell me just what we really are.

AUGUSTINE: List briefly what you wish to hear about the soul.

E.: That I shall do. For so long have I pondered these problems that I have them at the tip of my tongue. My questions on the soul are these. Whence is it? What type of thing is it? How big is it? Why was it joined to the body? What results when it enters and when it leaves the body?

A.: When you ask: "Whence the soul?" two meanings inevitably come to mind. For when we ask of a man: "Whence is he?" it is one thing to expect as an answer the land where he was born and quite another to be looking for information on his constitution, that is, on the things or elements from which he was made. When you ask: "Whence is the soul?" just what is it you want to know: Where it came from, its homeland as it were, or what it is in substance?

E.: Well actually I would like to know about both, but I prefer to leave it up to you which of these I ought to learn about first.

A.: Well I believe the soul's proper habitation, its homeland so to speak, is the God himself who created it. As for its substance, I am at a loss for a name. For I certainly do not believe it is made of any ordinary or familiar elements known to us such as earth, water, air, or fire, or of any combination thereof. Should you ask: What is a tree made of? I would list these four elements that we regard all such things to be composed of. But if you ask further: And what is earth itself, or air or fire made of? I would be unable to answer. In similar fashion, should you ask what man is made of, I could say: Of body and soul. Likewise, if you were to ask about the composition of the body, I would refer you to the same four elements. But since the soul seems simple and of a substance all its own, when you ask me what it is made of, I am as lost for an answer as when you ask what earth is composed of.

E.: I don't understand why you claim it has a substance all its own when you admit it was made by God.

A.: I can't deny earth was made by God, but I am unable to say what further bodies constitute it, so to speak. For earth is something simple by the very fact that it is earth. That is why it is called an element of anything composed of the four elements. There is nothing incompatible about our saying that the soul has a nature proper to itself and yet is made by God. For he himself made this nature that is peculiarly its own even as he made the distinctive natures of fire, air, earth, and water,—the elements of which all other things are composed.

CHAPTER 2

E.: What you say about the soul coming from God I accept for the present and shall ponder it carefully. Should some difficulty come to mind, I will mention it later. But now tell me what type of thing the soul is.

A.: It seems to me to be similar to God. For it is the *human* soul, I take it, that you ask about.

E.: How it is like to God is precisely what I would like explained. For while we believe God to be made by no one, the soul as you said before was made by God.

A.: What's the difficulty? That God should be able to make something similar to himself? Even we have that ability as you see from the variety of images we make of ourselves.

E.: But we see that what we create is not immortal, whereas the soul that God makes is, unless you possibly think otherwise.

A.: Do you expect men to turn out the same quality of products as God?

E.: Of course not! But if being immortal himself, in making something in his likeness God makes it immortal, should not we who have been made immortal by God also turn out immortal likenesses of ourselves?

A.: True, but only if you could paint a picture of what you believe to be immortal in yourself. But as things are now, it is a likeness of your body that you produce and that certainly is mortal.

E.: How then am I like to God, if unlike him I can make nothing immortal?

A.: If a statue or bodily image is unable to do what the body itself can, it is no wonder that your soul has not the same power as he in whose likeness it was made.

CHAPTER 3

E.: That is a good enough answer for the present. But now tell me how great the soul is.

A.: What do you mean by "How great?" For I know not whether you are asking how long or wide or firm it is, or about all these combined, or whether you want to know what it is able to do. For we are wont to ask: "How great is Hercules?" meaning, How many feet tall? And again, "How great a man was he?" meaning, What prowess or valor did he have?

E.: What I want to know is how great is the soul in both senses of "great."

A.: There is no way of speaking or thinking of the soul as being great in the first sense. For the soul must not be considered to have any length or width or bodily resistance. For all these, it seems to me, are properties of bodies. And so we would be asking about the soul questions that make sense only when applied to bodies. . . . I can give no answer to your question then, if you take it in this sense. I can only assert that the soul has no length or width or hardness nor any of the properties one usually looks for in measuring bodies. If you like, I shall give you my reason for thinking this.

E.: That would indeed please me. I am most eager to hear your reason for if the soul lacks all such properties, it would seem to amount to nothing.

A.: If you will, let me first prove to you there are many things you cannot call nothing, and still you cannot find anything in them comparable to the measurable properties you seek in the soul, so that far from regarding the soul as nothing because you find there no length or anything of that sort, you should consider it all the more precious because it possesses none of these properties. Afterwards, we shall see whether it actually is without such.

E.: Follow what order and method you like. I am willing to listen and learn.

CHAPTER 4

A.: Good! Now I want you to answer what I ask, for possibly you already know what I want to teach you. You have no doubt, I believe, that this tree is far from being absolutely nothing.

E.: Who could doubt that?

A.: What about justice being more excellent than this tree? You don't doubt that?

E.: It would be absurd to do so. There is no comparison between them.

A.: You are gracious to go along with me. Now consider this. Since it is so clear to you that this tree is so inferior to justice that you see no comparison between them and since you grant that this wood is certainly something, would you have us believe that justice itself is nothing?

E.: Who would be crazy enough to believe that?

A.: That's quite right! But perhaps you think this tree to be something because it has its proper height and girth and solidity, and that it would be nothing if you took these away.

E.: It looks that way.

A.: What about justice then? You admit it is not nothing. Indeed, you concede it is more divine and excels by far this tree. Does it seem to have any length?

E.: Not at all! Justice seems to me to lack length, breadth, and any thing of that sort I can think of.

A.: But if justice has none of these features and for all that is not nothing, why do you believe the soul to be nothing if it has no length?

E.: All right! I see now it does not follow that because the soul is neither long, nor wide, nor solid, it is nothing at all. But you know you have not yet made the point that it really is something of this sort. It may well be that there are many things lacking such properties that ought to be highly thought of. But I don't think we have to admit without further ado that the soul is to be classed among them.

A.: I recognize this point still remains to be resolved and I promised to go into it later. But the problem here is very subtle and requires a far deeper insight than we are wont to use in handling ordinary everyday affairs. For that reason I urge you not to be reluctant to follow the path I think we should pursue, nor become tired of the detours we must make, nor be put out because our progress is slower than you desired. For I shall begin by asking you this: Do you think there is any body without some length, breadth, or depth of its own?

E.: I'm not sure what you mean by "depth."

A.: I refer to that dimension that makes it possible to think of the body as having an interior or enables us to look into it if it is transparent like glass. As I see it, if this dimension were absent, bodies could not be sensibly perceived nor be thought of properly as bodies. I wish you would let me know what you think of this.

E.: I have no doubt bodies must have these dimensions.

A.: What about this? Can you think of these three things being anywhere but in bodies?

E.: I don't see how they can be anywhere else.

A.: And hence you think the soul is simply a body.

E.: Well, if you admit that even a breath of air is a body, I cannot deny that the soul seems to be a body, for I think it is something of this sort.

A.: If you were to ask me, I would admit that the wind is the sort of body that a flowing current is. For we feel the wind is simply an agitation or movement of the air about us. This can be confirmed by the little puff of air we feel when in a completely quiet and breezeless spot we flick away the flies. When this same thing occurs over a great portion of the world due to the unobserved movements of heavenly or earthly bodies we call it "wind" and give it different names according to the direction of of the heavens from which it comes. Or do you disagree?

E.: I have no other view and regard what you say as probable. But I didn't say the soul is wind as such but something akin to it.

A.: But tell me first whether this wind we were talking about has length, breadth, or depth? Then we shall see if the soul is something of this sort and we can thus investigate how far it extends.

E.: What could you readily find that extends further in length, breadth, or height than air? But when agitated, air is wind as you have just convinced me.

CHAPTER 5

A.: Right you are! But do you think your soul is anywhere save in your body?

E.: I think not.

A.: Is the soul only inside the body like the contents of a wine skin, as it were? Or is it merely on the outside like a cloak? Or is it both inside and outside?

E.: I feel it is the last, for were it not inside, what is under our skin would not be living. Were it not outside, we could not feel the mere prick of a pin the way we do.

A.: Why then ask further: "How great is the soul?" when you see it extends as far as the boundaries of the body allow.

E.: If that is what reason says, I shall seek no further.

A.: You do well not to go beyond what reason teaches. But does our present argument seem valid to you?

E.: It would seem so, since I see no rational alternative. But it poses a very puzzling question that I will raise when it is proper to do so, viz., Does the soul's shape remain the same when it departs from the body? I listed this last, if I recall, among the points to be discussed. There is a question pertaining to quantity, however, that ought not to be overlooked at this point, it seems to me, viz. "How many souls are there?" [i.e. is there one for each body or do we opt for transmigration?].

A.: That question is not irrelevant here, but first let us explicate a point that bothers me, if you don't mind, so that I too may learn something in the course of satisfying your curiosity.

E.: Ask what you please. For your seeming doubt makes me really question what I presumed we had just settled.

A.: Tell me then whether what is called memory seems to you to be a meaningless term.

E.: Who could view it as such?

A.: Do you regard it as belonging to the body or the soul?

E.: The question is ridiculous. Who would believe a lifeless body remembers or understands anything?

A.: Do you still remember the city of Milan?

E.: I recall it well.

A.: Now that we brought it up, do you recollect its size and the kind of city it is?

E.: Indeed I do. I remember nothing more vividly or more perfectly.

A.: Though you do not behold it with your eyes, you see it with your mind?

E.: That is right.

A.: I think you also recall how far it is from us here.

E.: That too I remember.

A.: Then you also envision with your mind the distance separating these places.

E.: I do.

A.: But your soul is here with your body and does not extend beyond the space this occupies, as our previous reasoning proves. How then does it see all these things?

E.: I presume it is through memory and not because the soul is present where they are.

A.: Memory then contains a likeness of these places?

E.: I think so, for I know not what is occurring there at present, as I would if my mind extended to those places and experienced what happens there just now.

A.: I think what you say is true. But surely these likenesses are of bodies.

E.: Obviously they must be, for neither cities nor such country places are something disembodied.

A.: Have you ever peered into a miniature mirror or seen the reflection of your face in the pupil of someone else's eye?

E.: Often enough.

A.: Why does it appear so much smaller than it really is?

E.: What do you expect? That it look larger than the reflecting mirror?

A.: Images of bodies must needs be small, then, if the bodies that reflect them are tiny?

E.: Unavoidably so!

A.: But if the soul is confined to a space no larger than that of the body how can such tremendous images be reflected in it as cities, or vast stretches of land, or any other enormous thing imaginable? I wish you would consider more carefully the greatness and multiplicity of objects contained in our memory, or more precisely in our soul. How profound, how deep, how immense the soul must be, then, to grasp all these things! Yet our previous proof seems to show it to be no greater than the body.

E.: I am at a loss for an answer. Nor can I explain the extent of my embarrassment about it all. It makes me laugh to think how quickly I was taken in by our earlier argument and agreed to limit the soul to the confines of the body.

A.: It no longer seems to you to be something like the wind then?

E.: Hardly! For even though this air, whose flow on good grounds we believe to be the wind, were to fill the whole world, the soul can envision innumerable worlds as great as this, though where it finds room for them all I have not the slightest suspicion.

A.: You see, then, how much better it is to believe that the soul, like justice, lacks all length or breadth or depth, as we said before.

E.: Readily would I accept that did it not leave me more at a loss than ever to understand how the soul, without length, breadth, or depth of its own, can comprehend countless images of such vast expanses.

CHAPTER 6

A.: Perhaps a studious investigation of length, breadth, and depth would provide you with an answer. Try then to think of length apart from any breadth.

E.: I can think of no such thing. Are we apt to think of anything more tenuous than a spider's web? Yet I cannot envision its length apart from such essentials as breadth and depth as well. No matter how diminished they be, I cannot deny they are present.

A.: While your answer is not entirely unreasonable, you surely recognize these as three distinct features of the spidery filament and know how one dimension differs from the other?

E.: How could I help knowing they differ? For how else would I know there is none missing in the spider's thread?

A.: But the same ability of mind that allows you to distinguish these dimensions permits you to think of length alone, provided you do not turn your mind to a particular body, for no matter what the latter may be, it will have all three dimensions. What I want you to conceive now is something incorporeal, for length in isolation cannot be discovered in a body but can be grasped by the mind alone.

E.: I see now what you mean.

A.: You see then you cannot split length longitudinally even in thought. If you could, it would also have width.

E.: That is clear.

A.: Such pure and simple length, if you agree, we shall call a [straight] line—which is the name most scholars give it.

E.: Call it what you will. I am not one to belabor the name so long as it is clear what it refers to.

A.: That is fine. I not only approve but also encourage you to be always more concerned with reality than with words. But let's get back to this line, which I believe you now understand correctly. Do you see that it can be extended endlessly in either direction, or does this tax your powers of mind too much?

E.: Nothing is easier to see.

A.: Then you also see that no line of this sort, no matter how far you extend it, will form a figure.

E.: I'm not sure what you mean by "figure."

CHAPTER 7

A.: For now I shall call any space enclosed by a line or lines a "figure." For instance if you drew a circle or joined four lines end to end in such a way that no extremity remained free or unjoined to another.

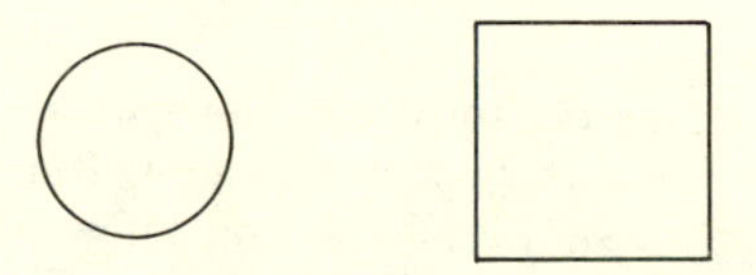

E.: I believe I understand what you mean by a "figure." Would I could see as well the bearing of all this, and what use you will make of it to show me what I want to know about the soul.

A.: I warned you at the outset about this and begged your patience with our somewhat circuitous approach. I repeat my request once more. For we are searching for something profound that is not readily known. If possible we want to make it plain and grasp it thoroughly. For it is one thing to take another's word for something and quite another to rely on our own reason. To believe an authority saves time and toil. If this is what you want, you can read in the extensive works of great and holy men what they thought ought to be said on such matters as a safe and easy guide for the ignorant, as it were. And they asked that such as could not be helped otherwise, either because they were too slow or preoccupied, believe implicitly what they said. For there are many people of this sort who when they try to reason to the truth are so easily deceived by sophisms that they fall into all kinds of harmful pitfalls from which they are unable to escape or manage to extricate themselves only with the greatest difficulty. People like these find it expedient to trust some extremely reliable authority and shape their conduct accordingly. If you think this the safer way, I shall not stop you, but shall give my wholehearted approval. But if you cannot restrain your inclination to arrive at truth through reason, you must be ready to follow the many and tortuous routes that reason takes—that reason at least which alone deserves the name, viz., right reason, which is also firm and free from all semblance of falsehood, assuming, of course, that man is able to reach a condition where neither false nor specious arguments can keep him from the truth.

E.: There is nothing I desire more. Let reason take me in hand and lead me where it will so long as it brings me to the goal.

CHAPTER 8

A.: This will God do, to whom alone we should turn for help, at least in matters such as these. But let us get back to our original subject. Now you know what a straight line is and what a figure is. Tell me whether any figure results from extending such a line at both ends or from drawing it out from one end to infinity.

E.: I'm convinced it cannot be done.

A.: What must one do then to form a figure?

E.: Make the line finite and draw it in the form of a circle until the ends meet. I see no other way of enclosing a space with a single line and so making a figure according to your definition.

A.: And if I wish to use only straight lines, can I make a figure with just one?

E.: Certainly not.

A.: With two?

E.: Not with two either.

A.: What about three?

E.: I see it can be done.

A.: You recognize and firmly hold, then, that no figure can be formed with fewer than three straight lines. Could any counter argument cause you to change your mind?

E.: Surely if someone could show me this is false, it would shake my confidence that I could know anything.

A.: Tell me then how you would construct a figure with three lines.

E.: By joining their ends.

A.: And where they meet, they form an angle?

E.: That is so.

A.: How many angles are in such a figure?

E.: As many as there are lines.

A.: Are the lines equal or unequal?

E.: Equal.

A.: And what about the angles? Is one more acute or obtuse than another or are all equal?

E.: They too are equal.

A.: Can such a figure whose three sides are equal have unequal angles, or is this impossible?

E.: It is impossible.

A.: But what if the figure consists of three straight but unequal lines? Can its angles possibly be equal.

E.: Absolutely not.

A.: You are correct. But tell me which figure seems better or more beautiful, the one whose sides are equal or unequal?

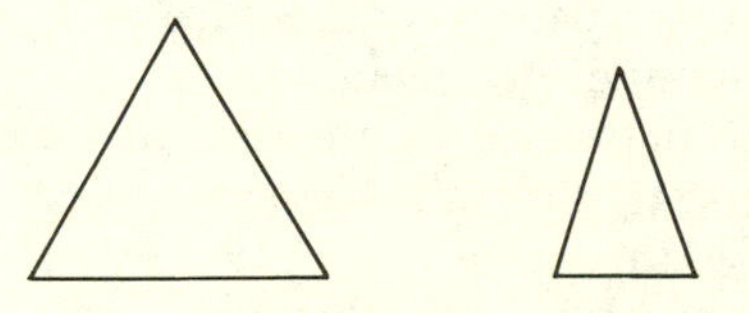

E.: Who can doubt that the one that excels in equality is more perfect?

CHAPTER 9

A.: So you value equality above inequality?

E.: Who would not?

A.: Consider the equiangular triangle. What faces each angle, a line or an angle?

E.: As I see it, a line.

A.: Suppose you have a figure, however, where an angle faces an angle and a side faces a side. Would it not have a greater measure of equality?

E.: I concede that of course, but I don't see how it is possible to make it with three lines.

A.: With four then?

E.: That is possible.

A.: Then a figure of four equal straight lines is better than one of three?

E.: Yes, since it has a greater measure of equality.

A.: Could a figure of four equal lines be constructed so that not all angles are equal, or is this impossible?

E.: I consider it possible.

A.: How?

E.: By widening one pair and closing the other.

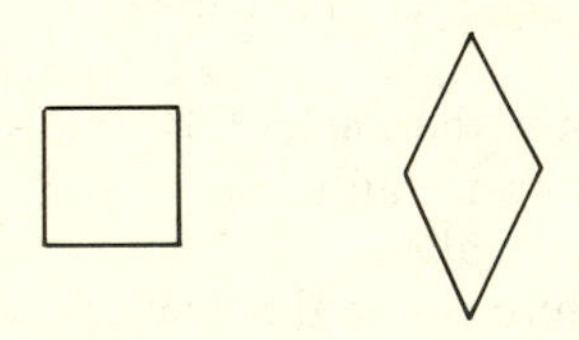

A.: Do you notice the acute angles face each other, like the obtuse pair?

E.: That is clearly the case.

A.: You see, then, that here too equality is preserved as far as possible. For it is clear that once you construct a figure of four equal lines, either all four angles are equal or at least they are paired equally face to face.

E.: That is my studied conviction.

A.: Aren't you impressed by the fact that even in such things there persists a certain kind of justice?

E.: What do you mean?

A.: Well we say, I believe, that justice is equity and equity stems from equality. What does the virtue of equity demand but "to each his own"? And would this be possible if all were equal and no differences existed? Or do you think otherwise?

E.: I fully agree.

A.: The practice of justice then requires as it were some measure of inequality and dissimilarity?

E.: I understand.

A.: Consider these equal-sided figures, the one with three, the other with four angles. Do they not seem to you to preserve some measure of justice in that the one whose opposite parts are unequal must of necessity have equal angles whereas the one whose opposite parts are equal allows for some angular inequality? Since this insight struck me so much, I had to ask you whether you also find this truth, this equity or equality, enchanting.

E.: I see what you mean and find it quite fascinating.

A.: But let us go on. Since you value equality above inequality, as I believe everyone with human sensitivity would, let us look for that figure, if you will, with the greatest measure of equality. For whatever it may be, we shall certainly prefer it to anything else.

E.: Fine. I am eager to know what it is.

CHAPTER 10

A.: Tell me first whether you think the figure with the four equal lines and angles is the best of those we've considered. As you see, it has equality as regards both angles and lines. In addition, line faces line and angle faces angle, something we don't find in a triangle.

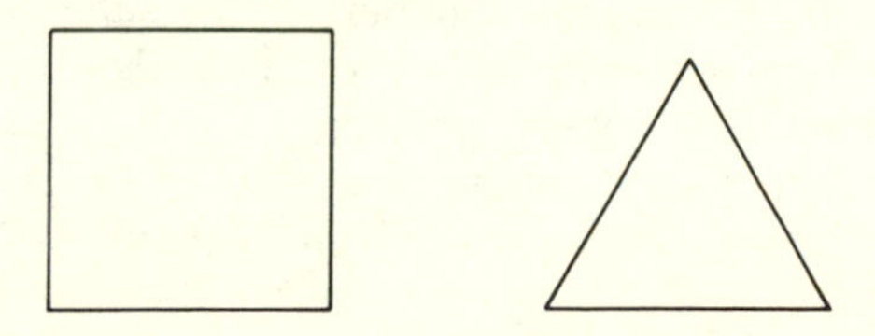

E.: It is just as you say.

A.: Do you think it has the greatest equality or not? If it has there is no point in looking elsewhere as we started to do. If it has not, I would like you to prove it to me.

E.: I think it has, for where the lines and angles are both equal I see no room for inequality.

A.: I do not agree, for a straight line has perfect equality until it forms an angle. For when it meets another line from the opposite side to form an angle, its equality, as you can see, is destroyed. Now does that portion of the figure enclosed by a line seem to have the same degree of equality as the portion enclosed by an angle?

E.: Not at all! I'm ashamed of my rash reply. What led me astray was discovering the parity between the angles as well as the sides. But who does not see the great difference between sides and angles?

A.: Take another clear instance of inequality. You surely see that both the equilateral triangle and the square have a center.

E.: I see that clearly.

A.: If we draw lines from the center to each part of the figure, will they all be equal or not?

E.: Unequal, of course, for the lines drawn to the angles must be longer.

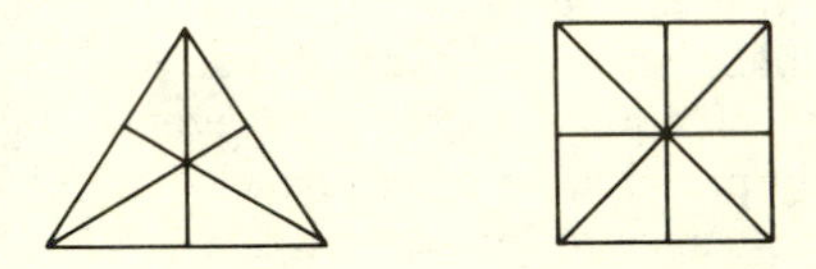

A.: How many such lines in the square and how many in the triangle?

E.: Four and three respectively.

A.: Of all the lines, which are shortest and how many of these has each figure?

E.: Those drawn to the midde of each side are the shortest and their number the same as the others.

A.: What you say is perfectly correct and there is no point in pursuing the matter further. What suffices for our purpose is to see that while there is a high degree of equality here, it is not yet perfect.

E.: I see that clearly and am most anxious to know what figure has the greatest [symmetry or] equality.

CHAPTER 11

A.: What else would it be, do you think, but a figure whose boundary is consistently the same, unbroken by any angle, and from whose center equal lines can be drawn to every part of the boundary?

E.: I think I understand. You are describing, it seems to me, a figure bounded by a single line drawn in a circle.

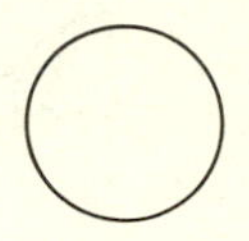

A.: That is right. Now consider this. Our previous reasoning revealed that a line is understood to have length alone. Being without breadth, it cannot be divided longitudinally. But do you believe we can find any figure without some breadth?

E.: No.

A.: Can you have breadth [i.e. an area] without length, even if you regard it simply as breadth, in the way we previously understood length to be without breadth? Or is this impossible?

E.: I see that is impossible.

A.: If I'm not mistaken, you also see that breadth can be divided every which way whereas a line cannot be divided longitudinally.

E.: That is clear.

A.: Which is more estimable: something divisible or that which cannot be divided?

E.: Surely that which is indivisible.

A.: You prefer a line then to breadth, for if the indivisible is to have preference, then we must prefer that which is less capable of division. Breadth can be divided in any direction whereas length can only be divided lengthwise, not widthwise. Hence it is superior to breadth. Or do you disagree?

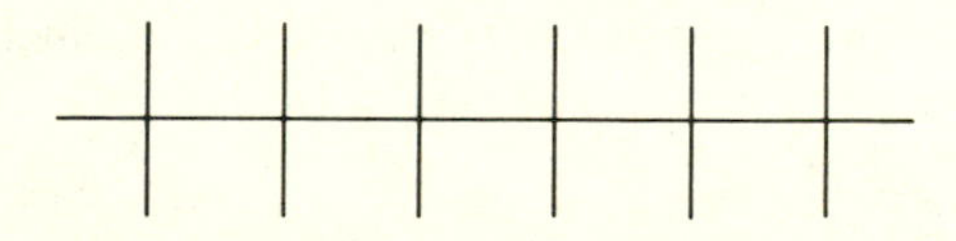

E.: Reason compels me to admit all you say.

A.: Following this train of thought, let us inquire, if you will, whether there is anything completely indivisible. In this respect, it will be ever so much better than a line, for the latter, as you see, can be cut crosswise countlessly. I leave you the task of discovering this thing for yourself.

E.: What we proposed as the center of the figure, from which lines were drawn to the borders, seems to me to be indivisible. For if it were divided, it would not be without length or even breadth. If it has length alone, it would be

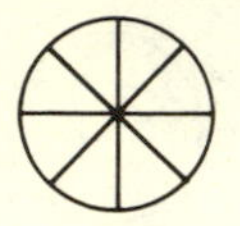

a line itself and not something from which lines were drawn. If it has breadth besides, this area would also have some center from which lines could be drawn to its borders. But reason rejects both assumptions. It must be this, then, which is indivisible.

A.: You are quite right. But don't you think the same is true of the starting point from which a line is drawn, even though we don't think of it as the center of a figure? I am talking about the initial point where length begins and want you to think of it as having no length whatsoever. For if you invest it with length, you simply fail to grasp that from which length itself takes its origin.

E.: I quite agree.

A.: I see you understand it, and of all the things we have pointed out so far, this is the most excellent since it admits of no division. If it is located in the center of a figure it is called "point." If it begins or ends a line or lines, or indicates something that must be understood to have no parts and still is not the center of a figure, we call it "sign." A sign then is a mark without parts. Such a mark in the center of a figure is a point. Every point, then, is a sign, but not every sign is a point. To avoid talking in circles, I would like to have mutual agreement on this usage. While some restrict "point" not to the center of any figure whatsoever, but only of a circle or sphere, we ought not belabor words too much.

E.: I agree.

CHAPTER 12

A.: Surely you also see how many functions a sign performs. It begins and ends a line. No figure can be constructed with straight lines unless it close the angles. Only through it can a line be cut, yet it cannot be sectioned itself. Only through it is line joined to line. And lastly, since reason reveals the circle surpasses in symmetry all other plane figures (we have said nothing of solids), what is the basis for this balance but the point in the center? Much more could be said on this subject, but I shall stop with this and leave further considerations to you.

E.: Just as you wish. If there is anything unclear, I shall not hesitate to bring it up. But I believe I see fairly well the multiplicity of ways in which a sign functions.

A.: Well then, consider this problem. You know now what a sign is, what length is and what breadth [or area] is. Of these, which appears so in need of the other that without the latter it could not exist?

E.: I see that breadth so requires length that you can't think of the former without the latter. I notice too that length needs no breadth, but without a sign it could not exist. The sign obviously stands alone without need of the others.

A.: What you say is so. But consider carefully whether breadth [or a flat surface area], though it admits of more division than a line, can be divided in any direction.

E.: I don't see why not.

A.: I believe you're forgetting something, something you must know. Let me prod your memory a bit. There is certainly no notion of depth in your conception of breadth.

E.: Certainly not.

A.: Add depth to breadth, then, and tell me whether the possibilities of division are augmented.

E.: You have indeed stirred my memory. For I see the combination is divisible not only horizontally or vertically but also laterally; in short, there is no direction impervious to division. Consequently, it is clear that breadth or area is not divisible along the depth axis.

A.: Since you know what length, breadth, and depth are, if I am not mistaken, tell me whether you can have depth without the other two dimensions.

E.: Not without length, but it seems depth without breadth is possible.

A.: Go back to your idea of breadth. If you see it as a surface lying flat, then turn it upright on any side as if you wished to shove it through the hairline crack between two closed doors. Do you understand what I mean?

E.: I understand what you say, but I still don't see what you're getting at.

A.: Just this. Does it seem to you that breadth [or a plane surface] by being placed upright has become depth and forfeited the name and description of breadth or is it still breadth despite its position?

E.: I believe it is now depth.

A.: Please recall our definition of depth [Chap. 4].

E.: I remember it now and I am ashamed of my answer. Even placed in this position, a plane surface admits of no division along the horizontal axis. Consequently, one cannot think of it as having any interior, although it is considered to have a center and boundaries. But according to your previous description of depth, if I recall, nothing is said to have depth unless you can conceive it to have an interior.

A.: What you say is correct. That is just what I wished you to recall. Now then, tell me this. You do prefer what is true to what is false, don't you?

E.: Had I any doubt about that, I would be incredibly stupid.

A.: Tell me then, I beg you, is that a true line that can be divided lengthwise? Is that a true sign [or point] that can be divided in any way? Is that a true plane figure which when turned upright can be divided edgewise?

E.: Nothing could be less true.

CHAPTER 13

A.: With your bodily eyes, did you ever see such a point, or such a line, or such a plane surface?

E.: Never. Such things are not corporeal.

A.: If, by reason of some marvelous affinity of natures, bodily things are seen with bodily eyes, must not the mind by which we see such incorporeal things be neither a body as such nor anything like a body? Or do you think differently?

E.: Well, I admit the mind is neither a body nor like a body. But tell me what it is.

A.: Consider, for the present, whether we have settled the matter of its having no quantity whatsoever, for that is the question we are discussing now. What the mind [or the soul] is, was the topic of our earlier discussion. I'm surprised you've forgotten. Remember you asked first: Whence is it? As I recall, we treated the question in two ways: one, in which we sought its place of origin, as it were; the other, in which we asked if it was derived from earth, fire, or any other element or from a combination of all or some of them. And we agreed it was as meaningless to ask what the mind or soul is made of as to ask what the earth or any other single element is made of. For it must be realized that while God made our mind, he gave it a substance all its own which is neither composed of earth, or fire, or air, or water; unless, perchance, one would believe that God gave earth the property of being just earth but did not do as much for the mind. If you wish a definition, and ask just what is mind [or soul], I have a ready answer. It seems to me to be some kind of substance, endowed with reason, equipped to rule the body.

CHAPTER 14

Consider then whether the mind has any quantity or spatial location, as it were. Since it is surely not a body, for if it were, it could not comprehend anything incorporeal as our previous reasoning proved, there is no doubt that it lacks such spatial characteristics as one measures bodies by. And that is why it is impossible to believe, or conceive, or think of the mind as having any quantity of this sort. If you wonder why without any quantity of this kind, the mind can encompass in memory such vast spaces of sky, sea, and earth, it is by virtue of its amazing power, some bit of which you must have surmised from our previous conclusions, depending upon your acumen. For if there is no body without length, breadth, or depth, as reason has already revealed, and if none of these properties can be present in a body apart from the other two, and for all that, one concedes the mind, by a kind of interior vision we call intelligence, can picture to itself a mere line, then I believe we must admit the soul is not a body, but something superior to it. Once this is conceded, there is no reason to doubt its superiority to a line, I would think. For since these three dimensions are essential to a body, would it not be absurd to believe that something superior to all three of these is not also superior to a body? But a line itself, which is clearly inferior to the soul, is superior to the other two dimensions, since it is less divisible than they are. What is more, the further these two dimensions are spatially stretched, the more they exceed a line in divisibility. But the only spatial dimension a line has is length. Take that away and it occupies no space at all. Hence anything more perfect than a line would not take up space, or be divisible in any way. It seems futile to me, consequently, to search for the mind's dimensions, since we admit it is more perfect than a line. If a circle is the most perfect of plane figures and reason reveals it contains nothing more perfect than a point, which no one doubts to be devoid of parts, is it surprising that the soul, which is not corporeal, or stretched lengthwise, or spread out in breadth, or solidified in depth still possesses such power over the body as to rule all its members and serve as the pivotal point of all bodily activity?

Since the center of the eye, called the pupil, is simply a point, so to speak, in the eye, and yet for all that, from an elevation it is able to survey half the heavens whose extent defies description, should it shock one that the mind lacks any tridimensional magnitude and still can picture any such magnitude to itself? Few are permitted to discern their own mind, that is, so that their mind sees itself. It is through intelligence that such insight occurs. Intelligence alone has the ability to discover that there is nothing more majestic or mighty in things than those characteristics conceivable apart from mass or bulk. Not without reason is the magnitude of a body referred to as "bulk." And if bulk were a matter of merit, then elephants would be wiser than we. Should someone who knows their ways call elephants wise (I've found them amazing and know that men might question this point), at least he will admit, I believe, that a bee shows greater brilliance than an ass, so that to judge intelligence by bulk would be worse than asinine. Or to return to what we said about the eye, who does not see an eagle's eye is much smaller than ours? Yet an eagle, soaring so high it can scarcely be discerned in broad daylight, has been known to sight a hare in a thicket or a fish beneath the waves. Size counts for nothing even in sense perception where only bodily things are perceived. Need one fear then that the human mind is nothing? Reason itself, which is its more excellent and almost sole power of perception, through which it discovers its own existence, convinces us it occupies no space or possesses any magnitude. Great things, believe me, should be ascribed to the mind, but not enormity in bulk. This discovery comes more easily to those well-instructed, who approach such subjects not in search of vainglory but prompted by a love of divine truth, or if not so well prepared for subtle study, turn away as far as possible from the tyranny of the senses and lend a patient and docile ear to what is good. By divine providence it cannot happen that religious souls searching purely, piously, and perseveringly for the truth about God and themselves should be denied the power to discover it.

On the Existence of God[8]

A.: To start with what is clearest, I ask you first: Do you exist? Or are you perhaps afraid of being deceived about this? [Remember], if you did not exist, you could not be deceived.

E.: No, no! Proceed!

A.: Since it is clear you exist, and since you would not see this were you not alive, it is also clear that you are alive. These two points, you understand, are absolutely true.

E.: I quite understand.

A.: Then this third point is also clear, namely that you understand.

E.: Obviously!

A.: Of these three, which is best?

E.: Understanding.

A.: Why?

E.: Well, we are dealing with three items: to exist, to live, and to understand. Now a stone exists, an animal lives; but I don't think a stone lives or an animal understands. Yet anyone who understands, most certainly exists and lives. That in which all three are present, I judge unhesitatingly to be more perfect than that in which either one or two are missing. For what lives, exists. That it also understands, however, does not follow. Animal life I think is this sort of thing. Neither does it follow that whatever exists also lives and understands. For I can say "Cadavers exist!" but no one would say they are alive or still less that something nonliving understands.

A.: Of the three, then, we maintain that two are wanting in a corpse, one in an animal, but none are absent in man.

E.: True.

A.: We also hold that of the three, understanding, which man has in addition to the other two, is the most excellent. For from his having this, it also follows that he is and lives.

E.: That we certainly hold.

A.: Tell me then whether you know that you have the common bodily senses of seeing, hearing, smelling, tasting, and touching.

E.: That I know.

A.: What do you think is proper to the sense of sight? That is, what do we perceive by seeing?

E.: Anything bodily.

A.: We do not perceive hardness or softness by sight, do we?

E.: No.

A.: What then pertains properly to the eyes? That is, what do we perceive through them?

E.: Color.

A.: And through the ears?

E.: Sound.

A.: And through the sense of smell?

E.: Odor.

A.: And taste?

E.: Flavor.

A.: And touch?

E.: The soft or hard, the smooth or rough, and many other such features.

A.: What about the shapes of bodies such as that they are large or small, square or round? Do we not perceive things of this sort both by touch and sight so that they are proper neither to vision nor touch but pertain somehow to both?

E.: That I understand.

A.: Then you also understand that each single sense has something it alone reports on whereas some report on things in common.

E.: This I also understand.

A.: It is not by any single sense, then, is it, that we judge what is proper to that sense or common to several?

E.: Of course not. That must be decided by something within us.

A.: Could this perhaps be reason which beasts lack? It does seem to me that it is by reason that we comprehend this and recognize it to be so.

E.: I rather think it is reason that recognizes the existence of an inner sense to which all is referred by the five familiar senses. For it is one thing by which a beast sees and quite another by which it seeks or shuns what it sees. The first sense resides in the eye; the second lies within the soul itself, for it is not only such things as they see, but also what they hear or perceive by the other senses that animals go for, if they are gratifying, or refuse and turn away from, if they are offensive. This sense is neither sight nor hearing nor taste nor smell nor touch, but something, I know not what, which presides over all these alike. While we can understand this by reason, as I have said, we cannot call this reason itself, because it is clearly something that exists in the brute animal as well.

A.: I acknowledge such, whatever it may be, and am not reluctant to call it an inner sense, but unless the information conveyed to us by the bodily senses passes beyond this inner sense, it cannot become knowledge. For what we know, we comprehend by reason. Now we do know that color is not perceived by hearing nor voices by the eyes, not to mention the other senses. When we know this, it is not by our eyes that we know it, nor by our ears or even by the interior sense we share with the brute animal. For there is no need to believe they know that light is not perceived by the ears nor the voice by the eyes, since this is something discovered only by reasoned reflection and thought.

E.: I cannot say this is evident to me. What if animals, by that inner sense you admit they have, do discern that colors cannot be perceived by hearing nor voices by seeing?

A.: Do you also think they can distinguish each of the following: the color perceived, the perception in the eye, this inner awareness in the soul, and reason which singles out and defines each of these?

E.: Of course not.

A.: Well, could these four be distinguished and their limits determined by reason, if colors were not referred to it by the ocular sense, and the latter's perception in turn by the interior sense supervising it? And could this interior awareness itself be referred to reason if there was not a distinction between the two?

E.: I don't see how it could.

A.: Well, don't you see that if color is perceived by the ocular sense, it is not the same sense that perceives this fact itself? You do not see that you see by the same sense that you see color.

E.: Of course not.

A.: Then try to distinguish the following as well, for I don't think you would deny that color is one thing, to see it is another thing, and it is still another, when color is absent, to possess the sense by which it could be perceived if it were present.

E.: I distinguish between them and concede each to be different.

A.: Of the three, it is only color you see with the eyes, is it not?

E.: Only that.

A.: Tell me then how you see the other two. For if they were not seen could you discriminate between them?

E.: I don't know. I just know it is so, that's all.

A.: You do not know, then, whether it is by this inner supervisory sense or by reason itself or by something else?

E.: No, I don't.

A.: Yet you recognize only reason can define these things and it can define only what is presented for its examination.

E.: Certainly.

A.: Clearly then this faculty which is able to perceive all that we know is a servant of reason, whatever else it may be. It presents and reports to reason whatever it contacts, so that whatever is perceived can be placed in its proper sphere and be grasped not only by perception but also by knowledge.

E.: True enough.

A.: Reason also distinguishes between itself and its servants. Recognizing the chasm between these and itself, it affirms it is more potent than they. But does reason comprehend reason by any faculty other than itself? Would you know you have reason, if reason itself did not perceive this?

E.: Surely not.

A.: When we see color, the sense by which we do so is not the same as that by which we perceive that we see. When we hear a sound, it is not our very hearing that we hear. Nor when we smell a rose, it is not our sensation that we smell. When we taste something, our mouth does not taste our tasting. And when we touch anything, it is not the sensation of touch that we touch. This being so, it is clear that the five senses cannot perceive themselves, though they perceive all bodily things.

E.: That is clear.

A.: I think it is also clear that the inner sense not only perceives what is presented by the body's five senses but also perceives these senses themselves. Otherwise the animal would make no move either to seek or avoid anything, were it unaware it perceives. But it does this not in such a way that it knows [in the proper sense of that term], for this is the task of reason. It only perceives this in such a way as to move, but this perception is not a function of any of the five senses. If this point is not clear, it will become more so if you consider a particular sense like sight. The animal could not possibly open its eye and turn towards what it wants to see, were it not aware it did not see with a closed eye or averted glance. If it is aware that it does not see when it does not, it must of necessity perceive that it sees when it does see. That it is aware of both situations is shown by the fact that it is not moved to turn its eye to see by the same impulse that would move it if it did not see.

But it is not so clear that this life which is aware of perceiving bodily things is also aware of itself as such, unless, on asking itself, it finds that all living things shun death; and since death is life's contrary, life—which shuns its contrary—must needs be aware of itself. But if this is still not obvious, let it go. For only by clear and certain proofs ought we to try to establish what we have in mind. Now these things are clear: bodily things are perceived by some bodily sense. This same sense cannot be perceived by itself, but it is some inner sense which perceives that corporeal things are sensed by a bodily sense as well as perceiving that bodily sense itself. But all this and reason itself is made manifest to reason and is a matter of knowledge [properly speaking]. Does it not seem so to you?

E.: It certainly does. . . .

A.: Tell me now, in which class of things do you think everything belongs that is perceived by the bodily senses such as the eye or any other bodily organ? That is, is it the class of what merely exists, or of what also lives, or of what understands?

E.: In the class of what just exists.

A.: In which of the three do you think the sense itself belongs?

E.: In the class of what lives.

A.: Which of the two is better, the sense or its object?

E.: The sense, of course.

A.: Why?

E.: Because anything that lives is better than something which merely exists.

A.: And what of the interior sense which we discovered to be beneath reason yet common to man and beast? Do you have any doubt that it is to be placed higher than a sense which perceives a body—which sense, you have said, is to be ranked above the body itself?

E.: No doubt at all.

A.: I would like to hear why you have no doubts on this score. It is not that the inner sense could be classed under things which understand, for it must be included among what exists and lives but lacks understanding, since it is present also in animals without intelligence. . . . If you say it is because the inner sense perceives this other sense, I don't think you will find any rule to assure us that everything which has perception is better than what it perceives. For this is false, since man understands wisdom yet he is not better than wisdom itself. Why then, do you think the inner sense should be preferred to a sense by which bodies are perceived?

E.: Because I know it acts as a moderator and judge of the other sense. If the latter be deficient in its function, the inner sense demands its debt from its servant, as we said a moment ago. For the ocular sense does not perceive whether it sees or does not see, and hence cannot determine what is sufficient or deficient. It is the inner sense which does this, warning the soul of the animal to open its closed eye and to do what it perceives needs to be done. No one can doubt however that what judges is better than that which is judged.

A.: Have you noticed that the bodily sense also passes judgment somehow upon bodies? Pleasure and pain are within its competence, a kind of verdict on whether it has been touched gently or has been bruised by the body. As the inner sense decides what is lacking or sufficient to the eyes, so the sense of sight rules on what is lacking or sufficient in color. As the inner sense passes judgment on hearing, whether it is attentive enough or not, so hearing in turn sits in judgment on sound, whether it is gentle or harsh. We need not take up the other senses, for I think you see what I mean. The interior sense pronounces judgment on the bodily senses, approving their adequacy and exacting what they owe. So too the bodily senses sit in judgment on bodies, welcoming a gentle touch and rejecting the opposite.

E.: Yes, I see that and agree it is so. . . .

A.: There is no need to ask whether reason judges the inner sense. For what is it but reason that tells us which is better, bodies, bodily senses or the interior sense? What but reason tells us of its own superiority? It could never do this without passing judgment on these things.

E.: Obviously!

A.: Now a nature, like the inanimate body which merely exists, but does not live or understand, is inferior to something like the animal soul which does not just exist, but also lives, even if it does not understand. The latter in turn is surpassed by something like the mind of man which exists and lives and has intelligence. Among the faculties which perfect our nature, I am sure you will find nothing nobler than the one we have put in this third place. Besides the body, we clearly have that kind of life that quickens a body and makes it grow—two things we recognize beasts also possess. But we also have a third something—a kind of "head" or "eye" of our soul, or whatever else more fitly describes the reason and understanding not possessed by beasts. Is there anything nobler in human nature, I pray, than this?

E.: I see nothing more noble.

A.: Should we find something you unhesitatingly recognize not only to exist, but to be more noble than reason, would you scruple to call this God?

E.: Not offhand would I call God anything that is better than the best in my nature. For it is not that to which my reason is inferior but that to whom no one is superior that I desire to designate as God.

A.: Rightly so! It is God himself who has empowered your reason to think so correctly and devoutly about him. But let me ask, if you find nothing above our reason save what is eternal and unchangeable, would you hesitate to call this God? Bodies, you know, are subject to change like the life that vivifies their varying moods. Reason itself proves mutable, for at times it tries to discover the truth whereas at other times it makes no effort. Sometimes, too, its search is successful, sometimes not. If reason on its own, without benefit of any organ or inferior sense, be it taste, touch or smell, or eyes or ears—if reason, I say, catches sight of something eternal and immutable, ought it not at the same time recognize its own inferiority and proclaim this something to be its God?

E.: What has no superior, I shall concede to be God.

A.: Good enough! I need but show then that such [an eternal and immutable] thing exists. Either you will admit this to be God, or if there be something above it, then you will grant that this is God. Whether or not there be something beyond this, it will be clear that God exists, when with his help I show, as I promised, that something superior to reason exists.

E.: Prove then what you promise.

A.: That I shall do. But first let me ask whether my bodily sense is the same as yours, or is mine mine and yours yours? Were the latter not so, I could see nothing with my eyes that you did not see.

E.: I quite agree that while they are of the same kind, each of us has his own individual sense of sight, hearing and so on. For one can not only see but also hear what another does not, and with any other sense, perceive what the other does not perceive. Your sense obviously belongs to you alone and mine to me.

A.: Would you say the same for the inner sense?

E.: Surely the case is no different. My inner sense perceives my senses and yours is aware of yours. That is why I am often asked by a person who sees something whether I see it too. While I perceive whether or not I see it, my questioner does not.

A.: Has each of us his own reason, then? For it can happen that at times I understand something you do not. And while you cannot know that I understand it, I can.

E.: Obviously we each have our own rational mind.

A.: But you cannot claim we each have our own sun, moon, or morning star, though we see each of these with our own sense.

E.: I would never claim that. . . .

A.: Tell me whether we can find anything all who reason see in common, each with his own mind and reason; something which is there for all to see, and yet is not used up by them or transformed like food and drink; something which remains complete and incorrupt, whether it be seen or not. Or do you think nothing of this sort exists?

E.: Quite the contrary, I find many such things, but it is enough to mention one—number's meaning and truth is there for all who reason. Each calculator tries to understand the truth of number with his own reason and intelligence. Some can do it easily, others with more difficulty. Yet number's truth presents itself alike to all who are able to grasp it. Neither is it converted into something consumed like food by him who learns it. Nor is it at fault, if one is mistaken about it. Rather it remains true and permanent, and the less one sees it, the more he is in error.

A.: Quite right. You are not unschooled in these matters, I see, and have quickly found your answer. But what would you say if someone were to tell you these numbers, being some sort of image of things visible, are impressed on our minds as a result of what we sensibly experience and not by virtue of their own nature? Would you agree?

E.: Not in the least. Even if it were by my bodily senses that I perceived numbers, I would still be unable in this fashion to discover the meaning of addition and subtraction. It is by the mind's light that I correct one who in adding or subtracting comes up with the wrong answer. I have no idea how long the earth or air I touch will last, or the bodies I perceive them to contain will endure. But three and seven add up to ten not only now but forever. Never did they come to anything else, and they will never add up to anything different. That is why I have declared this inviolable truth of number to be common to me and to anyone at all who reasons.

A.: I have no quarrel with you there. . . . [Consider too] there is no number that is not named from the number of times it contains an addition of one, yet the perception of "one" occurs through no bodily sense. And if we have not perceived "one" in that way, neither have we perceived any other number in that fashion. . . . [Or take a fact which holds for the whole of the number series.] No bodily sense makes contact with all the numbers, for they are innumerable. How do we know it holds good for them all? In what fantasy or sense image do we discern so sure a truth about innumerable numbers? Only an inner light of which the bodily sense knows nothing can yield so firm an insight.

By these and many similar arguments, men unclouded by obstinacy to whom God has given ingenuity, are forced to admit the law and truth of numbers is no concern of the bodily senses, but stands sure and unshakable, in common view of all who use their reason. Many other things one could cite that present themselves publicly and in common to reasoning men, things which remain inviolate and unaltered though each beholder sees them with his own mind and reason. Yet I was happy to hear that in answer to my question, it was the law and truth of numbers that first came to your mind. For not in vain does Holy Scripture conjoin number and wisdom, saying: "I turned my heart to consider, to seek out and to know wisdom and number."[9]

But now, I ask, what think you of wisdom itself? Has each man his own or is there but one which stands there in common for all, so that the more one partakes of it the wiser he becomes?

E.: I do not yet know what you mean by wisdom. I see men vary in their views of what is wisely said and done. Soldiers think they are acting wisely, while those who despise military service and devote all their care to agriculture praise this instead and call it wisdom. Those shrewd in devising ways to acquire money view themselves as wise, while those who leave all such things aside or abandon such temporal concerns to devote themselves wholeheartedly to the pursuit of truth, how they may know themselves and God, believe this to be the chief task of wisdom. Those who refuse to devote time to the search and contemplation of truth and who burden themselves with the duties of public office, advising their fellowmen and engaging in the just government and management of human affairs, deem themselves wise. Those who do both, busying themselves partly with the contemplation of truth and partly with toilsome duties they believe they owe to human society, are convinced they have captured the palm of wisdom. I shall say nothing of the innumerable groups which rank their own followers above all others, claiming they alone are wise. Since our discussion is concerned not with what we believe but what we ought to hold in the light of clear understanding, I am unable to answer your question until I know by reflection and reasoning as well that wisdom is what I believe it to be.

A.: You wouldn't regard wisdom as something other than the truth in which the supreme good is discerned and possessed, would you? For all the varied groups you mentioned seek good and shun evil. Their fragmentation comes from the fact that one sees this as good, another that. Now whoever seeks what he should not seek, errs even if what he pursues does seem good to him. But he cannot err who seeks nothing at all or who seeks what he should.

Insofar as all men are in quest of the happy life, they do not go wrong. To the extent that one strays from the path that leads to it, however, he is in error, even if he claims his sole desire is to find happiness. Error enters in when we follow a road that does not lead to where we wish to go. The more one errs in his mode of life, the less wise he is, since he has strayed that far from the truth in which the supreme good is discovered and possessed. When that good has been sought and obtained, each becomes happy—which beyond a doubt we all want.

Just as it is agreed we all wish to be happy, so too it is agreed we all wish to be wise, for who is happy without wisdom? For apart from the supreme good discovered and possessed in that truth we call wisdom, no one is content. But even before we are happy, we have impressed on our minds the notion of happiness. It is through this that we know and can confidently assert with no doubt whatsoever that we wish to be happy. In like fashion, even before we are wise, we have stamped on our minds a notion of wisdom. That is why each of us if asked if he wants to be wise, replies without a shadow of doubt that he does.

There is then some measure of agreement among us as to what wisdom is, even if, perhaps, you are unable to put it into words. For if your mind were not somehow aware of what wisdom was, you would never know you desire to be wise or that you should want to be wise—neither of which I think you will deny. What I wish you would tell me, however, is this. Is wisdom something like the law and truth of numbers, something presented in common to all who think? Or do you perhaps think that since there are as many minds as men and I cannot look in yours nor you in mine, there are as many "wisdoms" as there have been wise men?

E.: If the highest good be one for all men, then wisdom, as the truth in which it is envisioned and possessed, must also be one and common to all.

A.: Do you doubt that this supreme good, whatever it may be, is the same for all men?

E.: I certainly do, for I see different men rejoicing in different things as their highest good.

A.: Would that no one had any doubt about the highest good, just as no one has any doubt that unless he obtains the highest good, a man cannot be happy. Since this is a large question and may require a prolonged discussion, let us assume there are as many supreme goods as there are different things sought as such by different men. Does it follow that wisdom itself is not the same, shared in common by all men, just because the goods which men discern through it are many and varied? If that is what you think, you could also doubt that the light of the sun is one, because we see many different things in it. Of these, each person selects freely what he is going to enjoy through sight. One gazes delightedly at a mountain peak, another at the level plain, a third at a curving valley, still another at the green of the forests or the restless surface of the sea. Others still find their enjoyment in comparing several or all of these lovely sights. The scenes men choose to enjoy may be many and varied, but the sunlight that keeps them in view of each is one and the same. So too there may be many goods from which a man may choose what he wants to see and possess, making it his ultimate good to be truly and rightly enjoyed. Yet for all that the light of wisdom itself by which these things can be seen and grasped may very well be one and the same for all wise men.

E.: It's possible, I grant. Admittedly there is nothing to prevent there being one wisdom common to all even though the supreme goods be many and varied. But what I would like to know is whether this is the case. By conceding something to be possible, we do not immediately admit it is so.

A.: Nevertheless we do hold that wisdom exists, but whether it be one for all or whether each has his own wisdom, even as he has his own soul or mind, is something we do not know as yet.

E.: That is right.

A.: Where do we see these things—that wisdom or wise men exist and that all wish to be happy? I have no doubt that you see this and that it is true. Do you see all this to be true in the way you see your thoughts of which I am wholly ignorant unless you tell me of them? Or do you see it to be so in such a way that you understand I too can see it, even if you do not tell me?

E.: I have no doubt that you could see it too, even if I did not want you to.

A.: Is not the one truth common to us which we each see with our own mind?

E.: Most clearly so.

A.: I believe you do not deny we should strive for wisdom and that you grant this is true.

E.: I have no doubt at all.

A.: Can we deny this is true and one and in common sight of all who know it, even though each perceives it with his own mind and not with yours or mine or anybody else's? For what is seen is there in common for all alike to see, is it not?

E.: Of course.

A.: Do you agree that the following are also most true and there in common for you, me and all to see: "We ought to live justly," "The better should be preferred to what is worse," "Like should be compared with like," "Each ought to receive his due"?

E.: Agreed!

A.: Could you deny that what is incorrupt is better than what is corrupt, that the eternal is better than the temporal, the inviolable is better than the violable?

E.: Who would deny that?

A.: Could anyone call what is true his own when there it is, unalterable, for all to see who are able?

E.: No one could rightly call his own something which is as much one and common to all as it is true.

A.: Who denies the mind should be turned from corruption to incorruption, i.e., we should love the latter, not the former? And who admitting this to be true, does not recognize its unalterable character and that it is there in common sight for all who are able to see?

E.: How very true.

A.: Is not a life which no adversity can swerve from its set and honest course much better than one easily shaken or upset by passing troubles?

E.: Who would question it?

A.: But enough of such questions. It suffices if you see and grant, as I do, that it is surely the case that these norms and guiding lights, as it were, are true and unchangeable, and whether taken singly or all together, are there in common sight for each who with his own mind and reason can perceive them. But what I want to ask you is this. Do you regard these as belonging to wisdom, for I think you hold that man to be wise who has acquired wisdom?

E.: It seems they do.

A.: Could a person who lives a just life do so if he did not see which values are higher and which lower or on a par or if he did not perceive what is due to each?

E.: He could not.

A.: Would you deny that he who perceives these sees wisely?

E.: No.

A.: Does not the prudent person opt for incorruption, seeing that it ought to be preferred to corruption?

E.: Obviously.

A.: If he chooses to turn his mind to what no one doubts should be chosen, can anyone deny that he makes a wise selection?

E.: I would certainly not deny it.

A.: When he turns to the pursuit of a goal wisely selected, does he act wisely?

E.: Most certainly.

A.: And he who is undeterred by any threat or punishment from seeking the goal he wisely selected and chose to pursue, undoubtedly is behaving wisely?

E.: Without a doubt.

A.: It should be most clear then that what we have called the guiding lights or norms of virtue pertain to wisdom, since the more a man uses them to guide his life, the more wisely he lives and behaves. But nothing that is wisely done can be truthfully described as divorced from wisdom.

E.: That is quite true.

A.: Wisdom's norms then are as true and unalterable as the rules regarding number? . . .

E.: That I cannot doubt. . . .

A.: We might question whether number resides in or is derived from wisdom, or whether wisdom is derived from or resides in number, or whether both terms refer to a single thing. This much is certain, however. Both are true and immutably so. Hence you would not deny that some unchanging truth exists which contains all of these things that are unchangeably true and that it cannot be called exclusively mine or yours or any man's. It offers itself to all who discern things immutably true, like a light which in some strange fashion is both public yet concealed. . . .

You recall, I believe, what we said earlier of the sense of the body. Things that you and I both see and hear do not form an essential part of our eyes or ears but represent things that present themselves commonly to our sense perception. On the same grounds you will not claim that what you and I perceive in common, each with our own mind, pertains to the nature of either of our minds. We cannot say that what the eyes of two persons see simultaneously is part and parcel of the eyes of either, but is a third something on which the gaze of each is focused.

E.: That is something most obvious and true.

A.: What think you of this truth we've taken so long to describe and in which we see so many things? Is it superior, equal, or inferior to our minds? If it were inferior, we would not use it as a norm, but would pass judgment on it like we do on bodies beneath us when we say not merely that they are or are not so and so, but also that they ought or ought not to be so and so. We also know not only our state of mind but what it ought to be. We pass judgment when we say of bodies, for example, "This is not as bright as it should be," or "It is not square enough" and the like; or when we say of minds "This is not as capable as it should be," or "That is not gentle or eager enough," depending on what moral reason decides. And our judgment in all this is based on those interior norms of truth we discern in common. But we pronounce no judgment on these rules themselves. If one asserts the eternal is superior to the temporal, or that seven plus three makes ten, no one says, it ought to be so, but recognizing it to be such, he makes no attempt to correct the speaker but rejoices that he sees this.

On the other hand, if truth were merely on a par or equal to our minds, it too would be mutable. Sometimes our minds see more, sometimes less. Thus they recognize they are capable of change, but truth itself neither gains nor loses anything by our seeing more or less of it. It remains integral and whole, gladdening those who turn to it and punishing those with blindness who turn away. [If they were equal], how explain that while we have no jurisdiction over truth itself, we pass judgment on the mind itself according to the norms of truth? Do we not say a mind knows less than it should or as much as it ought to and that the closer it approaches and grasps immutable truth, the more it ought to understand.

Now if truth is neither below nor on a par with the mind, the only thing left is that it represents something superior which excels the mind.

If you recall, I promised I would show you something more sublime than our mind or reason. Behold, it is truth itself. Embrace and enjoy it if you can! . . . What more do you want than to be happy? And who is happier than he who enjoys this most excellent, firm, and immutable truth?

Men claim they are enthralled when they embrace the beautiful bodies of their wives or even courtesans. Do we doubt we are happy in the arms of truth? Men with throats parched with thirst cry out with joy when they find an abundant spring of pure water, or, if famished, when they discover a splendid dinner or supper. Shall we deny the happiness that comes from being given the food and drink that is truth? We frequently hear men say they are happy on a bed of roses or other flowers or inhaling the perfume of some fragrant ointment. But what is sweeter or more pleasant than the bouquet of truth? Many consider the happy life to consist in song or the music of strings or woodwinds. Without music they consider themselves miserable, with it they are entranced with joy. But when the silent truth penetrates our minds without tumult or oratorical tirade do we look further for the happy life or enjoy what is at hand and assured? Men enjoy what is bright and pleasant, the sheen of gold and silver, the sparkle of precious stones, the flash of color, the light itself which falls on the eye from the stars, sun, or moon, or some earthly fire. They think themselves happy if no trouble or want robs them of such pleasure and they desire to live forever. Should we fear to find life's happiness then in the light of truth? Since it is in that truth called wisdom that the supreme good is seen and grasped, let us turn to truth to possess and enjoy that good. Happy indeed is he who is enraptured by the highest good. For here is the truth that reveals all things that are really good, so that each man according to his lights selects one or more of them for his enjoyment. Of those who choose by the light of the sun what they wish to enjoy seeing, there are those who if they were endowed with stronger, more healthy, or vigorous eyes, would love to look at nothing better than the sun itself which sheds its light on all the other things that delight weaker eyes. So too a powerful and penetrating mind, having seen with certainty many unalterable truths, turns to truth itself wherein all is revealed, clinging to it as if forgetful of all else and enjoying in it everything at once. For whatever delights us in other truths, does so by reason of truth itself. . . .

No one possesses securely any good that can be lost in spite of what he wills. But no one can lose truth or wisdom unless he wills to do so, for what we call separation from truth and wisdom is nothing else than a perverted will in love with lesser things. In truth then we have something all may enjoy equally and in common. Here there is no dearth or defect. Truth receives all its lovers without arousing envy; it welcomes all and is chaste with each. No one says to another: "Get back that I too may approach; take away your hands that I too may embrace her." All cling to it and touch it together. No part of this food is consumed, you drink nothing from it that I cannot drink as well. Your share in it does not become something you alone possess, but what you take from it is there complete for me. To be inspired, I need not wait until you return what brought you inspiration. No part of truth becomes the private possession of one alone. All of it is open at once to all alike. What we taste, touch or smell is less like truth in this regard than what we see or hear. For each word is heard in full by all who hear it and by several at the same time. What lies before our eyes is seen simultaneously to the same extent by two as it is by one.

Despite such similarities, however, their difference is great. All speech is extended and protracted over a period of time, one part coming earlier, another later; the whole is not uttered at once. And the light from everything visible spreads out through space, as it were, and is not confined completely to a single place. And surely, through no will of our own, we may be robbed of such things and our enjoyment of them may be impeded. Suppose someone could sing sweetly forever, attracting students eager to hear him. The more that came, the more they would struggle for seats near the singer. As they heard him, they would be touched only by fleeting sounds with nothing lasting to remain with them. And if I wished and were able to gaze continually at the sun, at sunset it would desert me, clouds would cover it and many other obstacles would rob me of the pleasure of its sight despite my will. And even if sweetness of light and sound were ever present to eye and ear, what great thing has come to me that has not also come to the animal? But the loveliness of wisdom and truth lasts as long as you wish to enjoy it, never fading with time or fleeing from place to place. No surging, crowded audience to keep one away! No night to black it out or shadow to obscure it! No bodily sense it need depend on! Wherever it be in the whole wide world that its lovers reach out for it, all find it close by and always present. It abides in no place yet is absent from none. It admonishes us from without, it teaches us from within. All who behold it are changed for the better; by no one is it changed for the worse. No one passes judgment upon it or judges rightly without it. That is why it is clear beyond the shadow of a doubt that it is superior to our minds, none of which dares judge it, yet each of which becomes wise and a judge of all other things by means of it.

Now you granted that if I but showed you something superior to our minds you would admit it to be God, assuming there was nothing better. But in accepting your conditions, I declared it would suffice to prove the first. For if there be something superior to truth, then this would rather be God, but if not, then truth itself is God. But whichever be the case, you cannot deny that God exists. And this was the question we set out to discuss. Now if it bothers you that we have it on faith, from Christ's sacred teaching, that there is a "Father of Wisdom," remember it is also a tenet of our faith that this "Wisdom, begotten of the Father" is his equal. Let this be accepted for the present as settled by faith and let us question it no further. For [our present concern is that] God exists and he does so in the truest and highest sense of the word. It is not only by faith that we regard this beyond doubt but also, I think, by a certain, though tenuous form of knowledge. . . .

E.: Words fail to describe to you the almost incredible joy that I feel. What you have said I accept and proclaim as most certain. But within me a voice cries out by which I hope to be heard by truth itself and to cling to what I concede to be not just a good, but the Supreme Good, the source of happiness.

NOTES

1. *Contra Academicos* II, chap. 5, nn. 11-12, *Corpus Scriptorum Ecclesiasticorum Latinorum,* Vol. 63 (Vienna: Hölder, Pichler, Tempsky, 1922), 31-32.
2. *Ibid.,* III, chaps. 10-11, nn. 23-26, pp. 63-67.
3. *Ibid.,* chap. 12, nn. 27-28, pp. 67-68.
4. *Ibid.,* chaps. 15-16, nn. 34-36, pp. 70-75.
5. *De civitate Dei* XI, chap. 26, *Corpus Christianorum Series Latina,* Vol. 48 (Turnholti: Brepols, 1955), 345-46.
6. *De Trinitate* XV, chap. 12 n. 21, J.P. Migne, *Patrologia Latina,* Vol. 32 (Paris: 1845), cols. 1074-1075.
7. *De quantitate animae,* chaps. 1-14, J.P. Migne, *ibid.* cols. 1035-1049.
8. *De libero arbitrio* II, chaps. 3-15, *Corpus Scriptorum Ecclesiasticorum Latinorum,* Vol. 74 (Vienna: Hölder, Pichler, Tempsky, 1956), 42-75.
9. *Ecclesiastes* 7:26. Augustine quotes from the old Latin translation following the Septuagint.

II

BOETHIUS

ANICIUS MANLIUS TORQUATUS SEVERINUS BOETHIUS, of the distinguished senatorial family of the Anicii, was born in Rome about 480. After the death of his father, who had been consul in 487 and twice prefect of the city, the boy was adopted by the even more distinguished Symmachus, whose daughter he later married. Educated in Athens, where he became aquainted with the various schools of Greek philosophy, Boethius set himself the task of translating the complete works of Plato and Aristotle into Latin and showing the essential agreement of their basic philosophical principles. How much of this ambitious aim he actually realized is still a matter of dispute, as some of his writings have undoubtedly been lost. He did translate the whole of Aristotle's *Organon* plus Porphyry's introduction *(Isagoge)*, however, and thus became chiefly responsible for creating the technical Latin equivalents for Greek philosophical terms. He commented at length on both the *Categories* and *On Interpretation*, and twice on the *Isagoge*. In addition, he composed original treatises on the categorical and hypothetical syllogisms, on division, topics, rhetoric, arithmetic, and music, and also wrote several theological treatises in which he illustrated how rational analysis could be applied even to a revealed doctrine such as the Trinity.

Sharing Plato's conviction that civil government should be in the hands of wise men, he entered public service under the Arian King of the Ostrogoths, Theodoric, who ruled the western Roman empire as the deputy of the Eastern emperors in Constantinople. Though a Catholic, young Boethius quickly rose to political eminence under Theodoric. He became consul in 510 and saw his sons follow in his footsteps as joint consuls in 522. As Master of the

King's Offices, one of the highest positions in the western empire, he sought to eradicate corruption in government and to defend the traditional rights of the Roman Senate. Enemies made in the line of duty, however, turned Theodoric against him. Accused together with Symmachus of conspiracy against the king, Boethius seems to have become a victim of perjured testimony. He was imprisoned in Pavia in 523, and a year or so later was executed, after being cruelly tortured.

During his imprisonment he composed his philosophical classic, *On the Consolation of Philosophy*. The fact that over four hundred manuscripts of it are still extant attests to its popularity during the Middle Ages. The work is a mixture of poetry and prose, written in the form of a dialogue between Boethius and Lady Philosophy. Seeking to comfort the despondent prisoner abandoned by Fortune, Philosophy reminds him he is not the first of her faithful followers to suffer unjustly from evil men. Gradually she convinces him true happiness is not to be found in fame, fortune, or pleasure, but only in that that is all good, viz. God. Only by sharing in this good and thus becoming in a sense divine, can man be truly happy. Though the third book, with its impassioned plea for happiness, is often considered the climax of the work, it is only later Boethius probes such philosophical problems as how evil or the suffering of the innocent are compatible with an all good God (Book Four) or how God's perfect foreknowledge can be reconciled with human freedom (Book Five). Here we find his famous definition of eternity and one of the several ways in which medieval thinkers sought to explain how God knows the future.

The first selection, *Divine Foreknowledge of Human Actions*, comprises the whole of Book Five, with only the poetic interludes meant "to rest and refresh the reader" omitted. It was translated for this volume by A. B. Wolter from the text of L. Bieler. The second selection, *How Substances May be Good*, known to medieval schoolmen by the title *De hebdomadibus*, is numbered among the Theological Tractates. Its discussion of the goodness of creatures is, in fact, highly philosophical in character. It is translated in its entirety especially for this volume by J. F. Wippel.

Divine Foreknowledge of Human Actions[1]

1. "You said, [Lady Philosophy], that the problem of Providence involves other questions. From experience, I know this to be true. And in this connection I would like to know if you think chance to be anything at all, and if so, what?"

"My purpose," she said, "was to fulfill my promise of showing you the road back to your native land, and that as quickly as possible. And profitable though these other questions may be in themselves they digress to some extent from our main purpose. And I am afraid that tired out by such detours you may be unable to finish the trip."

"There is no danger of that," said I. "For it would give me much satisfaction to know about these things that delight me so much and to be so convinced of your argument that nothing that follows therefrom would occasion any doubt."

"I will do as you wish," she said, and went on to explain. "If one defines chance as an event produced by random movement without any causal connections, I assert categorically there is no such thing as chance. And apart from its present usage, I regard it as an empty word devoid of all reference. For what place is there for random behavior when God arranges all things in an orderly fashion? The statement that nothing comes from nothing is true and none of the ancients questioned it, though they understood the maxim of the material, rather than of the efficient cause, and made it a kind of basis for all their reasoning about nature. But if something occurred without a cause, it would appear to come from nothing. And if this cannot happen, then chance, as we just defined it, is also impossible."

"Is there nothing then," I asked, "that can correctly be called chance or fortune? Or is there perhaps something to which these words refer, even if it be something unknown to the man in the street?"

"My disciple, Aristotle," she said, "in his *Physics*[2] gave a short definition which comes close to the truth."

"And what," I asked, "did he say?"

"As often as something is done for a certain reason, but something other than what was intended takes place through the intervention of other causes, we call this chance. For instance, if a man turns over the soil to till it and discovers buried gold, this is believed to be a fortuitous event. But it does not come from nothing, for it has its own causes, whose concurrence, being unforeseen and unexpected, seems to have produced the effect by chance. For if the farmer had not dug into the earth where someone had buried his money, the gold would not have been found. Such are the causes of this good fortune. It results from a coincidence of causes and not by the intention of the agent. For neither he who buried the gold nor he who tilled the field intended the money to be found. But as I said, it was coincidental that the farmer dug where the other had hidden it.

"Chance may be defined, then, as an unexpected event produced by a concurrence of causes which had other ends in view. But the reason why these causes come together is to be traced to that order according to which things unfold in a pattern of inevitable connections, an order whose fountainhead is Providence which arranges all things, each in its proper place and time. . . ."

2. "I have noted what you say and I agree with it. But is there any room for freedom of will within this network of integrated causes or are all movements of men's minds also tied in with this fatal chain?"

"Of course there is freedom," she replied. "For there cannot be any rational nature that is not endowed with free will. For anything which by nature has the use of reason must also have the power to judge and make decisions. On its own, then, it differentiates what ought to be desired from what ought to be avoided. Everyone however seeks that which he considers desirable and rejects what he thinks should be shunned. Therefore in rational creatures there is freedom to like or dislike.

"Still I do not claim this freedom is the same in all. Supreme and divine substances possess perceptive judgment, an uncorrupted will and the effective means to attain what they desire. Human souls on the other hand have more freedom when engaged in contemplation of the divine mind than when joined to the body and are still less free when shackled with earthly fetters. But their greatest bondage is when they lose possession of their own reason by giving themselves to vice. For when they avert their gaze from the light of the supreme truth and look to lower and darker things, they are blinded by a cloud of ignorance and swayed by pernicious passions. By yielding and consenting to these they increase their slavery and are, as it were, made captives through their own freedom. Nevertheless, Providence from all eternity foresees all things and predestines each according to his merits. . . ."

3. "Now you have me even more confused and in still greater straits," I complained.

"Why is that?", she asked, "though I think I know what troubles you."

"Well," I replied, "that God should know all things beforehand and that any liberty should exist seem to be militantly and radically opposed to one another. For if God, who cannot be deceived, sees everything in advance, then whatever his Providence foresees will occur must of necessity come to pass. If from all eternity he knows not only the deeds of men, but also their deliberations and decisions, there can be no freedom of will. For no other deeds or decisions can exist save those foreseen by God's infallible Providence. For if something could be turned to any other end than such as was foreseen, God would have only uncertain opinion and not unshakable knowledge of future events, and to my mind it would be impious to believe this of God.

"Neither can I concede the validity of the reasoning which some believe will solve this problem. For they say it is not because Providence has foreseen the future that the events will happen. It is rather the reverse. What will occur cannot be hidden from divine Providence. Thus they switch the necessity to the other side. For they claim it is not necessary that the things happen which were foreseen, but it is necessary that those things be foreseen which will happen—as if the problem were which of the two is the cause of the other, viz. is the foreknowledge the cause of the necessity of future events or is necessity of the future events the cause of the foreknowledge? But our problem is rather to prove that no matter which way the causal sequence goes, it is necessary that the events foreseen should occur, even though the foreknowledge does not appear to imply that the events themselves occurred out of any necessity. For if someone were to sit down, the opinion that he is sitting must of necessity be true, and conversely, if the opinion that he is sitting be true, then he must needs be sitting. There is a 'must' for both; one on the side of the sitter, the other on the side of the truth. But the reason why the person sits is not because the opinion is true. Rather is such a statement true because the person is sitting. Thus though the cause for the truth stems from the one side only, necessity is characteristic of both.

"The same obviously holds of foreknowledge and future events. For even though such events are foreseen because they will occur, they do not happen because they are foreseen. Still it is necessary both that God foresees what will come to pass and that events foreseen will take place. And this alone suffices to rule out free will. And yet is it not preposterous to speak of the occurrence of temporal things as the cause of eternal foreknowledge? For to think that God foresees future events because they will take place is nothing else than to believe that things which happened later were the cause of that sovereign foreknowledge. And yet, if I know something to exist, it must needs be; so also then if I know something will happen, it must have to take place. Consequently, it follows that an event known in advance cannot fail to occur.

"And a final point, if anyone thinks a thing to be other than it is, this is not knowledge but fallacious opinion, which is a far cry from the truth we call knowledge. But if the outcome of something in the future is not certain and necessary, how can one know in advance what will happen? For just as certain knowledge is not marred by falsity, so what is conceived through such knowledge cannot be otherwise than as conceived. That is why such knowledge is not deceptive. Things have to be as true knowledge understands them to be. But then what? Can God have genuine foreknowledge of something uncertain? For if he thinks things will inevitably occur that may possibly not happen, he is deceived. This is as wrong to think as it is to say. But if he understands them to be just as they are, viz. something that may or may not occur, what kind of foreknowledge is this which does not grasp anything definite or certain? How is this better than Tiresias' parody on prophecy: 'Whatever I say will either be or not be'?[3] Or how would divine foreknowledge excel human opinion, if God judged, as do men, that uncertain events are doubtful? But if nothing can be uncertain to that most certain fountainhead of all things, then the occurrence of such events is certain which he knows will certainly take place. Hence there is no liberty in human decisions and actions, if the divine mind, foreseeing everything without error of falsity, limits them to one alternative. Admit this and see what ruin it entails for human affairs! For it is fruitless to propose rewards for the good and punishment for the wicked, if they do not merit such by any voluntary or free action. And to punish the wicked and remunerate the good, which now seems justified, will appear most unjust, if they are not ruled by their own will but by that inevitable necessity of what is to take place. There will be neither vice nor virtue and in their stead total confusion as to merits will prevail. And what is most blasphemous of all, the author of all good is made responsible for our vices since all ordering of things goes back to Providence and nothing is due to the decisions of men. There is no reason to hope or pray for anything. For what is the good of hope or prayer, when everything to be asked for results from an inflexible chain of events? Thus hope and prayer, man's only business with God, is taken from us. It is only the price of the humility that is our due that we merit the inestimable reward of divine grace and it is only in this way that as men we seem able to converse with God, being joined in supplication to that inaccessible light before receiving what we ask for. But if we believe these to have no force because we hold future events to be necessary, what remains to link us with the Sovereign Lord of things? Hence the human race, as you said before, will be cut off from its source and will pine away."

4. "This problem of Providence is an ancient one," she replied. "Marcus Tullius [Cicero] raised it in his work *On Divination*,[4] and you yourself have probed into it for a long time, but none of you have tried to solve it with sufficient vigor and diligence. The cause of the obscurity which shrouds the subject is that human reasoning as a step by step process cannot comprehend the simplicity of divine foreknowledge. Could we but understand the latter, no shadow of doubt would remain. This I shall try to clarify once I have explained the things that disturb you. For I would first ask why you consider insufficient the solution of those who see no threat to free will from foreknowledge inasmuch as it causes no necessity in what is to take place. For have you any proof for the necessity of future events other than this principle that things known beforehand have no choice but to occur? If foresight then does not make what will happen something

necessary, a point you have just conceded, why should voluntary actions be bound to take place in a certain way? For the sake of argument, that you may see what follows from it, suppose no foreknowledge exists. Would such things as occur arbitrarily become necessary on this account?"

"Not in the least."

"Let us then suppose foreknowledge exists but does not impose any necessity on things. Absolutely the same freedom of will would obtain *in toto*.

"Now you may say," she went on, "that foreknowledge is at least a sign future events must happen, even if it is not the knowledge as such that makes them necessary; and even in the absence of foreknowledge their outcome would still be necessary, since signs only show what is the case and do not produce what they point to. One must first demonstrate that everything happens by necessity, then, before showing that foreknowledge is a sign of such necessity. Otherwise, if there is no necessity, such knowledge cannot be a sign of what does not exist. Besides, it is clear that if the proof is to be solid, it should not rest on signs or extrinsic arguments but be deduced from suitable and necessary reasons."

"But how can things foreseen fail to happen?"

"We do not assume they will not happen if Providence has foreseen them. Rather we think that although they will come to pass, there is nothing in their natures that makes it necessary that they do so. For we see many things going on before our eyes just as the charioteer does as he directs the course of his chariot turning it here and there. So too with other things. Do you believe these things have to happen in the way they do?"

"Hardly! For in vain would art labor if all came about by necessity."

"Well if such things do not come into existence by necessity when they do take place, then they are hardly governed by necessity before they come to be. Consequently, the outcome of some future events at least is devoid of any necessity. For I think no one would deny that what is happening now was going to happen before it actually did occur. And some such events occur freely even though they were foreseen. Now just as the knowledge of present events does not entail that they occur of necessity, so neither does correct foreknowledge imply that the outcome of future events is necessitated.

"But, you will say, the point called into doubt is whether

foreknowledge is possible at all in regard to events whose outcome is not necessary. For these notions seem to clash, and you think that to be foreseen, the events must necessarily happen and if such necessity is wanting they cannot be foreseen, neither can anything be truly known if it be uncertain. If events whose outcome is not certain are foreseen as certain, this is obviously not truth of knowledge but obscurity of opinion, for you admit that to judge something to be other than it is, is a far cry from perfect knowledge. But your mistake lies in thinking that whatever is known is known only through the nature or by virtue of the things themselves, whereas it is quite the contrary. For everything known is known not according to its own power but according to the capacity of the knower. To illustrate this by a brief example: the curvature of a body is known differently by sight and touch. Sight at a distance takes in the whole thing at once by means of reflected radiation, but touch directly contacts the sphere and feeling around it grasps its curvature only gradually. Man himself is known differently by means of sense, imagination, reason, and intelligence. Where sense sees the figure as concretized in matter, imagination grasps it apart from the matter. But reason goes a step beyond weighing the universal features of the type or species found in particulars. Still higher is the eye of intelligence. It looks beyond the bounds of the universe to behold the simple form with the pure vision of the mind. What is most important to note about all this is that the higher power of comprehension includes the lower, but the lower can in no way come up to the higher. The senses are powerless where there is no matter; imagination also cannot grasp a universal type nor can reason see a simple form. But intelligence having grasped that form, looks down in judgment as it were on all beneath it, and the way in which it comprehends the form itself is unknown to any other power. For intelligence knows the universals of reason, the figures of the imagination, the material sensible, and all this without using reason, imagination, or the senses. It beholds all things, as I have said, and that by grasping their formal nature as it were and doing so with a single glance. Reason too, in considering what is universal, takes in all that can be imagined and sensed, but without using either senses or imagination. For instance, reason defines the universal she conceives like this: 'man is a two-footed, rational animal.' Now even though this is a universal conception, it leaves no one ignorant of the fact that man can be imagined or perceived by the senses—a fact which reason knows by a rational conception and not by imagination or sense. Imagination also, though it initially works with the senses in envisioning and forming figures, in the absence of sensory stimulation it still beholds the sensible objects but it does so not by some sense perception but by imagining them. See then how all these use their own powers to know things rather than the powers of the objects known! And rightly so, for since every judgment is an action performed by the one judging, he ought to accomplish it through his own resources rather than make use of another's. . . .

5. "In the case of a sentient organism, the qualities of the external objects affect the sense organs, and some physical sensation precedes the movement of the mind, stimulating it to act upon itself and to stir up the latent forms within it. Now if the mind, in sentient bodies, does not form its final impression from how it is passively affected, but judges by its own power the cause of the stimulation to which it was subjected, all the more so do minds freed from all bodily stimulation make use of their own abilities in arriving at their judgments rather than passively follow the impressions received from the objects. In line with this principle then, various kinds of substances would have different ways of knowing. Some immobile, animate organisms (e.g. those mollusks and other forms of marine life which feed while clinging to stones) have only sense impressions to rely on. Animals able to move, however, seem to have imagination and the impulse to go after some things and run away from others. Reason, on the other hand, is characteristic of mankind alone, just as intelligence is proper to what is divine.

"And so it is that the most excellent knowledge is that which in virtue of what it is, knows not only its own proper object but also the subject matter of all the other forms of knowledge. But now suppose, for instance, that sense and imagination were to gainsay reason, and declare that the *universal* which reason claims to see is sheer nothingness and that, since nothing sensible or imaginable can be universal, either reason is correct to claim there are no sensibles or else reason is inane to regard sensibles and singular things as if they were universal; but that they know there are many things subject to sense and imagination. What would you think of that? And suppose, further, that reason were to counter that she sees the sensible and imaginable under the aspect of universality, and that even though sense and imagination cannot aspire to such universal knowledge, since their cognition is unable to get beyond the bodily figure, we ought still to trust the judgment of the more perfect and potent power in matters of knowledge. In such a controversy, ought we not, with our ability to reason as well as to imagine and to sense, side with the claims of reason?

"Now the situation is similar if human reason supposes that divine intelligence views future events only as she herself sees them. For you argue that just because some things seem not to have any necessary or certain outcome, certain knowledge of them beforehand is not possible. Consequently, you claim there is no foreknowledge of such things, or if you do believe such foreknowledge exists, you insist there is nothing whose outcome is not controlled by necessity. But if we, who now share in reason, could possess the discernment of the divine mind, we would judge that just as sense and imagination should accede to reason, so is it most reasonable for human reason to submit itself to the divine mind. If we can then, let us rise to the plane of the highest intelligence; for from there reason will see what it cannot intuit on its own, viz. how certain and definite foreknowledge even of those events of uncertain outcome is possible and that this is not mere conjecture but rather is part and parcel of that supreme science which in its simplicity is without bounds. . . .

6. "Seeing that whatever is known is known according to the nature of the knower and not according to its own nature, as was just shown, let us, as far as we may, look at the situation in the divine substance to see what its knowledge is like. Now it is the common judgment of all rational creatures that God is eternal. So let us consider what eternity is, since this will make both the divine nature and divine knowledge clear to us.

"Eternity then is endless life possessed all at once in its totality and perfection. This becomes clear in contrast to temporal things. For whatever lives in time, lives in the present, proceeding from past to future. But nothing so temporally constituted can embrace at one time the whole of its life span. For yesterday it has already lost and tomorrow it has still to experience. Even today's life you do not live outside of a moving, passing moment. Whatever is subject to such temporal conditions, then, could not rightly be regarded as eternal, even if its life span were coextensive with infinite time, without beginning or end—as Aristotle thought was the case with the world. For it does not comprehend or embrace the total sweep of this infinite life all at once, since it does not have the future which is still to come. Only that deserves to be called eternal which comprehends and possesses the entire plenitude of endless life all at once with none of the past or future missing. It is also necessary that, with full possession of its mental powers, it not only always be present to itself but also have in its presence at every moment the infinitude of passing time.

"They are mistaken then who when they hear Plato believed this world to be without temporal beginning or end,[5] think that on such an assumption the world becomes coeternal with its creator. For it is one thing to endure an endless life, which is what Plato ascribed to the world, and quite another to embrace the whole of this boundless life as present all at once. Obviously this latter is what is proper to the divine mind. Neither should we consider God to be older than his creation because of the amount of time he has existed, but see his priority to creation rather as a consequence of the simplicity of his nature. This motionless life where all is ever present, the infinite motion of temporal things tries to imitate, but being unable to equal or reproduce the same, it turns from immobility to motion, from the simplicity of the 'now' to an infinite sequence of 'befores' and 'afters.' And since it cannot have the fullness of its life all at once, it sets out to imitate to some degree what it cannot fully express by never ceasing to exist in some way and by binding itself to a kind of present in this minute, passing moment, which in virtue of its resemblance to that changeless present invests whatever it touches with a semblance of existence. Yet unable to remain quiet, it undertook an infinite journey through time and thus by moving it extends that life whose fullness it could never embrace by standing still. If we wish to label things properly then, taking our cue from Plato,[6] let us call God eternal but the world perpetual.

"Since all power of discernment apprehends according to its own nature what is submitted to it, and since God lives in an eternal present, his knowledge too transcends all temporal change and abides in the simplicity of his 'now.' Embracing the infinite stretch of past and future, it views all things in its simple comprehension as if they were going on now. If you wish to appreciate that 'present' by which it knows all things, you will evaluate it more correctly as knowledge of a never fading instant than as foreknowledge of the future. Hence it is called providence rather than prevision, for located far above all lesser things it looks down upon them all from on high.

"Why then do you require the events illumined by this divine light to be necessary, when not even men impose necessity upon what they see? Does your vision invest the events you see before you with any necessity?"

"Not at all!"

"Well then, if the analogy of the divine and human vision of the present is a fitting one, then just as you see things at present, so he views things in his eternal 'now.' Consequently, this divine foreknowledge does not change the nature or properties of things, but envisions them at present in the way they will eventually turn out to be. Neither is his judgment confused, but with a single glance of the mind, he encompasses all future events, be they necessary or not. Even as you possess the ability to distinguish between the voluntary and involuntary, though you see both at once (e.g. when you see simultaneously the sun rising in the sky and a man walking on the ground), so the divine vision looking down on all does not alter the nature of what is present before it, though in terms of time, the events are in the future. Consequently God does not have mere opinion, but knowledge based on truth.

"You may object at this point that what God sees will be, has to be, but whatever has to be, happens by necessity. Now if you tie me down to this word 'necessity,' I'll admit there is a most solid truth at stake here, but hardly anyone will arrive at it who does not contemplate the divine. For I grant by way of answer that the same future event seems to be necessary with reference to God's knowledge but independent and free as regards its own nature. For there are two types of necessity, one simple like the necessity of all men being mortal, the other conditional like this. If you know someone to be walking he must be walking. For whenever anyone knows something, it cannot be otherwise than it is known to be. But this condition does not entail simple necessity, for the necessity in the second case arises only when the condition is added and does not come from the proper nature of the thing in question. No necessity compels the steps of the voluntary walker, but when he walks he has to take steps. So too if Providence sees something present, it is necessary that it be, even though it may not be of a necessary nature. But those future things which result from free will God sees as present. With reference to the divine sight they become necessary on condition of divine knowledge, whereas considered in themselves they lose nothing of the absolute freedom of their nature. There is no doubt then that all will be which God knows will be, but some of these events result from free will. And though they come to pass, they do not by existing lose what is essential to their nature. Now one such property is that, before they happened, they could also have been avoided. But you may ask what is the import of saying such things are not necessary, if in virtue of the condition of divine knowledge, they take place as though they were necessary? The point is the same as in the example I proposed earlier of the man walking and the sun rising. At the moment both are happening, it is not possible that both are not happening, yet before they occurred, only for one of the two was it necessary that it should happen. So too all those events God has present before him will indubitably exist, but some of them happen out of the necessity of things, whereas others are in the power of those who make them occur. Not improperly then did we refer to the latter as necessary only in reference to divine knowledge, whereas considered in themselves they are free from the bonds of necessity. It is like something perceptible to the senses, which is singular in itself but is a universal with reference to reason.

"But you may say, if it is in my power to change my mind, I could frustrate Providence, since I could change something which it perhaps foresaw. To this I answer that you may indeed alter your decision, but since the present truth of Providence sees not only that you can, but also whether you will, you can no more frustrate divine foreknowledge than you could escape the eye of one watching you now by freely changing the course of your actions. Still you may wonder about this. Is the divine knowledge altered by my decisions so that if I were to switch my choice, divine knowledge would be changed correspondingly? Certainly not! For the divine vision anticipates every future event making it part and parcel of its own present knowledge. It does not change, as you might think, foreseeing in turn first this then that, but in one unchanging glance it envisions and comprehends all your changes. This ability to see and comprehend all things as present is something God gets, not from the way future events turn out, but from that simplicity which is proper to himself. This also accounts for a point you made a moment ago, viz. that it would not be fitting to speak of our future actions as the cause of God's knowledge. For it is a characteristic of this knowledge which envisions all things as present, to be itself the measure of all else and to owe nothing to what will take place later. This being so, the freedom of will of mortals remains inviolate, and it is not unjust to have laws which propose punishment or rewards to voluntary agents unshackled by necessity. And there is one who looks down on us all, a provident God dispensing rewards to the good and punishment to the wicked, and who correctly envisions the future quality of our actions, since his eternity is copresent to all time. Not in vain are our hopes and prayers directed to God, for if they be just they cannot fail. Stand firm then against vice and cultivate virtue. Let hope elevate your soul. Send your humble prayers to heaven. The need for acting virtuously is very great, if you but face it, for all your actions are performed before an all-seeing judge."

How Substances May Be Good in Their Essence Without Being Good of Their Essence[7]

[INTRODUCTION]

You ask me to develop and clarify the obscure question treated in our *Hebdomades*[8] as to how substances may be good in that which they are [i.e. in their essence] without being good *of* their essence *(substantialia bona.)*[9] And you point out that this should be done since the method of presentation in this type of writing is not clear to all. I myself bear witness as to how eagerly you entertained this topic before. I prefer to expound my *Hebdomades* to myself, however, and entrust my thoughts to my own memory rather than to share them with those who are so flippant and querulous that they will not tolerate anything that is not amusing. Do not take umbrage then at the obscurity that results from brevity, since it is the faithful guardian of mystery and has this advantage that it speaks only to those who deserve to understand.

[AXIOMS]

As is customary in mathematics and other disciplines, I have proposed [the basic] terms and rules according to which I shall develop all that follows.

I. A conception common to the mind is a proposition admitted by anyone as soon as it is heard. Of these there are two types. One is so common that it will be admitted by all. Thus, "If equals be subtracted from equals the remainders are equal." No one who understands this proposition will deny it. The other type is understood only by the learned, but it too comes from such conceptions common to the mind. For instance, "Incorporeals do not occupy space" and the like are propositions admitted by the learned but not the uneducated.

II. Being *(esse)* and the subject which exists are different. For it is still not being as such, but a subject which has received its form of being that exists and subsists.

III. What exists can participate in something but in no way does being itself participate in anything. For only when something exists is there participation. But something exists only when it has received being.

IV. The subject which exists admits of possible addition to what it is. But being itself admits of no admixture of anything besides itself.

V. Merely to be something[10] is one thing; to be something in essence is another. For accident is signified in the first instance whereas substance is signified in the second.

VI. Everything that is participates in being[11] in order to exist. But it participates in something else in order to be something. Hence the subject which exists participates in being in order to exist. But it exists in order to participate in something else.

VII. In every simple entity, its being and that which it is are one and the same.

VIII. In every composite entity, its being and that which it is are not one and the same.

IX. All diversity repels, but likeness is to be desired. As regards that which desires something else, its being is naturally manifested to be of the same kind as that which it desires.

Therefore, these preliminaries will suffice. Each point will be buttressed with appropriate argumentation by the intelligent follower of this discussion. Now this is the problem. Those things which exist are good. It is the general consensus of learned men that everything that exists tends to the good and that everything tends to its like. Therefore, those things that tend to the good are themselves good. But we must determine how they are good, whether by participation or by substance. If [they are good] by participation, then they are not good of themselves in any way. For that which is white by participation is not white of itself in its essence. And the same is true of the other qualities. If, therefore, they [things that exist] are good by participation, they are not good of themselves in any way. Therefore, they will not tend to the good. But this point [that they do tend to the good] has already been granted.

Therefore, they are not good by participation but by substance.

But those things whose substance is good are good *of* their essence. But their essence [that which they are] derives from being itself. Therefore, their being is good. Therefore, the being of all things is good. But if their being is good, those things that exist are good in their essence and their being will be the same as the being of the Good. Therefore, because they do not participate in goodness, they are good *of* their essence. But if their very being is good, there is no doubt but that, since they are good *of* their essence, they are similar to the first good. And by reason of this they will be this good itself. For nothing other than it is like it. From this it follows that all things that exist are God, which is a reprehensible assertion. Therefore, such things are not good *of* their essence and hence, goodness of being is not found in them. Therefore they are not good *in* their essence. But neither do they participate in goodness. For in no way do they tend to the good. Therefore, they are good in no way whatsoever.

[SOLUTION]

The following solution may be presented to this question. There are many things that can be separated in the order of thought even though they cannot be separated in fact. For instance, even though no one can in fact separate a triangle or other [mathematical figure] from its underlying matter, nevertheless by mental separation one can view the triangle itself and its properties apart from matter. For a moment, therefore, let us remove the presence of the First Good from our minds, whose existence is indeed evident from the consensus of all men, both learned and unlearned, and can be ascertained from the religious beliefs of barbarian peoples.

Having abstracted from the First Good for the moment, let us suppose that all things that exist are good and let us consider how they could be good if they did not in any way derive from the First Good. In this way I am led to note that for them to be good is one thing, for them to be is another. Let us suppose that one and the same substance is good, white, heavy, and round. Then the substance will be one thing, its roundness another, its color another, and its goodness another. For if these particular aspects were the same as the substance, then weight would be the same thing as color or as goodness and goodness would be the same thing as weight—which is contrary to nature. Therefore, in such entities being would be one thing and being something[12] would be another. Thus they would indeed be good but their being itself would not be good. Therefore, if they did exist in any way at all, they would neither be from the good, nor good, nor the same as good, but for them being would be one thing and goodness another.

But if there were absolutely nothing else but good things and if they were neither heavy nor colored nor subject to spatial dimension and if they were free from every quality with the exception of goodness, then *it* (not they) would seem not to be things but the principle of things. For there is only one thing which is of this type, which is only good and nothing else. But since such things are not simple they could not exist at all unless that being which is the only Good willed them to be. Hence, they are said to be good because their being flows from the will of the First Good. For the First Good, because it is, is good in its essence. But a second good is itself good because it flows from that whose very being is good. But the very being of all things derives from that which is the First Good and which is good in such a way as to be rightly said to be good in its essence. Therefore, their being is [also] good; thus [they are good] in that [which they are, i.e., in essence].[13]

Thereby the question is resolved. Therefore, although they may be good in their essence, nevertheless, they are not like the First Good, since their being itself is not good under every aspect. And since the being of such things cannot itself be given unless it derives from the First Being, i.e., the First Good, therefore, their being is good and yet is not similar to that from which it derives. The former [the First Good] is good in essence under every aspect. For it is nothing else than good. The latter [a secondary being] might perhaps be good but could not be good in essence if it did not derive from the former. For then it might perhaps participate in good; but their very being, not deriving from the Good, could not itself be good.

Therefore, when one separates the First Good from such beings by a mental process, although they would be good, they could not then be good in essence. And since they could not exist *in act* unless that which is truly the Good had produced them, therefore, their being is good, and yet that which flows from the substantial Good is not like it. And unless they did derive from it, even though they might be good, nevertheless they could not be good in essence since they would be distinct from the good itself and would not derive from it, while it itself is the First Good and being itself and goodness itself and essential goodness.

But it will not be necessary for things that are white to be white in their essence; for they flow from the divine will insofar as they exist but not insofar as they are white. Being is one thing, being white is another. This is so because he who brought them into being is indeed good, but he is not white. Therefore, it is in accord with the will of one who is good that they be good in essence. But it is not in accord with the will of one who is not white that such be the property of a thing that it be white in essence. Nor did they flow from the will of one who is white. Thus, they are white [but not in essence] simply because one who was not white willed them to be white. But they are good in essence because one who was good willed them to be good.

But according to this reasoning, must all things be just because one who is just willed them to be? Not at all! Being good has to do with essence whereas being just has to do with action. In Him [the Good] being and action are one and the same and therefore being good is the same as being just. But for us being and action are not one and the same. For we are not simple beings. Therefore, being good and being just are not one and the same for us. But being in essence[14] is the same for all of us. Therefore, all things are good but not all things are just. Moreover, the good is something general whereas the just is something specific and this species does not extend to all things. Wherefore, some things are just, others are something else, but all things are good.

NOTES

1. *Boethii Philosophiae consolatio,* V, ed. L. Bieler, *Corpus Christianorum Series Latina,* Vol. 94 (Turnholti: Brepols, 1957), 90-105.
2. Aristotle, *Physics* II, 4-5; see also *Metaphysics* V, 30.
3. Horace, *Satires* II, 5, 59.
4. Cicero, *De divinatione* II, 8ff.
5. Plato, *Timaeus,* 28ff.
6. *Ibid.,* 37ff.

7. *Quomodo substantiae in eo quod sint bonae sint cum non sint substantialia bona,* ed. E. K. Rand, *Boethius: The Theological Tractates* (Cambridge, Mass.: Loeb Classical Library, 1918, repr. 1962), 38-50.

8. It was this reference to a work apparently lost that caused the schoolmen to refer to this treatise of Boethius by the shorter title *De hebdomadibus.*

9. Literally, they are not "substantial goods." Unlike God, who is goodness itself, they are not "good *of* their essence." Yet their goodness is not merely extrinsic and hence they are to be described as "good *in* their essence," or literally "in that which they are" *(in eo quod sint).*

10. "Merely to be something" is our translation of *tantum esse aliquid.* As used here and in Axiom VI *(alio vero participat ut aliquid sit)* it refers to being something in a particular or qualified way, as distinguished from being something in essence or substantially.

11. Literally, "that which is being" *(eo quod est esse).*

12. Cf. note 10 above.

13. The text found in Migne contains a longer reading: *Tunc enim in eo quod essent non essent bona, si a primo bono minime defluxissent.* PL 64: 1313. In our translation we have followed the Rand text which ends more abruptly: *tunc enim in eo* (46:127). Following a suggestion made by Gilbert of Poitiers in his commentary on the *De hebdomadibus,* we understand the concluding words *in eo* as an introduction to the frequently recurring expression: *in eo [quod sunt, bona sunt],* with the words in brackets to be supplied by the reader. For Gilbert's text cf. N. Häring, *The Commentaries on Boethius by Gilbert of Poitiers* (Toronto: Pontifical Institute of Mediaeval Studies, 1966), 221:96-100.

14. Literally, "being in that which we are" *(esse . . . in eo quod sumus).* Hence since we are good *in* essence though not good *of* our essence, all of us are good.

III

FRIDUGIS

FRIDUGIS (also *Fredegis, Fredegisus*), the deacon, was one of several of Alcuin's Anglo-Saxon students at York who joined his master (*ca.* 796) as a teacher in Charlemagne's palace school. When Alcuin died in 804, Fridugis succeeded him as abbot of St. Martin of Tours. Under Charlemagne's son, Louis the Pious, he served as chancellor (819-832). He died in 834.

His only extant writing is the present letter to Charlemagne *On Nothing and Darkness,* composed during his tenure at the palace school. Interpretation of the Sacred Scriptures was the only "advanced study" in its extremely primitive curriculum. A contemporary, Agobard, criticizes Fridugis' predilection for "dialectical-syllogistic" proofs of his interpretations and chides him for believing that the human soul is created from some "unknown matter" which is to be identified with "nothing."

To understand the point of Fridugis's argument, one must keep in mind that he treats the Latin *nihil* as a "definite noun" (*nomen finitum*). Aristotle, we recall, in *De interpretatione,* chap. 2, distinguishes a true noun like "man" from the expression "nonman." To the latter he gave the name "indefinite noun" *(onoma aoriston),* which Boethius translated as *nomen infinitum,* reserving *nomen finitum* for a true or definite noun or name. Medieval logicians called attention to the ambiguities inherent in such indefinite nouns and verbs as "nonman" and "is not-healthy," since they may be referred to both existent and nonexistent things. *Nihil* is not as obviously indefinite in the way its English equivalent *nothing* (i.e. non-thing) is. By treating it as definite, Fridugis creates a problem reminiscent of that posed by Meinong, which Russell set up his "theory of descriptions" to solve.

The following translation from Dümmler's critical edition was made expressly for this volume by Hermigild Dressler.

Letter on Nothing and Darkness[1]

Fridugis the Deacon to all the faithful and to all at the sacred palace of our lord the most serene prince Charles.

1. On Nothing

With careful reflection and consideration I have finally decided to take up the question concerning nothing which has been raised for a very long time by many persons and which they have left unconsidered and unexamined as a question which it is impossible to explain. Clearing up the serious difficulties in which it seemed to be involved I have brought it to a conclusion and explained it, and brought it to light clearing away the obscurities, and I have made provision that it be secured for the memory of posterity in all ages to come.

This is the nature of the question: "Is nothing something or not?" If one replies: "It seems to me that nothing exists," the very negation of it which he assumes to be the case forces him to admit that nothing is something in that he says: "It seems to me that nothing exists." This statement is such as if he were to say: "It seems to me that nothing is something." If it seems to be something how can it appear not to exist in some way? Consequently it remains that it seems to be something. If, however, this reply be given: "It seems to me that nothing is not something," we must counter this assumption first by reason, insofar as human reason permits, and then by authority, not any kind of authority, but by divine authority which is the only authority and which alone leads to a firm conclusion. Let us therefore approach the question by reason.

Now every definite name signifies something, as man, stone, wood. As soon as these names have been mentioned we understand immediately the things they signify. For the name man, abstracting from individual differences, signifies the universality of men. Stone and wood likewise comprise their generality. Therefore nothing, if it is a noun at all as the grammarians maintain, is a definite noun. But every definite noun signifies something. For it is impossible that something definite should not be something; it is impossible that something definite should not exist, and it is impossible that nothing which is definite should not be something. Likewise nothing is a word that has signification. But every signification has reference to that which it signifies. From this it is proved that something cannot be nonexistent. Likewise every signification is signification of what is. Nothing, however, signifies something. Nothing, therefore, is the signification of what is, that is, something existing.

Now since it has been established by reason with a few examples though many of this kind could be adduced to prove that nothing is not only something, but something great, it is our pleasure to turn to divine authority which is the bulwark and firm support of reason since indeed the whole Church, taught by God, born from the side of Christ, nourished by the food of His most sacred flesh and the cup of His precious blood, instructed from its very beginning in deep mysteries confesses that it holds with unwavering faith that divine power has made out of nothing earth, water, air, and fire, light too and angels, and the soul of man. Our mental capacity, therefore, must be lifted up to the authority of such eminence which can be shaken by no reasoning, refuted by no arguments, impugned by no power. It is this authority which proclaims that those which are the first and foremost among creatures have been created out of nothing. Therefore, nothing is something great and remarkable, and its magnitude from which so many and such noble things have been produced cannot be grasped. For indeed one of these things which has been brought forth from it cannot be known and defined as it is to be known. Who has completely judged the nature of the elements? Who has comprehended the substance and nature of light, or of an angel or a soul? If then we have been unable to grasp by human reason these matters I have mentioned, how will we understand the magnitude and nature of that to which they trace their origin and species?

I could have submitted very many other arguments, but we believe that enough has been instilled by these in the hearts of all capable of learning.

2. *Concerning Darkness*

Since I have fittingly concluded with these brief remarks I have next turned to an explanation of those matters which not undeservedly seemed to diligent readers worth investigating. It is indeed the opinion of some that darkness does not exist, and that it is impossible that it should exist. The prudent reader will understand how easily this opinion can be refuted by citing the authority of Sacred Scripture. Let us therefore see what the account of the book of Genesis says on this point. "And darkness was upon the face of the deep" (Gen. 1:2). If darkness did not exist by what logic is it said that it "was"? He who says that darkness exists, by his affirming posits a thing, however, he who says that it does not exist, by his negation takes away a thing. As when we say: Man exists, we affirm a thing, that is, man. When we say: Man does not exist, by negating we take away a thing, that is, man. For this is the nature of a substantive verb, that to whatever subject it is joined without negation it asserts that subject to exist. By declaring therefore in the passage that was cited: "Darkness was upon the face of the deep" a thing is affirmed which no negation separates or removes from existence. Again, "darkness" is the subject, "was" is declarative. By this statement the text declares that darkness exists in some way. Behold unvanquished authority with reason following in its train, and reason also acknowledging authority proclaim one and the same thing, namely: darkness exists.

Even though these points cited for the sake of example are sufficient to prove what we have said, nevertheless that no occasion for contradiction be left to any opponents let us make it plain adding a few divine testimonies, chosen from among many, that frightened by them they may no longer dare to raise their impertinent voices against them. Indeed when the Lord on account of the oppression of the people of Israel chastised Egypt with dreadful plagues he also covered the land with darkness so thick that it could be felt; not only did the darkness rob men's eyes of the power to see but in keeping with its density it was subject to the touch of the hand. Whatever can be touched and felt must of necessity exist, whatever must be, it is impossible that this does not exist. And by this it is impossible that darkness does not exist because it has been proved that it must exist from the fact that it is palpable. And this point too must not be overlooked that when the Lord made a division between light and darkness, He called the light day and the darkness night. If the name day signifies something, the name night cannot not signify something. Day, however, signifies light, and light is something great. Day both exists, and is something great. What then, is darkness to signify nothing? Since the name night has been given it by the same creator who gave the name to the light is divine authority to be rejected? By no means, for it is easier that heaven and earth pass away than that divine authority be overthrown. For the creator gave names to the things He created so that each thing called by its name would be recognized. Neither did he fashion anything without a name nor did He assign a name except to that for which existence was decreed. But if this were the case the name would seem entirely superfluous and it may not be said that God did this. If, however, it may not be said that God established a superfluous thing, the name which God gave darkness can in no way seem superfluous. If it is not superfluous it is according to due measure, and if it is according to due measure it is also necessary because it is needed to recognize the thing which is signified by it. It is therefore certain that God made things and names according to due measure because they are mutually necessary. The holy prophet David, too, filled with the Holy Spirit, knowing that darkness is not an empty sound like that of the wind, clearly stated that it is something, because he says: "He sent darkness" (Psalm 104:28). If darkness does not exist how is it sent? But what can be sent can also be sent to a place where it is not. But what does not exist cannot be sent in any direction because it exists nowhere. Darkness is therefore said to have been sent because it existed. Again, "He placed darkness as his covert" (Psalm 17:12). What existed he placed and placed it in a certain way in order to place the darkness which existed as his covert. Likewise another passage reads: "Like his darkness" (Psalm 138:12) where it is shown that darkness is possessed and by this it is clear that it exists. For everything that is possessed exists; darkness, however, is possessed, therefore it exists.

Although these great and weighty arguments are sufficient and provide an impregnable stronghold against all assault from which they can easily hurl back the shafts at those who throw them, some arguments should nevertheless be sought from the authority of the Gospel. Let us therefore take the words of the Saviour Himself, "The children of the kingdom," he says, "will be put forth into the exterior darkness" (Matt. 8:12). It is to be noted, however, that he calls the darkness exterior. 'Outside' *(extra)*, from which 'without' *(exterius)* is derived, signifies a place. There would be no exterior darkness unless there was also interior darkness. Now whatever is outside must necessarily be in a place. But that which does not exist is nowhere. Therefore, darkness is not only exterior, but also has a place. In the passion of the Lord the evangelist says that darkness was made from the sixth to the ninth hour of the day. How can that which was made be said to be nonexistent? What was made cannot be made out as not to have been made. But that which does not always exist, nor ever is made, never exists. Darkness, however, was made, therefore it cannot be brought about that it does not exist. Likewise in another place we find "If the light that is in thee is darkness how great will the darkness itself be?" (Matt. 6:23., Luke 11:34). I believe that no one doubts that quantity has been attributed to bodies which are all distinguished through quantity and quantity belongs to bodies as an accident. But accidents either exist in a subject or are predicated of a subject. By the statement which is made "How great will the darkness itself be," quantity in a subject is indicated. Consequently from the argument given as proof it is gathered that darkness not only exists, but is also corporeal.

I have therefore put in writing these few proofs taken from reason and authority for your greatness and prudence, that clinging to them firmly and unalterably you may by no lure of false opinion stray from the path of truth. But if by chance something shall be said by anyone at variance with this our explanation, by referring to it as norm, you can disprove foolish trickery by its sound teachings.

NOTES

1. *Epistola de nihilo et tenebris,* ed. Ernest Dümmler, *Monumenta Germaniae Historica, Epistolae Karolini Aevi,* tom. II (Berlin: apud Weidmannos, 1895), 552-55.

IV

JOHN SCOTUS ERIUGENA

PRACTICALLY NOTHING is known about the place, the time, or the circumstances of either the birth or death of this unusual scholar who appeared in France at the court of Charles the Bald around the middle of the ninth century. John Scotus Eriugena was probably born sometime between 800 and 815 in Ireland, since *Scotus* (the Scot) in the ninth century commonly designated a native of that land, and *Eriugena* (or Erigena) means "born of the people of Erin." He probably functioned as headmaster of Charles' palace school when in 850, at the request of Hincmar, Archbishop of Rheims, he composed a treatise, *On Predestination,* against the teaching of Gottschalk. Eriugena's own views on the subject, however, were later condemned at the Synod of Valence in 855 and the condemnation was renewed by the Synod of Langres in 877. Charles himself seems to have commissioned Eriugena to do a new Latin translation of the Greek works ascribed to Dionysius the Areopagite as well as a translation of the *Ambigua* of St. Maximus, Confessor, wherein certain statements of St. Gregory Nazianzus are clarified in the light of Pseudo-Dionysius. The Neoplatonic views of these Greek theologians provided the inspiration for the Weltanschauung Eriugena presents in his masterwork *On the Division of Nature,* as well as the concept of Christ as *Logos* that we find in the extant fragments of his commentary on the Gospel of St. John. There is some evidence that he was involved in a doctrinal controversy on the Eucharist around 870. After that date he drops from sight. The legend that in 883 he was recalled to England by Alfred the Great, became abbot of Malmesbury, and was stabbed to death by the pens of his students is unreliable and seems based on a confusion of similar names.

Most of the following selections are taken from *On the Division of Nature.* They include a lengthy section covering some twelve chapters, more-or-less consecutive from Book One, to give the reader some indication of Eriugena's style. This is preceded and followed by a number of shorter selections, to give some general idea of his notion of philosophy and its divisions, along with the overall plan of his metaphysical-theological synthesis.

From these works it becomes apparent that Eriugena understood philosophy in its etymological sense as the "pursuit of wisdom." "Wisdom," in addition to its more usual abstract meaning, is concretely identified with God and specifically with the *Logos* or Second Person of the Christian Trinity as the locus of the Platonic ideas or Stoic *logoi spermatikoi.* Man attains the fullness of this wisdom only in the beatific vision and union with God in the afterlife. In this sense no one can enter heaven without having been a philosopher or lover of wisdom. Nevertheless, even a partial understanding of the deeper meaning of the Scriptures through a use of reason is a kind of anticipation of this supreme happiness already in this life.

Eriugena then belongs to the tradition of Augustine and Anselm of Canterbury, whose "philosophy" is the result of faith seeking understanding. Unlike Augustine, however, who knew of Byzantine thought only through the little that was available in Latin translation, Eriugena made direct use of such Christian writers as the three great Cappadocians (St. Gregory Nazianzus, known as the Theologian, and the two brothers, St. Basil the Great and St. Gregory of Nyssa). He especially used that enigmatic writer, probably a contemporary of Boethius, who used the pseudonym Denis or Dionysius the Areopagite and who throughout the Middle Ages was regarded as St. Paul's disciple (Acts 17:24). It is the speculative insights Eriugena found in these Christian Neoplatonists that give his own synthesis its unusual character and that have caused him, probably unjustifiably, to be regarded as holding pantheistic views.

The translations are by A. B. Wolter especially for this volume.

Philosophy, Faith, and Reason

1. [PHILOSOPHY AS THE QUEST FOR WISDOM][1]

As St. Augustine puts it: "A principal point about man's salvation is the belief and teaching that philosophy or the pursuit of wisdom is not something other than religion, for those whose teaching we disapprove of are precisely those who do not share our religion."[2] What is the practice of philosophy but explaining the rules of the true religion in which God, the supreme and principal cause of all things, is humbly worshiped and rationally investigated? It follows from this that true philosophy is true religion, and conversely, true religion is true philosophy. Every type of perfect and godly teaching wherein the rational grounds for anything is sought most earnestly and found most clearly stated is in that branch of learning the Greeks customarily call philosophy. . . .

2. [PHILOSOPHY BEGINS WITH FAITH]

"There came a Samaritan woman to draw water" (John 4: 7). As we have pointed out Samaria is a symbol for the Gentiles. The woman who came out of the city is the Church, gathered from among the Gentiles, and after having accepted faith, now desires to drink of the fountain of truth itself, i. e. Christ. The woman going out of the city also represents human nature in its natural quest for the fountain of reason to quench its thirst, i.e. its inborn desire for true knowledge. This desire could never be fully satisfied prior to the incarnation of the Creator, who is the font of life. In investigating nature's Creator and cause along with the nature of things by means of a study of their physical activity, man found he could drink only with great effort of the natural spring of reason.

"Jesus said to her, 'Give me to drink'; for his disciples had gone away into the town to buy food" (John 4:8-9). Jesus sitting at the well begs of the primitive Church, which he had chosen from the Gentiles, the drink of faith through which men believed in him. But he also asks of nature the drink of reason by which the Creator and Redeemer is investigated. The disciples, gone into the city for food, represent the apostles sent into the world in order to purchase spiritual food. This food by which the spiritual masters of the Church are satisfied consists of faith, action, and knowledge. The first of these they ask for is faith which enables them to preach, next are actions that are in accord with this faith, and finally there is rational investigation of the truth. The latter is not only the reason why the faith is preached, but it is that through which both action and knowledge come to perfection. . . .

The deep well, as we said, signifies either the profundity of man's nature or the lowliness of the sense perceptible or bodily creature, for in the entire universe of created things there is nothing below a corporeal nature. While it is physics [or natural philosophy] that investigates human substance or the creature as perceptible to the senses, the pitcher by which fresh water is brought forth from the intimate recesses of nature is the study of wisdom [i.e. first philosophy].[3]

O blessed John! . . . Your name means "to whom it is given." Not unjustly then are you called John. For to what theologian was given what has been granted to you, namely, to penetrate the veiled mysteries of the Supreme Good and to give some hint to man's mind and senses of what was revealed and declared to you? Tell me, I beg, to whom has been given such and so great a grace? Perhaps to Peter, the prince of the Apostles, you will say. When the Lord asked him "Who do you say that I am?" Peter replied, "Thou art the Christ, the Son of the living God." But I do not think it rash to say that in uttering these words, Peter typifies faith and action more than knowledge and contemplation. And if Peter is presented as the symbol of faith and action, it is John who typifies knowledge and contemplation. One rested his head on the Lord's chest, the symbol of contemplation; the other frequently faltered, a symbol of hesitant action. For before behavior in accord with the divine commandments becomes a matter of habit, action is at times guided by the pure face of virtue, but at other times its judgment fails, clouded by miasmata of carnal thoughts.

But the eye of inner contemplation, having once looked upon the face of truth, will never turn away again; it will never be deceived or clouded with darkness.

Still both [apostles] ran to the sepulcher. Christ's tomb typifies the divine scriptures in which the deepest mysteries of divinity and humanity lie protected in rock. But John ran faster than Peter, for the power of contemplation completely cleansed penetrates the inner secrets of the divine workings more rapidly and subtly than action still to be purified. Still Peter entered the sepulcher first, and John afterwards. As both ran, so both entered; Peter indeed as a symbol of faith, John as the symbol of understanding. But because it is written: "If you will not believe, you shall not understand," faith must be the first to enter the place where sacred scripture lies buried and only then does understanding follow for which faith has prepared the entrance. Peter knew Christ and man as something made in the course of time when he declared: "Thou art the Christ, the son of the living God." He soared high indeed, but he who understood this same Christ to be "God of God," begotten before all time, soared still higher. And it was he who uttered those words: "In the beginning was the Word." . . .[4]

3. [REASON AND AUTHORITY]

DISCIPLE: You urge me to discuss matters reasonably, but I wish you would add something in the way of support from the authority of the holy fathers [of the Church] to strengthen what you say.

MASTER: But you are not ignorant I think which is of greater worth: what is prior by nature or what is prior in the order of time.

D.: This is indeed known to all.

M.: We have been taught that reason is prior by nature, authority is prior in the order of time. For although nature has been created simultaneously with time, nevertheless authority did not begin to exist from the very beginning of time and nature. But reason did have its origin along with nature and time from the very beginning of all things.

D.: This reason itself teaches us. Authority indeed proceeds from true reason, reason never proceeds from authority. For all authority which true reason does not endorse is seen to be weak. True reason, however, being ratified and rendered immutable by virtue of itself, needs no additional assent from authority to strengthen it. For true authority, it seems to me, is nothing else but the truth which was uncovered by the power of reason and set down in writing by the holy fathers for the benefit of posterity. Or does it, perhaps, seem otherwise to you?

M.: Not at all. Therefore we must first use reason in those things we shall discuss and only then authority. . . .[5] No authority should frighten you away from what reasonable persuasion based on correct contemplation teaches. For true authority is not opposed to right reason nor right reason to authority. Indeed there can be no doubt that both spring from a common source, namely, divine wisdom.[6]

4. [THE REWARDS OF PHILOSOPHY]

The reward of those who labor in Sacred Scripture is pure and perfect understanding. O Lord Jesus, no other reward, no other happiness, no other joy do I ask of you except to understand your words which were inspired by the Holy Ghost, purely and without error due to false speculation. For this is my supreme felicity. It is the goal of perfect contemplation, because even the purest soul will not discover anything beyond this, for there is nothing beyond it.[7]

No one can enter heaven except by philosophy![8]

5. [THE CONTENT AND METHOD OF PHILOSOPHY]

Wisdom properly so-called is that capacity by which the contemplative mind, be it human or angelic, considers what is divine, eternal, and immutable, whether this be the First Cause of all things or whether it be the primordial causes of all things, which the Father has produced simultaneously and all at once in his Word. This phase of reason wise men call *theology*. Knowledge *(scientia)*, on the other hand, is that capacity by which the speculative mind, be it human or angelic, treats of the natures of things which come forth from the primordial causes in the process of generation and are divided into genera and species by means of differences and properties. It makes no difference whether these natures are subject to accidents or are free of them, whether they are joined to bodies or not, whether they are distributed through space and time or transcend both and are inseparably one by reason of their simplicity. This phase of reason is called physics. For physics is that natural science which treats of natures perceptible to the senses or intellect.[9]

Philosophy may be divided in many different ways, of course, but here we single out four principal parts [or techniques] which are required for the solution of any question. The Greeks were wont to call these *diaeretic, horistic, apodictic,* and *analytic;* the same role or part in Latin we could call *divisoria, definitiva, demonstrativa,* and *resolutiva.* Of these, the first by *dividing* separates the one into many; the second in *defining* collects one from among many; the third by a process of *demonstration* reveals what is hidden by means of what is manifest; the fourth by a process of dissolution *resolves* composite things into simple things.[10]

The Dialectic of Nature

1. [THE NATURE OF DIALECTIC]

Does not that art which the Greeks called *dialectic* and which is defined as the science of disputing well begin first of all with *ousia* (essence) as its proper starting point? For with this, all division and multiplication into those things about which this art disputes begins and continues downward from the most general genera [i.e. the ten categories], through the intermediary genera to the most specialized of the species. And then by a series of complicated rules it proceeds upward through the same series of steps by which it descended until it returns again to that *ousia* from which it came; for as the sole intelligible or the most intelligible, *ousia* satisfies that for which it always thirsted.[11]

Though the Greeks frequently use *physis* and *ousia* interchangeably, properly speaking *ousia* or essence is predicated of that which cannot perish or be increased or decreased in any creature, visible or invisible. *Physis* or nature, on the other hand, refers to the spatial and temporal generation of the essence in some matter, where it can perish or be increased or decreased or be affected by accidents.[12]

2. [DIALECTIC AS THE LAW OF NATURE][13]

That art called dialectic, then, which divides genera into species and resolves species into genera once more, is not of man's making, but was implanted in the very nature of things by the Author of all that is truly art. Wise men discovered it and skilled men make use of it in their inquiry into things.

3. [THE DUAL ASPECT OF DIALECTIC][14]

DISCIPLE: There is no rational division, whether of essence into genera, or genus into forms and numbers, or of the whole into its parts (called "Partition"[15]), or of the whole universe into those things which reason contemplates in it, there is no rational division, I say, which cannot be retraced through the same set of steps by which unity was diversified until one arrives again at that initial unit which remains inseparable in itself. It seems to me, however, that you should say a few words about the etymology of the term *analytic,* for it is not quite clear to me.

MASTER: *Analytic* comes from the verb *analyo* meaning "I return" or "I am dissolved." From this the term *analysis* is derived. It too can be translated "dissolution" or "return," but properly speaking, *analysis* refers to the solution of questions that have been proposed, whereas *analytic* refers to the retracing of the divisions of forms back to the source of their division. For all division, which was called *merismos* by the Greeks, can be viewed as a downward descent from a certain definite unit to an indefinite number of things, that is, it proceeds from the most general towards the most special. But all recollecting, as it were, is a return again and this begins from the most special and moves towards the more general. Consequently, there is a "return" or "resolution" of individuals into forms, forms into genera, genera into substance, substances into wisdom and prudence, where all division both begins and ends.

On the Division of Nature[16]

1. [INTRODUCTION]

MASTER: The first and supreme division of everything that can be perceived by the soul or transcends its vision is into (1) things which are and (2) things which are not. After frequently reflecting on this classification and looking into it as diligently as my powers permit, it struck me that there is a general term that comprises both classes. In Greek it is called *physis,* in Latin *natura.* Do you agree?

DISCIPLE: Yes indeed. Though I am but a tyro in regard to reasoning, I can see this is so.

M.: Nature then is the common name for all things which are and which are not.

D.: Certainly, for nothing could occur in the universe to which that name would not apply.

M.: Since we agree on the general designation, I wish you would tell me its specific subdivisions, or would you rather I do the dividing and you the evaluating?

D.: Go right ahead, please. I'm impatient to learn the truth from you.

M.: It seems to me that nature is subdivided into four species or kinds by four differences or distinguishing marks: (1) a nature which creates but is not created; (2) a nature which creates and is created; (3) a nature which is created and does not create; (4) a nature which neither creates nor is created. Among these four there are two pairs of opposites, however, for the third is opposed to the first and the fourth to the second. The fourth, however, falls into a class which includes impossible things whose characteristic is their inability to exist. Does such a division seem correct to you or not?

D.: Correct, indeed! But I wish you would elaborate on the opposition between the four to make it clearer.

M.: If I mistake not, you see the first and third are opposed.

For the first, viz. that which creates and is not created, has as its [logical] contrary that which is created and does not create. The second is opposed to the fourth, since what is both created and creates, which is the second, is universally contradicted by the fourth, viz. that which neither creates nor is created.

D.: I see that clearly. But the fourth species you have added puzzles me. About the other three I feel no hesitation, for I imagine the first refers to the cause of all things which are and which are not, while the second refers to the primordial causes, and the third to what we know is produced at various times and places. As I see it, however, it is necessary to discuss each of these in greater detail.

M.: You are quite right about that, but in what order? Which species or kind, in other words, do you think should be discussed first?

D.: I would think whatever light the mind is permitted to throw upon the matter should be directed to the first, before discussing the others.

M.: Let it be so. But first of all I think we should speak briefly about the initial and highest division of all things, viz. the division into those things that are and those that are not.

D.: It is reasonable and prudent to do so. Not only is this the primary distinction among things but it is also the most obscure. I see it is fitting to begin our speculation with this.

M.: There are various ways of interpreting this primordial distinction for classifying all things. Of these, the first is this. Whatever is perceptible by the intellect or bodily senses can reasonably be said to be, whereas anything which in virtue of the excellence of its nature eludes not only every material sense but even intellect and reason, by the same token can correctly be said not to be. The only things properly included in this latter class are God, the basic substrate, the ideal natures and essences of all things made by him. And justly so, for only he who alone truly exists, is the essence of all things. As Denis the Areopagite puts it: "The being of all things is the superbeing, divinity." Gregory the theologian also adduces many reasons to prove no mind can grasp just what any substance or essence is, be it that of a visible or invisible creature. For even as no intellect can understand what God is in himself as transcending every creature, so neither is that substance comprehensible which constitutes the most secret core of every creature that is made by him and exists in him. Whatever corporeal sense or intellect perceives of any creature is something which is incidental, so to speak, to its incomprehensible essence. It is the fact that something is, not really what it is, that we know in terms of quality, quantity, form, matter, a kind of specifying difference, and time or place. . . .

Let the second way of being and not being come from considering the various grades and differences found among created natures. This order begins with that nature whose intellectual powers make it most excellent and nearest to God and extends downwards to the lowest of rational and irrational creatures. To put it more plainly, the hierarchy starts with the highest angel and descends to the lowest part of the rational and irrational soul, to that part, I say, which is concerned with such life functions as nutrition and growth. For the lowest portion of the soul in general is that which nourishes the body and causes it to grow. Now every grade or order, down to the very lowest which is that of bodies, where the sequence ends, can be said both to be and not to be in a very special sense. For to affirm the inferior is to negate the superior and to negate the inferior is to affirm the superior. In the same way affirmation of the superior is negation of the inferior, whereas a negation of the superior will be an affirmation of the inferior. Affirmation of man as still mortal is a negation of the angel, and vice versa. For if man is a rational animal, mortal and visible, certainly the angel is neither a rational animal, nor mortal nor visible. Likewise if the angel is an essential intellectual activity, contemplating God and the causes of things, then obviously man is not something of this sort. The same rule holds for all heavenly essences until the highest order or grade is reached. Negation in the upward direction ends there, for to negate this creature is not to affirm some superior creature. Topping the hierarchy are three orders of which the first comprises the Cherubim, Seraphim, and Thrones, the second the Virtues, Powers, and Dominations; the third the Principalities, Archangels, and Angels. At the bottom the lowest, that of bodies, only affirms or negates something superior to itself, for there is nothing below to be affirmed or negated, since this order precedes nothing lower and is preceded by everything higher. Every grade or order of rational and intellectual creatures in this hierarchy can be said both to be and not to be. Each is, to the extent that it is known either by itself or something higher, whereas it is not, to the extent that it is incomprehensible to what is below it.

The third way is best seen in those things which represent the full flowering of this visible world and in their anterior causes planted in nature's most secret womb. Whatever has sprung from these germinal causes, appearing in formed-matter in the course of time and at a particular place, men customarily say exists, whereas things still latent in the womb of nature, which have not yet appeared in formed-matter or have been invested with temporal, spatial, or other accidental characteristics, by the same custom, are said not to exist. There are many obvious examples of this. Take human nature especially. Now God did not produce all men simultaneously in this visible world, yet he made them all at once in that one, first [ideal or prototype] man, created in his image. But this nature, which was constituted all at once, he brings forth as a visible essence according to a certain order of space and time known to himself. Those men whom we see now or who have already appeared are said to be. Those to appear in the future, but latent at present, are said not to be. Now the first and third way differ in this that the first applies generally to all things which were made all at once and together in their causes and effects. The third applies especially to those things which are partly latent in their causes and partly apparent in those effects, which properly speaking make up this world. Considerations concerning the power of the seed, be it animal, tree, or herb, would come under this third way. For the power of the seed, at the time it reposes silently in the recesses of nature, is said not to be, since it is not yet manifest, but as soon as animals, flowers or fruits are born and begin to grow, it is said to be.

The fourth way is that of the philosophers who claim, not improbably, that only those things truly exist which are grasped by the intellect, whereas anything that can undergo change, be it generation, or corruption, an expansion or contraction of matter, or temporal or spatial change, as is the case with all bodies subject to generation and corruption, is not said to exist in any true sense of the word.

The fifth way is applicable to human nature alone. When it has destroyed through sin the dignity of the divine image in which it properly subsists, and has thus deservedly lost its existence, it is therefore said not to be. But when it is restored by the grace of God's only begotten Son to its original substantial status wherein it represented an image of God, then it begins to be in Him who was made in God's image. . .

But I think we should return to the subject matter we set out to discuss, namely to the division of nature. . . .

2. [GOD AS UNCREATED CREATOR][17]

M.: Of the aforesaid divisions of nature, the first member was into that which creates and is not created. And rightly so, for this kind of nature is correctly predicated of God alone, for only he is understood to create all and yet is himself without any beginning or source. And because he is the principal cause of all that is made from and through him, he is also the end of all that comes from him. For all things seek him. He is then, the beginning, the middle, and the end. Beginning, for from him are all things which derive their essence from him; middle, because they subsist and are moved in him and through him; end, because they gravitate towards him seeking rest and unchanging perfection.

D.: This I most firmly believe. . . . But this bothers me. I frequently find in the books of the holy fathers, when attempting to discuss the divine nature, that they not only claim it creates all that exists, but that it is also created. If this be so, I don't readily see how our position can be held.

M.: With good reason you are disturbed. . . . I think we should first consider the name, which Sacred Scripture uses most frequently, that is "God." For though the divine nature is called by many names like "Goodness," "Essence," "Truth," and the like, nevertheless scripture most often uses this name [viz. "God" or "theos"].

D.: Obviously so!

M.: Etymologically the name is from the Greek. Either it derives from the verb *theoreo* (i.e. I see) or *theo* (i.e. I run), or more probably from both, since they contain one and the same meaning. For when *theos* [God] is derived from the verb *theoreo,* he is regarded as seeing. For he sees in himself all that exists because he sees nothing outside himself, since nothing is outside of him. When *theos* is derived from the verb *theo, theos* [God] is justly understood as running, for he flows through all things and is in no sense stagnant, but fills all things moving through them. As it is written: "Swiftly runs his Word" [Ps. 147: 16]. Yet despite it all he is in no way moved. Indeed God is most truly said to be movement that is stable and stability that is mobile. For in himself, God is incapable of change; his natural immobility is never lost. Nevertheless, he does move himself in regard to everything that subsists essentially through him, so that these things come to exist. For it is because he moves that they come to be. Hence the two interpretations of the name "God" are to be understood in a single sense. For his running through all things is nothing else than seeing all things, even as it is through his seeing and flowing through all things that they come to exist through him.

D.: So much for the etymology of the name, which is convincing enough. But I still do not see sufficiently how he moves himself—he who is everywhere and without whom nothing can exist and outside of whom nothing is situated, since he represents the locus and limit in which all is confined.

M.: I did not say that God is moved by something outside himself, but rather by himself, and in himself, and with respect to himself. For one ought to credit him with no motion apart from that entailed by the desire of his will by which he wills that all things come to be. Similarly his state of rest should not be understood as something following upon motion, but as the unalterable proposal of his will by which the immutable constitution of all things is established. Actually neither rest nor motion in any proper sense are to be ascribed to him. For these opposite states are seen to be mutually repugnant, and true reason forbids the attribution of opposites to him, particularly since the state of rest properly terminates a state of motion. But God is not initially moved to attain any state. Hence names of this sort, like many others, are derived from created things and referred to the Creator by a kind of divine metaphor. And this is not unreasonable, since he is the cause of all things at rest or in motion. For as the principle or beginning of all things, it is through him that they begin their course towards existence and it is through him that they gravitate towards him by their natural motion so that they may eventually rest in him immutably and eternally. For it is he in whom all things terminate and come to rest, for they desire nothing beyond himself. They find the beginning and end all of their activity in him. That is why God is said to be "running." It is not that he who remains immutable in himself and who fills everything, runs [or overflows] his boundaries, but rather he makes everything "run" from nonexistence to existence.

D.: What you say seems reasonable. Let us return then to what we proposed to treat.

M.: What proposal did you have in mind? When we digress, we often lose sight of our initial questions.

D.: Did we not set out to investigate as far as possible the reasons why those who discuss the divine nature claim it both creates and is created? That this nature does create all things surely no intelligent person would question, but I don't see sufficiently why it is said to be created.

M.: You are right. But I think the basis for answering this question is to be found in what we have already said. For we have agreed that the movement of the divine nature means nothing else than the proposal of the divine will to create those things that are to be made. Now what is said "to be made" [or "to come to be"] in anything is the divine nature which is not something other than the divine will. For in that nature being is not something other than willing, but in establishing all things he sees are to be made, his being and willing are one and the same. For example, one could say that the movement of the divine will comes down to this: that those things which exist, exist. To that extent it creates all things, bringing them forth from nothing, so that they may be in being from nonbeing. On the other hand, it is created because except for it nothing exists essentially, for it is the essence of all things. Just as there is no natural good besides it, but everything which is called good is good by participating in the highest good, so everything which is said to exist does not exist in itself, but by participating in that nature which truly exists. Not only is the divine nature fashioned in those who are reformed by faith, hope, charity, and the other virtues, so that the Word of God is born in a wonderful and ineffable manner as the Apostle speaking of Christ says: "Who is made in us wisdom and justice and redemption" [1 Cor. 1:30], but the divine nature, being invisible in itself, reveals itself in all things which exist and consequently it is not improperly said to be made. Consider our intellect. Before it begins to think or recall, it is not unreasonably said not to be, for it is not visible as such, being known only to God and self. But when it begins to think and take form from certain sense images, it is not unreasonably said to be made. For the intellect which was uninformed prior to bringing something to mind, is fashioned as it were by so doing, receiving certain forms of things or words or colors or other sensibles. It receives a second formation, as it were, when it is informed by certain signs of forms or words (I refer to letters, which are signs of words and mathematical figures, which are signs of forms) or other sensible signs, by which [its presence] is suggested to the senses of those who perceive these signs. Though this analogy does not do justice to the divine nature, still I think it can help us to understand how that nature which creates all things and can be created by nothing—is for all that "created" in a marvelous fashion in all those things which stem from it. Just as the mind's intelligence, intention, or purpose, or whatever you wish to call this innermost movement of ours, when it finds expression first in thought, then through sense images, and finally in sensible signs like words or gestures, not unreasonably can be said to be made, so too the divine essence, which as subsisting in itself transcends every intellect, can justly be said to "be created" in those things which are made by it, in it, through it, and for its sake, so that it is able to be known in these things by the intellect, if they be intellectual, or by the senses, if they be sensible, by those who investigate this essence by proper study.

D.: I think we have said enough on this point. . . . But I would like to know what theology teaches us about the ineffable and incomprehensible creative and causal nature. I would like to know whether it exists, what it is, the kind of a thing it is, and how it is defined.

M.: Does not theology, as you now call it, which deals either exclusively or principally with the divine nature, persuade those looking into the matter of this truth, viz. that from the things it creates we know only that it subsists essentially; we do not know what its essence is? For it not only is beyond the grasp of human reason, as we have frequently said, but also beyond the most pure minds of the celestial essences as well. Nevertheless, theologians, by means of an upright mind, have discovered its existence from the things that do exist; that it is wise from the way these things are divided into essences, genera, species, differences, and individuals; and that it lives from the constant motion of all things and their mobile state. Also by such reasoning they have found the cause of all three subsists. For, as we have pointed out, from the essences of the things which are it is understood to exist; from the wonderful order of things it is known to be wise; and from their movements it is found to be living. The creative nature or cause of all things, then, exists, is wise and is alive. . . .

D.: I am sufficiently convinced of all this, and I see this to be most true. Indeed it is not possible to say what it is or what kind of a thing it is. For what cannot be understood at all cannot be defined. . . .

M.: That is why either one must be silent and entrust everything to the simple and true faith . . . or if one wishes to discuss these things, he must make use of the two principal parts of theology, one affirmative which the Greeks call *catafatica,* the other negative, called *apofatica.* The latter denies that the divine essence or substance is any of the things which exist, i.e. which can be understood and described. The other way, however, predicates of that nature everything which exists and therefore is called affirmative. Not that it establishes this nature to be some one of the things that are, but it suggests that all things which exist by reason of this nature can be predicated of it. For it is reasonable that something causal can be described in terms of what it causes. For that reason [this ineffable nature] is said to be truth, goodness, essence, light, justice, the sun, a star, wind, water, a lion, a city, a worm, and countless other things. . . . But it is not our purpose to discuss these things now, for they are treated adequately in the symbolical theology of St. Denis the Areopagite. . . .

D.: But names like essence, goodness, truth, justice, wisdom, and others of this kind not only seem to be divine, but to be most divine, and to signify exclusively the divine substance or essence. Why then does the aforesaid most holy father and theologian declare that they are used only metaphorically, i.e. in a sense transferred from creatures to the creator? One would think he had some mystical or secret reason for speaking in this fashion.

M.: You are sharp enough. I see we cannot avoid considering this point. But I would like you to answer this. Do you think God has the opposite trait or that such a trait, though not part of his essence, is something he happens to have coeternally? By the opposite trait, I mean either that God is deprived of or simply lacks the aforesaid trait, or that he has it only in a relative sense, or that he has some contrary trait. By something he just happens to have, I mean something associated with him eternally but not essential to him.

D.: I see clearly what you have in mind, and I would not dare to say he has the opposite trait nor that the trait in question is something he only happens to have, i.e. that it is in essence something other than himself. . . . For if this were conceivable or were found to be the case, it would follow necessarily that all things have not a single principle or source, but that there are two or more, each differing from the other. And this is something true reason would not hesitate to deny and rightly so, for while all things could originate from one source, where two or more are required nothing would begin to be.

M.: I think you are quite right. If the aforesaid names include a reference [by contrast] to names opposed to these, then what they properly signify must also have contrary things opposed to it. Consequently, they could not be predicated properly of God to whom nothing is opposed or with whom nothing differs by nature coeternally. For true reason can find none of the aforesaid names or those like them to which some other name in the same general class is not opposed. And we know what holds for names, holds also for the things they signify. Nevertheless, there are innumerable divine expressions which Sacred Scripture predicates of God in a sense transferred from creatures to the Creator—if one can speak properly of anything being predicated of God, a point we must consider elsewhere. Though it is impossible for our weak reason to find or gather them all, a few examples ought to be cited. Thus God is said to be essence, but properly speaking he to whom nothing is opposed is not essence; he is *hyperousia,* i.e. superessential. Similarly he is called goodness, but he is not properly goodness, for evil is opposed to goodness; he is rather *hyperagathos,* i.e. more than good, and *hyperagathotes,* i.e. more than goodness. He is called "God," but he is not God, for blindness is opposed to vision and unseeing to seeing; therefore, he is more than God, if *theos* be interpreted as seeing. If it is regarded as derived from *theo* (I run), the same applies, for not running is opposed to running just as tardiness is opposed to quickness. Therefore, he will be *hypertheos,* i.e. more than running, as it is written: "Swiftly runs his Word." For this is understood of God the Word who "runs" ineffably through all things which exist in order that they may be. We must take truth in the same way. For falsity is opposed to truth. Hence God is not properly truth, but *hyperalethes,* i.e. more than true, and *hyperaletheia,* i.e. more than truth. The same rule must be observed in all the divine names. For he is not properly called eternity, since eternity is opposed to temporality; he is *hyperaionios* and *hyperaionia,* that is, more than eternal, more than eternity. One should not think that there is nothing opposed to wisdom and therefore it can be properly predicated of God, for to wisdom and wise are opposed foolish and foolishness. Therefore, God is truly and correctly called *hypersophos,* that is, more than wise, and *hypersophia,* more than wisdom. In like fashion, he is more than life, since death is opposed to life. The same applies to light, for to light darkness is opposed. I think we have said enough about this.

D.: I grant we have said enough. [Let us go on to something else.]

M.: I wonder at the sharpness of your perception, however, which up to now seemed keen enough.

D.: Why do you say that?

M.: Did we not say that no word, no name, no sensible sound or any significant thing could properly signify this ineffable nature? And this you admited. For it is in a transferred sense, and not properly, that essence, truth, wisdom, and other such things are asserted. But superessential, more than truth, more than wisdom and such like are asserted. Does it not seem as if these are proper names as it were? And if essence is not predicated properly, superessential is? Likewise, if truth or wisdom is not properly predicated, more than truth and more than wisdom is asserted properly. Hence, proper names are not wanting. . . .

D.: Indeed, the divine substance does not seem to be ineffable if one can speak about it properly. . . .

M.: I see now you are awake.

D.: I am awake, all right, but I don't see how to answer the question you raise.

M.: Go back to what we agreed on a little earlier. If I am not mistaken, we said there were two most sublime parts to theology, and this not on our own authority but on that of St. Denis the Areopagite. He states most clearly that theology is bipartite: *catafatica* and *apofatica,* which Cicero translates as *intention* and *repulsion.* But to bring out the meaning of the words more clearly, we preferred to translate them as *affirmative* and *negative.*

D.: I believe I recall all this. But I must confess I don't see its bearing on the present problem.

M.: You see, don't you, that affirmation and negation are mutually opposed?

D.: I see that clearly enough. Indeed, I don't think anything could be more opposed.

M.: Pay close attention, then. For when you attain the insight that comes with perfect reasoning, you will see these two seeming contraries are not in opposition to one another so far as the divine nature is concerned, but in every respect are in perfect harmony with each other. To make this clearer, let us use a few examples. For instance, *catafatica* declares [the divine nature] is truth, *apofatica* declares it is not truth. Here we seem to have a certain form of contradiction, but if it is examined more closely, there is no disagreement to be found. For the statement that it is truth, does not affirm that the divine substance is truth in the proper sense of the term, but that it can be called by this name by way of metaphor taken from the creature and applied to the creator. Even when invested with such words, the divine essence remains bare of all proper meaning. Now the negative way which says it is not truth, clearly recognizing the divine nature to be incomprehensible and ineffable, does not deny that it exists, but that it is not properly truth, nor is it properly called such. Every signification with which *catafatica* invests the divinity, *apofatica* knows how to remove. For the one which says it is wisdom, invests it, for example, whereas the other which asserts it is not wisdom, removes it. Hence the one says it can be called this, but it does not say this properly; the other says it is not this, but it can be called such.

D.: If I am not mistaken, I now see most clearly that what up to now seemed to me to be opposed is really not in disagreement when considered in connection with God. But I confess I don't see how this leads us closer to solving our present question.

M.: Then pay closer attention and tell me, if you can, to which part of theology these designations mentioned above pertain. I refer to superessential, more than truth, more than wisdom and such like. Are they applied affirmatively or negatively?

D.: I don't dare settle this myself. For when I consider the aforesaid designations lack the negative particle "not," I fear to relegate them to the negative part of theology. If I put them with the affirmative part, however, I recognize this does not agree with what I know of them. For one who asserts [God] to be superessential clearly denies that he is essential. And consequently, although the negation does not appear in the words, it is evident to one who considers the matter carefully that it is not lacking in the understanding. For that reason, I think, I am forced to admit the aforesaid designations which seem to lack any negation are more in harmony with negative than affirmative theology by reason of the way they are understood.

M.: I see you replied most observantly and cautiously and I much approve of the way you discovered most subtly the negative meaning in the verbal affirmation. Let us then, if you please, solve the present question in this fashion. All that is predicated of God with the addition of the prefix "super" or the words "more than" such as "superessential," "more than truth," "more than wisdom," and so on is most comprehensively dealt with in both the aforesaid parts of theology. The verbal form in which they are presented is affirmative, but in virtue of the way they are understood, they pertain to the negative way. Let us conclude with this brief example. "[God] is essence"—affirmation! "He is not essence"—negation! "He is superessential"—both affirmation and negation! For what superficially seems to lack negation is strongly negative in meaning. One who asserts God to be superessential does not say what he is, but what he is not, for he declares he is not essence, but more than essence. But one who asserts God is not any of the things which are, but is more than these, does not express just what this is, which is more than essence. In other words, he does not in any way define what this being is.

D.: I think we have dealt with this question sufficiently. . . .

3. [CREATURES AS IDEAS IN THE LOGOS][18]

"All things were made through him" (John 1:3). Through the Word, who is God himself or through the Word himself, God made all things. And what does this "all things were made through him" mean except that he was born of the Father before all and that all things were made with him and through him? For his generation from the Father is itself the establishment of the cause of all, and of all things which proceed from causes into various genera and species, it is the operation and execution. Through the generation indeed of God from God as a principle all things were made. Hear the divine and ineffable paradox, the inscrutable secret, the invisible, incomprehensible, profound mystery! Through what was begotten but not made, all things were made but not begotten.[19] The principle from which are all things is the Father, the principle through which are all things is the Son. The Father by speaking his Word, i.e. by begetting his wisdom, makes all things. As the prophet said: "Thou hast made all things in Wisdom" [Psalm

103:24], and speaking elsewhere in the person of the Father: "My heart hath uttered . . ." [Ps. 44:2]. And what has his heart uttered? The prophet himself explains: "a good word," i.e. I speak a good word, I beget a good Son. The "heart" of the Father is his own substance, from which the proper substance of the Son is begotten. The Father does not precede the Son by nature . . . . The Son, however, does precede naturally all things which are made through him. The substance of the Father and Son is coeternal. But the substance of those things which are made through him have begun to exist in him before worldly time, not indeed *in* time, but *with* time. For time itself is among the other things that were made; it was not created *before,* but *with* [them]. And what is the consequence of the Word uttered by the mouth of the Most High? . . . The Father speaks, the Word is begotten, all things are made. Hear the prophet, since he says: "And they were made," i.e. [the Father] begot his Word, through whom all things were made. And lest you might think that those things which were in truth made through the Word, were either made outside of him or had existence of or through themselves so that not "all that is and is not" are referred back to a single principle, he [John] adds: "without him was made nothing that has been made," i.e. nothing was made outside or without *[extra]* him. For he embraces and comprehends within himself everything. Nothing however is understood to be coeternal, consubstantial, or coessential with him except his Father and his Spirit which proceeds from the Father through him.

4. [ACTUAL CREATION IS RADICALLY OTHER THAN GOD]

MASTER: The primary intention and principal topic of our "Physiology" [i.e. *On the Division of Nature*] was to stress that this superessential nature is the creative cause of all that exists and does not exist. It itself is not created, but is the one beginning or principle, the one universal fount and origin of all things. . . .[20]

DISCIPLE: When I hear that the divine goodness created everything from nothing, I do not understand what this term "nothing" stands for, whether it refers to a privation of essence or substance, for instance, or to something which *is* only accidentally, or whether it refers to the [ineffable] excellence of the divine superessentiality itself.

M.: I would not easily concede that the divine superessentiality is nothing or that it can be called by such a privative term as this. For although it may be said "not to be" by theologians, they do not wish to imply that it is nothing, but rather that it is more than being *(esse)*. For how could the cause of all things which exist be understood to be nothing in the way of essence, when all things that exist teach us that this cause truly *exists,* even though we cannot determine from anything they say just *what* this cause is? If by reason of its ineffable excellence and incomprehensible infinity the divine nature is said not to be, it does not follow that it is nothing at all, since there was no other reason for predicating "nonbeing" of it, except that it was superessential, and that among the number of those things which exist, true reason was not permitted to enumerate it, since it is understood to be above all things which are understood to be or not to be.

D.: What then am I to understand, I beg of you, when I hear you say: "God made everything which exists from nothing?"

M.: Understand that by the power of the divine goodness, from the nonexistent, existent things have been made. For those things which were not, received existence from nothing, for they have been made, since before they were made, they did not exist. The word "nothing" here does not refer to some kind of material, or even to some kind of cause of what exists, or to any procession, or to a mere occasion or opportunity which may have exercised some influence on their production. Neither does it mean anything coessential or coeternal with God, nor any self-subsisting entity that is not God, or anything he might have made use of as a kind of material from which to fabricate the world. The name then indicates the total deprivation of anything essential. Indeed, it would be more true to say, simply the word designates the absence of the whole essence. For "privation" refers to the removal of some characteristic it had. But how can there be talk of any privation before anything was possessed? Now before all things which exist had received subsistence, there was simply nothing they had.

D.: The word "nothing" then indeed means an absence or

negation of all essence or subsistence of everything which in the realm of nature has been created.

M.: That is what I think. For practically all the expositors of scripture agree on this that the Creator of all creatures made those things he willed to make from absolute nothingness and not from anything at all.[21]

5. [ONLY METAPHORICALLY HAS CREATION ISSUED FROM GOD][22]

MASTER: God is not a genus with respect to the creature, nor the creature a species of [what is divine or] God. Neither is the creature a genus with respect to God nor God a species of creature. The same can be said for the relation of whole and part, for God is not the whole of the creature nor the creature a part of God. Neither is the creature the whole of God nor God a part of a creature.

Nevertheless, in a metaphorical sense, God is called "genus," "whole," "species," and "part" according to the more lofty viewpoint of Gregory the Theologian since we who share in human nature are said to be a "part of God . . . in whom we live, move and have our being."[23] For everything which is in him and from him can with reason and piously be affirmed of him. When we spoke briefly then in the first book of the general division of all nature or the universe—where by universe, I mean God and creation, it was by a kind of exercise in intellectual contemplation and not as if there was an [actual] division of a genus into its forms or a whole into its parts.

6. [ON THE RETURN OF MAN, THE MICROCOSM, TO GOD]

[Of the fourfold divisions of Nature] two are brought together through an analytic or reductive resolution. For the first and the fourth are one, since they both refer to God alone. For he is the principle of all things that were created by him and he is also the end of all things that seek him in order that they may find their rest. Indeed, the cause of all can be said to create when those things created by him and after him, by a kind of marvelous divine multiplication proceed to become genera, species, and individuals and all the other various things which are considered as established in nature. But because all those things which came forth from this selfsame cause will return to it as their end, it is designated as the goal of all and is referred to as neither creating nor created. For once all things will have returned to it, nothing further will come forth from it to become genera and forms generated in time and space; in it all will remain at rest, and one, immutable individual. But this fourth consideration of the universe, which is understood to apply to God alone like the first division, we shall discuss to the extent that we shall be granted the light to do so.[24]

If the [Logos or] Word of the Father, in whom all things are and in whom all things have been made, is the cause of all things visible and invisible, is he not also the "cause of causes" or finis of the world, in whom it will come to an end? Is there any goal beyond him that any creature could desire? Especially when it is the case that everything reaching out for something has as the goal of its endeavor something which was first established in him who is the Word of God. There is nothing beyond him to which they could tend or which they could seek. The Word of God then is in truth the goal of all creation. He is consequently the one in whom both the beginning and the end of the world is to be found, and if I may speak even more openly, the beginning and end are the Word itself, which is a multiple end without end and a beginning without a beginning, i.e. with no source or principle other than the Father. That is why we can sum up what we have tried by many arguments to suggest, defining him thus: The one from whom and unto whom are all things, for he is both beginning and end. This too is what the Apostle most obviously infers when he says: "For from him and through him and unto him are all things" [Romans 11:36]. Here we have most clearly propounded on apostolic authority, as Maximus points out in his *Ambiguities* (chap. 37), not only the origin of all that was made, by the fivefold division, but also the return and reunion through the selfsame divisions and the resolution of the whole of creation into one and ultimately into God himself.

Indeed the first of all the divisions of nature is that which separates the created from what is not created, i.e. God. The second divides the created into the sensible and the intelligible. The third differentiates the sensible world into heaven and earth. The fourth separates paradise from the rest of the terrestrial world. The fifth and last division is that of man into masculine and feminine. In him, namely in man, all visible and invisible creatures were constituted. Therefore he is called "that in which all things were fabricated," for all that was posterior to God is contained in man. For that reason he is also referred to as a mediator, for composed as he is of body and soul, he holds in himself widely divergent extremes, namely the spiritual and the corporeal, and gives them unity. Therefore the divine history [Genesis] introduces him at the very close of the fashioning of all things, signifying by this that in him is contained all that has been made so far. Therefore it is from the division of man into the aforesaid two sexes that the ascent and reunion begins.[25]

First there is a reversal of human nature, when the body is dissolved and summoned [in death] to return to the four elements of the sensible world from which it was called. The second stage occurs in the resurrection, when each one receives back his own body from the common fund of the four elements. The third step occurs when the body is transformed into spirit.[26]

The great Gregory of Nyssa, as I have said, in [one of his] sermons gives persuasive arguments for the thesis that "matter is nothing else than a kind of combination of what is accidental, such that visible matter comes from elemental factors that are themselves invisible." And this position is not without its merits, for if the essence of this bodily matter which is dissoluble were in fact simple, immutable, and in no way capable of dissolution, then there would be no way in which it could disintegrate. But the fact remains that it does disintegrate. Therefore there is nothing in it which cannot be dissolved. . . . If we may use a simile, a shadow is created by a body and light, but neither the body nor the light are changed into the shadow. When the shadow disappears, however, it is understood to be dissolved into its causes, namely light and a body. . . . Do not be surprised then that bodies can be created from incorporeal causes and can be dissolved into them again. But these causes as created have come from him who is the same one Creator of all that exists.[27]

In the resurrection sexual differences will disappear and nature will be reunited so that there will just be man as he would have been had he not sinned.[28] Next, the earth will be rejoined to paradise and there will be only paradise. Then the earth will be reunited to the heavens and there will be only the heavens. Note throughout that it is always the inferior that is transmuted into the superior. Sex is indeed transformed into man, because it is something beneath man; the terrestrial earth, into paradise, because it is inferior to paradise. Earthly things, since they are inferior, will be transmuted into heavenly bodies. Then the whole of sensible creation's reunion and transmutation into what is intelligible takes place, so that every creature will become intelligible. Afterwards the whole creation will be united with the Creator and it will be one in him and with him. And this represents the destiny or goal of all things visible and invisible, because all things visible are transformed into intelligibles and the intelligibles into God by a marvelous and ineffable union, but not—as we have frequently insisted—by a confusion or annihilation of their essences or substances.[29] Then God will be all in all, when there is nothing but God. Not that we are trying to say that the substance of things will perish, but that they will return through the aforementioned stages to become something better. And how can anything perish when it turns into something better? Hence the change of human nature into God should not be thought of as a destruction of its substance, but as a wonderful and ineffable return to that pristine state it lost through sin. For if everything which understands in a pure fashion becomes one with that which it understands, is it surprising that when our nature comes to contemplate God face-to-face in the person of those individuals who have been found worthy, that nature should become one with him and in him to the extent that, having been elevated to the vision of God, it is privileged to contemplate him?[30]

NOTES

1. *Liber de praedestinatione,* chap. 1, J.P. Migne, *Patrologia Latina,* Vol. 122 (Paris: 1865), cols. 357-358.

2. *De vera religione,* I, chap. 5, n. 8.

3. *Commentarius in S. Evangelium secundum Joannem,* fragmentum 2, J.P. Migne, *op. cit.,* 333-34.

4. *Homilia in prologum S. Evangelii secundum Joannem,* J.P. Migne, *op. cit.,* 283-85.

5. *De divisione naturae,* I, 69, J.P. Migne, *op. cit.,* 513B.

6. *Ibid.,* 66, 511B.

7. *Ibid.,* V, 38, 1010.

8. *Annotationes in Marcianum,* ed. C. Lutz (Cambridge, Mass.: Medieval Academy, 1939), 64.

9. *De divisione naturae,* III, 3, J.P. Migne, *op. cit.,* 629A.

10. *Liber de praedestinatione,* chap. 1, J.P. Migne, *op. cit.,* 358A.

11. *De divisione naturae,* V, 4, J.P. Migne, *op. cit.,* 868-69.

12. *Ibid.,* 3, 867A.

13. *Ibid.,* IV, 4, 749A.

14. *Ibid.,* II, 1, 526A.

15. The term refers to the rhetorical division into parts or headings, but it was also used as the title of rhetorical treatises.

16. *Ibid.,* I, 1-7, 441-45.

17. *Ibid.,* 10-14, 451-62.

18. *Homilia in prologum S. Evangelii secundum Joannem,* J.P. Migne, *op. cit.,* 287.

19. The distinction here is between the eternal generation of the Logos, or only begotten Son of the Father (who, though a distinct person, shares the same nature or substance with the Father) and the production of the archetypal ideas. The latter are said to be created or made in the sense that they are given that peculiar intentional mode of existence characteristic of pure thought objects. The analogy is that of the creative artist who first envisions in his mind what he later creates in stone or marble. Though their production is timeless, the ideas can only be called "coeternal" in a secondary or derivative sense, for according to the Boethian definition of eternity, only the divine nature or a divine person can be called eternal.

20. *De divisione naturae,* IV, 1, J.P. Migne, *op. cit.,* 741C.

21. *Ibid.,* III, 5, 634-35.

22. *Ibid.,* II, 1, 523-24D.

23. *Acts of the Apostles,* 17:28-30. St. Paul says that as children of God, men are of the same race or stock *(genus)* as God.

24. *De divisione naturae,* II, 2, J.P. Migne, *op. cit.,* 526-27.

25. *Ibid.,* V, 20, 892-93.

26. *Ibid.,* 8, 876A.

27. *Ibid.,* I, 36, 58, 479B, 501B-D. Eriugena recognizes that this view of St. Gregory of Nyssa is not the common view of the Fathers, but he believes that if the archetypal ideas represent what is essential to any creature, then the substance of the body must be spiritual or intelligible. He argues: "Now the substance of the body is completely intelligible and therefore it is not incredible nor opposed to reason that intelligible substances be reunited so that they become one and each does not cease to have its proper nature and subsistence, but in such a way that the inferior is contained in the superior." *De divisione naturae,* V, 8, J.P. Migne, *op. cit.,* 879A.

28. This idea that the sexual differences in man are somehow due to an original sin also comes from St. Gregory of Nyssa, who derived it from Origen. Origen who, like Plotinus, had been a student of Am-

monius Saccas, used this theory to explain why creatures created in the image of God were not all alike angelic natures. According to Gregory and Eriugena, however, it seems this idealized and sexless form of human nature never actually existed; God, foreseeing that man would sin, in his mercy created man with a material body in a visible universe so that by transcending its limitation he might return to the state originally planned by God had there been no sin. Cf. *De divisione naturae,* II, 12, J.P. Migne, *op. cit.,* 540B.

29. *De divisione naturae,* V, 20, J.P. Migne, *op. cit.,* 893-94.

30. *Ibid.,* 8, 876B.

V

ST. PETER DAMIAN

PETER DAMIAN was born at Ravenna in 1007. After a brief teaching career there, he entered the religious life and eventually became prior of a congregation of hermits whose form of life he revised, using ideals drawn from the Rule of St. Benedict. A great deal of his life was spent in various diplomatic missions for the Pope or in Church reform projects. In 1057 he was made Cardinal. He died at Faenza in 1072.

Though he wrote extensively, his works are almost exclusively of a purely religious character. He is usually cited, in contrast to saints like Augustine or Anselm, as an almost fanatical opponent of philosophy. He is known for statements to the effect that if philosophy were necessary, Christ would have chosen philosophers instead of fishermen equipped, like Samson, with the jawbone of an ass. Pure philosophy was an invention of the devil. As the first professor of grammar, he taught our protoparents to decline God in the plural. While it is best not to know philosophy, since not every monk who has the "jawbone of an ass" is necessarily a Samson, philosophy may at times be of help to the theologian, the world being what it is. But philosophy must always be kept in its place as a handmaid or servant. As Moses required an Israelite to treat a captive girl he wished to marry (Deuteronomy 21: 10-13), so should the monk treat philosophy, shaving off her hair (useless theories of philosophy), cutting her nails (works of superstition), and taking away her old clothes (fables and pagan superstitions). Only then may he marry her. But these statements taken out of context do not do him justice. One of the great stylists of the Middle Ages, Damian was a master of epigrams. Many of his quips occur in a work entitled *On Holy Simplicity,* written to console a monk who is worried about his lack of education. One must consider also the status of education in his day. The Western world was only beginning to recover from the unbelievably low level to which classical studies had fallen during the politically turbulent tenth century. Since it was inspired largely by what Boethius had made available in his translations from the Greek, Christian speculation of this period began with dialectics. Like the sophists at the time of Socrates, however, the new breed of dialecticians emerging from the monastic schools frequently behaved as if the art of debate were little more than an amusing sport. In displaying their own skill they did not hesitate to challenge the hallowed beliefs of their less educated elders. Even the more serious thinkers among them were proposing theologically debatable positions about the Eucharist based on philosophical theories about matter and form. Because this controversy stressed the role of divine omnipotence, some believe it was the occasion for this dissertation of Peter's. Be that as it may, Peter seems more proximately concerned with those who would ascribe some kind of impotence to God on the authority of Holy Writ, St. Jerome, or even his friend, Desiderius. The more effectively to answer their objections, Peter addressed this letter to the latter, the cardinal and abbot of Monte Cassino (later to become Pope Victor III). Peter's first concern is to show that the problems being raised are actually pseudo-problems (nonproblems) that arise only because these dialecticians have allowed themselves to be bewitched by language and have paid too little attention to the "logic of speech." Real questions, such as whether God can restore a sinner or fallen virgin, should not be confused with the quite different problem as to why the past is said to be unchangeable. In his first approach to solving the latter problem, Peter points out that "necessity" and "impossibility" in this context do not refer to "the nature of things" but to "the logical consequences of speech." Put in more modern terminology, we are dealing with a tautology of the form "p implies p," which says nothing about reality or the situation expressed by "p." The implication, Peter asserts, holds good regardless of whether the proposition be stated in the present, past, or future tense. The fact expressed is always something that could be either true or false, or logically speaking, it is always something possible. Since possible in this context means "able to be accomplished," its logical correlative is "able to accomplish." From Damian's viewpoint, the objective basis for this possibility reduces to God's creative power or omnipotence, and much of this lengthy letter is concerned with establishing this point, together with that of God's timeless mode of existence. The latter suggests a new approach to the problem, that developed in the "epilogue" numbered XVI. Here we see a primitive attempt to distinguish between the "logical form" of ordinary language and an "ideal language" adequate to the timeless reality that is God. In this ideal language, as Damian envisages it, it would be impossible even to state that there is something God cannot do.

In the following selection, we have omitted those sections of the letter irrelevant to Damian's general argument and have inserted section XVI between V and VI, where this "epilogue" seems to fit more naturally. The translation was made by Owen J. Blum especially for this volume.

On Divine Omnipotence[1]

To the Lord Desiderius, the most reverend abbot of the monastery of Monte Cassino, and to all his holy community, the monk Peter, the sinner, sends the kiss of peace in the Holy Spirit.

For him who alone was rescued from the swells of a high-flowing sea it would be an act of inhumanity if, while seeing his boat still foundering amid threatening and towering waves and in danger of rocks and cliffs, he did not deplore the condition of his companions who were fighting for their lives. And so, after putting down the episcopal burden, I rejoice as one who safely reached the shore; but with brotherly solicitude I am concerned that you are still shaken by winds and storms. . . .

I. As you might remember, one day as we both sat talking at table, the topic turned to this passage of St. Jerome: "I speak boldly," he said, "while God can do all things, he cannot cause a virgin to be restored after she has fallen. He may, indeed, free her from guilt, but he cannot award her the crown of virginity which she lost."[2] "I confess," I said, "that this opinion has never satisfied me; and I consider not by whom a thing is said, but what is said. It seems altogether unbecoming that impotence be so lightly ascribed to him who can do all things, unless it be affirmed on the secret evidence of a higher intelligence." On the other hand, you replied that it is certain and quite worthy of belief that God cannot cause a virgin to be restored after defloration. Then after we had gone far afield with long and wordy argument, you at length reduced your thinking to this brief statement: God is unable to do this for no other reason than that he does not wish it. To which I replied: "If God can do none of the things that he does not wish to do, he does nothing but that which he wishes; therefore, he can do none of the things at all that he has not done. Consequently, if I may speak freely, God does not cause it to rain today because he is unable to do so; therefore he does not heal the bedridden because he is unable; for the same reason, he does not destroy the unjust nor free the faithful from their oppression. These and many other deeds God does not perform because he is unwilling, and because he does not so wish, he is unable. It follows, therefore, that whatever God does not do, he is totally unable to do. This seems clearly to be so absurd and so ridiculous, that such an assertion not only fails to agree with divine omnipotence, but is incompatible even with the weakness of man, since there are many things that we do not do, and yet are able to do."

However, if in Holy Scripture we should find such statements having mystical and allegorical significance, we should accept them cautiously and with reverence, rather than interpret them boldly and freely in a literal sense. Such an instance is had when the angel spoke to Lot who was hurrying to Segor: "Make haste," he said, "seek safety there for I can do nothing till you arrive there" (Gen. 19:22). . . . If, then, statements of this kind are found included in Sacred Writ, they must not be quickly and indiscriminately publicized with a daring and self-conceited air, but treated with restraint in temperate and modest language. For if the assertion should reach the common folk that God were in any sense impotent —which would be an impious thing to say—unlettered people would be immediately confused and the Christian faith would be disturbed to the grave detriment of souls.

II. In the same sense that one asserts that God cannot do a thing one may also say that he is ignorant of something: namely, since he cannot do anything that is evil, he does not know how to do evil. Thus he has neither the power nor the knowledge to lie, or to commit perjury or any injustice. . . . The statement that God is unable to do or to know something evil, then, does not refer to ignorance or impossibility, but to the uprightness of the eternal will. Precisely because he does not wish evil, it is correct to say that he can neither know nor do something evil, according to the evidence of Scripture: "But though you have might at your disposal, you judge with clemency, and with much lenience you govern us; for power, whenever you will, attends you" (Wisdom 12:18).

III. The will of God is truly the cause of the existence of all things, whether visible or invisible, in that all created things, before appearing in their visible forms, were already truly and essentially alive in the will of their Creator. "All that came to be," says John, "had life in him" (John 1:4). And he testified in the Apocalypse to the same statement by the twenty-four elders: "You are worthy, O Lord our God, to receive glory and honor and power, because you created all things; by your will they have their being and were created" (Apoc. 4:11). In the first place it is said "they have their being," and then that "they were created," because the things that were externally expressed by their making, already existed internally in the providence and in the design of the Creator.

Moreover, as the will of God is the cause by which the things that were not yet made originally came into being, so it is no less the efficient cause whereby those things that have been lost might return to the integrity of their state. "Have I any pleasure in the death of the wicked, says the Lord, and not rather that he should turn from his way and live?" (Ez. 18:23). What could hinder God from restoring a virgin after she has fallen? Is it for the reason that he is unable because he is unwilling, and that he does not wish it because it is evil, as was said before, that God neither wishes nor is able to lie, to swear falsely, or to commit an injustice? . . .

IV. That a virgin may be restored after her fall is to be understood in two ways: either in relation to the fullness of merits, or in relation to bodily integrity. Let us see, then, whether God is not able to do both. In reference to merit, the apostle calls the community of the faithful a virgin when speaking to the Corinthians: "For I betrothed you to one spouse, that I might present you a chaste virgin to Christ" (2 Cor. 11:2). Certainly, there were not only virgins in this people of God, but also many women who had married or who had lived in continence after they had abandoned virginity. And the Lord said in the words of the prophet: "If a man divorces his wife, will he ever return to her? Would not that woman be thought impure and contaminated? You have played the harlot with many lovers; nevertheless, return to me, says the Lord" (Jer. 3:1). This return to the Lord, insofar as it concerns the quality of merit, is exactly that by which a woman becomes pure after she has lost her virtue, or by which a virgin is won back from prostitution. For this reason the spouse repeats his words: "And I will no longer remember any of your sins" (Jer. 31:34). . . .

In my opinion, and I state and affirm this without fear of abuse or captious arguments to the contrary, the omnipotent

God has power to restore virginity to any woman, no matter how many times she has been married, and to renew in her the seal of integrity, just as she was when taken from her mother's womb. I have said these things, however, not to lessen respect for St. Jerome, who spoke with pious purpose, but to refute with invincible reasons of faith those who take occasion from his words to charge God with impotence.

V. And now I feel obliged to respond to an argument which, on the subject of this controversy, many put forward on the strength of your holiness's opinion. They say: "If God," as you assert, "is omnipotent in all things, can he act so that things that were made become things that were not made? He can certainly destroy all things so that they no longer exist, but it is impossible to understand how he can cause things that were made to become unmade. One might grant that it is possible that from this moment on and thereafter, Rome does not exist, since it can be destroyed; but there is no way to explain how it is possible that it was not founded in antiquity."

As I prepare to reply to these objections, as God may inspire me, I feel obliged in the first place to call my critic's attention to the words of Solomon, where he says: "With what is too much for you meddle not, and do not search out the things which are beyond you" (Sir. 3:22). Then one must say: what God makes is something; what God does not make is nothing. . . . Citations from Scripture testify that God made that which was not, and did not destroy that which existed; that he created future things without forgetting things past, although one often reads that God had overthrown something to make provision for something better, for example, the earth by means of the flood, and the Five Cities (Pentapolis) by means of fire.[3] These things, in fact, he so deprived of being and of future being so as not to deprive them also of past being. But if you should closely note the deeds of the evil men who were then destroyed, seeing how in pursuing vain and worthless things they tended not toward being but toward nothing, you might reasonably conclude that they had not existed. For this reason Scripture asserts that they cry out from the fullness of their affliction. . . . "Hereafter we shall be as though we had never been" (Wis. 2:2). This they say because even at the time when they seemed to be, they belonged rather to nonbeing than to real being. "I AM WHO AM," he said, and "Say this to the people of Israel: 'I AM has sent me to you' " (Ex. 3:14). But he who withdraws from him who truly is, must cease to be, because he tends towards nothing. . . .

Countless similar statements are to be found in the Scripture, in which wicked men are compared to the smallest or the most trifling things, or are said to be nothing, even at the time they seem to be powerful. . . .

XVI. Consequently, when the question is asked in these words: "How can God bring it about that something that has happened will not have happened," a brother endowed with a sound faith should reply that if whatever happened was evil, it was not something but nothing. Hence, it must be considered not to have existed because it did not possess the grounds for existence, which the maker of all things had not provided so that it might exist. However, if what happened was good, it was surely made by God: "For he spoke, and it was made; he commanded, and they were created" (Ps. 32:9). "And through him all things came to be: not one thing had its being but through him" (John 1:3). So it is much the same thing to ask: "How can God bring it about that what once happened did not happen?" or "Can God act in such a way that what he once made, he did not make?" as to assert that what God has made, God did not make. And indeed, whoever affirms this proposition should be thought contemptible. He is not worthy of a reply, but should rather be sentenced to branding.

Nevertheless, for purposes of confuting wicked and sharp-tongued men, one should call to mind what was said above, which, at this point, however, I avoid mentioning even briefly, so that verboseness of style may not annoy my reader; for I did not set out to compose a book, but a letter. Among the things that I noted, however, this point should not be forgotten: that as the ability *[posse]* to do all things is coeternal to God, the Creator of all things, so also is his power to know all things; and that he contains, determines, and forever confirms within the compass of his wisdom all times past, present, and future in such a way that nothing new at all can happen to him, nor can anything pass away through forgetfulness. And so we might ask: What sort of power is this by which God can do all things, and what is the nature of the wisdom by which he knows all things? Let us inquire of the Apostle: "Christ," he says, "is the power of God and the wisdom of God" (1 Cor. 1:24). In him, surely, there is true eternity and true immortality; in him there exists that eternal today that never ends; in him an everlasting present is so firmly and perpetually fixed that it is capable of neither passing away nor of changing at some time into the past. If, therefore, I must refute the insolence of these impudent opponents for whom the above solution to this question is still not satisfactory, I can say without appearing foolhardy that God, in that immutable and ever uniform eternity of his, is able to bring about that what had happened relative to our passing time, did not happen. For example, we may say: God *can* so cause it to happen that Rome, founded in antiquity, would not have been founded. In saying *can [potest]*, that is, in the present tense, we use the word properly insofar as it relates to the unalterable eternity of God; but in relation to us, in whom there is continuous movement and perpetual change, we should more correctly say *could have [potuit]*, as we normally do, and as we may also understand the following: God can so act that Rome would not have been founded, that is, in respect to himself with whom "there is no variation, no play of passing shadows" (James 1:17). For us, however, this is equivalent to saying "God could have." But in respect to his eternity, whatever God could do, he also can do, because his present never turns into the past, his today does not change into tomorrow or into some other alteration of time; and hence just as he is always what he is, so also whatever is present to him is always present. Wherefore, as we may rightly say that God *could* cause Rome before it was established to be nonestablished, so no less rightly may we also say: God has that power after Rome was founded that it be notfounded; that is, he *could have* caused it not to have been founded relative to us; he *can*, relative to himself. Indeed, the very potency that God possessed before Rome existed remains forever immutable and intransient in the eternity of God, so that we can say about anything that God is able to cause it, since his potency which is coeternal to him remains forever fixed and immutable. Only in relation to ourselves can we say that God has been able *[potuisse]*; relative to himself, however, there is no "has been able," but always a motionless, constant, and unchangeable potency: for whatever God could do, he doubtless also is able to do.

In truth, as there is with him no being and having been, but only everlasting being, so consequently there is no having been able and being able, but always a perpetual potency that can never change. For, just as he did not say: "I am who was and am," but rather, "I AM WHO AM," and "I AM has sent me to you" (Exodus 3:14), so it undoubtedly follows that he does not say: "I am who could and can," but says, "who unalterably and eternally can." In fact, the potency that was in God before all ages is the same today; and the same potency that he possesses today was his before all ages, and it eternally endures still firm and immutable through all the ages yet to come. Since, therefore, God could have caused things not to exist before anything was made, so even now he has that power that the things which were made should not have existed. For the same potency that he then possessed has neither changed nor been removed, but just as he always is what he is, so also God's potency cannot be changed. Truly, it is he who speaks through the prophet: "Surely I, the Lord, do not change" (Mal. 2:6), and in the Gospel: "Before Abraham was born, I am" (John 8:58). For, in the manner of our human condition he does not change from future being to present being, or from present being to past being, but is always the same and is always what he is. Therefore, since God is always one and the same, so in him the power to do all things is always present, is unfailing, and cannot pass away. Moreover, as in all truth and without any fear of contradiction whatsoever I say that God is now and forever what he was before all time, so in all truth I say now and forever God is able to do what he was able to do before all time. If, therefore, in every instance God is always able to do whatever he could do from the beginning, if he was able before the creation of things to cause whatever now exists not to have existed in any way, he has the power, consequently, that the things that were made would not have been made at all. Indeed, his potency is fixed and eternal, so that whatever he could have done at any moment he always has the power to do, nor does the diversity of times suggest the presence of the slightest change in eternity. As he is the same as he was in the beginning, so also has he the ability to do everything that he could have done before time began.

We must, therefore, allow the following conclusion to the problem here set forth. If the potency to do all things is coeternal to God, then it follows that God could have caused things that have happened not to have happened. And hence we must firmly and surely assert that God, just as he is in fact said to be omnipotent, can in truth, without any possible exception, do all things, either in respect to events that have happened or in respect to events that have not happened. . . .

VI. But what is the purpose of these vain men, of these sacrilegious innovators in doctrine, who, while devising their ensnaring questions for others were not aware that they themselves had first been trapped in them, and of those who, while placing obstacles of frivolous investigation in the path of simple wayfarers, themselves stumbled over the "stumbling-stone" (Romans 9:32)? They ask: "Can God bring it about that once something happened, it did not happen?" as if this impossibility should appear to be restricted only to past events and were not to be found similarly in things present and to come. For truly, whatever exists at the moment, so long as it exists, must undoubtedly exist.[4] For it is not true that so long as something exists, it is possible for it not to exist. In like manner, for something that will happen, it is impossible for it not to happen, even though there may be some things whose happening or not happening is a matter of indifference, as, for example, my riding or not riding today, seeing or not seeing a friend, our having rain or clear weather. These and similar cases secular scholars are wont to call "indifferent alternatives" *[utrumlibet]*, because generally they are just as likely to happen as not to happen; but these are called "indifferent alternatives" more properly in relation to the variable nature of things than to the logical consequence of speech. Thus, according to the natural order of inconstant phenomena, it can happen that today it may rain, and it can also happen that it may not rain; but by the logic of words, if it is going to rain, it is absolutely necessary that it rain. Likewise, what is said of past events may be applied with equal cogency to present and future things; in this sense, that, just as everything that happened necessarily had to happen, so also everything that exists must exist so long as it exists, and everything that will happen must happen in the future. And so in relation to the logical order of speech, for whatever was, it is impossible not to have been; for whatever is, it is impossible not to be; and for whatever will be, it is impossible that it will not be.

Notice, therefore, how the blind foolhardiness of these pseudointellectuals who investigate nonproblems by boldly attributing to God those things that refer to the art of rhetoric cause him to become completely impotent and deprived of strength, not only regarding things past, but also relative to things present and to come. These men, indeed, because they have not as yet learned the elements of style, lose their grasp of the fundamentals of simple faith as a result of the obscurity produced by their dull tricks; and still ignorant of those things boys study in school, they heap the abuse of their contentious spirit on the mysteries of God. Moreover, because they have acquired so little skill in the rudiments of learning or of the liberal arts, they obscure the study of ecclesiastical doctrine by the cloud of their indiscreet curiosity.

Clearly, conclusions drawn from the arguments of dialecticians and rhetoricians should not be thoughtlessly addressed to the mystery of divine power; dialecticians and rhetoricians should refrain from persistently applying to Sacred Scripture the rules devised for their progress in using the tools of the syllogism or in the fine style of oratory, and from setting their inevitable conclusions against the power of God. However, if the techniques of the humanities be used in the study of revelation, they must not usurp the rights of the mistress, but should humbly assume a certain ancillary role as a maidservant to her lady, so as not to be led astray in assuming the lead, nor to lose the enlightenment of deepest virtue, nor to abandon the right road to truth by attending only to the superficial meaning of words.

Surely, it is obvious to all that, if one should trust these arguments based on the meaning of words, the power of God would appear impotent on many occasions. For, in keeping with this abusive and frivolous inquisition, God would be unable to act so that things that had already happened should not have happened; nor, contrariwise, that things which did not happen should have happened; nor that those things which now exist, so long as they exist, should not exist; nor that things that will happen should not exist in the future; nor, on the contrary, that things which will not happen should happen in the future. Many of the ancient authorities in the liberal arts, not only pagans but also members of the Christian faith, have studied this question at length; but none of them dared to promote the mad opinion that would attribute the quality of impotence to God, and especially, if he were a Christian, to doubt his omnipotence. But they disputed the problems of dialectical necessity or impossibility in such a way as to keep them solely within the framework of this art, without ever mentioning God in the course of their arguments. But those who today take up this ancient problem, while striving to comprehend things beyond their capacity, instead blunt the keenness of their minds because they have not feared to offend the very Author of light.

Therefore, this question, in that it is proven that it pertains neither to the investigation of the power of divine majesty, but rather to the skills of the art of dialectic, nor to the perfection or the nature of things, but rather to the method and order of speech and to the relationship of words, has no place amidst the mysteries of the Church, which are loosely discussed by young lay students in the schools. This question, in fact, does not relate to the norms of faith nor to the probity of conduct, but relates to the fluency of speech and to the elegance of language.

Wherefore, we are satisfied that in this brief summary we have defended the faith which we hold, while granting to the wise of this world the things that are theirs. Let those who wish, retain the letter that brings death, so long as, by the mercy of God, the life-giving Spirit does not depart from us.[5]

NOTES

1. *De divina omnipotentia* (Epist. 2, 17). P. Brezzi, *De divina omnipotentia e alteri opusculi* (Florence: Vellechi, 1943), pp. 50-82; cf. also J.P. Migne, *Patrologia Latina,* Vol. 145, cols. 595-622.
2. St. Jerome, *Epist.* 22, 5, *Corpus Scriptorum Ecclesiasticorum Latinorum,* Vol. 54, 150.
3. Cf. *Wisdom* 10:6; *Genesis* 14:2.
4. Aristotle, *De interpretatione* I, c. 9, 18b 8.
5. Cf. 2 *Corinthians* 3:6.

VI

ST. ANSELM AND GAUNILON

St. Anselm was born of a noble family in Aosta, northern Italy, in 1033. Despite the objections of his father, he decided to become a Benedictine monk and in 1059 went to Bec in Normandy, where his countryman Lanfranc was famous as a teacher. He entered the order the following year, succeeded Lanfranc as Prior in 1063, and became Abbot in 1078. It was during this interval that he composed his main works. In 1093 he succeeded Lanfranc as Archbishop of Canterbury and Primate of England, in which office he remained until his death in 1109.

In contrast to Peter Damian, Anselm believed strongly in the utility of the rational methods of the dialecticians for clarifying and defending Christian revelation, and for this reason he is frequently regarded as the father of scholasticism.

Undoubtedly the most provocative of his views was the argument for the existence of God developed in the *Proslogion*. It is presented in the following pages, together with the criticism of Gaunilon, a monk of Marmoutier, and Anselm's reply to the same.

The translations were made from the critical edition of F. S. Schmitt, O.S.B., by A. B. Wolter especially for this volume.

St. Anselm on the Existence of God[1]

PREFACE

Some time ago at the pressing invitation of some brethren I did a small work as a sample of meditation based on faith. The work was written in the person of one seeking to throw light on an area of ignorance by silently reasoning with himself. Reflecting that what I had woven together was really a chain of many arguments, I began to ask myself whether one might not be able to find a single argument, needing no proof beyond itself, which would suffice by itself to link together such conclusions as that God truly exists, that he is the highest good—needing no other but needed for the existence and well-being of all else—and whatever else we believe to be true of the divine being. Diligently and often did I pursue this quest. Sometimes the solution seemed almost at hand; at other times it simply eluded the grasp of my mind. Finally I decided in despair to cease the search for something so impossible to find. But when I tried to put the matter out of mind lest I waste time that might profitably be spent on other matters in such a fruitless quest, it continued to importune me despite my unwillingness and efforts at resistance. And so it was that one day when I was weary of struggling against this obsession the solution I had despaired of finding suddenly appeared amidst the welter of my conflicting thoughts and I eagerly seized the idea I had been so strenuously fending off.

Thinking that, if I put down in writing what I was so happy to find, others too would find pleasure reading it, I did the following little tract which takes up this and some allied matters from the viewpoint of one who tries to bring his mind to contemplate God and seeks to understand what he believes. Neither this nor the earlier treatise seemed to deserve to be called a book or bear their author's name. Still I felt they should not be put out without some title to invite those in whose hands they fell to read them. To each I gave a name, calling the first *An Example of Meditation Based on Faith* and the second *Faith Seeking Understanding*. But when both had been copied frequently under these titles, I was urged to add my own name thereto, especially by Hugh, the reverend archbishop of Lyons and apostolic delegate to France, who commanded me by his apostolic authority to do so. That this might be more fittingly accomplished, I called the earlier work *Monologion* (i.e. a soliloquy) and the present work *Proslogion* (i.e. an allocution).

CHAPTER I

. . . It is not your sublimity, O Lord, I seek to penetrate, for my mind is no match for it, but I do desire to understand something of your truth which I believe and love in my heart. For I seek not to understand that I may believe, but I believe that I may understand. For this too I believe: "Unless I believe, I shall not understand!"

CHAPTER II

O Lord, who grants understanding to faith, make me, so far as is good for me, to understand that you exist, as we believe, and that you are what we believe you to be. Now we believe you to be something greater than which we can conceive of nothing. Could it be then that there is no such nature, since "the fool says in his heart, 'There is no God' " [Ps. 13:1]? But surely this same fool, when he hears me say this, "something than which we can conceive of nothing greater," understands what he hears and what he understands is in his understanding even if he does not understand it to exist. For it is one thing for something to be in the understanding and quite another to understand that the thing in question exists. When a painter thinks of the work he will make beforehand, he has it in his understanding, but he does not think that what he has yet to make exists. But once he has painted it, he not only has it in his understanding but he understands that what he has made exists. Even the fool then must be convinced that in his understanding at least there is something than which nothing greater can be conceived, for when he hears this, he understands it and whatever is understood is in the understanding. But surely if the thing be such that we cannot conceive of something greater, it does not exist solely in the understanding. For if it were there only, one could also think of it as existing in reality and this is something greater. If the thing than which none greater can be thought were in the mind alone, then this same thing would both be and not be something than which nothing greater can be conceived. But surely this cannot be. Without doubt then there exists both in the understanding and in reality a being greater than which nothing can be conceived.

CHAPTER III

So truly does such a thing exist that it cannot be thought of as not existing. For we can think of something as existing which cannot be thought of as not existing, and such a thing is greater than what can be thought not to be. Wherefore, if the thing than which none greater can be thought could be conceived of as not existing, then this very thing than which none greater can be thought is not a thing than which none greater can be thought. But this is not possible. Hence, something greater than which nothing can be conceived so truly exists that it cannot be conceived not to be.

O Lord, our God, you are this being. So truly do you exist that you cannot even be thought of as nonexistent. And rightly so, for if some mind could think of something better than you, then the creature would rise above the Creator and would judge him, which is absurd. It is possible indeed to think of anything other than you as nonexistent. Of all beings then you alone have existence in the truest and highest sense, for nothing else so truly is or has existence in so great a measure. Why then does the fool "say in his heart, 'There is no God,' " when it is so evident to a reasoning mind that of all things you exist in a supreme degree? Why indeed save that he is stupid and a fool!

CHAPTER IV

But how did he come to say in his heart what he could not think? Or why was it he could not think what he said in his heart? For after all, *to say in one's heart* and *to think* are the same. And if it be true, or rather, since it is true that he thought it because he said it in his heart, and it is also true that he did not say it in his heart because he could not think it, it follows that there is not just one way to think of something or to say it in one's heart. In one sense, we think of something when we think of the word that signifies that something; in another sense, we think of it when we think of the thing itself. In the first sense, then, God can be thought of as not existing, but in the second sense, he cannot be thought of as not existing. For no one who really understands what God is can think that he does not exist, despite the fact that these words may be said in his heart either without any meaning whatsoever or with some peripheral sense. For God is that than which none greater can be thought, and whoever understands this correctly must understand that he so exists that he cannot even be thought of as nonexistent. Hence, he who understands that God exists in this way cannot think of him as nonexistent.

My thanks to you, good Lord, my thanks to you! For now I understand by your light what I once believed by your grace, so that even if I were to refuse to believe that you exist, I should be unable not to understand this to be true.

. . .

CHAPTER XV

And so, O Lord, you are not merely that than which nothing greater can be thought; rather you are something greater than can be thought. For it is possible to conceive that there is something of this sort [i.e. something we cannot know exhaustively], and if you are not this being, then something greater than you can be thought—but this cannot be.

A Reply to Anselm on Behalf of the Fool[2]

by Gaunilon, a Monk of Marmoutier

1. If one doubts or denies there is some such nature that nothing greater than it can be conceived, he is told that the existence of this being is proved, first, from the fact that in doubting or denying such he already has such a being in his understanding, for in hearing about it, he understands what is said. Next he is told that what he understands must needs exist not only in the intellect but in reality as well. And the proof of this is that a thing is greater if it also exists in reality than if it were in the understanding alone. Were it only in the intellect, even something that once existed would be greater than it. And so what is greater than all is less than something and thus not really greater than everything, which is clearly contradictory. It is necessary then that something greater than all, already proved to exist in the understanding, exists in reality as well, for otherwise it could not be greater than all. To this he might reply:

2. The only reason this thing is said to be in my understanding is because I understand what is said. But could I not be said equally to have in my understanding all manner of pseudo-things, even such as have absolutely no existence in themselves, simply on the grounds that if someone speaks of them I would understand what he said? Unless perhaps one shows this being to be so constituted that one has it in thought in a way other than that of the unreal or dubious thing. And therefore I am not said to think of what I hear or have it in thought, but to understand it and have it in my understanding, because the only way I can think of this being is to understand it, i.e. to include in my knowledge of it the fact that it exists.

But if this be the case, it would do away, for one thing, with the distinction between what is temporally prior (i.e. having the thing in the understanding) and what succeeds it in time (i.e. the understanding that such exists), as in the example of the picture which is first in the mind of the painter and only afterwards exists as a work. Furthermore it is scarcely credible that this being when spoken of or heard of cannot be thought of as nonexistent in the way that God can be thought not to exist. For if it cannot, what is the point of constructing an argument against one who doubts or denies that there is such a nature?

Finally, you must prove to me that this is such a thing that you simply can't think of it without your understanding quickly grasping in all certainty its indubitable existence. But you must prove this to me by an incontestable argument and not by one I don't accept, viz. that what I understand when I hear it, already is in my understanding. For anyone whose words I understand can mention all sorts of dubious or unreal things. And I still think such things are in my understanding in the same way as this being is, or even more so if I am deceived and believe such words, as often happens.

3. Hence the example of the painter who already has in his understanding what he is about to paint is not to the point. For before the picture is made the painter's art contains it. But such things are there only as a part of his understanding, as it were. "A carpenter about to make a box," says St. Augustine, "first has it in his art. The box that will be made is not life, but as it exists in his art it is life, for the artisan's soul is alive. And all these things are there before they are produced." Why then are these things life in the living soul of their maker if it is not because they are nothing else but the knowledge or understanding of the soul itself? Now take anything which when heard or thought of is perceived to be real. Except for such things as are known to pertain to the very nature of the mind, no doubt the real object will be one thing and the understanding grasping it will be another. Hence even if it be true that there is something greater than which none can be conceived, such a thing when heard of or understood is not like a prospective picture in the mind of the painter.

4. Another point touched on can be attacked, viz. that this being which is greater than all that can be thought of is said to be none other than God himself. So far as actual knowledge of such is concerned, be it of a specific or general nature, I am as little able to conceive of this being when I hear of it or to have it in my understanding as I am to conceive of or understand God himself. It is for this very reason indeed, that I can conceive him to be nonexistent. For I have no direct

knowledge of the reality itself which God is nor can I figure out what it is from things that are like it, because on your own claim there can be nothing like this reality. Suppose I heard something said of a man I never knew and of whose existence I was unaware. By reason of the special or general knowledge I have of what a man is or what men are, I could think of this individual in terms of that reality itself which a man is. And still it might be that the man I conceived of was nonexistent, for example, if the man who spoke of him were lying, for I was not thinking of him according to that reality that would make him just this man but in terms of what is true of any man whatsoever. But when I hear "God" or "something greater than all else," I do not have this in my thought or understanding in the same way that I had this nonexistent man, since I can think of the latter in terms of some real and familiar thing, whereas I can only think of the former in terms of mere words and one can never or scarcely ever think of anything real in this signification rather than the word itself we think of. The word (i.e. the sounds and syllables) are real enough. Neither is it like the case of one who knows what a word is wont to signify, namely one who thinks of it in terms of the reality signified. Rather it is like the case of one who does not know the actual signification of the word, but when he hears the word in his mind tries to imagine what it would be. And it would be surprising if he could ever arrive at the truth in this fashion. And yet it is just in this way and no other that the object is in my understanding when I hear and understand a person who says there is a being greater than all conceivable beings. So much for the claim that this supreme nature exists already in my understanding.

5. Now the proof I am given that such a being exists not only in the understanding but also in reality is this. If such were not the case, then whatever really exists would be greater than this thing already proved to exist in the intellect. Hence the latter will not really be greater than everything else. To this I reply. Should one say that there is in the understanding something which cannot be conceived as actual, I would not deny it is in me in this way. But since this does not guarantee it any real existence, I shall not admit it has such until unquestionable proof be given. Now he who says: "This being which is greater than all exists, because otherwise it would not be greater than all" does not pay sufficient attention to what he

is saying. For I would still not admit, indeed I would doubt or deny, that this [thing in the understanding] is greater than any real thing. Neither would I grant it any other existence (if it should be called "existence") than you have when the mind, on the basis of a word one only hears, tries to imagine something it has no knowledge of. But how do you prove to me this has any greater claim to real existence because it is assumed to be greater than all other things? For I deny or doubt that it is in my intellect or thought in any greater measure than are many dubious and uncertain things. For you must first assure me that it really exists somewhere and then, from the fact that it is greater than everything else, it will be clear that it also subsists of itself.

6. For example, they say that somewhere in the ocean there is an island, which because of the difficulty, or better, the impossibility of finding what does not exist, some call the lost island. And they say this island is inestimably wealthy, having all kinds of delights and riches in greater abundance even than the fabled "Fortunate Islands." And since it has no possessor or inhabitant, it excels all other inhabited countries in its possessions. Now should someone tell me that there is such an island, I could readily understand what he says, since there is no problem there. But suppose he adds, as though it were already implied: "You can't doubt any more that this island, which is more excellent than any land, really exists somewhere, since you don't doubt that it is in your understanding and that it is more excellent not to be in the understanding only. Hence it is necessary that it really exists, for if it did not, any land which does would excel it and consequently the island which you already understand to be more excellent would not be such." If one were to try to prove to me that this island in truth exists and its existence should no longer be questioned, either I would think he was joking or I would not know whether to consider him or me the greater fool, me for conceding his argument or him for supposing he had established with any certainty such an island's existence without first showing such excellence to be real and its existence indubitable rather than just a figment of my understanding, whose existence is uncertain.

7. This then is an answer the fool could make to your arguments against him. When he is first assured that this being is so great that its nonexistence is inconceivable, and that this in

turn is established for no other reason than that otherwise it would not excel all things, he could counter the same way and say: "When have I admitted there really is any such thing, i.e. something so much greater than everything else that one could prove to me it is so real, it could not even be conceived as unreal?" What we need at the outset is a very firm argument to show there is some superior being, bigger and better than all else that exists, so that we can go on from this to prove all the other attributes such a bigger and better being has to have. As for the statement that it is inconceivable that the highest thing of all should not exist, it might be better to say its nonexistence or even its possibility of nonexistence is unintelligible. For according to the true meaning of the word, unreal things are not intelligible, but their existence is conceivable in the way that the fool thinks that God does not exist. I most certainly know I exist, but for all that, I know my nonexistence is possible. As for that supreme being which God is, I understand without doubt both his existence and the impossibility of his nonexistence. But whether I can conceive of my nonexistence as long as I most certainly know I exist, I don't know. But if I am able to, why can I not conceive of the nonexistence of whatever else I know with the same certainty? But if I cannot, then such an inability will not be something peculiar to God.

8. The remaining portions of the book are so accurately, so brilliantly, and so splendidly argued and are so full of usefulness, and have such an aura of devotion and holy feeling that they should not be rejected simply because these initial points, though rightly sensed, are weakly argued, but rather this argumentation should be strengthened so that the whole work will be received with great respect and praise.

Anselm's Reply to Gaunilon[3]

It was a fool against whom I argued in my little work. But since my critic is far from a fool, and is a Catholic speaking in the fool's behalf, it is enough for me if I can answer the Catholic.

CHAPTER I

Whoever you be, you say the fool could argue as follows: This existence in the understanding is no different in truth for a being than which none greater can be conceived than it is for anything else whatsoever, provided only that it can at least be thought of. To argue from this that the former exists both in the understanding and in reality is no more valid than to infer that a lost island most certainly exists from the fact that when it is described in words, the hearer has no doubt that it is in his understanding.

But I say: if a being than which none greater can be thought does not exist either in the intellect or in thought, then either God isn't such a being that one cannot think of something greater or else he is not understood or thought of and hence is not in the understanding or thought. But for proof that the consequent is false, I appeal both to your faith and to your conscious experience. Consequently, such a being is truly being understood and thought of and therefore is also in the understanding and in thought. Either the basis on which you try to refute me is not true or else the inference you think follows is invalid.

Now you think that just because someone understands "a thing such that a greater is inconceivable," it does not follow it exists in the understanding. Nor if it is in the understanding, it also exists in reality. But surely I say if it can be conceived at all, it must exist. For one cannot think of it as existing if it were not without a beginning. Whatever does not exist, but can be thought to exist, however, can be thought of as beginning to exist. Consequently whatever does not exist, but can be thought of as existing, simply is not such a thing that one could not conceive of a greater. If it can be conceived to exist, it has to exist.

Furthermore, if such a thing can be thought of at all, it is necessary that it exist. For no one who denies or doubts there is such a being that a greater is inconceivable denies or doubts that if such existed, its nonexistence could neither be the case nor be in the intellect. Otherwise it would not be such a thing that one could think of no greater. Take something that does not exist, but can be thought of. If it did exist, its nonexistence would have been both a real and conceivable possibility. Now if one could even conceive of such a being that to be greater is inconceivable, it cannot be nonexistent. Assume for the sake of argument it doesn't exist, but that one could conceive of it. Now what does not exist but can be thought of, if it were to exist, would not be such that a greater is inconceivable. It would follow then that if there were such a thing that a greater is inconceivable, it would not be such a thing that a greater is inconceivable, which is too absurd. Consequently, it is false to say a thing of this kind does not exist, if it can be conceived; and all the more so if it can be understood and can be in the intellect.

I will even go further; there is no doubt that if there is any time and place at which a thing does not exist, even if it does exist at some other time and place, one could conceive of it as nonexistent for all times and places in the way it is nonexistent at a particular time and place. Take something which is today, but yesterday was not. One could think of it always being the way it was yesterday. What is not here but elsewhere, could be conceived to be nowhere even as it is not here. So too with something that has parts which do not all exist at the same place or time; all its parts and hence the whole thing can be conceived to be nowhere for all time. For though time may be said to exist always and the universe to be everywhere, yet the whole of time does not exist at every moment, nor the entire universe at every place. And just as one part of time does not exist when another does, so each can be conceived never to have existed. Or as each part of the universe does not exist where another part does, so each can be thought of as being nowhere. What is composed of parts can be dissolved in concept and could be nonexistent. But if there can be such a thing that a greater is inconceivable, it cannot be thought of as nonexistent. Otherwise, if it does exist, it would not be such that one could not conceive of something greater; which is inconsistent. There is no time or place, then, where it does not exist as a whole, but it is present always and everywhere in its entirety.

Do you believe a thing understood to have such properties can somehow be conceived or understood or can exist in concept or in the understanding? For if not, one could not think such things about it. But if you claim that what is not perfectly understood is simply not understood and is not in the understanding, then you should also say that one who cannot stare directly at the light of the sun does not see the light of day, which is nothing else than sunlight. Certainly then "a being greater than which nothing can be conceived" is understood and is in the intellect, if such properties are understood of it.

CHAPTER II

In the argument you attack, then, I have said that when the fool hears "a being than which no greater is conceivable" he understands what he hears. Certainly one who does not understand a familiar tongue when it is spoken either is without any understanding or is very dull witted.

Then I said that if this is understood, it is in the intellect. But if you can prove something must in fact exist, is there no intellect in which it is? You may say that even though it is in the intellect, it does not follow it is understood. But notice that it does follow that it is in the intellect, if it is understood. For just as what is conceived, is conceived through a conception, and what is conceived through a conception is there in the way it is conceived, so also what is understood, is understood through the understanding, and what is understood through the understanding is there in the way it is understood. What could be clearer?

After this, I have said that if it is only in the understanding, it could be conceived to be also existing in reality, and this is greater. If it is only in the understanding, then one and the same thing is such that one both can and cannot conceive of anything greater. Which follows more logically, I ask: that it exists in the intellect alone, but cannot be thought to exist also in reality, or that it can be thought to exist in reality, and one who thinks this thinks of something greater than if it were only in the intellect? What follows more logically than this: if a being than which none greater is conceivable is only in the understanding, then it is not such that none greater can be conceived? But surely in no intellect will you find a thing with both these properties, viz. "greater than which something is conceivable" and "greater than which nothing is conceivable." Does it not follow then that if "a thing greater than which nothing is conceivable" is in any understanding, then such a thing is not only in the understanding? For if it were, it is "a thing greater than which something is conceivable," which is not consistent.

CHAPTER III

But you claim our argument is on a par with the following. Someone imagines an island in the ocean which surpasses all lands in its fertility. Because of the difficulty, or rather impossibility, of finding what does not exist, he calls it "Lost Island." He might then say you cannot doubt that it really exists, because anyone can readily understand it from its verbal description. I assert confidently that if anyone finds something for me, besides that "than which none greater is conceivable," which exists either in reality or concept alone to which the logic of my argument can be applied, I will find and give him his "Lost Island," never to be lost again. But it now seems obvious that a thing such that none greater can be conceived cannot be thought of as nonexistent since it exists on such firm grounds of truth. For otherwise it would not exist at all. If anyone says he thinks it does not exist, then I declare that when he thinks this he either thinks of something than which a greater is inconceivable, or else he does not think at all. If he does not think, then neither does he think that what he is not thinking of is nonexistent. But if he does think, then he thinks of something which cannot be thought of as not existing. For if it could be conceived as nonexistent, it could be conceived as having a beginning and an end. Now this is impossible. Hence if anyone thinks of it, he thinks of something that cannot even be conceived to be nonexistent. Now whoever conceives it thus doesn't think of it as nonexistent, for if he did he would conceive what can't be conceived. Nonexistence is inconceivable, then, of something greater than which nothing can be conceived.

CHAPTER IV

You claim moreover that when we say this supreme reality cannot be conceived of as nonexistent, it would be perhaps better to say that its nonexistence or even the possibility of its nonexistence is not understandable. But it is better to say it cannot be conceived. For had I said that the reality itself could not be understood not to exist, perhaps you, who insist that according to proper usage what is false cannot be understood, would object that nothing existing could be understood not to exist. For it is false to claim that what exists does not exist. Hence it would not be peculiar to God to be unable to be understood as nonexistent. If any one of the things that most certainly exist can be understood to be nonexistent, however, then other certain things can also be understood to be nonexistent. But this objection cannot be applied to "conceiving," if this is correctly understood. For though none of the things that exist can be understood not to exist, still they can all be conceived as nonexistent, except the greatest. For all—and only—those things can be conceived as nonexistent which have a beginning or end or consist of parts or do not exist in their entirety in any time or place, as I have said. Only that being which cannot be conceived to be nonexistent must be conceived as having no beginning or end or composition of parts but is whole and entire always and everywhere.

Consequently you must realize that you can conceive of yourself as nonexistent, though you most certainly know that you exist. You surprise me when you say you are not sure of this. For we conceive of many things as nonexistent which we know to exist and of many things as existent which we know do not exist. And we conceive them thus not by judging but by imagining them so. We can indeed conceive of something as existent even while we know it does not exist, because we are able to conceive the one at the same time that we know the other. But we cannot conceive nonexistence while knowing existence, because we cannot conceive existence and nonexistence at the same time. If anyone distinguishes between the two senses of the statement in this fashion, then, he will understand that nothing, as long as it is known to be, can be conceived not to be, and that whatever exists, with the exception of a thing such that no greater is conceivable, can be conceived of as nonexistent even when it is known to exist. This inability to be conceived of as nonexistent, then, is peculiar to God, even though there are many objects which cannot be conceived not to be while they are. As for the way in which God can still be said to be conceived as not existing, I believe this has been explained clearly enough in my little book itself.

CHAPTER V

Even for a man of little wisdom it is easy to detect the weakness of the other objections you urge against me in behalf of the fool, and I had not thought it necessary to answer them. But since I hear some who have read them think they tell against me, I shall discuss them briefly.

First of all, you often repeat that I assert that what is greater than all other beings is in the understanding, and if it is there it exists also in reality, for otherwise a being greater than all would not be a being greater than all. But nowhere in my writings do you find such a proof. For "greater than all" and "than which nothing greater can be conceived" are not in the same category when it comes to proving that what you are talking about exists. If someone states that a subject having the property "than which nothing greater can be conceived" has no real existence or that it is possible that it does not exist, or even that it can be conceived as nonexistent, his assertion can be readily refuted. For what does not exist can not exist, and what can not exist can be conceived of as not existing. But whatever can be conceived of as not existing, if it does exist, is not such that something greater than it cannot be conceived. And if such a thing does not exist, or for that matter if it does exist, it is not the sort of thing than which one cannot conceive of something greater. But it cannot be truly said of a subject with the property "than which something greater cannot be conceived" that if it exists, it is not such that it has this property, or that if it would be, it would not be something "than which something greater cannot be conceived." Consequently, it is evident that something of this sort is not without existence, nor could it be nonexistent or even be conceived as nonexistent. For otherwise, if it did exist, it would not be what it is said to be; and if it did exist, it would not exist.

But it is not so easy to prove all this of a subject with the property "greater than all." For it is not so clear that what can be conceived not to exist is not greater than all things which actually do exist, as it is clear that such a being is not that than which no greater can be conceived. One could also question whether a being greater than all, if it does exist, is identical with a being than which no greater can be conceived, or if it would exist, whether it might not be something other than this. But there is no such uncertainty about a subject with the property "greater than which nothing can be conceived." For what if someone were to say that there is something greater than all things which actually exist, and yet, for all that, such a thing could still be conceived of as not existing, and that something greater than it, although it does not exist at the moment, can still be conceived of? Can one so readily rule out the possibility in this case that such a being is not greater than all other existing things as one could most readily rule out that it is not a being greater than which nothing can be conceived? For the former requires something additional in the way of argument besides the statement that it is greater than all. In my argument however nothing more is needed than the assurance that no greater than this can be conceived. But if one cannot prove of a subject with the property "greater than all" what can be proved of one with the property "no greater can be conceived," then you chide me unjustly for saying what I did not say, since it differs so much from what I actually did say.

But if the other argument is valid, then you should not censure me for asserting what can be proved. Whether or not it can be proved, however, he will easily decide who knows that a being than which nothing greater can be conceived can be proved. For a thing than which nothing greater is conceivable cannot be understood to be anything other than that which alone is greater than all else. Hence, just as that than which no greater can be conceived is understood and is in the understanding and is therefore asserted to really exist, so that which is said to be greater than all else is understood and is in the understanding and is necessarily inferred to really exist. Was it right, then, to compare me to the fool who, solely because he understands its verbal description, is willing to assert the lost island exists?

CHAPTER VI

But you also object that any unreal or dubious thing can be understood and be in the understanding in the same way as the thing I was talking about. It surprises me that you should raise this objection, since I intended to prove what was dubious, and was first content with showing the thing in question was somehow understood and was in the understanding, before going on to consider whether it was only in the understanding like something unreal or whether it also existed in reality. For if unreal or dubious objects are understood in this fashion and are in the understanding simply because the hearer understands what the speaker means when he talks about them, then there is no reason why the thing I spoke of should not be understood and be in the understanding. But how do you reconcile these statements? On the one hand, you say you would understand what someone was saying if he spoke about any kind of unreal thing; and yet on the other hand, you claim that when you hear of this thing which is not held in concept the same way that unreal objects are, you do not conceive of what you hear or have any conception of it, but you understand it and have it in your understanding. For you cannot conceive of it in any other way than by understanding it, that is, by including in your knowledge of it that it exists in reality. How, I ask, are these to be reconciled: that what is unreal is understood and that to understand is to comprehend in your knowledge that something exists? I don't care about the contradiction. That's your problem. But if unreal things are somehow understood and your definition applies not to all, but to a certain kind of understanding, you should not blame me for saying that a thing greater than which nothing can be conceived is understood and is in the understanding, even before it was certain that such really exists.

CHAPTER VII

You go on to say that it is scarcely credible that when one hears this being spoken of, he could not conceive of it as nonexistent in the same way in which even God could be conceived not to exist. Even those who have achieved but little dialectical skill could answer this for me. Does it make sense to deny the existence of something one understands just because it is said to be identical with something whose existence he denies because he doesn't understand it? Or if that which is somehow understood is at all times denied and identified with what is not understood at all, is it not easier to prove what is still in doubt about that which is somehow understood than what is doubtful about that which is not understood at all? That anyone denies the existence of a being greater than which nothing is conceivable, which he understands to some extent when he hears it, simply because he denies the existence of God whose meaning he does not conceive at all, is scarcely credible, therefore. Or if he denies something because he doesn't understand it completely, is it not easier to prove the existence of what is partly understood than what is not understood at all? Not without reason then have I presented to the fool, to prove that God exists, this notion "than which nothing greater can be conceived," since he would understand this to some extent whereas he would in no wise understand God.

CHAPTER VIII

Moreover, there was no need to prove so carefully that a being than which none greater can be conceived is not on a par with the still unpainted picture in the understanding of the painter. The reason for suggesting the preconceived picture was not that I wished to assert the being was of this nature but to show that what is not understood to exist can be in the understanding.

You say too that when you hear of a thing than which no greater is conceivable, you cannot conceive of it with reference to any real object you know of either specifically or generically, nor can you have it in your understanding. For you claim you don't know of such a thing in itself nor are you able to form an idea of it from anything resembling it. Yet this is clearly untrue, because everything that is less good, to the extent that it is good, resembles the greater good. It is therefore clear to any reasoning mind that by ascending from the lesser to the greater good, we can go far towards forming a notion of a being than which a greater is inconceivable. Who, for instance, cannot conceive of the following, even if he does not believe that what he conceives of really exists? He knows of some good that has a beginning and an end, and then he conceives that a good with a beginning but no end would be still better. And just as the latter is better than the former, so a good that has neither beginning nor an end, though it is always passing from the past through the present to the future, is even better than the second? And far better still—whether any such exist or not—is a being that neither requires nor is compelled to undergo any change or motion. Can one not conceive of this, or is something greater conceivable? Is this not to form an idea from things than which a greater is conceivable of the being than which a greater is inconceivable? The fool who does not accept sacred authority, then, can be readily refuted if he denies that a notion may be formed from other objects of something than which no greater is conceivable. But if any Catholic were to deny this, let him recall that "Since the creation of the world God's invisible attributes are clearly seen—his everlasting power also and divinity—being understood through the things that are made" (Rom. 1:20).

CHAPTER IX

But even were it true that a being than which no greater is conceivable cannot be conceived or understood, it still would not be false that "a being than which a greater cannot be conceived" is conceivable and intelligible. There is nothing to stop one from pronouncing "ineffable," though what is said to be ineffable cannot be spoken of. "Inconceivable" is conceivable, although that to which the word "inconceivable" applies is not conceivable. So when one says "that than which no greater is conceivable," there is no doubt that what is heard is conceivable and intelligible, although that thing itself than which a greater is inconceivable cannot be conceived or understood. Should there be a man so foolish as to say there is no being such that a greater is inconceivable, he will not be so impudent as to say he cannot understand or conceive of what he is talking about. Or if such a person were found, perchance, not only should what he says be rejected but he himself should be despised. Consequently whoever denies the existence of a thing than which none greater can be conceived at least understands and conceives of the denial he makes. This denial however, he cannot understand or conceive of without its component terms and one term of this statement is "a thing such that none greater can be conceived." Whoever makes such a denial therefore understands and conceives of that than which no greater can be conceived. It is obvious also that in similar fashion it is possible to conceive of and to understand a being whose nonexistence is impossible. He who conceives of this conceives of a greater thing than one whose nonexistence is possible. Consequently when a thing than which no greater is conceivable is conceived, if it is a thing whose nonexistence is possible that one conceives, then it is not that being than which no greater is conceivable. But a thing cannot be simultaneously conceived of and not conceived of. Hence one who conceives of a thing than which no greater is conceivable does not conceive of something whose nonexistence is possible, but of something whose nonexistence is impossible. Consequently, what he conceives of must exist; for anything whose nonexistence is possible is simply not what he conceives of.

CHAPTER X

I believe I have shown in my former book, by an argument that is not weak but necessary enough, that I did prove the actual existence of a thing than which nothing greater can be conceived; and I believe that the cogency of this argument cannot be weakened by the force of any objection. For the signification of this utterance is so powerful that, from the very fact that the subject under discussion is conceived or understood, it follows necessarily that it exists in reality and has whatever we believe should be ascribed to the divine substance. For we attribute to the divine substance anything that absolutely speaking we think it would be better to be than not to be. For example, it is better to be eternal than not to be eternal, to be good than not to be good, indeed, to be goodness itself rather than not to be goodness itself. A being greater than which nothing is conceivable, however, could not but be a thing of this sort. Consequently, this thing than which none greater can be conceived must of necessity be whatever we believe the divine essence should be.

My thanks to you then for your kindness in both blaming and praising my book. For since you were so generous in your praise of those parts you regarded worthy of acceptance, it is quite clear that your criticism of those parts you regarded as weak stemmed from a benevolent rather than any malevolent attitude.

NOTES

1. *Proslogion,* ed. F.S. Schmitt, *Sancti Anselmi Cantuariensis Archiepiscopi Opera Omnia,* Vol. 1 (Edinburgh: Thomas Nelson and Sons, 1946), 93-104, 112.

2. *Quid ad haec respondeat quidam pro insipienti,* ed. F.S. Schmitt, *Sancti Anselmi Cantuariensis Archiepiscopi Opera Omnia,* Vol. 1 (Edinburgh: Thomas Nelson and Sons, 1946), 125-29.

3. *Quid ad haec respondeat editor ipsius libelli,* ed. F.S. Schmitt, *Sancti Anselmi Cantuariensis Archiepiscopi Opera Omnia,* Vol. 1 (Edinburgh: Thomas Nelson and Sons, 1946), 130-39.

VII

HONORIUS OF AUTUN

MAN'S IDEA of the universe at various stages of his intellectual development provides the conceptual background against which many of the philosophical and theological speculations of a period have to be understood. The medieval period was no exception; fortunately, there is no scarcity of medieval documents concerning the physical universe. The following extract gives an idea of how the average educated or literate man of the twelfth century pictured the world. It was written around 1122 by a Benedictine monk of Regensburg, whose works were popular but whose life is still something of a puzzle, since to avoid fame he used the pseudonym *Augustodunensis*. The name means literally the hill (dunum) of Augustus, the site of a supposed victory of Charlemagne near Regensburg. In addition to *The Key to Nature (Clavis physicae)*, a work influenced by Eriugena, he wrote in all probability the *Clarification (Elucidarium)* or *Dialogue on the Whole of Christian Theology,* which was translated into medieval French, Provençal, Italian, German, Old Norse, Swedish, Gaelic, Welsh, and English. It deals with the spiritual significance of the universe, whereas the present work *(De imagine mundi)* is more concerned with its physical features.

From the following excerpts it is evident that universe formed an immense continuous material sphere balanced between two spiritual poles, heaven and hell. From further elaboration of their details in the *Clarification* we see already the rough plan of Dante in the *Divine Comedy.*

Writers of this period derived almost all of their conceptions from the encyclopedic works of Isidore of Seville (d. 636) and Rhabanus Maur (d. 856). Their concern about etymological meaning stems from the conviction that the real name of a thing is the key to its hidden nature and mystical power, a belief that drew its inspiration from the description in the Book of Genesis (2:19) of how God brought all the birds and beasts to Adam "to see what he would call them; for that which the man called each of them would be its name."

The conceptions of this period are certainly primitive. With the influx of Aristotelian literature and Arabic commentaries in the thirteenth century medieval Europe recovered the physical knowledge of the ancient world and in the fourteenth century initiated a development that gave birth to the modern sciences.

The translation was made by A. B. Wolter especially for this volume.

A Picture of the World[1]

1. The world *[mundus]* gets its name from *undique motus,* as it were, for it is in perpetual motion. It is round like a ball, yet it has distinct parts like an egg. A shell completely covers the outside of the egg. Inside the shell is the clear albumen; within the latter lies the yolk; within the yolk, the fatty germ. In similar fashion heaven covers the whole of the world like a shell, next comes the sphere of pure aether like the clear albumen, then the sphere of turbulent air like the yolk, and finally, like the fatty germ, comes the earth.

2. There are five ways of writing about the creation of the world. One has to do with the way the immensity of the universe is conceived before all ages in the divine mind. This conception is called the archetypal world, of which it is written: "Whatever has been made found life in him [the Logos]" (John 1). The second refers to the moment when this world, perceptible to the senses, was embodied in matter according to the archetype. Of this it is written: "He that liveth forever created all things together" [Eccles. 18:1].[2] The third refers to the six days during which this world was given form by fashioning the various kinds of things, as it is written: "For six days God made his wonderfully good things" (Genesis 1). The fourth has to do with one thing being born of another as man from man, beast from beast, tree from tree, and each from seed of its own kind, as it is said: "My father works even until now" [John 5:17]. The fifth refers to the future renovation of the universe, as it is written: "Behold I make all things new" (Apoc. 21).

3. The elements composing all things are called *elementa,* which comes from *hyle* and *ligamenta* (i.e. the bands in which matter is wrapped), *hyle* being Greek for *matter*. They are fire, air, water, and earth. In themselves they revolve in cyclic fashion, until fire turns into air, air into water, water into earth and back again, earth into water, water into air, and air into fire. Each has its own qualities that are like arms, so to

speak, which clasp each other and merge their discordant natures into a peaceful alliance. For the dry, cold earth is linked with cold water, while water, being cold and wet, is in turn connected with humid air. Air, being damp and warm, is joined to fire with its heat. Fire, being hot and dry, is tied in again with the dry earth. Of these elements, earth is the heaviest and occupies the lowest place, whereas fire as the lightest rises to the highest. The two remaining elements occupy an intermediate position, supplying a kind of stable bond. Of these, water is the heavier and nearest to the earth; air is the lighter and has the place next to fire. Walking things like men or beasts are destined for the earth; things that swim like fish, for the water; things that fly like birds, for the air; radiant things like the sun and stars, for the sphere of fire.

4. The lowest element is known by seven names: *terra, tellus, humus, arida, sicca, solum,* and *ops*. *Terra,* derived from *terendo,* "treading upon," refers to the element earth as a whole. *Tellus* [land], derived from *tollens fructus,* [bearing fruits], refers to what is suitable for farming or is planted with vineyards or fruit-bearing trees. *Humus,* from *humor* [fluid], refers to swampy, nonarable areas. *Arida,* "without water," are desert lands like Lybia, which are always kept dry by the heat of the sun. *Sicca* are places like Judea, which, though watered by rain at times, are quickly desiccated. *Solum* [ground] from "solidity," applies to mountainous regions. *Ops* [property, wealth] applies to lands like India, where treasures like gold and precious stones abound.

5. The form of the earth is round, hence it is called an orb. If someone were situated high in the air, looking down upon it, its mighty mountains and concave valleys would appear to be smaller than the finger of one who held a huge ball in his hand. The circumference of the earth, however, is measured at 180,000 *stadia,* which is estimated to be 12,502 miles. The earth is located in the center of the world, like a point in the exact center of a circle. Since the position it occupies as its own represents an end point, it rests on no other element for support, but is held where it is by the power of God, as is written: "Do you not fear me, says the Lord, who hangeth the earth on nothingness, founding it on its own bases" (Ps. 103).[3] The ocean encompasses it like a girdle, as is written: "The deep like a garment is its clothing" *(ibid)*. Its dryness is irrigated throughout by channels of water within it like the veins of blood in the body. That is why wherever one digs into the earth, water is to be found.

6. The earth is divided into five zones or circles. Of these the two extremes where the sun never approaches are uninhabitable because of the cold. The central zone from which the sun never recedes is uninhabitable because of the heat. The two intermediary zones are habitable being tempered on the one hand by the heat and on the other by the cold. If a fire, for instance, is kindled outside in the winter it sets up five areas of which the two extremes are icy, the center hot, and the two in between temperate. If it moved in a circle like the sun, these would become five circular zones. Of the earth's zones, the first is called the arctic, the second gets its name from the summer solstice, the third from the equinox, the fourth from the winter solstice, and the fifth is called antarctic. Only the second we know to be inhabited.

7. The habitable zone in which we dwell is divided into three parts by the Mediterranean Sea. One of these is Asia, the other Europe, and the third Africa. Asia extends from the north by way of the east to the south; Europe, from the west to the north; Africa, from the south to the west.

8. Asia gets its name from a queen by the same name. The first region of this in the east is paradise, a place renowned for its pleasantness, but inaccessible to men because it is surrounded by a fiery wall extending up to heaven.

9. In it is the tree of life, namely the tree the fruit of which is such that whoever eats of it will remain in a state of immortality. Here also is the fountain that splits up into four rivers. Within paradise they flow together over the earth but outside they spread out over great distances.

[Chapters 13-36 contain descriptions, some mythical, some factual, of the various regions of the earth, concluding with a brief mention of various known and legendary islands.]

. . . Among these is that great island of which Plato writes which sank into the sea with its inhabitants. It exceeded Africa and Europe in size and was located where the present Mare Concretum is. And there is a certain ocean island, known as the "Lost Island," which surpasses all others on earth in pleasantness and productivity, but its whereabouts is unknown to man. It was once discovered by chance and when men tried to find it afterwards without success, it came to be called the "Lost Island."

37. Hell *[infernus]* is so called because it lies below *[inferius]*. For just as the earth is in the center of the sphere of air, so hell is in the center of the earth. That is why it is also called the end of the earth. But it is actually a place, broader

below and narrower at the top—a horrible place of fire and brimstone. It is also called the "Lake of the Dead" or "Land of the Dead" because the souls that descend into it are truly dead. It is also called the "Pool of Fire" because souls sink into it like stones into the sea. It is also referred to as the "Dark and Gloomy Land" because it is clouded by smoke and a murky stench. It is also known as the "Land of the Forgotten" because those who dwell there have forgotten God and are forgotten by his mercy. It is also called *Tartarus,* which is etymologically linked with "horror" and "tremor," for here there is "weeping and gnashing of teeth" (Matt. 8). Another name for it is *Gehenna,* i.e. "land of fire," for *ge* means a land, whose fire puts ours into the shade. Its deepest recesses, filled with dragons and fiery snakes, is called *Erebus.* This is also called an "open mouth" and a *Barathrum* [deep pit] because it is a kind of *atra vorago* or "black pit." The places emitting fetid vapors are called "Acheron" which means air-holes that breathe forth a filthy smell. Here is located the river Styx, which in Greek means "sadness." It is also called "Phlegeton," which means "infernal river" because of the proximity of fire and brimstone. It is horrible by reason of the heat and stench. There are many other dreadful places and islands of punishment, some by reason of the cold or raging winds, others by reason of the ever-burning fire and brimstone. Having reviewed the fiery places of hell, let us now turn to the cooling sphere of the waters.

38. Water, the second element, gets its name from *aequalitas* [equality]. Hence the surface of the sea is level. Water collects in the sea, is scattered in rivers, is divided in springs, and is connected by flowing streams. It girds the entire earth, dividing all regions and provinces. Its deepest part is called *abyssus* [abyss] from *abest fundus* (i.e. having no bottom). Actually it does have a bottom, but it is exceedingly deep.

39. The ocean *[oceanus]* gets its name from *ocior annis* [swifter than years][4] or *limbus* [hem or border] of the zones, because it surrounds them like a hem.

40. The tides of the ocean, i.e. its ebbing and flowing, are caused by the moon, whose inhalation causes high tide and exhalation low tide. . . .

53. Air is the name given to everything resembling the void, extending from the earth to the moon, from which vital breath is drawn. Because [this element] is moist, birds fly in it

as fish swim in water. Air is the place where demons dwell awaiting with horror the day of judgment; from it they fashion bodies when they appear to men.

54. From air the wind is created, which is nothing else but air that has been agitated and stirred up. . . .

67. The fourth element is fire or *ignis* which gets its name from *quasi non gignis* [not begotten as it were].[5] It extends from the moon to the firmament. It is more subtle than air, even as air is more tenuous than water or water less dense than earth. This is also called *aether* which is *purus aer,* as it were, i.e. pure or refined air. From this the angels take their bodies when they are sent on missions to men.

68. In this fire sphere, seven stars go their own way against [the general movement of] the world and because of their wandering course are called planets, i.e. erratic things. The immense velocity of the firmament carries them from east to west, though their natural course is in the opposite direction. They are like the fly carried about on the mill wheel. Nevertheless their proper motion seems to be counter to the direction of the revolution of the firmament. Because of the obliquity of the zodiac they do not wander above or below it. Being impeded by the rays of the sun, however, they become eccentric and move backwards or remain stationary.

69. The moon is the first of the planets and the smallest star. But to us it appears to be bigger because it is carried along on the first sphere next to the earth. It is a globe-shaped body, of a fiery nature, but mixed with water. Hence it does not glow with a light of its own but, like a mirror, it is illumined by the light of the sun. That is why it is called *luna,* because it is, as it were, *lucina,* i.e. *a luce nata* [born from light]. The little clouds seen on it are believed to come from the water in its substance. For it is said that if water were not intermixed with it, it would shed its rays on earth like the sun. But in such a case, because of its proximity it would devastate the earth with its heat, for this globe is much larger than the earth. Still, because of the distance of its orbit, it appears to be hardly a half-measure larger. The moon shines by that portion of its surface which faces the sun, whereas the portion turned away from the sun is in darkness. At full moon it is most remote from the sun, neither waxing nor waning. But when it is in opposition to the earth its light is obscured. Although it is carried violently through the firmament every day from east to west, it strains against this motion and passes

through all the signs of the zodiac in twenty-seven days. Its path is said to oscillate over a period of nine or ten years. On the fourth day after the new moon, if the moon has the hue of ruddy gold, it portends windy weather; if the upper horn is darkened with spots, it is the beginning of a month of rain; if it is the central portion that is clouded, come full moon, it will be serene.

70. The second planet is Mercury. It is also known as Stilbon. It has a spherical form and is formed of fire. Its size is in the neighborhood of the moon and it receives light from the sun. It moves around the zodiac in 339 days.

71. The third planet is Venus(also known as Hesperus, the son of Aurora and Cephalus). It is both the Morning Star and Evening Star. It too is formed of fire, is round, and moves like Mercury through the zodiac, but in 348 days.

72. The fourth planet is the sun *[sol]* or Phoebus. It is called *sol* from *solus* [sole], because when all the other stars are obscured, it is the sole thing that shines. It too is of spherical form and of the nature of fire. Over eight times the size of the earth, its light exceeds that of all the other stars. Borne from east to west by the impetus of the firmament, it has a gradual counter movement that takes it through the zodiac in a period of 365 days. The periodic variation of its path is believed to take twenty-one years. Its presence brings about day; its absence, night. Just as it shines above the earth during the whole day, so it shines below the earth during the entire night. When it travels in the northern part of the heavens it produces long days and the summer; when it moves in the southern part of the heavens it brings winter and shorter days.

73. At daybreak, if the sun is hazy or hidden by clouds, it augurs a rainy day; if it looks pallid, stormy weather is in the offing; if the sun appears concave, emitting bright rays towards the north and south, it forebodes damp and windy weather; if it is pale at sunset or covered with black clouds, the wind will be from the north.

74. Mars, also called Pyrois, is the fifth planet. It is globular, fiery hot, and takes two years to move through the zodiac.

75. The sixth planet is Jupiter. Round and temperate, it moves around the zodiac in twelve years.

76. The seventh planet is Saturn. It is also called Phaeton, the son of Helios.[6] . . . It is spherical, icy, and moves through the zodiac in thirty years.

All of these orbits change periodically. After a span of 532 years the cycle begins again.

77. With respect to the center of the earth, the higher apsis of each orbit occurs when Saturn is in Scorpio, Jupiter in Virgo, Mars in Leo, the sun in Gemini, Venus in Sagittarius, Mercury in Capricorn, the moon in Aries. Halfway around each orbit is the lower apsis, the point closest to the center of the earth.

78. Each planet has its peculiar shade. Saturn is white; Jupiter, clear and bright; Mars, fiery; the Morning Star, whitish; the Evening Star, refulgent; Mercury, radiant; the moon, serene; the sun, burning.

79. The zodiac, or circle of the twelve signs, through which the planets move is divided laterally into twelve bands. The sun moves only through the two middle bands; the moon through them all; Venus wanders two degrees beyond; Mercury moves through eight of them, four above, two in the middle, and two below. Saturn, like the sun, stays in the middle two.

80. Delightful music is produced by these seven spheres revolving in sweet harmony, but tremendous though it be, we hear it not, for our ears are not attuned to it and it originates beyond the atmosphere. The only sounds that we can hear, however, are such as occur in the atmosphere. Celestial music is measured on a scale that extends from earth to firmament, but our scale is said to be modeled upon it.

81. If, on earth, one puts *A* in the moon, *B* in Mercury, *C* in Venus, *D* in the sun, *E* in Mars, *F* in Jupiter and *G* in Saturn, the musical scale becomes immediately apparent, for from earth to the firmament seven tones are to be found. From earth to moon is one tone; from moon to Mercury, a halftone; from Mercury to Venus, a halftone; from Venus to the sun, three halftones; from the sun to Mars, a whole tone; then to Jupiter, a halftone; from there to Saturn, a halftone, and from Saturn to the zodiac, three halftones. A tone consists of 15,625 miles; a halftone of 7,812½ miles. Altogether the tones add up to seven. The reason the philosophers have distinguished nine Muses is because they discovered nine consonances between earth and heaven, consonances which are implanted by nature in man.

82. For as the tones in our world add up to seven, and we have seven notes in our music, so the human composite represents a sevenfold blend. The body is a harmony of the four

elements; the soul, of three powers; and nature has brought them together through the art of music. That is why man is called a microcosm, or smaller world, when he is thus recognized to be numerically in tune with the music of the spheres.

83. The distance from earth to moon is 12,600 *stadia,*[7] which equals 15,625 miles; from moon to Mercury, 7,812½ miles; from there to Venus, the same; from it to the sun, 23,-437½ miles; from the sun to Mars, 15,625 miles; to Jupiter, 7,812½ miles; to Saturn, the same; from there to the firmament, 23,437½ miles. From earth to heaven therefore it is 109,375 miles.

With the planetary spheres we pass beyond fire; let us push on to the heavenly spheres.

84. Heaven is called *coelum,* since it is like a *casa ilios* [i.e. a home of the sun] or like a *vas coelatum* [i.e. an embossed vase], since it is set with stars. It is of a subtle, fiery nature. Being everywhere equally distant from the center of the earth, it has a round shape. Consequently, from all quarters, it appears as a hemisphere and it rotates daily with an indescribable rapidity. If the heavens are red in the evening, it portends a fine day; if they are so at dawn, it betokens stormy weather. There are two "Gates of Heaven," the east from which the sun comes forth, the west into which it enters.

85. The climes or regions of heaven are four: eastern, southern, western, and northern. . . .

86. The orient is named after *ortus solis* [where the sun rises]; the occident from *occasus solis* [where the sun sets]; the meridian from *medidies* [midday] and the north *[septentrio]* from the seven stars known as the seven *[septem]* ploughing oxen *[triones.]* The first letter of the Greek names for these celestial zones can be arranged to spell the name of Adam, who is a microcosm.

87. The superior heaven[8] is called the firmament, for it is like firm land in the midst of waters. It has a spherical form, is of an aqueous nature, and is everywhere adorned with stars. But the water, like ice, is solidified in crystal form. Hence it is called "firmament."

88. There are two poles, so called from *polire* [to smooth or polish]. One is the north pole, always visible to us; the other, the south pole, which we never see because the swelling of the earth prevents us from viewing the point on the sphere directly opposite to us. The heavens turn on these like a wheel on its axle.

89. The heavens are studded everywhere with stars but they do not appear to us during the day because they are blotted out by the brightness of the sun, even as the sun does not shine when clouds cover the sky. A star *[stella]* gets its name as it were from *stans luna* [i.e. a "standing moon"], for they stand fixed in the firmament and do not fall despite the amazing speed at which they are whirled about. While one star is called *stella,* many together are called *astra* or *sidera.*

90. *Sidera* comes from con*sider*ing, since those who are sailing or are traveling study the stars. All the stars are round and fiery. Only God knows how they are arranged or ordered. He who numbers the stars alone knows their names, their distinctive traits, their capacities, the course they run, their time and place. But the wise of this world give to them the names of animals or men so that we might tell them apart.

91. In the midst of the firmament are the twelve signs which divide equally the circular path [through which the planets seem to move]. In Greek, it is called *zodiacus;* in Latin, *signifer,* because it contains the signs *[signa]* which bear the names of animals, *zoön* meaning "animal."

[Chapters 92-135 list the signs of the zodiac and explain how they and the principal other constellations got their names.]

136. The Milky Way is so white because all the stars pour their light into it.

137. Comets are stars with tails of flame, which appear towards the northern part of the Milky Way. They portend political revolutions, plague, war, tornadoes, scorching heat, or drought. They appear for seven days, or if longer, for eighty days.

Many untrue and vicious things we have seen ascribed to the stars, however. Let us look higher then to the Morning Star and the Sun of Suns.[9]

138. Suspended above the firmament are water-like clouds which are said to move through the heavens in a circular path and are referred to as the *aqueous heaven.*

139. Above this is a spiritual heaven unknown to men. It is the habitation of the nine orders or choirs of angels. Here is the paradise of paradises where the souls of the saints are received. It is this heaven that was created in the beginning with the earth, according to what we read [in the Scriptures].

140. Far surpassing even this is the heaven of heavens in which the King of Angels dwells.

NOTES

1. *De imagine mundi libri tres,* ed. J. P. Migne, *Patrologia Latina,* Vol. 172 (Paris: J. P. Migne; 1854), cols. 121-46. The text used here is in general better than either the Latin or early Italian translation edited by V. Finzi in *Zeitschrift für romanische Philologie,* XVII (1893), 490-543; XVIII (1894), 1-73, though the latter can be consulted with profit occasionally for an interpretation of a specific passage.

2. The Latin text reads: *Qui manet in aeternum creavit omnia insimul.* The author seems to be alluding to St. Augustine's interpretation in *De Genesi ad litteram, liber imperfectus,* 4:33-34; 5:23; 6:3 that God created everything simultaneously, in germ at least. This, though later repudiated by Augustine, contains the basic conceptual framework for a contemporary Christian interpretation of evolution, such as that of Teilhard de Chardin.

3. The text quoted by the author, seemingly from memory, appears to be a composite of several scriptural texts. Cf. e.g. Job 26:7.

4. Many of Honorius's etymological explanations seem to be elaborations or modifications of those found in Isidore of Seville. In the latter's *Etymologiarum libri xx,* XIII, chap. 15 (Oxford: Clarendon Press, 1911) we read that *oceanus* in Greek and Latin designates *eo quod in circuli modum ambiat orbem* (something which goes about the orb like a circle), or which because of its swiftness designates *eo quod ocius currat.* In terms of what such etymological explanations were presumed to be achieving, Honorius's represents an advance over that of Isidore.

5. Fire was considered the most refined of the four elements, incapable of generation or corruption, unlike terrestrial elements. It is obviously being identified here with Aristotle's fifth element, "ether," of which celestial bodies are exclusively composed.

6. Phaethon, son of Helios, was identified with Jupiter; Phaenon with Saturn by the Greeks (Cf. Isidore, *Etymol.,* III D, 71, 20). Honorius here seems to be conflating the two.

7. Though various interpretations have been given to the numerical equivalent of a *stadium,* it is obvious that the equivalent values in miles (presumably Roman miles or 4,854 English feet) given here do not agree with the equivalents given earlier in chapter 5.

8. *Superior* heaven seems to be taken relative to what are sometimes called the heavens of the planets. Cf. e.g. Dante's *Divina Commedia.*

9. The "Morning Star" refers to Mary, the Mother of Christ; the "Sun of Suns," to Christ or God.

VIII

PETER ABELARD

PETER ABELARD was born of a noble family at Pallet, Brittany, in 1079. His love for dialectical disputation, he tells us, caused him to turn away from the military career his father had planned for him and to "wander about the various provinces like the peripatetics wherever I heard the pursuit of this art was vigorous." After studying in the school of Roscelin the nominalist, Peter eventually came to Paris where he enrolled in the school of William of Champeaux, a realist, but he soon became unwelcome because of his open disagreement with his master on the theory of universals. Peter opened his own school, first at Melun, then at Corbeil, and finally at Paris. His skill and brilliance brought him fame as a teacher, but his utter ruthlessness in public debate earned him many enemies. From logic, he turned to the study of theology, entering the school of Anselm of Laon. But again he soon was quarreling with his teacher, this time about the method of presenting this subject. Again he opened his own school, first at Mont Sainte-Geneviève and then at Notre Dame in Paris (1113). His use of dialectics revolutionized the traditional method of teaching theology, but also aroused the criticism and suspicion of many influential theologians, especially St. Bernard of Clairvaux.

After his famous and tragic love affair with Heloise, he entered the Benedictine monastery of Saint-Denis. There he continued to teach until 1121, when he was called to the Council of Soissons to defend his teaching on the Trinity against the charge of heresy. His condemnation, together with a violent quarrel with the monks of Saint-Denis because he denied that their founder, the Apostle of Gaul, was also Dionysius, the disciple of St. Paul, made his residence at the monastery unbearable, and he obtained permission to retire to the solitude of Maisoncelle near Nogent-sûr-Seine, where he built an oratory dedicated to the Paraclete. Soon disciples gathered about him to form another school, but the flux of students and Abelard's growing fame drew the attention of his enemies. As an escape from his difficulties, he accepted his election as abbot of St. Gildas in his native Brittany (1128), but he soon felt threatened by his own monks and in his depression wrote his autobiographical *The Story of My Misfortunes*. On his return to teaching in Paris, his theological interpretations brought him into conflict with his most formidable adversary, St. Bernard. The latter's concern for orthodoxy led to Peter's summons before the Council of Sens (1141), where a number of his tenets were condemned. He set out for Rome to appeal to the Pope, unaware that this avenue had been closed to him by Bernard's letters. His friend Peter the Venerable, abbot of Cluny, persuaded Abelard to give up the struggle and seek reconciliation with Bernard. Abelard stayed with Peter, devoting the last months of his life to work, meditation, and monastic exercises. He died April 21, 1142.

Though he had a considerable following as a theologian, Abelard is perhaps best known for his solution of the problem of universals. The present selection is taken from his glosses entitled *Logica "Ingredientibus"* (so-called because of its opening words). Though he does not name his adversary, it is clear from other writings that it is William of Champeaux. The latter tried to explain the basis of universal predication by assuming that each individual literally shared in one and the same essence, differing from one another only in terms of their diverse accidental forms. Even the analogy of different forms being impressed on wax does not do justice to William's position, since the same wax does not constitute different statues at the same time, but the universal substance "man," for example, is presumed to be in every respect identical in each and every individual. Against this position, Abelard argued persuasively that this theory, among other things, would allow one and the same substance to be subject simultaneously to contrary accidents, a point already shown by Aristotle to be untenable. As a result of Abelard's criticism, William modified his realism, substantially claiming merely that the essence of humanity in which the individual shares is only "indifferently the same." Put in another way, each man has his own essence, so that what is in one is not in the other; in Abelard's words they are discrete both as to form and as to matter. Hence individuation by forms is discarded; still, one can say that though two men are different by themselves they still agree "in man." Abelard, while admitting that this comes closer to the truth, still attacks its fuzzy formulation. This "indifference" of their common essence must be interpreted either negatively or positively. If Plato differs from Socrates by a "negative indifference," this would mean that they do not differ in man. But, Abelard argues, they also do not differ in their not being a stone, a brute animal, and so on. Hence, negative indifference does not do justice to why Socrates and Plato are alike. If we interpret this indifference positively, then we have all the confusion of the earlier theory, for everything positive in Socrates and Plato is individual. If Socrates agrees with Plato "in man," then since the only men are Socrates or other individuals, Socrates must agree with Plato as Socrates or as some other person, such as Zeno. Clearly neither of these alternatives can be the case. Hence, Abelard concludes, we must not try to identify the "common denominator" as a physical thing, be it substance or accident. It is to be sought rather in the fact that they have this in common: The same predicate can be affirmed of them. They are alike "in being men" rather than "in man." What is more, the universal is not a mere word (a *flatus vocis*); there is also a common concept that the mind forms on the basis of a real similarity between things. Hence Abelard's position, like that of Ockham, is more aptly described as a "realistic conceptualism." Unlike Ockham, however, who adopted and then abandoned this view, Abelard makes a sharp distinction between the act of understanding or thinking an object (be it singular or universal) and the content of the thought. The former is a quality of the mind or soul, to use Aristotle's categorical framework; but the inner thought object has a purely "intelligible being" and cannot be called properly either substance or accident. Universal names refer directly to individual things, but signify them only indeterminately or indiscriminately; they also "name" directly this "common conception."

The following translation by A. B. Wolter was made especially for this volume.

On Universals

Porphyry, as Boethius points out [in his Commentary on the *Isagoge*], raises three profitable questions whose answers are shrouded in mystery and though not a few philosophers have attempted to solve them, few have succeeded in doing so. The first is: Do genera and species really exist or are they simply something in the mind? It is as if [Porphyry] were asking whether their existence is a fact or merely a matter of opinion. The second is: Granting they do exist, are they corporeal or incorporeal? The third is: Do they exist apart from sensible things or only in them? For there are two types of incorporeal things. Some, like God or the soul, can subsist in their incorporeality apart from anything sensible. Others are unable to exist apart from the sensible objects in which they are found. A line, for example, is unable to exist apart from some bodily subject.

Porphyry sidesteps answering them with the remark: "For the present I refuse to be drawn into a discussion as to whether genus and species exist in reality or solely and simply in thought; or if they do exist whether they are corporeal or incorporeal, or whether, on the admission they are incorporeal, they are separated from sensibles or exist only in and dependent upon sensible things, and other things of this sort."

"Other things of this sort" can be interpreted in various ways. We could take him to mean: "I refuse to discuss these three questions and other related matters." For other relevant questions could be raised that pose similar problems. For instance, what is the common basis or reason for applying universal names to things, which boils down to explaining to what extent different things agree; or how should one understand those universal names wherein one seems to conceive of nothing, where the universal term in a word seems to have no referent? And there are many other difficult points. By understanding "other things of this sort" in this way, we can add a fourth question: Do genera and species, as long as they remain such, require that the subject they name have some reality or, if all the things they designate were destroyed, could the universal consist simply in its significance for the mind, as would be the case with the name "rose" when no roses are in bloom which it could designate in general? . . .[1]

Since genera and species are obviously instances of universals and in mentioning them Porphyry touches on the nature of universals in general, we may distinguish the properties common to universals by studying them in these samples. Let us inquire then whether they apply only to *words* or to *things* as well.

Aristotle[2] defines the universal as "that which is of such a nature as to be predicated of many." Porphyry, on the other hand, goes on to define the singular or individual as "that which is predicated of a single individual."[3]

Authorities then seem to apply "universal" to things as much as they do to words. Aristotle himself does this, declaring by way of preface to his definition of the universal, that "some things are universal, others individual. Now by 'universal' I mean that which is of such a nature as to be predicated of many, whereas 'individual' is not something of this kind."[4] Porphyry too, having stated that the species is composed of a genus and difference, proceeds to locate it in the nature of things. From this it is clear that things themselves fall under a universal noun.

Nouns too are called universals. That is why Aristotle says: "The genus specifies the quality with reference to substance, for it signifies what sort of thing it is."[5]

"It seems then that things as well as words are called universals. . . .[6]

However, things taken either singly or collectively cannot be called universals, because they are not predicable of many. Consequently it remains to ascribe this form of universality to words alone. Just as grammarians call certain nouns proper and others appellative, so dialecticians call certain simple words particulars, that is, individuals, and others universals. A universal word is one which is able to be predicated of many by reason of its intention, such as the noun "man," which can be joined with the names of particular men by reason of the nature of the subject on which they are imposed. A particular word, however, is one which is predicable only of a single subject, as *Socrates* when it is taken as the name of but one individual. For if you take it equivocally, you give it the signification not of one word but of many. For according to Priscian, many nouns can obviously be brought together in a single word.[7] When a universal then is described as "that which is predicable of many," *that which* indicates not only the simplicity of the word as a discrete expression, but also the unity of signification lacking in an equivocal term. . . .[8]

Now that we have defined "universal" and "particular" in regard to words, let us investigate in particular the properties of those which are universal. For questions have been raised about universals, since serious doubts existed as to their meaning because there seemed to be no subject to which they referred. Neither did they express the sense of any one thing. These universal terms then appeared to be imposed on nothing, since it is clear that all things subsisting in themselves are individuals and, as has been shown, they do not share in some one thing by virtue of which a universal name could be given to them. Since it is certain then that (a) universals are not imposed on things by reason of their individual differences, for then they would not be common but singular, (b) nor can they designate things which share in some identical entity, for it is not a thing in which they agree, there seems to be nothing from which universals might derive their meaning, particularly since their sense is not restricted to any one thing. . . . Since "man" is imposed on individuals for an identical reason, viz. because each is a rational, mortal animal, the very generality of the designation prevents one from understanding the term of just one man in the way, for example, that one understands by Socrates just one unique person, which is why it is called a particular. But the common term "man" does not mean just Socrates, or any other man. Neither does it designate a collection, nor does it, as some think, mean just Socrates insofar as he is man. For even if Socrates alone were sitting in this house and because of that the proposition "A man sits in this house" is true, still by the name "man," there is no way of getting to Socrates except insofar as he too is a man. Otherwise, from the proposition itself, "sitting" would be understood to inhere in Socrates, so that from "A man sits in this house," one could infer "Socrates sits in this house." And the same applies to any other individual man. Neither can "A man sits in this house" be understood of a collection, since the proposition can be true if only one man is there. Consequently, there is not a single thing that "man" or any other universal term seems to signify, since there is not a single thing whose sense the term seems to express. Neither does it seem there could be any sense if no subject is thought of. Universals then appear to be totally devoid of meaning.

And yet this is not the case. For universals do signify distinct individuals to the extent of giving names to them, but this significative function does not require that one grasps a sense which arises out of them and which belongs to each of them. "Man," for example, does name individual things, but for the common reason that they are all men. That is why it is called a universal. Also there is a certain sense—common, not proper—that is applicable to those individuals which one conceives to be alike.

But let us look carefully now into some matters we have touched on only briefly, viz. (a) what is the common reason for imposing a universal name on things, (b) what is this intellectual conception of a common likeness, and (c) is a word said to be common because of some common cause by virtue of which all the things it designates are alike, or is it merely because we have a common concept for all of them, or is it for both of these reasons?

Let us consider first the question of the common cause. As we noted earlier, each individual man is a discrete subject since he has as proper to himself not only an essence but also whatever forms [or qualifications] that essence may have. Nevertheless, they agree in this that they are all men. Since there is no man who is not a discrete or distinct individual thing, I do not say they agree "in man," but "in being a man." Now if you consider the matter carefully, man or any other thing is not the same as "to be a man," even as "not to be in a subject" is not a thing, nor is there anything which is "not to undergo contrariety" or "not to be subject to greater or lesser degrees," and still Aristotle says these are points in which all substances agree. Since there is no *thing* in which things could possibly agree, if there is any agreement among certain things, this must not be taken to be some *thing*. Just as Socrates and Plato are alike in being men, so a horse and donkey are alike in not being men. It is for this reason that they are called "nonmen." Different individuals then agree either in being the same or in not being the same, e.g. in being men or white, or in not being men or being white.

Still this agreement among things (which itself is not a thing) must not be regarded as a case of bringing together things which are real on the basis of nothing. In point of fact we do speak of this agreeing with that to the extent of their having the same status, that of man, i.e. the two agree in that they are men. But what we perceive is merely that they are men, and there is not the slightest difference between them, I say, in their being men, even though we may not call this an essence. But "being a man" (which is not a thing) we do call "the status of man" and we have also called it "the common cause for imposing on individuals a universal name." For we frequently give the name "cause" to some characteristic that is not itself a thing as when one says "He was beaten because he did not wish to appear in court." His not wishing to appear in court, cited here as a cause is not a [constitutive] essence [of his being beaten].

We can also designate as "the status of man" those things themselves in a man's nature which the one who imposed the word conceives according to a common likeness.

Having shown how universals signify, namely by functioning as names of things, and having presented what the reason for imposing such general names is, let us indicate just what these universal meanings consist of.

To begin with, let us point out the distinguishing features of all intellectual conception or understanding. Though sense perception as well as intellectual conception are both functions of the soul, there is a difference between the two. Bodies and what inhere in them are objects of sensory knowledge, e.g. a tower or its sensory qualities. In the exercise of this function, however, the soul makes use of corporeal instruments. In understanding or conceiving something intellectually, the soul needs no corporeal organ and consequently no bodily subject in which the thought object inheres is required. It is enough that the mind constructs for itself a likeness of these things and the action called intellection is concerned with this [cognitive content]. Hence, if the tower is removed or destroyed, the sense perception that dealt with it perishes, but the intellectual conception of the tower remains in the likeness preserved in the mind. As the act of sense perception is not the sensed thing itself, so the act of the intellect is not itself the form understood or conceived intellectually. Understanding is an activity of the soul by virtue of which it is said to understand, but the form toward which understanding is directed is a kind of image or construct (*res ficta*) which the mind fashions for itself at will, like those imaginary cities seen in dreams or the form of a projected building which the architect conceives after the manner of a blueprint. This construct is not something one can call either substance or accident.

Nevertheless, there are those who simply identify it with the act itself through which it is understood or conceived. Thus they speak of the tower building itself, which I think of when the tower is not there and which I conceive to be lofty, square, and situated in a spacious plain, as being the same as thinking of a tower. But we prefer to call the [conceptual] image as such the likeness of the thing.

There is of course nothing to prevent the act of understanding itself from being called in some sense a "likeness" because it obviously conceives what is, properly speaking, a likeness of the thing. Still, as we have said—and rightly so—the two are not the same. For, I ask: "Does the squareness or loftiness represent the actual form or quality possessed by the act of understanding itself when one thinks of the height and the way the tower is put together?" Surely the actual squareness and height are present only in bodies and from an imagined quality no act of understanding or any other real essence can be constructed. What remains then but that the substance, like the quality of which it is the subject, is also fictive? Perhaps one could also say that a mirror or reflected image is not itself a true "thing," since there often appears on the whitish surface of the mirror a color of contrary quality. . . .[9]

Having treated in general the nature of understanding, let us consider how a universal and a particular conception differ. The conception associated with a universal name is an image that is general and indiscriminate *[imago communis et confusa],* whereas the image associated with a singular word represents the proper and characteristic form, as it were, of a single thing, i.e. it applies to one and only one person. When I hear the word "man," for instance, a certain likeness arises in my mind which is so related to individual men that it is proper to none but common to all. But when I hear "Socrates," a certain form arises in my mind which is the likeness of a particular person. . . . Hence it is correct to say "man" does not rightly signify Socrates or any other man, since by virtue of this name no one in particular is identified; yet it is a name of particular things. "Socrates," on the other hand, must not only name a particular thing, but it must also determine just what thing is its subject. . . . To show what pertains to the nature of all lions, a picture can be constructed which represents nothing that is the peculiar property of only one of them. On the other hand, a picture suited to distinguish any one of them can be drawn by depicting something proper to the one in question, for example, by painting it as limping, maimed, or wounded by the spear of Hercules. Just as one can paint one figure that is general and another that is particular, so too can one form one conception of things that is common and another conception that is proper.

There is some question, however, and not without reason, whether or not this [universal] name also signifies this conceptual form to which the understanding is directed. Both authority and reason, however, seem to be unanimous in affirming that it does.

For Priscian, after first showing how universals were applied commonly to individuals, seemed to introduce another meaning they had, namely the common form. He states that "the general and special forms of things which were given intelligibility in the divine mind before being produced in bodies could be used to reveal what the natural genera and species of things are."[10] In this passage he views God after the fashion of an artist who first conceives in his mind a [model or] exemplar form of what he is to fashion and who works according to the likeness of this form, which form is said to be embodied when a real thing is constructed in its likeness.

It may be all right to ascribe such a common conception to God, but not to man. For those works of God like a man, a soul, or a stone represent general or special states of nature, whereas those of a human artisan like a house or a sword do not. For "house" and "sword" do not pertain to nature as the other terms do. They are the names not of a substance but of something accidental and therefore they are neither genera nor ultimate species. Conceptions by abstraction [of the true nature of things] may well be ascribed to the divine mind but may not be ascribed to that of man, because men, who know things only through the medium of their senses, scarcely ever arrive at such an ideal understanding and never conceive the [underlying] natures of things in their purity. But God knew all things he created for what they were and this even before they actually existed. He can discriminate between these individual states as they are in themselves; senses are no hindrance to him who alone has true understanding of things. Of those things which men have not experienced through the senses, they happen to have opinions rather than understanding, as we learn from experience. For having thought of some city before seeing it, we find on arriving there that it is quite different than we had thought.

And so I believe we have only an opinion about those forms like rationality, mortality, paternity, or what is within. Names for what we experience, however, produce understanding to the extent they can do so, for the one who coined the terms intended that they be imposed in accord with the [true] nature or properties of things, even though he himself was unable to do justice in thought to the nature or property of the thing. It is these common concepts, however, which Priscian calls general and special [i.e. generic and specific], that these general names or the names of species bring to the mind. He says that the universals function as proper names with regard to such conceptions, and although these names refer to the essences named only in an indiscriminate fashion, they direct the mind of the hearer immediately to that common conception in the same way that proper names direct attention to the one thing that they signify.

Porphyry too, in distinguishing between things constituted only in the likeness of matter and form and those actually composed of matter and form, seems to understand this common conception by the former. Boethius also, when he calls the conception gathered from a likeness of many things a genus or a species, seems to have in mind this same common conception. Some think that Plato subscribed to this view, i.e. to these common ideas—which he located in the *nous*—he gave the names of genus and species. On this point, perhaps, Boethius indicates some disagreement between Plato and Aristotle, where he speaks of Plato claiming not only that genera, species, and the rest should be understood to be universals, but also that they also have true existence and subsistence apart from bodies, as if to say that Plato understood these common concepts, which he assumed to exist in a bodiless form in the *nous*, to be universals. He means here by universal "a common likeness of many things" perhaps, rather than "predicable of many" as Aristotle understood the term. For this conception [itself] does not seem to be predicated of many in the way that a name is able to be applied to each of many things.

But his [i.e. Boethius'] statement that Plato thinks universals subsist apart from sensibles can be interpreted in another way, so that there is no disagreement between the philosophers. For Aristotle's statements about universals always subsisting in sensibles is to be understood of the way they actually do exist, because the animal nature (which the universal name "animal" designates and which is called a kind of universal in a transferred sense of the term) is never found to exist in anything which is not sensible. Plato, however, thinks this nature has such a natural subsistence in itself that it would retain its existence if it were not subject to sense [i.e. if it were not clothed with sensible accidents]. Hence what Aristotle denies to be actually the case, Plato, the investigator of the nature, ascribes to a natural capacity. Consequently there is no real disagreement between them.

Reason too seems to agree with these authorities in their apparent claim that the universal names designate these common concepts or forms. For what else does to conceive of them by name mean but that names signify them? But since we hold that these forms conceived are not simply the same as the acts of knowing them, there is in addition to the real thing and the act of understanding a third factor, viz. the signification or meaning of the name. Now while there is no authority for holding this, still it is not contrary to reason.

At this point, let us give an answer to the question we promised earlier to settle, namely whether the ability of universal words to refer to things in general is due to the fact that there is in them a common cause for imposing the words on them, or whether it is due to the fact that a common concept of them exists, or whether it is for both of these reasons. Now there seems to be no ground why it should not be for both of these reasons, but if we understand "common cause" as involving something of the nature of the things, then this seems to be the stronger of the two reasons.

Another point we must clarify is the one noted earlier, namely that these universal conceptions are formed by abstraction, and we must show how one can speak of them as isolated, naked, and pure without their being empty. But first about abstraction. Here we must remember that while matter and form are always fused together, the rational power of the mind is such that it can consider matter alone or form alone or both together. The first two are considerations by way of abstraction, since in order to study its precise nature, they abstract one thing from what does not exist alone. The third type of consideration is by way of synthesis. The substance of man, for instance, is a body, an animal, a man; it is invested with no end of forms. But when I turn my attention exclusively to the material essence of a substance, disregarding all its additional forms or qualifications, my understanding takes the form of a concept by abstraction. If I direct my attention, however, to nothing more than the corporeity of this substance, the resulting concept, though it represents a synthesis when compared with the previous concept (that of substance alone), is still formed by abstraction from the forms other than corporeity, such as animation, sensitivity, rationality, or whiteness, none of which I consider.

Such conceptions by abstraction might appear to be false or empty, perhaps, since they look to the thing in a way other than that in which it exists. For since they consider matter or form exclusively, and neither of these subsists separately, they clearly represent a conception of the thing otherwise than the way it is. Consequently, they seem to be vacuous, yet this is not really the case. For it is only when a thing is considered to have some property or nature which it does not actually possess that the conception which represents the thing otherwise than it is, is indeed empty. But this is not what happens in abstraction. For when I consider this man only in his nature as a substance or a body, but not as an animal, a man, or a grammarian, certainly I do not think of anything that is not in that nature, and still I do not attend to all that it has. And when I say that I attend only to what is in it, "only" refers to my attention and not to the way this characteristic exists, for otherwise my conception would be empty. For the thing does not only have this, but I only consider it as having this. And while I do consider it in some sense to be otherwise than it actually is, I do not consider it to be in a state or condition other than that in which it is, as was pointed out earlier. "Otherwise" means merely that the mode of thought is other than the mode of existing. For the thing in question is thought of not as separated, but separately from the other, even though it does not exist separately. Matter is perceived purely, form simply, even though the former does not exist purely nor the latter simply. Purity and simplicity, in a word, are features of our understanding, not of existence; they are characteristic of the way we think, not of the way things exist. Even the senses often function discriminatively where composite objects are concerned. If a statue is half gold, half silver, I can look separately at the gold and silver combined there, studying first the gold, then the silver exclusively, thus viewing piecemeal what is actually joined together, and yet I do not perceive to be divided what is not divided. In much the same way "understanding by way of abstraction" means "considering separately" but not "considering [it] as separated." Otherwise such understanding would be vacuous. . . .[11]

But let us return to our *universal* conceptions, which must always be produced by way of abstraction. For when I hear "man" or "whiteness" or "white," I do not recall in virtue of the name all the natures or properties in those subjects to which the name refers. "Man" gives rise to the conception, indiscriminate, not discrete, of animal, rational and mortal only, but not of the additional accidents as well. Conceptions of individuals also can be formed by abstraction, as happens for example when one speaks of "this substance," "this body," "this animal," "this white," or "this whiteness." For by "this man," though I consider just man's nature, I do so as related to a certain subject, whereas by "man" I regard this nature simply in itself and not in relation to some one man. That is why a universal concept is correctly described as being *isolated, bare,* and *pure:* i.e. "isolated from sense," because it is not a perception of the thing as sensory; "bare," because it is abstracted from some or from all forms; "pure," because it is unadulterated by any reference to any single individual, since there is not just one thing, be it the matter or the form, to which it points, as we explained earlier when we described such a conception as indiscriminate.

Now that we have considered these matters, let us proceed to answer the questions posed by Porphyry about genera and species. This we can easily do now that we have clarified the nature of universals in general. The point of the first question was whether genera and species exist. More precisely, are they signs of something which really exists or of something that merely exists in thought, i.e. are they simply vacuous, devoid of any real reference, as is the case with words like "chimera" or "goat-stag," which fail to produce any coherent meaning? To this one has to reply that as a matter of fact they do serve to name things that actually exist and therefore are not the subjects of purely empty thoughts. But what they name are the selfsame things named by singular names. And still, there is a sense in which they exist as isolated, bare, and pure only in the mind, as we have just explained. . . .

The second question, viz. "Are they corporeal or incorporeal?" can be taken in the same way, that is, "Granting that they are signs of existing things, are these things corporeal or incorporeal?" For surely everything that exists, as Boethius puts it, is either corporeal or incorporeal, regardless of whether these words mean respectively: (1) a bodily or a bodiless substance, (2) something perceptible to the senses like man, wood, and whiteness, or something imperceptible in this way like justice or the soul. (3) "Corporeal" can also have the meaning of something discrete or individual, so that the question boils down to asking whether genera and species signify discrete individuals or not. A thoroughgoing investigator of truth considers not only what can be factually stated but also such possible opinions as might be proposed. Consequently, even though one is quite certain that only individuals are real, in view of the fact that someone might be of the opinion that there are other things that exist, it is justifiable to inquire about them. Now this third meaning of "corporeal" makes better sense of our question, reducing it to an inquiry as to whether it is discrete individuals or not that are signified. On the other hand, since nothing existing is incorporeal, i.e. nonindividual, "incorporeal" would seem to be superfluous in Boethius' statement that everything existing is either corporeal or incorporeal. Here the order of the questions, it seems, suggests nothing that would be of help except perhaps that corporeal and incorporeal, taken in another sense, do represent divisions of whatever exists and that this might also be the case here. The inquirer in this case would seem to be asking, in effect: "Since I see that some existing things are called corporeal and others incorporeal, I would like to know which of these names we should use for what universals signify?" The answer to this would be: "To some extent, 'corporeal' would be appropriate, since the *significata* are in essence discrete individuals. 'Incorporeal' would be a better description, however, of the way a universal term names things, for it does not point to them in an individual and specific fashion but points only in an indiscriminate way, as we have adequately explained above." Hence universal names are described both as corporeal (because of the nature of the things they point to) and as incorporeal (because of the way these things are signified, for although they name discrete individuals, universals do not name them individually or properly).

The third question ("Do they exist apart from or only in sensible things?") arises from the admission that they are incorporeal, since, as we noted [in the opening paragraph], there is a certain sense in which "existing in the sensible" and "not existing in the sensible" represent a division of the incorporeal. Now universals are said to exist in sensible things to the extent that they signify the inner substance of something which is sensible by reason of its external forms. While they signify this same substance actually existing in sensible garb, they point to what is by its nature something distinct from the sensible thing [i.e. as substance it is other than its accidental garb], as we said above in our reinterpretation of Plato. That is why Boethius does not claim that genera and species exist apart from sensible things, but only that they are understood apart from them, to the extent namely that the things conceived generically or specifically are viewed with reference to their nature in a rational fashion rather than in a sensory way, and they could indeed subsist in themselves [i.e. as individual substances] even if stripped of the exterior or [accidental] forms by which they come to the attention of the senses. For we admit that all genera and species exist in things perceptible to the senses. Since our understanding of them has always been described as something apart from the senses, however, they appeared not to be in sensible things in any way. There was every reason, then, to ask whether they could be in sensibles. And to this question, the answer is that some of them are, but only to the extent, as was explained, that they represent the enduring substrate that lies beneath the sensible.

We can take corporeal and incorporeal in this second question as equivalent to sensible and insensible, so that the sequence of questions becomes more orderly. And since our understanding of universals is derived solely from sense perceptions, as has been said, one could appropriately ask whether universals were sensible or insensible. Now the answer is that some of them are sensible (we refer here to the nature of those things classed as sensible) and the same time not sensible (we refer here to the way they are signified). For while it is sensible things that these universals name, they do not designate these things in the way they are perceived by the senses, i.e. as distinct individuals, and when things are designated only in universal terms the senses cannot pick them out. Hence the question arose: "Do universals designate only sensible things, or is there something else they signify?" And the answer to this is that they signify both the sensible things themselves and also that common concept which Priscian ascribes above all to the divine mind.

As for the fourth question we added to the others, our

solution is this. We do not want to speak of there being universal *names*[12] when the things they name have perished and they can no longer be predicated of many and are not common names of anything, as would be the case when all the roses were gone. Nevertheless, "rose" would still have meaning for the mind even though it names nothing. Otherwise, "There is no rose" would not be a proposition.[13]

NOTES

1. *Peter Abaelards philosophische Schriften,* ed. B. Geyer in *Beiträge zur Geschichte der Philosophie des Mittelalters* XXI (Münster: Aschendorff, 1933), 7-8.
2. Aristotle, *De interpretatione,* chap. 7 (17a 38).
3. Cf. Boethius, *In Isagogen Porphyrii commenta,* ed. G. Schepss and S. Brandt, *Corpus Scriptorum Ecclesiasticorum Latinorum,* Vol. 48 (Vienna: Tempsky, 1906), 148.
4. Aristotle, *loc. cit.*
5. Aristotle, *Categoriae,* chap. 5 (3b 20).
6. Abelard, *op. cit.,* 9-10.
7. Priscian, *Institutiones grammaticae,* XVII, in H. Keil, *Grammatici latini.* Vol. 3 (Lipsiae: in aedibus B. G. Teubneri, 1858), 145[22].
8. Abelard, *op. cit.,* 16.
9. *Ibid.,* 18-21.
10. Priscian, *op. cit.,* 135.
11. Abelard, *op. cit.,* 21-26.
12. When Abelard speaks of "there being universal names," he has in mind terms that have actual reference; he distinguishes in a word between signification in the sense of having meaning or sense and denominating, i.e. actually naming or referring to existing things.
13. Abelard, *op. cit.,* 27-30.

IX

PETER LOMBARD

PETER LOMBARD, known as the Master of the Sentences, was born probably at Lumello in the commune of Novara in Lombardy (Italy) around 1095. He studied at Bologna, Reims, and at the school of St. Victor in Paris. He was certainly acquainted with Abelard's works and may even have attended his lectures around 1136. He taught at the Cathedral School in Paris (*ca.* 1140) and at Reims. Sometime between 1158 and 1159 he became Archbishop of Paris, but died shortly afterwards (*ca.* 1160).

His *Book of Sentences,* composed at Paris between 1155 and 1158 in the tradition of Abelard's *Sic et Non,* represents an attempt to construct some kind of theological synthesis in which the views of the fathers of the church are assembled in topical fashion for the convenience of the student who does not enjoy the luxury of an extensive library. With the exception of John Damascene (d. *ca.* 749) who is quoted in the newly finished translation of Burgundio of Pisa, the Greek fathers are sparsely represented, but the Latin fathers, especially St. Augustine, are cited extensively, together with contemporary writers like Abelard, Hugh of St. Victor, and Gratian. This work, together with the *Decretum* of Gratian of Bologna (*ca.* 1140), represents for many of the medieval theologians the chief source of their knowledge of the fathers.

Though Peter makes no claim to originality and though his citations from the fathers merely present their views without any accompanying speculation, his work is not without merits. He managed to steer a middle course between the extremist dialecticians and those who advocated a complete divorce of reason and revelation, thus continuing the tradition of Augustine and Anselm of "faith seeking understanding." Though his aim was principally to present the views of others, his attempted solutions to a good many problems provoked the curiosity of the students and led professors in commenting on him to give an extended presentation of their own views.

Alexander of Hales was the first to substitute the *Sentences* for the Bible as the basis for his ordinary lectures in theology at Paris, shortly before the University strike of 1229. It soon became the standard textbook in theology, not only at Paris but in all medieval universities, until the sixteenth century. At first the commentaries took the form of simple glosses like those composed by Alexander in 1223-29, but they soon became independent studies, which used the *Sentences* as the occasion for posing certain problems or as a guideline for a sequence of lecture topics. Presenting commentaries of this form became the proper task of a bachelor preparing to become a master of theology.

The *Sentences* of Peter are divided into four books (which were further subdivided by Alexander into "distinctions"). Book I, after taking up Augustine's distinction between goods to be used (*uti*) and the Good to be enjoyed (*frui*) as an end, takes up the subject of God, the absolute good, as both one and triune. Book II treats of created goods that were meant to be used as means to union with God; it includes an account of the six days of creation, the fall of the angels, man's creation and sin. Book III deals with the incarnation, redemption, virtues, and the decalogue. Book IV treats of the sacraments and the four "last things," viz. death, judgment, hell, and heaven.

This general plan is typical of all the "Commentaries on the Sentences" of medieval writers and has also shaped, to some extent, the sequence of topics in such theological *Summae* as those of Alexander of Hales and Thomas Aquinas.

The short selection that follows deals with the subject of God's existence and trinitarian nature. It provoked extensive discussion on such topics as to what extent God is knowable from nature, how the divine Persons are related to each other and to the divine Nature, or how nature, and especially the human soul, mirrors in some fashion the Trinity.

The translation is by A. B. Wolter especially for this volume.

How Creatures Manifest God As One and Triune[1]

The Apostle says: "Since the creation of the world his [God's] invisible attributes are clearly seen–his everlasting power also and divinity–being understood through the things that are made" [Rom. 1:20]. [According to the *Ordinary Glosses,*] 'creation of the world' refers to man, either "because he excels all other creatures by reason of his eminent position or else because he embodies something of the perfection of every other creature."[2] With his mind's eye, then, man has been able to grasp, or has seen, God's invisible attributes by means of the visible and invisible creation. That the truth might be made clear to him, man was given two things to help him: a nature that is rational and works fashioned by God. That is why the Apostle says: "God manifested this to him," namely when God created works that provide some evidence of who made them.

As [Pseudo-] Ambrose says: "That God, who is invisible by nature, might also be known from what is visible, he fashioned a work which by its visibility made its maker manifest, so that the uncertain might be known from what is certain and that he who made what man cannot may be believed to be the God of all."[3] Therefore, they could have known, or did know, that he transcends every creature who produced what nothing created could either make or destroy. Let a creature possess such power and let it fashion such a heaven and such an earth and I shall admit that it is God. But because no creature can make such things, it is clear that he who did produce them surpasses every creature. By this was the human mind able to know that he is God.

Reason could have led, and did lead them to the truth about God in still another way. As Augustine says in *The City of God:* "The most exalted philosophers recognized no body could be God and, therefore, in their quest for him they went beyond everything bodily. Convinced also that nothing mutable could be the most high God, the principle or source of all things, they looked beyond every soul or spirit subject to change. Then they saw that what is mutable can only exist in virtue of him who exists in an unqualified and incommunicable sense. They realized then that he had made all these things and was himself made by none of them.

"They considered also that whatever subsists is either a body or a spirit and that a spirit is better than a body. Better by far, however, is he who made both body and spirit.

"They also understood the beauty of a body to be sensible and the beauty of the soul to be intelligible, and they preferred intellectual to sensible beauty. We call 'sensible' such things as can be seen or touched and 'intelligible' such as can be perceived by mental vision. Once they perceived various degrees of beauty in mind and body, they realized if all form or beauty were lacking, things would cease to exist. They recognized there was something which produced these beautiful things, something in which beauty was ultimate and immutable, and therefore beyond compare. And they believed, with every right, that this was the source of all things, that source which itself was never made but is that by which all else was made."[4] See in how many ways, then, the truth of God could have been known. Though God is but one simple essence, which does not consist of different parts or accidents, the Apostle, nevertheless, speaks in the plural of the "invisible attributes of God" because there are many ways in which the truth about God is gleaned from the things that he made. The perpetuity of creatures indicates their maker is eternal; the greatness of creatures argues to his omnipotence, from their order and arrangement he is known to be wise, from their governance he is recognized as good. All these attributes refer to divine nature as a unity.

What remains to be shown is whether the things that were made contain some trace or slight indication that God is a Trinity. On this point Augustine says: "When we speak of the mind beholding the Creator in what he has made, we should understand this of the Trinity. For creatures do contain some trace or vestige of the Trinity. Everything produced by divine artistry manifests (a) unity, (b) form or beauty, and (c) order. Consider what creature you will and you find it to be one (e.g. bodies or souls), to have some form or beauty (e.g. bodily shapes or qualities, learning, and mental skills), and that it strives for or maintains some position or order (e.g weights, bodily complexes, intellectual loves, or mental delights). Consequently some trace of the Trinity is to be found in creatures. For it is the Trinity that represents the ultimate origin, the most perfect beauty, and the ultimate delight of everything."[5] As Augustine shows in his work *Of True Religion,* the ultimate origin refers to God the Father, from whom are all things, from whom also are the Son and the Holy Spirit. "The most perfect beauty" refers to the Son, who is the Truth of the Father in whom and with whom we venerate the Truth. "He is in all respects like the Father and is the form of all things that have been made by the One and which strive for unity. But all things would not have been made by the Father through the Son, nor would they be preserved safe within their boundaries, if God were not supremely good. He begrudges no one anything, for to all he has given the possibility of being good. By 'goodness' we understand the Holy Spirit, who is the Gift of God, whom we worship and hold to be equally unchangeable with Father and Son in a Trinity of one substance. From the consideration of creatures, then, we understand a Trinity of one substance, one God, namely, the Father, from whom, the Son through whom, and the Holy Spirit in whom we have our being, i.e. a principle to which we have recourse, a form which we imitate, and the grace by which we are reconciled. In a word, there is one God by whom we were made, and his likeness by whom we are formed for unity, and his peace whereby we cleave to unity; God who spoke and it was done; and the Word by whom all was made that has substance and nature; and the Gift of his benignity by which he was pleased that nothing made through the Word and reconciled with its author, should perish."[6]

See that it has been shown here just how some likeness at least of the Trinity is found in creatures. Without interior revelation or a revelation of this doctrine, however, adequate knowledge of the Trinity neither was nor can be obtained from contemplation of creatures. That is why ancient philosophers could only see this trinitarian truth in a haze, as it were, and from afar. Like Pharaoh's magicians after the third plague [Exod. 8:19], their recognition of God was defective. Nevertheless our belief in what we cannot see is helped by means of the things that were made.

NOTES

1. Book I, distinction 3, chap. 1 from Petrus Lombardus, *Libri IV Sententiarum,* 2 ed. (Ad Claras Aquas: ex typographia Collegii S. Bonaventurae, 1916) tom. I, 30-33.

2. Anon., *Glossa ordinaria,* Epistle to the Romans, chap. 1, v. 20 (PL 114, col. 472).

3. Pseudo-Ambrose (Ambrosiaster), *Epistle to the Romans,* chap. 1 (Cf. PL 17, col. 57).

4. Augustine, *The City of God,* Bk. VIII, chap. 6.

5. Augustine, *On the Trinity,* Bk. VI, chap. 10.

6. Augustine, *On True Religion,* chap. 55.

X

RICHARD OF ST. VICTOR

RICHARD was born in Scotland during the first quarter of the twelfth century. At an early age, he seems to have joined the Canons of St. Augustine at the Abbey of St. Victor in Paris, where he became subprior in 1159 and prior in 1162. He succeeded his teacher, Hugh of St. Victor, as master of the famous abbey school and remained there until his death, March 10, 1173.

Though he is known primarily for his writings in mystical theology and his exegesis of Scripture, his six-volume theological treatise *On the Trinity* holds the greatest interest for the philosopher. In the Anselmian tradition of "faith seeking understanding," this work is an attempt to find a rational justification for the various attributes ascribed in the Athanasian Creed to the triune God. Anselm was once reproved by his teacher Lanfranc for preferring dialectical argument to scriptural support in his theological speculations. Richard in similar fashion seeks "necessary reasons" why God should be both one and three. Most medieval thinkers have considered the trinitarian character of the divine nature to be the most profound of all the mysteries of the Christian faith. While reason may at best refute objections to a trinity of persons in one nature, it can hardly be expected to provide positive support for the doctrine. Richard, on the contrary, believed that St. Anselm had found the key to the "divine processions" in the fact that God is perfect love, with all that this implies.

His arguments as to why God must contain more than one person yet no more than three are reminiscent to some extent of C. S. Peirce's reasoning as to why the triad is the most fundamental of all relations.

Though Richard's explanation of the Trinity was not generally followed by subsequent theologians, his mystical theology had considerable influence during the Middle Ages, through St. Bonaventure and the Franciscan school.

Two modern editions of Richard's *De Trinitate* are available, the critical text of J. Ribaillier (Paris, 1958) and the Latin text with a French translation by G. Salet (Paris, 1959). They were used as the basis for the following translations by A. B. Wolter, made especially for this volume.

On the Trinity

[SELECTIONS FROM BOOK ONE][1]

If we wish to proceed wisely in ascending to the knowledge of sublime things, the price of achievement, to begin with, is knowing in what ways knowledge of things is acquired. If I am not mistaken, there are three ways in which we come to know things. Experience is our test for some; others we gather from reasoning; still others we hold to be certain on faith. Knowledge of temporal things we know from experience; but we rise to a knowledge of eternal things sometimes by reasoning, sometimes by belief. For some of the things we are commanded to believe seem to be not only above reason but even against it if they are not studied deeply and subtly, or rather, if they are not made manifest by divine revelation. In our knowledge or affirmation of such things then, we are prone to rely more on faith than on reason, more on authority than on argument, according to those words of the prophet, "Unless you believe, you will not understand" (Isa. 7).[2] But here something else should be carefully noted. This text does not rule out understanding categorically but only conditionally, since it says, "*Unless you believe,* you will not understand." Those with trained minds then should not despair of such understanding, so long as they feel themselves to be firm in faith and to be of proved constancy in affirming their faith throughout it all. . . .

It is indeed by faith that we enter upon the knowledge of those things of which it is correctly said, "Unless you believe, you will not understand." But we must not just stand there at the entrance, but with all zeal and diligence hasten onward to master their deeper and more interior aspects so that day by day we may advance in our understanding of those things we hold by faith. For it is in the full knowledge and perfect grasp of such things that we obtain eternal life. To know such things is of the greatest benefit. To contemplate them brings the greatest joy. They are our supreme treasure. The pleasure they bring never ends. To taste such is the height of sweetness. To enjoy them is infinite delight. In the present work then we intend to deal not with everything we are required to believe by the rule of our Catholic faith but only with those things which are eternal. We shall not treat of the sacred mysteries of our redemption, which occurred in the course of time and which we are also commanded to believe in and do believe in. But the manner of treating such is different from the way one deals with eternal things.

It will be our intention then, insofar as God grants us to do so, to present in this work not only probable but also necessary reasons[3] for what we believe, and to season the lessons of our faith with a development and explanation of the truth. For I believe without a doubt that not merely probable but necessary arguments can be found to explain anything which necessarily exists, although they may at times remain hidden despite our best efforts to reveal them. For if anything, through the benevolence of the Creator, in time begins to be, it is both possible for it to exist and possible for it not to exist. And that is why its existence is not inferred by reasoning but is established by experience. Those things which are eternal, however, cannot be completely nonexistent. Just as there never was a time when they did not exist, so surely there never will be a time when they do not exist. What is more, they always are what they are and never can be anything else or exist in any other way. And while it seems wholly impossible that any necessary thing should not exist or should lack a necessary reason for existing, nevertheless not every soul is able to draw such reasons forth from where they lurk in the depths of nature's labyrinthine heart or to bring them into common view, as it were, from out of wisdom's most secret hiding place. Many are not worthy or fit or studious enough to do so. And we seldom or scarcely ever think of matters that should always be before our eyes. With what eagerness and desire, I ask, should we not take up this task; should we not stand open-mouthed before this spectacle on which the supreme blessedness of those who are to be saved depends. I believe I shall have accomplished something, at least, if it be granted me that by this work of mine I have been able to assist eager minds even a little in this pursuit or to arouse tepid minds to take up the same.

I have often read there is but one God, Lord of all, from

whom everything that exists is; that he is eternal, uncreated, immense, almighty, totally present everywhere without being divided into parts. I have read that my God is both one and three, one in substance but three in persons. All this have I read, but nowhere do I recall reading how these points are proved. I have read that in true divinity there is but one substance and that in the unity of substance there are several persons, each differentiated from the others by a distinctive property, [viz.] that there is one person who is of himself and not from any other; that there is another who is not of himself but is from one alone; and that there is a person who is not from one but from two. Daily[4] do I hear of these three that they are not three eternals, but one Eternal; not three uncreateds or three infinites, but one Uncreated and one Infinite. I hear of the three that they are not three almighties, but one Almighty. I hear further that they are not three gods, but one God, not three lords, but one Lord. I find the Father to be neither made nor begotten, the Son to be begotten but not made, and the Holy Spirit to be neither begotten nor made, but proceeding [i.e. eternally from Father and Son as from a single principle or source]. All these things I often hear or read, but I do not remember having read how these points are proved. In these matters statements from authorities abound, but they are not matched by arguments. Empirical knowledge of such things is wanting and arguments for them are rare. As I said above, then, I think I shall have accomplished something if I can aid minds eager to pursue such matters in some small way, even if it be not given to me to satisfy them wholly.

To make it plain and evident that the series of steps in our reasoning process is grounded, as it were, on some firm and unshakeable truth, lest anyone have reason to doubt or cause to draw back, let us begin with such statements as these. Everything which is or can be either exists eternally or begins to be in the course of time. Everything which is or can be either has existence of itself or from something other than itself. Generally speaking then, there is a threefold basis for classifying each case of existence. For either existence will pertain to an existing thing eternally and of itself; or, contrariwise, neither eternally nor of itself; or what is between these two extremes, eternally but not of itself. For nature itself would never suffer the existence of what might seem to be a fourth alternative, since nothing whatsoever can exist of itself which is not eternal. For whatever in the course of time begins to be, was once nothing. But while it was nothing, it had nothing whatsoever nor could it do anything whatsoever. Consequently, it could not bring it about that either itself or anything else would exist or that something could exist. Otherwise it would give what it did not possess and do what it was unable to accomplish. Conclude then from this that it would be impossible for anything whatsoever to exist of itself, and yet not be eternal. Behold how by evident reason then we arrive at the threefold classification of what exists or can exist.

Our starting point then should be some kind of thing about which there can be no doubt whatsoever, and from what we know by experience we reason to what we ought to think about those things which transcend experience. This starting point should be indeed that mode of existence which is not eternal and thereby—for the aforesaid reason—not of itself. Of this kind of existence we are assured by daily and manifold experience. We continually see one thing succeeding another and what at first did not exist becoming actual. In the case of men and animals we see this repeatedly. Daily experiences show the same holds good of trees or vegetation. It is the same whether it be works of nature or of human industry that are concerned. What we experience then from day to day does not permit us to remain blind to the fact that there are innumerable things existing which were not always so. Superior reason[5] discovers that anything not eternal cannot exist of itself. Otherwise it would be clear to us that at a moment when it had nothing and could do nothing, something gave itself initial existence. The complete impossibility of this, however, is by no means hidden from the mind of man. It is clear then that all those things which begin to be in the course of time have this in common: they do not exist from all eternity and by that very fact, as has been said, neither do they exist of themselves. Behold then this type of existence of which we speak, about which there can be no doubt, inasmuch as it is something which daily experience proves to be the case.

But from that form of existence which is neither eternal nor of itself we gather by inference the existence of that which is of itself and therefore is also eternal. For if nothing existed of itself, there would be nothing whatsoever from which those things which neither have nor could have existence of themselves could have come to exist. Hence one is convinced that something exists of itself, and by that very fact, as has been said, that it is also eternal. For otherwise there would have been a time when it did not exist and, if this were so, then at no future time would it have been able to exist, because who would or could give this or anything else its initial existence? And so nothing whatsoever would be, which the very evidence and experience of existing things proves to be false. And thus it is true that we see eternal things from what is transitory, heavenly things from what is mundane, and the divine from what is human. "For since the creation of the world his invisible attributes are clearly seen—being understood through the things that are made" (Rom. 1:20). . . .

It is necessary then to speak further about this existence which is of itself. From what has been said, it is clear that this existence is eternal. Such most certainly exists, and therefore I believe that no one can doubt that among such a variety of existing things and so many different degrees of existence there must be something which is the greatest. But we call that the greatest than which nothing is greater, nothing better. Now there is no doubt that a rational nature is better than one that is irrational. It must needs be then that some rational substance is the greatest of all, and is that which holds the highest place in the universe of things. Now it cannot be the case, however, that such a thing has received what it is from something inferior to itself. It must needs be, then, that there is some substance which has both characteristics, viz. it holds the highest place and it exists of itself. For as we have stated and proved above, if nothing existed of itself, there would be nothing eternal and then there would be neither any beginning nor any succession of things. Evidence of things experienced, then, convinces one that some substance must needs exist of itself. For if nothing existed of itself, then there would be none of those things which originate from other things and which cannot exist of themselves. That substance, then, which exists only of itself, I say, belongs to that being which is eternal and without a beginning.

What has been said of the highest substance can be substantiated by an additional argument. For it is most certain that nothing can exist in the entire realm of things if it has no possibility of being either of itself or by reason of another. For what cannot exist is completely nonexistent. In order that something may exist, then, it is necessary that its capacity to exist be derived from something which has power over its existence. Everything, then, which subsists in the universe has received existence from some such power. But if all things come from it, the latter must exist of itself, and whatever properties it possesses, it has of itself. But if all things come from it, then all essence, all power, all wisdom stem from it. If all being comes from it, then it is itself the highest essence. If all possibility is from it, it is most powerful. If all wisdom stems from it, then it is most wise. For it is impossible that anything give more than it has. It is true that one who possesses wisdom can give all of it and at the same time retain it all. But you cannot give more wisdom than you possess. Hence, that from which all wisdom originates must be most wise. Where there is no rational substance, wisdom cannot be present at all, for only a rational substance can possess wisdom. There exists a rational substance, then, which is the greatest of all and which possesses the highest wisdom. That from which every essence is derived, be it of an irrational or a rational nature, is, I say, the greatest thing of all. Consequently, this power over existence is not something distinct from the highest substance. Such power which exists of itself, therefore, must be identical with this greatest of substances, and the latter is not then something other than its power over existence. And so it is clear that everything which exists is from this highest substance. But if everything is from this, then there is nothing other than this substance which exists of itself. And if all existence, all potency, all "having something" stems from it, there is no doubt that whatever this substance has, it has of itself. Rightly then is that called primordial, from which every existing thing has its source or beginning.

Let us turn our consideration for the present to what we said about the supreme substance being most powerful. Now it is most certainly the case that its being most powerful is something derived from power itself and its being wise is something derived from wisdom itself. It has already been proved however that all this being has, it has of itself. But in order to have of itself whatever it owes to power itself or to wisdom itself, it must needs be that these perfections are not something distinct from itself. Otherwise this being, which could be neither powerful nor wise apart from power itself or wisdom itself, would owe to another rather than to itself what stems from these perfections. But if each of these is really identical with the supreme substance then each is really identical with the other.

At this point it is most important to notice that if this thing which is most powerful is itself a substance, it cannot be a substance other than the substance of that being itself. Otherwise substances which are diverse would constitute one substance and one substance would consist of diverse substances, which is completely impossible. But you might say: Perhaps there could be diverse substances, each of which had the highest of powers even if these were not identical with the highest power itself. Would they not be equipowerful if they both had the highest of powers? Well, I would categorically assert without the shadow of doubt that if there were one of these which could have, but not be, the highest power, it would not be equal in power to something which could both have and be the highest power. For to have in part and to lack in part what *in toto* is possible for another is not a characteristic of the plenitude of power but is the mark of something which only participates in power. But it is far greater and more excellent to possess the plenitude of what is great than to have it only by participation. From such considerations then it is amply evident that the primordial substance has no equal, even as it is clear from what has been said that it has no superior.

It seems to pertain to the very nature of this substance, then, that it excels all else having neither a superior nor an equal. For whatever is in it substantially undoubtedly is intrinsic to its nature. From the fact then that the primordial substance and that which is the highest power are one and the same thing, it follows that it is of the nature of such a thing to be all powerful and to be incapable of having anything that would equal or excel it. Let us see whether it might have some inferior associate as something proper to its nature. But how, I ask, could any such substance be inferior to the primordial essence if it naturally shares with that essence the property of having no equal or superior? For on such an assumption, each would be part of the nature of the other; the one and the same thing would be both superior and inferior, both more and less than itself. It is impossible then that the primordial substance have any associate as a property of its nature.

According to the preceding argument, we can already hold as certain that this highest substance is the sole source of whatever it is, and all it possesses it owes to itself. But if this substance is the root of all that is there, it is also the source of divinity itself. Now if it were to bestow divinity on another thing without retaining divinity for itself, there would be something superior to it. But from what we have just proved, this substance has no superior. That it retains and possesses divinity, then, is an established fact. But anyone who has deity is God and the fact that this being is God it owes to its deity. But if this highest substance (which has nothing it does not have of itself) owes to its divinity the fact that it is God, it follows that deity itself is not something distinct from this supreme substance. Consequently, it could not bestow deity on another substance (I do not say, "to have deity," but, "to be deity"). For otherwise it would have an equal, which is impossible. From all this one gathers that true divinity exists in a unity of substance and true unity of substance in divinity itself. Consequently God can be only one in substance.

Hear then how easily we can prove that there is but one God. From the fact that this substance possesses nothing it does not owe to itself it follows that divinity as such is not something distinct from this substance, for otherwise one would have to conclude that what it owes to its divinity it has in virtue of something other than itself. Divinity itself, however, will be either something incommunicable or something common to more than one subject. If it is incommunicable, it follows there is but one God. If it be common to several, that substance which is identified with divinity itself will also be common to them. But one substance cannot be something common to several substances. Otherwise one and the same thing will be both one and more than one, which is something notoriously false. But if we say divinity is common to more than one person, from what has been said it follows that to these persons the substance identified with divinity will also be common. Accordingly then there will be several persons but only one substance in the one divinity. But whether one claims there be one or more than one person in divinity, it still remains the case that God is only one in substance. One and only one God, therefore, exists of himself and by that very fact exists from all eternity. Since the highest substance proved to be identical with God, it follows that all God has he has of himself and that he is power itself and wisdom itself.

But if God's wisdom and God's power are absolutely one and the same reality then no measure of perfection or fullness that one possesses will be lacking in the other. There will be nothing greater or better in his knowledge than there is in his power, and therefore in his being, since his power is not something other than his being. Hence whatever his wisdom may discover or define that is excellent or distinguished, it all comes under the plenitude of his power, it is all bound together by the integrity of his essence. For if the intellect at the peak of its perfection could conceive of something that exceeded the full scope of his power, he would be undoubtedly more magnificent by reason of his wisdom than he would be by virtue of his power. Then one and the same substance would be both greater and less than itself. For since the substance of God is not something other than his power or wisdom, if he ranged further by his wisdom than he did by his power, or if he could span more with the one than he could with the other, then assuredly one and the same substance viewed as power would be greater than itself through its wisdom, and the same substance viewed as wisdom would be less than itself through its power. Nothing then is greater or better than God, nay, God himself cannot define or grasp anything of the sort.

But if divine knowledge cannot grasp intellectually anything more perfect than God, all the more is human knowledge unable to conceive of anything greater or more perfect than God. For what human thought can grasp could not be hidden from divine intelligence. It is a species of madness to think that man can ascend in thought to something surpassing God, when with all his investigation he cannot reach that unique "this" which God is.[6] The better and the more perfect such human knowledge becomes then, the more it approaches, yet never quite reaches, that unique individuality that makes God God.

It seems to be almost a natural endowment that causes the erudite as well as those less learned to adopt as their wont and to hold as a kind of rule that whatever is best is unhesitatingly deemed to be God's. And if clear reasoning does not teach us, then without doubt devotion persuades us of such attributes as accord with this rule. Hence it is that even those who are ignorant of how such points may be proved, unhesitatingly affirm God to be immense, eternal, immutable, supremely wise, and omnipotent. To attribute to God all that human thought regards as sublime while axiomatic for the learned is like a common conviction for the generality of mankind. Even the greatest of masters when they wished to discuss the divine properties in a more profound and grave fashion, generally took as their point of departure this firm starting point which has its roots, as it were, in the heart of truth.

That God is all-powerful is sufficiently established from what was said above, but one can still raise this question: is he called all-powerful because no one excels him in strength or is he all-powerful in the sense that he can do all things and is truly omnipotent. Now if we do not grant that God is omnipotent, it is because we are convinced that we can think of something greater than what God is able to do. For to have omnipotence is something greater than any power whatsoever which lacks something of the plenitude of omnipotence. But anything man is capable of understanding is certainly not hidden from divine wisdom. Now if God knows of something he lacks which pertains to the plenitude of omnipotence, however, his knowledge would be more extensive than his power, even though both are identical with his very being. Hence, according to our reasoning above, one and the same being would be both greater and less than itself, and nothing could be more impossible. Hence we conclude without a doubt that he has the ability to do anything that implies true power. For there are many things that are called "powers" or "abilities" that were better styled "debilities," such as power to grow less, the ability to fail, the ability to be destroyed and annihilated. Things of this sort are more forms of impotence than of power. They are more a badge of weakness than a mark of majesty. Therefore he can do all those things and only those things which imply some true power, as we have said. For more truly and correctly do we call him omnipotent whom we have freed from all charges of weakness in power.

One can raise the same question of divine wisdom as was posed of divine power. Is it called supreme because there is none greater than it, or is it truly supreme in the sense that it is all-perfect? Now it is most certainly the case that where omnipotence is, the plenitude of wisdom cannot be wanting. For if so far as the fullness of his wisdom goes there was some degree of perfection that God could not have, he would not be unequivocally omnipotent. It is established then that God's wisdom lacks not an iota of perfection as to knowledge or prudence, the addition of which would make it better or greater. Take note that from a consideration of divine wisdom we learn of the fullness of his power, and conversely, from a consideration of omnipotence we are convinced of the fullness of his wisdom.

But we can give another proof for speaking of the fullness of divine wisdom. For it must be that whoever is wise is wise because he has the fullness of wisdom itself or because he has a share of wisdom. But we have previously established that God's wisdom is the same thing as the divine substance. Now who but a fool would say that God's substance of itself possesses wisdom but only partially, i.e. in part it lacks wisdom and it is not able of itself to have the fullness of wisdom? Just as it is not possible for God's substance not to have itself in full so it is not possible for it to lack the fullness of wisdom.

By a similar reasoning what was said earlier of omnipotence is confirmed. For just as someone who is wise is so either in virtue of the fullness of wisdom or through participation in wisdom, so too is one powerful either by virtue of the fullness of power or because he has a share in the same. But it is impossible that anyone have only a share of himself. The fact that God is powerful however cannot be because he only participates in power, for the fullness of power is not something distinct from himself. It is the case, then, that he is powerful by virtue of the plenitude of power. But where there is plenitude of power, no ability can be lacking. Consequently he has omnipotence and is truly almighty in whom all ability is present.

It is impossible, however, that there be several almighties. For whoever is truly omnipotent could easily bring it about that the others could do nothing; otherwise he would not truly be almighty. But what kind of omnipotent beings are those who are so readily reduced to total impotence! See how easy it is to be convinced that the very nature of things permits of but one Almighty. However, we have shown by clear reasons that God is omnipotent and are unable any longer to doubt it. But if there can be but one Almighty, then there can be but one God.

What faith affirms and what we have already stated is therefore proven to be the case, viz. that true divinity occurs in a unity of substance and unity of substance in true divinity.

Behold that we have said much already of the unity of divinity; it remains to say something of the nature of this singular being.

[SELECTIONS FROM BOOK THREE][7]

Up to now we have discussed as best we could the unity and proper attributes of the divine substance. In what follows however we propose to examine what we ought to think about the plurality of persons and their properties.

The first question it seems we should discuss is whether in that true and simple divinity there is a plurality of persons and whether they are three in number as we believe. . . .

We have learned from what was said earlier [in Book Two] that in the highest and universally perfect good there is the plenitude and perfection of all goodness. Where the fullness of goodness exists, however, true and supreme charity or love cannot be absent, for nothing is better or more perfect than charity. Now no one is said to have charity by virtue of the private love he has for himself, since to be charity, love must tend towards another; and where there are not several persons, charity simply cannot exist.

But perhaps you will say: Even if there were but a single person in that true divinity, he still could, and indeed would have charity towards his creatures. But surely he could not have the supreme degree of charity for a person who was created. For if he loved supremely one unworthy of supreme love, his charity would be inordinate. But it is impossible that inordinate charity should exist in goodness that is also supremely wise. A divine person then could not have the highest charity towards a person unworthy of supreme love. For charity to be supreme and all-perfect then, it must be so great that it could not be greater and of such quality that it could not be better. But as long as one loves only himself, this private love he bears himself shows he has yet to reach the highest degree of charity. A divine person would have no one he could fittingly love as himself had he no deserving person as his peer. But no person who was not God would be a worthy peer of a divine person. In order to have the plenitude of charity in that true divinity, therefore, what any divine person must have is the companionship of a person who is his peer in dignity and who is therefore divine.

See how easily then reason proves a plurality of persons must be present in true divinity. Certainly God alone is supremely good; God alone then is to be loved supremely. A divine person consequently could not display the highest love towards a person who lacked divinity. But the fullness of divinity could not be present if complete goodness was missing; and complete goodness could not be present without the fullness of charity, nor the complete charity without a plurality of divine persons. . . .

It is clear that there is a plurality of divine persons, but it is not yet evident that they constitute a trinity. For there can be plurality without a trinity. Duality itself is a plurality. Let us ask the same witnesses about trinity that attested to the presence of a plurality. And, if you will, let us see first what sovereign charity has to say on the subject.

Sovereign charity must be perfect on all counts. To be supremely perfect, however, charity must be such that it can be neither greater nor better. No degree or kind of excellence could be missing. Now to wish that another be loved as we are loved seems to be the sort of thing that should be present in true charity. Where love is ardent and mutual, nothing is rarer, nothing more admirable than the desire that another be loved to the same degree as you by the one whom you love supremely and by whom you are supremely loved. The proof of consummate charity then is this desire to share the love shown to oneself. Surely one who loves supremely and desires to be loved supremely would be wont to find perfect joy in the fulfillment of that desire, in obtaining the love desired. Never to have the satisfaction of sharing such perfect joy, therefore, is proof that perfect charity is not present. To be unable to enjoy this companionship of love is a sign of weakness. But if it is great to be *able* to do so, it is still greater to do so *in fact,* and greatest of all if one *must* do so. The first is a great good, the second a greater good, the third the greatest good. Such excellence we owe to the Supreme Being; to the best we owe the best.

Our earlier discussion revealed the presence of two persons united in mutual love. The perfection of each, however, if it is to be consummate, requires that each for the same reason have someone to share the love shown to himself. For if either did not want what perfect goodness requires, where would the plenitude of power be? Hence reason clearly reveals that where some defect of power or will precludes such sharing in love, such participation of perfect joy, there the supreme degree of charity and plenitude of goodness cannot exist. Each of these persons who is and should be supremely loved must needs require by common desire a third person to be loved and must needs possess such a one in perfect harmony as they desire.

See then how the consummation of charity demands a trinity of persons without which it could not subsist whole and entire! Where something universally perfect is present in its entirety, neither integral charity nor true trinity can be absent. Hence there is not only plurality but also true trinity in true unity, and true unity in true trinity. . . .

Note indeed in these divine persons that the perfection of one demands it be joined to another and consequently the perfection of the pair requires their union with a third. For, as we said above, if each of the pair deserves the supreme love of the other, each must be supremely perfect. As the pair must be one in wisdom and power, so too in supreme generosity. But the hallmark of the highest and most perfect generosity is that it share with another the full measure of its richness. But if each of the two has the same generosity, they must share the same desire for the same reasons; both require a third partner to share their supreme joy. For where a loving pair are seized by supreme desire and each delighted by the supreme love of the other, then the supreme joy of the one comes from his intimate love of the other, and conversely, the supreme joy of the second stems from his intimate love of the first. But so long as one is loved only by the other, he seems to be the sole possessor of his supremely sweet delight; similarly with the other, so long as he has no partner in the love shown him, he misses sharing this supreme joy. But that both can share their own delight, they need another loved one. Where such colovers are so generous, then, that they want to share whatever perfection they possess, both, by common desire and for equal reasons, need to have another who is loved even as they and, by virtue of the plenitude of their power, to possess what they desire.

NOTES

1. Of the 25 chapters in Book One, only chapters 2, 9, and 10 have been omitted as irrelevant to the main course of the argument.

2. Text of the Septuagint.

3. Theologians distinguish between revealed truths, which are necessary since they depend upon the immutable nature of God, and those that depend upon the free decrees of God, such as the Incarnation, the Redemption, and indeed the whole of salvation history. Richard, like St. Anselm of Canterbury before him, argues that in principle, if not in practice, it should be possible to find necessary reasons for such non-contingent truths about God. The contrast between "probable" and "necessary" reason suggests acquaintance with Aristotle's requirements for demonstrative knowledge.

4. The liturgical books from the Abbey of St. Victor indicate that the Athanasian Creed from which these various assertions are taken was recited almost daily by the Canons.

5. Following St. Augustine, scholastics of this period distinguish between "superior" and "inferior" reason, representing two facets of man's mental abilities. When the mind looks upward, i.e. contemplates God and spiritual realities, it functions as "superior reason," whereas when it looks downward, i.e. considers the material sensible world about us, it functions as "inferior reason." The former requires no bodily organ, whereas "inferior reason" makes use of the senses and imagination.

6. Such knowledge would require a direct experience or face-to-face vision of God, such as the blessed in heaven are said to possess; knowledge of God in this life is by way of inference and description, not by acquaintance, to use Russell's distinction.

7. Chapters 1, 2, 11, and 15.

XI

AVICENNA

Avicenna (Ibn Sīnā), perhaps the greatest medieval Islamic philosopher, was born in Afshana, near Bukhārā, in 980. Although his nationality has been disputed, the best available evidence points to Persian ancestry. For an account of his life we are fortunate in having a partial autobiography, dictated to his pupil and secretary al-Juzjānī and completed by him. According to this account, Avicenna's learning was prodigious. After surpassing his teachers in the study of the religious sciences, logic, geometry, and astronomy, he proceeded to master medicine and philosophy. Aristotle's *Metaphysics* proved too difficult for him, however, until he chanced upon a commentary on it by al-Fārābī. While serving as court physician for the Sultan of Bukhārā, he took fullest advantage of the royal library to continue to broaden himself intellectually. He seems to have begun writing in his early twenties. But the changing political fortunes of his patron soon necessitated his departure from Bukhārā. He began a period of traveling to different cities in Transoxiana and Iran and served various princes. In spite of pressing political responsibilities, a short period in prison, enforced flights, the pillaging of his library, and his service as court physician, his writing activity was not curtailed. The final period of his life was spent in the service of the Emir of Ispahān, in relative calm. He died in 1037 from ill health while accompanying his patron on a military expedition.

Over one hundred of Avicenna's writings survive and deal with philosophy, medicine, science, and various religious topics. Among his writings on medicine, *The Canon of Medicine* must be mentioned. His great encyclopedia of philosophy, *The Healing (al-Shifā')* was translated in large part into Latin in the twelfth and thirteenth centuries, and exercised profound influence on Latin scholasticism.

Avicenna is a leading representative of the Arabic-speaking group known as the school of the *falāsifa* (philosophers), i.e., those thinkers who followed the tradition of Greek philosophy. While being deeply indebted to Aristotle, his thought was open to too many other influences to be described simply as Aristotelian. Neoplatonic influences are quite strong as, for instance, in his complicated theory of a necessarily and eternally emanating universe. Certain works dating from the last period of his career refer to an *Oriental Philosophy,* apparently never completed. Surviving fragments of this work suggest an even greater Plotinian influence. Nevertheless, he represented himself as a sincere Muslim believer. As the following short treatise suggests, however, he was not unaware of possible conflict between certain philosophical positions and the views of the theologians of his day. Perhaps this accounts in part for the brevity and reserved nature of the work. The translation is by G. F. Hourani.

Essay on the Secret of Destiny*

In the name of God, the Merciful, the Compassionate.

Someone asked the eminent *shaykh* Abū 'Alī b. Sīnā (may God the Exalted have mercy on him) the meaning of the Ṣūfī saying, 'He who knows the secret of destiny is an atheist'. In reply he stated that this matter contains the utmost obscurity, and is one of those matters which may be set down only in enigmatic form and taught only in a hidden manner, on account of the corrupting effects its open declaration would have on the general public. The basic principle concerning it is found in a Tradition of the Prophet (God bless and safeguard him): 'Destiny is the secret of God; do not declare the secret of God'. In another Tradition, when a man questioned the Prince of the Believers, 'Alī (may God be pleased with him), he replied, 'Destiny is a deep sea; do not sail out on it'. Being asked again he replied, 'It is a stony path; do not walk on it'. Being asked once more he said, 'It is a hard ascent; do not undertake it'.[1]

The *shaykh* said: Know that the secret of destiny is based upon certain premisses, such as [1] the world order, [2] the report[2] that there is Reward and Punishment, and [3] the affirmation of the resurrection of souls.

[1] The first premiss is that you should know that in the world as a whole and in its parts, both upper and earthly, there is nothing which forms an exception to the facts that God is the cause of its being and origination and that God has knowledge of it, controls it, and wills its existence; it is all subject to His control, determination, knowledge, and will. This is a general and superficial account, although in these assertions we intend to describe it truly, not as the theologians understand it;[3] and it is possible to produce proofs and demonstrations of that. Thus, if it were not that this world is com-

*From George F. Hourani, "Essay on the secret of destiny," *Bulletin of the School of Oriental and African Studies,* London, Vol. 29, Pt. 1, 1966, pp. 31-33. Reprinted with permission of the publishers.

posed of elements which give rise to good and evil things in it and produce both righteousness and wickedness in its inhabitants, there would have been no completion of an order for the world. For if the world had contained nothing but pure righteousness, it would not have been this world but another one, and it would necessarily have had a composition different from the present composition; and likewise if it had contained nothing but sheer wickedness, it would not have been this world but another one. But whatever is composed in the present fashion and order contains both righteousness and wickedness.

[2] The second premiss is that according to the ancients Reward is the occurrence of pleasure in the soul corresponding to the extent of its perfection, while Punishment is the occurrence of pain in the soul corresponding to the extent of its deficiency. So the soul's abiding in deficiency is its 'alienation from God the Exalted',[4] and this is 'the curse', 'the Penalty', [God's] 'wrath' and 'anger', and pain comes to it from that deficiency; while its perfection is what is meant by [God's] 'satisfaction' with it, its 'closeness' and 'nearness' and 'attachment'. This, then, and nothing else is the meaning of 'Reward' and 'Punishment' according to them.

[3] The third premiss is that the resurrection is just the return of human souls to their own world: this is why God the Exalted has said, 'O tranquil soul, return to your Lord satisfied and satisfactory'.

These are summary statements, which need to be supported by their proper demonstrations.

[*a*] Now, if these premisses are established, we say that the apparent evils which befall this world are, on the principles of the Sage,[5] not purposed for the world—the good things alone are what is purposed, the evil ones are a privation, while according to Plato both are purposed as well as willed; [*b*] and that the commanding and forbidding of acts to responsible beings, by revelation in the world, are just a stimulant to him of whom it was foreknown [by God] that there would occur in him [performance of] the commandments, or (in the case of a prohibition) a deterrent to him of whom it was foreknown that he would refrain from what is forbidden. Thus the commandment is a cause of the act's proceeding from him of whom it is foreknown that it will proceed, and the prohibition is a cause of intimidation to him who refrains from something bad because of it. Without the commandment the former would

not have come to desire the act; without the prohibition the latter would not have been scared. It is as if one were to imagine that it would have been possible for 100 per cent of wickedness to befall in the absence of any prohibition, and that with the presence of the prohibitions 50 per cent of wickedness has befallen, whereas without prohibitions 100 per cent would have befallen. Commandments must be judged in the same way: had there been no commandments nothing of righteousness would have befallen, but with the advent of the commandments 50 per cent of righteousness has occurred.

[*c*] As for praise and blame, these have just two objects. One is to incite a doer of good to repeat the like act which is willed to proceed from him; the second is to scare the one from whom the act has occurred from repeating the like of it, and [ensure] that the one from whom that act has [not] occurred will abstain from doing what is not willed to proceed from him, though it is in his capacity to do it.

[*d*] It is not admissible that Reward and Punishment should be such as the theologians suppose: chastisement of the fornicator, for example, by putting him in chains and shackles, burning him in the fire over and over again, and setting snakes and scorpions upon him. For this is the behaviour of one who wills to slake his wrath against his enemy, through injury or pain which he inflicts on him out of hostility against him; and that is impossible in the character of God the Exalted, for it is the act of one who wills that the very being who models himself on him should refrain from acts like his or be restrained from repeating such acts. And it is not to be imagined that after the resurrection there are obligations, commandments, and prohibitions for anyone, so that by witnessing Reward and Punishment they should be scared or refrain from what is proscribed to them and desire what is commanded to them. So it is false that Reward and Punishment are as they have imagined them.

[*e*] As for the [system of] penalties ordained by the divine Law for those who commit transgressions, it has the same effect as the prohibitions in serving as a restraint upon him who abstains from transgression, whereas without it it is imaginable that the act might proceed from him. There may also be a gain to the one who is subject to penalty, in preventing him from further wickedness, because men must be bound by one of two bonds, either the bond of the divine Law or the bond of reason, that the order of the world may be completed.

Do you not see that if anyone were let loose from both bonds the load of wickedness he would commit would be unbearable, and the order of the world's affairs would be upset by the dominance of him who is released from both bonds? But God is more knowing and wiser.

NOTES

1. These Traditions do not explain the meaning of the original saying, they merely reaffirm the prohibition.

2. 'Report' (*hadīth*) seems to hint that after-life Reward and Punishment in the usual sense are only traditional doctrines, not known by science. This view is confirmed below, and elsewhere, e.g. *Shifā'*: *Ilāhiyyāt,* ed. I. Madkur, M. Y. Musa, S. Dunya, and S. Zayed, Cairo, 1960, IX, 7, pp. 414 ff.

3. 'Truly', i.e. according to the Neoplatonic system of causal determination, not the voluntaristic conceptions of Muslim *kalām,* Mu'tazilite and other. Thus Ibn Sīnā's 'destiny' should not be called 'predestination'.

4. All the words put here within quotation marks are Islamic religious expressions which Ibn Sīnā is interpreting in his own way.

5. *al-ḥakīm,* the epithet of Aristotle.

XII

AVERROËS

Averroës (Ibn Rushd) is to be counted among the outstanding figures of medieval Islamic philosophy. He was born at Córdoba in 1126 into a family of distinguished judges. His grandfather had served as chief *qāḍī*. Not surprisingly, Averroës himself was trained in this legal tradition. In addition, he was well grounded in theology, medicine, and philosophy. Very little is known about his early philosophical education, but his first writings seem to have included treatises on medicine (the *Kullīyāt*), law, and perhaps some summaries of Aristotle. Averroës was introduced by the philosopher and court physician, Ibn Ṭufail, to the caliph Abū Ya'qūb, a great patron of learning. Impressed by Averroës and well versed in philosophy in his own right, the caliph made known to Ibn Ṭufail his desire for some clarifying treatises on Aristotle, and Ibn Ṭufail conveyed the request to Averroës. Thus, with the caliph's encouragement, Averroës began the long series of commentaries that would eventually win for him the title "The Commentator." He also seems to have been entrusted with certain important public offices, probably as *qāḍī* of Seville and then as *qāḍī* of Córdoba. In 1182 he became court physician and continued to enjoy high favor until about 1195/6, when he was suddenly banished to a small village by the caliph Abū Yūsuf. Various reasons have been proposed for this surprising turn of events, but it seems likely that Averroës himself was caught in a general reaction against philosophy. Whatever the cause, his period of disgrace was short-lived. Recalled and restored to a position of honor, he died soon thereafter, in 1198.

Averroës' subsequent influence was far greater in the Latin West than in the Muslim world. Many of his commentaries, translated into Latin in the early thirteenth century, exercised great influence in the rediscovery of and deepening appreciation for Aristotle during the rise of scholasticism at that time. His Aristotelian commentaries fall into three classes: great commentaries, which reproduce and comment on the entire Aristotelian original; middle commentaries, which follow the order of the original but only reproduce the opening words of the respective paragraphs of the Aristotelian text; and paraphrases, which follow the order deemed most suitable by Averroës himself, not necessarily that of the Aristotelian original. In addition to the Aristotelian commentaries, Averroës composed other philosophical treatises of a more independent nature, such as his *De substantia orbis*. As a believing Muslim and a philosopher, the relationship between philosophy and religion was of vital concern to him. Charges that he defended a theory of "double truth" do not appear to be well grounded. Rather, one finds him defending the accord of philosophy and religion and treating of certain problems involved in his attempted reconciliation in works such as *The Decisive Treatise,* his *Letter to a Friend* (about God's knowledge of singulars), *The Incoherence of the Incoherence* (directed against Algazel's *Incoherence of the Philosophers*), and his *Exposition of the Methods of Arguments concerning the Belief of Truth.* The following selections include the "Letter to a Friend," a short excerpt from the *Great Commentary on the Metaphysics,* also treating of divine knowledge, and an extract from the *Exposition of the Methods of Arguments . . . ,* "The Future Life." The first and third items were translated by George F. Hourani. The second was translated by Richard M. Frank especially for this volume.

On God's Knowledge

SELECTION I*

[We shall try to solve your problem about God's Knowledge.]

May God prolong your power, continue to bless you, and keep you out of sight of misfortunes!

By your superior intelligence and abundant talents you have surpassed many of those who devote their lives to these sciences, and your sure insight has led you to become aware of the difficulty that arises about the eternal, Glorious Knowledge, on account of Its being connected with the things originated by It. It is therefore our obligation, in the interests of truth and of ending your perplexity, to resolve this difficulty, after formulating it; for he who does not know how to tie a knot cannot untie it.

[The problem: How can God be aware of a change in reality without a corresponding change occurring in His eternal Knowledge?]

The difficulty is compelling, as follows. If all these things were in the Knowledge of God the Glorious before they existed, are they in their state of existence [the same] in His Knowledge as they were before their existence, or are they in their state of existence other in His Knowledge than they were before they existed? If we say that in their state of existence they are other in God's knowledge than they were before they existed, it follows that the eternal Knowledge is subject to change, and that when they pass from nonexistence to existence, there

*From *Averroës On the Harmony of Religion and Philosophy,* trans. and ed. by George F. Hourani (Printed for the Trustees of the "E. J. W. Gibb Memorial" and published by Messrs. Luzac and Co., London, 1961), pp. 72-75. Reprinted with permission of the publishers.

comes into existence additional Knowledge: but that is impossible for the eternal Knowledge. If on the other hand we say that the Knowledge of them in both states is one and the same, it will be asked, 'Are they in themselves', i.e. the beings which come into existence, 'the same before they exist as when they exist?' The answer will have to be 'No, in themselves they are not the same before they exist as when they exist'; otherwise the existent and the non-existent would be one and the same. If the adversary admits this, he can be asked, 'Is not true Knowledge acquaintance with existence as it really is?' If he says 'Yes', it will be said, 'Consequently if the object varies in itself, the knowledge of it must vary; otherwise it will not be known as it really is'. Thus one of two alternatives is necessary: either the eternal Knowledge varies in Itself, or the things that come into existence are not known to It. But both alternatives are impossible for God the Glorious.

This difficulty is confirmed by what appears in the case of man: His knowledge of non-existent things depends on the supposition of existence, while his knowledge of them when they exist depends [on existence itself]. For it is self-evident that the two states of knowledge are different; otherwise he would be ignorant of things' existence at the time when they exist.

[God's foreknowledge of all change does not solve the problem, as the theologians think, for the actual occurrence of the change presumably adds something new to His knowledge.]

It is impossible to escape from this [difficulty] by the usual answer of the theologians about it, that God the Exalted knows things before their existence as they will be at the time of their existence, in respect of time, place and other attributes proper to each being. For it can be said to them: 'Then when they come to exist, does there occur any change or not?'—with reference to the passage of the thing from non-existence to existence. If they say 'No change occurs', they are merely being supercilious. But if they say 'There does occur a change', it can be said to them: 'Then is the occurrence of this change known to the eternal Knowledge or not?' Thus the difficulty is compelling. In sum, it can hardly be conceived that the knowledge of a thing before it exists can be identical with the knowledge of it after it exists. Such, then, is the formulation of this problem in its strongest possible form, as we have explained it to you in conversation.

> *[Nor is Ghazālī's solution satisfactory. He regards God's Knowledge as a term in a relation, which does not change in itself when that to which it is related, the known object, changes its relation to it. But knowledge is a relation, not a related term.]*

The [full] solution of this difficulty would call for a lengthy discourse; but here we shall only go into the decisive point of the solution. Abū Ḥāmid in his book entitled *The disintegration* wanted to resolve this difficulty in a way which carries no conviction. He stated an argument the gist of which is as follows. He asserted that knowledge and the object known are related; and as one of two related things may change without the other changing in itself, this is just what seems to happen to things in the Knowledge of God the Glorious: they change in themselves, but the Knowledge of God the Glorious about them does not change. A parallel case of related things would be if a single column were first on the right of Zayd and then came to be on his left: meanwhile Zayd would not have changed in himself. But this [argument] is not correct. For the relation has changed in itself: the relation which was a right-handed one has become a left-handed one, and the only thing which has not changed is the subject of the relation, i.e. its bearer, Zayd. If this is so, and knowledge is the relation itself, it must necessarily change when the object known changes, just as, when the column changes [its position], the relation of the column to Zayd changes, coming to be a left-handed relation after having been a right-handed one.

> *[The correct solution is that the eternal Knowledge is the cause of beings, not their effect as originated knowledge is. Therefore It does not change when they change.]*

The way to resolve this difficulty, in our opinion, is to recognize that the position of the eternal Knowledge with respect to beings is different from the position of originated knowledge with respect to beings, in that the existence of beings is a cause and reason for our knowledge, while the eternal Knowledge is a cause and reason for beings. If, when beings come to exist after not having existed, there occurred an addition in the eternal Knowledge such as occurs in originated knowledge, it would follow that the eternal Knowledge would be an effect of beings, not their cause. Therefore there must not occur any change such as occurs in originated knowledge. The mistake in this matter has arisen simply from making an analogy between the eternal Knowledge and originated knowledge, i.e. between the suprasensible and the sensible; and the falsity of this analogy is well known. Just as no change occurs in an agent when his act comes into being, i.e. no change which has not already occurred, so no change occurs in the eternal Glorious Knowledge when the object of Its Knowledge results from It.

Thus the difficulty is resolved, and we do not have to admit that if there occurs no change, i.e. in the eternal Knowledge, He does not know beings at the time of their coming into existence just as they are; we only have to admit that He does not know them with originated knowledge but with eternal Knowledge. For the occurrence of change in knowledge when beings change is a condition only of knowledge which is caused by beings, i.e. originated knowledge.

[The philosophers hold that God knows particulars with eternal Knowledge, not that He does not know them at all. Indeed, they consider that His knowledge is the cause of their coming into existence, also that It sends premonitions of particulars in dreams.]

Therefore eternal Knowledge is only connected with beings in a manner other than that in which originated knowledge is connected with them. This does not mean that It is not connected at all, as the philosophers have been accused of saying, in the context of this difficulty, that the Glorious One does not know particulars. Their position is not what has been imputed to them; rather they hold that He does not know particulars with originated knowledge, the occurrence of which is conditioned by their occurrence, since He is a cause of them, not caused by them as originated knowledge is. This is the furthest extent to which purification [of concepts] ought to be admitted.

For demonstration compels the conclusion that He knows things, because their issuing from Him is solely due to His knowing; it is not due to His being merely Existent or Existent with a certain attribute, but to His knowing, as the Exalted has said: 'Does He not know, He who created? He is the Penetrating, the Omniscient!' But demonstration also compels the conclusion that He does not know things with a knowledge of the same character as originated knowledge. Therefore there must be another knowledge of beings which is unqualified, the eternal Glorious Knowledge. And how is it conceivable that the Peripatetic philosophers could have held that the eternal Knowledge does not comprehend particulars, when they held that It is the cause of warning in dreams, of revelation, and of other kinds of inspiration?

[Conclusion]

This is the way to resolve this difficulty, as it appears to us; and what has been said is incontestable and indubitable. It is God who helps us to follow the right course and directs us to the truth. Peace on you, with the mercy and blessings of God.

SELECTION II[1]

[Aristotle] means: Because of its not intellecting anything outside its own essence (since it is simple), its intellection of its own essence is something which can be subject to no mutation through all eternity; nor can there be any doubt regarding the fact that it is not subject therein to any weariness such as is the case in our intellection. The situation must be the same in the case of the rest of the separated intellects, save that the First is the simplest of them and for this reason is the One absolutely, since there is no multiplicity whatsoever in it, either through the intellect's[2] being other than the intelligible or through the multiplicity of the intelligibles. For the multiplicity of intelligibles in one and the same intellect (as is the situation with our intellection) is something that is consequent on the otherness which exists in it, *scil.,* between the act of intellection and the intelligible. For when the intellect and the intelligible are united in a perfect union it follows that the many intelligibles which belong to that intellect and that intellect [itself] are united so as to become one thing, simple in all respects; but when the intelligibles that are actual in the single intellect remain many they are not united with its essence and its essence, then, is other than them.

This is what escaped Themistius where he holds that it is possible for the intellect to understand many intelligibles simultaneously. This contradicts our statement that it understands its own essence and understands nothing extrinsic to it and that the intellect and what it understands are one in all respects. He says that it understands all things by virtue of its understanding that it is a principle of theirs. All of this exemplifies the speech of one who does not grasp Aristotle's proofs here. Indeed, a disgraceful conclusion may follow, viz., that God is ignorant of what is here. Because of this, some people have said that he knows what is here through a universal knowledge, not through a particular knowledge. The truth is that since he knows his own essence alone he knows existent beings in that existence which is the cause of their [individual] existences. For example, one does not say of him who knows the heat of fire alone that he has no knowledge of the heat that is present in hot things but on the contrary it is he who knows the nature of heat *qua* heat. Thus it is the First (Be He Praised) who knows the nature of the existent *qua* existent absolutely which [existent] is his essence.

NOTES

1. From Averroës, *Great Commentary on the Metaphysics* (*Tafsîr mâ ba'd aṭ-ṭabî'a*) ed. M. Bouyges 3 (*Bibliotheca Arabica Scholasticorum,* série arabe, VII) Beyrouth: Imprimerie Catholique, 1948, 1705-1708 (*Lâm,* Comment 51, *ad Metaphysics* 1075a10).

2. Note that there is but a single term (*'aql*) for intellect and the act of intellection as also there is only one term *(ma'qûl)* for the *intellectum* (the actually known) and the intelligible (that which is capable of being the object of understanding).

The Future Life*

[Corporeal symbols are more effective than spiritual ones in instructing the masses about the life beyond, and are used in the Qur'ān *which is primarily concerned with the majority.]*

All religions, as we have said, agree on the fact that souls experience states of happiness or misery after death, but they disagree in the manner of symbolizing these states and explaining their existence to men. And it seems that the [kind of] symbolization which is found in this religion of ours is the most perfect means of explanation to the majority of men, and provides the greatest stimulus to their souls to [pursue the goals of] the life beyond; and the primary concern of religions is with the majority. Spiritual symbolization, on the other hand, seems to provide less stimulus to the souls of the masses towards [the goals of] the life beyond, and the masses have less desire and fear of it than they do of corporeal symbolization. Therefore it seems that corporeal symbolization provides a stronger stimulus to [the goals of] the life beyond than spiritual; the spiritual [kind] is more acceptable to the class of debating theologians, but they are the minority.

[There are three interpretations of the symbols by Muslims. (1) The life beyond is the same in kind as this one, but it is permanent, not limited in duration. (2) It differs in kind: (a) The life beyond is spiritual, and is only symbolized by sensible images for the purpose of exposition. (b) It is corporeal, but the bodies are other, immortal ones not these perishable ones. This opinion is suitable for the élite. It avoids the absurdity of (1), arising from the fact that our bodies here provide material for other earthly bodies and so cannot at the same

*From *Averroës On the Harmony of Religion and Philosophy,* trans. and ed. by George F. Hourani (Printed for the Trustees of the "E. J. W. Gibb Memorial" and published by Messrs. Luzac and Co., London, 1961), pp. 76-78. Reprinted with permission of the publishers.

time exist in the other world. But every opinion is permissible except total rejection of another life.]

For this reason we find the people of Islam divided into three sects with regard to the understanding of the symbolization which is used in [the texts of] our religion referring to the states of the future life. One sect holds that that existence is identical with this existence here with respect to bliss and pleasure, i.e. they hold that it is of the same sort and that the two existences differ only in respect of permanence and limit of duration, i.e. the former is permanent and the latter of limited duration. Another group holds that there is a difference in the kind of existence. This [group] is divided into two subdivisions. One [sub-] group holds that the existence symbolized by these sensible images is spiritual, and that it has been symbolized thus only for the purpose of exposition; these people are supported by many well-known arguments from Scripture, but there would be no point in enumerating them. Another [sub-] group thinks that it is corporeal, but believes that that corporeality existing in the life beyond differs from the corporeality of this life in that the latter is perishable while the former is immortal. They too are supported by arguments from Scripture, and it seems that Ibn 'Abbās was one of those who held this opinion, for he is reported to have said, 'There is nothing in this lower world like the next world except the names.'

It seems that this opinion is more suitable for the élite; for the admissibility of this opinion is founded on facts which are not discussed in front of everyone. One is that the soul is immortal. The second is that the return of the soul to other bodies does not involve the same absurdity as [its] return [to] those same [earthly] bodies. This is because it is apparent that the materials of the bodies that exist here are successively transferred from one body to another: i.e. one and the same material exists in many persons at different times. Bodies like these cannot possibly all exist actually [at the same time], because their material is one: for instance, a man dies, his body is transformed into dust, that dust is transformed into a plant, another man feeds on that plant; then semen proceeds from him, from which another man is born. But if other bodies are supposed, this state of affairs does not follow as a consequence.

The truth in this question is that every man's duty is [to believe] whatever his study of it leads him to [conclude], provided that it is not such a study as would cause him to reject the principle altogether, by denying the existence [of the future life] altogether; for this manner of belief obliges us to call its holder an unbeliever, because the existence of this [future] state for man is made known to people through their Scriptures and their intellects.

[The basic assumption of all the permissible views is the immortality of the soul. It can be proved from the Qur'ān, *which equates death with sleep; now since we know that the soul is not dissolved in sleep, the same applies to death. In both cases the organ, not the soul itself, ceases.]*

The whole of this [argument] is founded on the immortality of the soul. If it is asked 'Does Scripture contain an indication of the immortality of the soul or [at least] a hint of it?', we reply: This is found in the precious Book in the words of the Exalted, 'God receives the souls at the time of their death, and those which have not died He receives in their sleep', [and so on to the end of] the verse. The significant aspect of this verse is that in it He has equated sleep and death with respect to the annihilation of the soul's activity. Thus if the cessation of the soul's activity in death were due to the soul's dissolution, not to a change in the soul's organ, the cessation of its activity in sleep [too] would have to be due to the dissolution of its essential being; but if that were the case, it would not return on waking to its normal condition. So since it does return to it, we know that this cessation does not happen to it through anything which attaches to it in its substantial nature, but is only something which attaches to it owing to a cessation of its organ; and [we know] that it does not follow that if the organ ceases the soul must cease. Death *is* a cessation; it must therefore be of the organ, as is the case in sleep. As the Philosopher says, 'If the old man were to find an eye like the young man's eye, he would see as the young man sees'.

This is as much as we see fit to affirm in our investigation of the beliefs of this religion of ours, the religion of Islam.

XIII

MOSES MAIMONIDES

Moses Maimonides (son of Maimon), the most distinguished Jewish philosopher of the middle ages, was born in Córdoba in 1135. He received his earliest education from his learned father. In addition to a solid grounding in rabbinical studies, Maimonides profited from the Greco-Arabic learning then available in Islamic Spain and North Africa. When Córdoba fell into the hands of the Almohads in 1148, his family was forced to flee because of the religious intolerance of the new conquerors. After a long period of wandering through Spain, they sought refuge in Fez, Morocco. Religious persecution threatened them there as well, and it was only through the aid of a friendly Muslim poet-theologian that they managed to escape. In 1165 they departed for Palestine and eventually settled in Egypt. The family then suffered a severe financial reverse. In order to cope with these new difficulties, Maimonides began to practice medicine, and he eventually became court physician. He was appointed *nāgîd* or chief of the Jewish communities in Egypt, and apparently was held in high regard both by Jew and by Muslim. He died in 1204.

Maimonides' writings include works on law, logic, medicine, a popular treatise on the resurrection, and various letters and responses. By far his greatest contribution to philosophy, however, is his *Guide of the Perplexed.* This work was originally written in Arabic in 1190, and was translated into Hebrew with the author's approval in 1204. It was well known to the thirteenth-century scholastics because of a Latin translation that appeared during the first half of that century. Interestingly, Maimonides did not regard it as a philosophical work. He rather addressed it to Jewish believers who were well grounded in their own religious heritage and who had some acquaintance with Greek learning. They might easily be led into a state of "perplexity" before apparently conflicting claims of philosophy and religion. His purpose seems to be to guide such "perplexed" individuals to a deeper insight into philosophical truths without compromising their religious commitment and, at the same time, to increase their appreciation of Scripture itself. In so doing he displays vast philosophical erudition and a great debt to Aristotle and certain classical commentators such as Alexander of Aphrodisias (*ca.* 200) and Themistius (*ca.* 317-*ca.* 387). At times he agrees with Avicenna and at times he differs with him. The following selection will illustrate something of his attitude towards and usage of the Peripatetics in achieving his purpose. It was translated by Shlomo Pines.

The God of the Philosophers*

In the name of the Lord, God of the World[1]

[INTRODUCTION]

The premises[2] needed for establishing the existence of the deity, may He be exalted, and for the demonstration that He is neither a body nor a force in a body and that He, may His name be sublime, is one, are twenty-five—all of which are demonstrated without there being a doubt as to any point concerning them. For Aristotle and the Peripatetics after him have come forward with a demonstration for every one of them. There is one premise that we will grant them, for through it the objects of our quest will be demonstrated, as I shall make clear; this premise is the eternity of the world.

1. The first premise: The existence of any infinite magnitude is impossible.

2. The second premise: The existence of magnitudes of which the number is infinite is impossible—that is, if they exist together.[3]

3. The third premise: The existence of causes and effects of which the number is infinite is impossible, even if they are not endowed with magnitude. For instance, the assumption that one particular intellect, for example, has as its cause a second intellect, and that the cause of this second intellect is a third one, and that of the third a fourth, and so on to infinity, is likewise clearly impossible.

4. The fourth premise: Change exists in four categories: it exists in the category of substance, the changes occurring in a substance being generation and corruption. It exists in the

*Reprinted from Moses Maimonides, *The Guide of the Perplexed*, Part II, trans. Shlomo Pines (Chicago, 1963), pp. 235-52, by permission of The University of Chicago Press.

category of quantity, namely, as growth and decrease. It exists in the category of quality, namely, as alteration. It exists in the category of place, namely, as the motion of translation. It is this change in the category of place that is more especially called motion.

5. The fifth premise: Every motion is a change and transition from potentiality to actuality.

6. The sixth premise: Of motions, some are essential and some accidental, some are violent and some are motions of a part—this being a species of accidental motion. Now essential motion is, for example, the translation of a body from one place to another. Accidental motion is, for example, when a blackness existing in this particular body is said to be translated from one place to another. Violent motion is, for example, the motion of a stone upwards through the action of something constraining it to that. Motion of a part is, for example, the motion of a nail in a ship; for when the ship is in motion, we say that the nail is likewise in motion. Similarly when any compound is in motion as a whole, its parts are likewise said to be in motion.

7. The seventh premise: Everything changeable is divisible. Hence everything movable is divisible and is necessarily a body. But everything that is indivisible is not movable; hence it will not be a body at all.

8. The eighth premise: Everything that is moved owing to accident must of necessity come to rest, inasmuch as its motion is not in virtue of its essence. Hence it cannot be moved forever in that accidental motion.

9. The ninth premise: Every body that moves another body moves the latter only through being itself in motion when moving the other body.

10. The tenth premise: Everything that is said to be in a body is divided into two classes: either it subsists through the body, as do the accidents, or the body subsists through it, as in the case of the natural form. Both classes are to be considered as a force in the body.

11. The eleventh premise: Some of the things that subsist through body are sometimes divided through the division of the body and hence are divisible according to accident, as for instance the colors and the other forces that are distributed through the whole of the body. In a like manner some of the things that constitute a body are not divisible in any way, as for instance the soul and the intellect.

12. The twelfth premise: Every force that is found dis-

tributed through a body is finite because the body is finite.

13. The thirteenth premise: It is impossible that one of the species of motion be continuous, except local motion, and of this only that which is circular.

14. The fourteenth premise: Local motion is the primary and the first by nature among all motions; for generation and corruption are preceded by alteration, and alteration is preceded by the approach of that which alters to that which is to be altered; and there is no growth and diminution except when they are preceded by generation and corruption.

15. The fifteenth premise: Time is an accident consequent upon motion and is necessarily attached to it. Neither of them exists without the other. Motion does not exist except in time, and time cannot be conceived by the intellect except together with motion. And all that with regard to which no motion can be found, does not fall under time.

16. The sixteenth premise: In whatsoever is not a body, multiplicity cannot be cognized by the intellect, unless the thing in question is a force in a body, for then the multiplicity of the individual forces would subsist in virtue of the multiplicity of the matters or substances in which these forces are to be found.[4] Hence no multiplicity at all can be cognized by the intellect in the separate things, which are neither a body nor a force in a body, except when they are causes and effects.

17. The seventeenth premise: Everything that is in motion has of necessity a mover; and the mover either may be outside the moved object, as in the case of a stone moved by a hand, or the mover may be in the body in motion, as in the case of the body of a living being, for the latter is composed of a mover and of that which is moved. It is for this reason that when a living being dies and the mover—namely, the soul—is lacking from it, that which is moved—namely, the organic body—remains at the moment in its former state, except that it is not moved with that motion. However, inasmuch as the mover that exists in that which is moved is hidden and does not appear to the senses, it is thought of living beings that they are in motion without having a mover. Everything moved that has a mover within itself is said to be moved by itself—the meaning being that the force moving that which, in the object moved, is moving according to essence, exists in the whole of that object.

18. The eighteenth premise: Everything that passes from potentiality to actuality has something other than itself that causes it to pass, and this cause is of necessity outside that

thing. For if that cause were that thing and there were no obstacle to prevent this passage, the thing would not have been for a certain time in potentia but would have always been in actu. If, however, the cause of the passage from potentiality to actuality subsisted in the thing, and if there was at the same time an obstacle to it, which was subsequently removed, there is no doubt that the factor that put an end to the obstacle is the one that caused that potentiality to pass into actuality. Understand this.

19. The nineteenth premise: Everything that has a cause for its existence is only possible with regard to existence in respect to its own essence. For it exists if its causes are present. If, however, they are not present, or if they become nonexistent, or if their relation that entails the existence of the thing in question has changed, that thing does not exist.

20. The twentieth premise: Everything that is necessarily existent in respect to its own essence has no cause for its existence in any way whatever or under any condition.

21. The twenty-first premise: Everything that is composed of two notions has necessarily that composition as the cause of its existence as it really is, and consequently is not necessarily existent in respect to its own essence, for it exists in virtue of the existence of its two parts and of their composition.

22. The twenty-second premise: Every body is necessarily composed of two things and is necessarily accompanied by accidents. The two things constituting it are its matter and its form; and the accidents accompanying it are quantity, shape, and position.

23. The twenty-third premise: It is possible for whatsoever is in potentia and in whose essence there is a certain possibility, not to exist in actu at a certain time.

24. The twenty-fourth premise: Whatsoever is something in potentia is necessarily endowed with matter, for possibility is always in matter.

25. The twenty-fifth premise: The principles of an individual compound substance are matter and form. And there is no doubt about the necessity of there being an agent, I mean to say a mover that moves the substratum so as to predispose it to receive the form. That is the proximate mover, which predisposes the matter of a certain individual. At this point it is necessary to engage in speculation with regard to motion, the mover, and the moved. However, with regard to all this, every-

thing that it was necessary to explain has already been explained. The text of the words of Aristotle is: Matter does not move itself.[5] This therefore is the capital premise calling for an inquiry concerning the existence of the Prime Mover.

Of the twenty-five premises that I have put before you in the form of a preface, some become manifest with very little reflection and are demonstrative premises and first intelligibles or notions approaching the latter, as may be seen in the epitome we have made of their orderly exposition. Others require a number of demonstrations and premises leading up to them. However, all of them have been given demonstrations as to which no doubt is possible. With regard to some of them, this has been done in the Book of "Akroasis"[6] and its commentaries; with regard to others, in the Book of "Metaphysics" and its commentary. I have already made it known to you that the purpose of this Treatise is not to transcribe the books of the philosophers and to explain the most remote of the premises, but to mention the proximate premises that are required for our purpose.

I shall add to the premises mentioned before, one further premise that affirms as necessary the eternity of the world. Aristotle deemed it to be correct and the most fitting to be believed. We shall grant him this premise by way of a hypothesis[7] in order that the clarification of that which we intended to make clear should be achieved. This premise, which among them is the twenty-sixth, [consists in Aristotle's statement] that time and movement are eternal, perpetual, existing in actu.[8] Hence it follows of necessity, in his opinion, that there is a body, moving with an eternal movement, existing in actu; and this is the fifth body. For this reason, he says that the heaven is not subject to generation and corruption. For according to him, movement is not subject to generation and corruption; for he says that every movement is necessarily preceded by another movement either of the same species as itself or of other species, and that what is thought with regard to living beings—namely, that their local movement is not preceded at all by another movement—is not correct. For the cause of their movement after rest goes back finally to things calling for this local movement; these things being either an alteration of temperament necessitating a desire to seek what agrees with the living being or to flee from what disagrees with it, or an imagination, or an opinion occurring to it. Accordingly, any one of these three factors sets the living being in motion, and every one of them is necessitated by other movements. Similarly he says that in the case of everything that comes about in time, the possibility of its coming-about precedes in time its coming-about. From this there follow necessarily several points liable to validate his premise.[9] According to this premise, a finite moving object moves upon a finite distance an infinite number of times, going back over the same distance in a circle. Now this is impossible except in circular movement, as is demonstrated in the thirteenth of these premises. According to this premise, that which is infinite must necessarily exist as a succession and not simultaneously.[10]

This is the premise that Aristotle constantly wishes to establish as true. Now to me it seems that he does not affirm categorically that the arguments he puts forward in its favor constitute a demonstration. The premise in question[11] is rather, in his opinion, the most fitting and the most probable. However, his followers and the commentators of his books claim that the premise is necessary and not merely possible and that it has already been demonstrated. On the other hand, every Mutakallim desires to establish that it is impossible. They say that there can be no mental representation of the coming-about in succession of an infinite number of things occurring in time. The strength of their argument is that it constitutes, in their opinion, a first intelligible. But to me it seems that the premise in question is possible—that is, neither necessary, as is affirmed by the commentators of the writings of Aristotle, nor impossible, as is claimed by the Mutakallimūn. It is not the purpose now to explain the arguments of Aristotle, or to raise our doubts concerning him, or to explain my opinion concerning the creation of the world in time. But the purpose at this point is to circumscribe the premises that we need for our three problems; after first having set forth these premises and having agreed to take them as granted, I shall set out explaining what necessarily follows from them.

NOTES

1. Religious invocation from Gen. 21:33.

2. No example prior to Maimonides of a list of twenty-five or twenty-six "premises" seems to be known.

3. Or: simultaneously.

4. Literally: of their matters and substrata.

5. *Metaphysics* xii.6.1071b29-30. The quotation is accurate.

6. Aristotle's *Physics* is meant.

7. I read *taqdīr* instead of the word *taqrīr* found in the Arabic text. Graphically this emendation is very slight. It is in conformity with Ibn Tibbon's Hebrew translation.

8. Cf. *Physics* viii.1.251b20ff.; *Metaphysics* xii.6.1071b5ff.

9. Concerning the eternity of movement.

10. Or: together.

11. The Arabic pronoun for which the words, "the premise in question," are substituted in this translation, may alternatively refer to "the arguments" mentioned in the preceding sentence. This was Ibn Tibbon's opinion. However, the sentences that follow appear to prove the correctness of the translation propounded in the text.

CHAPTER 1

It follows necessarily from the twenty-fifth premise that there is a mover, which has moved the matter of that which is subject to generation and corruption so that it received form. If now it is asked: what moved this proximate mover?—it follows of necessity that there exists for it another mover either of its own species or of a different species; for motion exists in four categories,[1] and sometimes these different kinds of change are called motion in a general way, as we have mentioned in the fourth premise. Now this does not go to infinity, as we have mentioned in the third premise. For we have found that every movement goes back, in the last resort, to the movement of the fifth body, and no further. It is from this movement that every mover and predisposer in the whole lower world proceeds and derives. Now the sphere moves with a movement of translation, and this is prior to all other movements, as has been mentioned in the fourteenth premise. Similarly every movement of translation goes back, in the last resort, to the movement of the sphere. It is as if you say: this stone, which was in motion, was moved by a staff; the staff was moved by a hand; the hand by tendons; the tendons by muscles; the muscles by nerves; the nerves by natural heat; and the natural heat by the form that subsists therein, this form being undoubtedly the first mover. What obliges this mover to move could be an opinion, for instance an opinion that the stone should be brought by the blow of the staff to a hole[2] in order to stop it, so that blowing wind should not enter thereby toward the man who had this opinion.[3] Now the mover of this wind and the factor causing it to blow is the movement of the sphere. In a similar way you will find that every cause of generation and corruption goes back, in the last resort, to the movement of the sphere. Now when, in the last resort, we have gone back to this sphere, which is in motion, it follows necessarily that it must have a mover, according to what has been set forth before in the seventeenth premise. Now the mover cannot but be either in the moved or outside it, for this is a necessary division. Now if the mover is outside the sphere, it cannot but be either a body or not a body; in which latter case it should not be said to be outside the sphere, but separate from it, for what is not a body is not said to be outside a body except through an extension of the meaning of the expression. If, however, its mover is in it—I mean the mover of the sphere—it cannot but be either that the mover is a force distributed in the whole of the body of the sphere and divisible through the latter's being divided—as heat in fire—or that it is a force in the sphere that is not divisible—as are the soul and the intellect—just as has been expounded before [in] the tenth premise. There is, accordingly, no doubt as to the mover of the sphere being one of these four: either another body outside it, or separate from it,[4] or a force distributed in it, or an indivisible force.

Now the first supposition—namely, that the mover of the sphere is another body outside the sphere—is absurd, as I shall point out. For if it is a body, it must—as has been set forth in the ninth premise—be in motion when moving another body. Now in that case, this sixth body[5] likewise must be in motion when moving another body. Accordingly it would necessarily follow that it is moved by a seventh body. This in its turn must be supposed to be in motion. Accordingly it would follow necessarily that an infinite number of bodies must exist and that only in that case is the sphere in motion. Now this is absurd, as has been set forth before in the second premise.

The third possibility—namely, that the mover of the sphere is a force distributed in the latter—is likewise absurd, as I shall point out. For the sphere is a body and in consequence necessarily finite, as has been set forth before in the first premise. In consequence its force must be finite, as has been set forth in the twelfth premise. Hence this force must be divisible if the sphere is divided, as has been set forth in the eleventh premise. Hence it cannot move something for an infinite time, as we have supposed that it does in the twenty-sixth premise.

As for the fourth possibility—namely, that the mover of the sphere is an indivisible force subsisting in the sphere, as for example man's soul does in man—it is likewise absurd that this mover alone should be the cause for this perpetual motion, even if it is indivisible. The explanation of this lies in the fact that if this mover is the first mover of the sphere, it also must be in motion according to accident, as has been mentioned in the sixth premise.

I shall add here the explanation that follows. When, for example, the soul of a man, which is his form, moves him to go up from the house to an upper chamber, it is the body that is in motion according to essence, the soul being the first mover according to essence. However, the soul is in motion according to accident, for through the transporting of the body from the house to the upper chamber, the soul, which was in the house, was transported and came to be in the upper chamber. Now if the action of moving exerted by the soul would come to rest, that which was moved by it, namely, the body, also would come to rest. But then through the fact that the body would come to rest, the accidental motion, which had come to the soul, would be abolished. Now, everything that is moved according to accident must of necessity come to rest, as has been mentioned in the eighth premise. When, however, it comes to rest, that which is moved by it likewise comes to rest. It follows accordingly of necessity that the first mover in question necessarily must have another cause subsisting outside the whole, which is composed of a mover and of a moved. When this cause, which is the beginning of movement, is present, the first mover, which subsists in this whole, moves that in it which may be moved. When, however, it is not present, that which may be moved in the whole is at rest.[6] For this reason the bodies of animals are not perpetually in motion, even though there is in every one of them an indivisible first mover. For this mover does not move them perpetually according to essence, for the factors that incite it to cause to move are matters outside it: either quest for what agrees with that particular animal, or flight from what disagrees with it, or again an imagination or a representation in the case of those animals that have representations.[7] When acted upon by these factors, the mover causes movement. When doing this, it itself is moved accidentally. And accordingly there is no doubt about its coming to rest at a certain time, as we have mentioned. If, however, the mover of the sphere were in it in this manner, it would not be able to be in motion eternally.

Accordingly, if the motion in question is perpetual and eternal, as is stated by our adversary–and this is possible, as has been mentioned in the thirteenth premise–it follows necessarily, according to this option,[8] that the first cause of the movement of the sphere conforms to the second possibility; I mean to say that it is separate from the sphere according to what is required by the above division.[9] It accordingly has been demonstrated that it is necessary that the mover of the first sphere, if the movement of the latter is regarded as eternal and perpetual, should not at all be a body or a force in a body; in this way the mover of this sphere would have no movement, either according to essence or to accident, and would not be subject to division or to change, as has been mentioned in the seventh and the fifth of the premises. Now this is the deity, may His name be sublime; I am referring to the first cause moving the sphere. And it is absurd that there should be two or more of them because it is absurd that there should be multiplicity in the separate things, which are not bodies, except when one of them is a cause and the other an effect, as has been mentioned in the sixteenth premise. It has also been made clear that this first cause does not fall under time because it is impossible that there should be movement with regard to it, as has been mentioned in the fifteenth premise. Accordingly this speculation has led by means of a demonstration to the knowledge that it is impossible that the sphere should move itself in an eternal motion; that the first cause to which its being set in motion is due, is not a body or a force in a body; and that this first cause is one and unchangeable because its existence is not conjoined with time. These are the three problems with regard to which the most excellent among the philosophers gave demonstrations.

A second speculation made by them. Aristotle propounded, by way of introduction, a premise that runs as follows: Supposing that there exists a thing composed of two things and that one of these two things exists separately outside this compound thing, it follows necessarily that the other thing also must exist outside the compound thing.[10] For if the existence of these two things had required that they exist only together, as do matter and natural form, one of them would not have existed in any way without the other. Accordingly, the fact that one of them exists separately is a proof for the absence of an obligatory mutual connection. Consequently the second thing, which enters into the compound thing, must necessarily exist separately. The following example for this may be adduced: if oxymel exists and honey likewise exists by itself, it follows necessarily that vinegar must exist by itself. After having explained this premise, he says: We find that many things are composed of a mover and a moved. He means to say thereby that these things move other things, and, when moving the latter, are themselves moved by other things. This is manifest with regard to all the things that have an intermediate status as far as causing to move is concerned. Now we find that there exists a thing that is moved and does not at all cause to move; this is the last of the moved things. It follows accordingly that there must exist a mover that is not moved at all; this is the first mover.[11] And inasmuch as no motion is possible in it, it is not divisible and not a body, and it does not fall under time, as has become clear in the preceding demonstration.

A third philosophic speculation about this subject is taken over from Aristotle's argumentation, even though he sets it forth with a view to another purpose. This is how the argument is ordered. There is no doubt that there are existent things. These are the existent things that are apprehended by the senses. Now there are only three possible alternatives,[12] this being a necessary division: namely, either no existents are subject to generation and corruption, or all of them are subject to generation and corruption, or some of them are subject to generation and corruption whereas others are not. Now the first alternative is clearly absurd, for we perceive many existents that are subject to generation and corruption. The second alternative is likewise absurd, the explanation of this being as follows: if every existent falls under generation and corruption, then all the existents and every one of them have a possibility of undergoing corruption. Now it is indubitable, as you know, that what is possible with regard to a species must necessarily come about. Thus it follows necessarily that they, I mean all existents, will necessarily undergo corruption. Now if all of them have undergone corruption, it would be impossible that anything exists, for there would remain no one who would bring anything into existence. Hence it follows necessarily that there would be no existent thing at all. Now we perceive things that are existent. In fact we ourselves are existent. Hence it follows necessarily, according to this speculation that if there are, as we perceive, existents subject to generation and corruption, there must be a certain existent that is not subject to generation and corruption. Now in this existent that is not subject to generation and corruption, there is no possibility of corruption at all; rather, its existence is necessary, not possible. He also says that, with reference to this existent's being necessary of existence, there are two possibilities: this may be either in respect to its own essence or in respect to the cause of this existent. In the latter case, its existence and nonexistence are possible in respect to its own essence, but necessary in respect to its cause. Thus its cause would be necessary of existence, as has been mentioned in the nineteenth premise. Now it has been demonstrated that, of necessity, there can be no doubt that there is an existent that is necessary of existence in respect to its own essence. For without it, there would be no existent at all, neither one that is subject to generation and corruption, nor one that is not subject to them—if there is a thing that exists in this manner, as Aristotle states; I mean to say a thing that is not subject to generation and corruption because of its being an effect caused by a cause that is necessary of existence. This is a demonstration concerning which there can be no doubt, no refutation, and no dispute, except on the part of one who is ignorant of the method of demonstration. After this we shall say that it follows necessarily that the existence of everything that is necessary of existence with respect to its own essence can have no cause, as has been set forth in the twentieth premise; and that in anything that is necessary of existence there cannot be a multiplicity of notions, as has been mentioned in the twenty-first premise. Hence it follows necessarily that, as has been set forth in the twenty-second premise, it is not a body or a force in a body. It thus has been demonstrated in this speculation that there is an existent that is necessary of existence and is so necessarily with respect to its own essence, and that this existent has no cause for its existence and has no composition in itself, and for this reason is neither a body nor a force in a body. It is he who is the deity, may His name be sublime. Similarly it can be easily demonstrated that it is impossible that necessity of existence in respect to essence should exist in two beings. For the species, necessity of existence, is a notion that would be superadded to the essence of each one of these two supposed beings. Accordingly, none of them would be necessary of existence in virtue only of itself, but it would be necessary of existence in virtue of the notion representing the species—necessity of existence—a species subsisting both in that particular being and in another one. Now it has been made clear in a number of ways that no duality at all, nor the existence of an equal or of a contrary, can be true with reference to the necessary of existence. The cause of all this is the latter's absolute[13] simplicity and absolute[13] perfection—leaving no residue outside its essence that pertains to the species, the necessary of existence—as well as the nonexistence in any way of a primary or secondary cause[14] for it. Accordingly, nothing at all can be associated with the necessary of existence.

The fourth speculation, likewise philosophic. It is well known that we constantly see things that are in potentia and pass into actuality. Now everything that passes from potentiality into actuality has something outside itself that causes it to pass, as has been mentioned in the eighteenth premise. It is also clear that this something, which in one particular case causes to pass from potentiality to actuality, had been a cause of this passage in potentia and then only became such a cause in actu. Now the reason for its having been in potentia might lie either in an obstacle subsisting in its own right or in a relation—which had been absent before—between it and the thing it is to cause to pass from potentiality to actuality. When this relation is realized, it actually causes the thing to pass from potentiality to actuality. Now these two explanations necessarily require something that causes to pass from potentiality to actuality or a factor that puts an end to a hindrance. And the same thing must necessarily be said of the second something that causes to pass from potentiality to actuality or of the second factor that puts an end to a hindrance. And this series of causes or factors cannot continue to infinity. There is no doubt that, in the last resort, one must come to something that causes the passage from potentiality to actuality, that is perpetually existent in one and the same state, and in which there is no potentiality at all. I mean to say that in it, in its essence, there is nothing in potentia. For if there were possibility[15] in its essence, the thing in question would at some time become nonexistent, as has been mentioned in the twenty-third premise. It is further impossible that the thing in question should be endowed with matter; rather is it separate from matter, as has been mentioned in the twenty-fourth premise. Now the being that is separate from matter, in which there is no possibility whatever, but that exists in virtue of its essence, is the deity. And it has already been made clear that He is not a body and that He is one, as has been mentioned in the sixteenth premise.

All these are demonstrative methods of proving the existence of one deity, who is neither a body nor a force in a body, while believing at the same time in the eternity of the world.

There is also a demonstrative method of refuting the belief in the corporeality of [God] and of establishing [God's] unity. For if there were two deities it would follow necessarily that they must have one separately conceivable thing in which they participate, this being the thing in virtue of which each one of them merits being called a deity. They also must necessarily have another separately conceivable thing in virtue of which their separation came about and they became two. Now in virtue of the fact that in each of them there must be a separately conceivable thing other than the one subsisting in the other deity, each one of them must be composed of two separately conceivable things. Accordingly, as has been explained in the nineteenth premise, none of them can be a first cause or necessary of existence in respect to its own essence, but each of them must have several causes. If, however, the separately conceivable thing causing the separation between them exists in only one of them, the one in which the two separately conceivable things[16] exist, is not according to his essence, existent of necessity.

Another method with regard to the belief in unity. It has already been established as true by means of a demonstration that all that exists is like one individual whose parts are bound up with each other, and that the forces of the sphere pervade this lowly matter and fashion it. At the same time it is impossible—and this has already been established as true—that one deity should be exclusively concerned with one part of what exists, and the other deity[17] with another part; for one part is bound up with the other. According to the division of possibilities, the only hypotheses that remain open are that one deity acts during a certain time and the other during another time, or that both of them always act together so that no act is perfect unless it has been carried out by both of them together. Now the supposition that one of them acts during a certain time and the other during another time is absurd from several points of view. For if it were possible that during the time in which one of them acts the other should act also, what could be the cause necessitating that one of them acts during that time whereas the other remains inactive? If, however, it were impossible for one of them to act during the time in which the other acts, there consequently must be another cause that necessitates that at a given time it is possible for one of them to act whereas for the other it is impossible. For there is no differentiation in time as a whole; and the substratum for the action[18] is one, and its parts are bound up with one another, as we have made clear. Furthermore, according to this supposition, each one of them would fall under time inasmuch as his work would be tied up with time. Furthermore, each one of them, at the time of his action, would have to pass from potentiality to actuality, and, in consequence, each one of them would need something that would cause him to pass from potentiality to actuality. Furthermore, possibility would subsist in the essence of each of them. If, however, they were supposed always to make together everything that is in existence, so that one of them would not act without the other, that also would be absurd, as I shall set forth. For in the case of any complex composed of parts, which cannot cause a certain act to become perfect except through the co-operation of each one of its parts, none of these parts is an agent in respect to its own essence or the first cause of the act; that first cause is the coming-together of the parts of the complex. Now it has been demonstrated that it is a necessary conclusion that what is necessary of existence can have no cause. Moreover the coming-together of the parts of the complex represents a certain act, which requires another agent, namely, one who causes the parts of the complex to come together. Now if the agent who causes the parts of the complex to come together—without which the act cannot become perfect —is one, he is indubitably the deity. If, however, this agent who causes the parts of this complex to come together is another complex, the same conclusions follow necessarily with regard to this second complex as with regard to the first. Thus there can be no doubt about ultimately reaching One who is the cause of the existence of this existent, which is one,[19] whatever the manner of this may have been: whether through creating it in time after it had been nonexistent, or because it proceeds necessarily from this One. It has thus become clear, also according to this method, that the fact that all that exists is one, indicates to us that He who caused it to exist is one.

Another method of refuting the belief in the corporeality [of God]. As has been mentioned in the twenty-second premise, every body is a compound. Now there can be no doubt that every compound requires an agent, which is the cause of the subsistence of its form in its matter. Now it is most clear that every body is divisible and has dimensions. Accordingly, it is indubitably something to which accidents must be attached. Hence a body cannot be one, both because of its divisibility and because of its being a compound—I mean to say, because of its being two as far as statement is concerned. For every body is a certain body only because of some separately conceivable thing subsisting in it that is superadded to the fact of its being a body. In consequence, every body is necessarily provided with two separately conceivable things. Now it has been demonstrated that in the necessary of existence there is no composition in any way at all.

After having first set forth these demonstrations, I shall start to give an epitome of that method which is emphatically ours, as we have promised.

CHAPTER 2

The fifth body, namely, the sphere, cannot but be either subject to generation and corruption—in which case movement would likewise be subject to generation and corruption—or, as the adversary says, not be subject to generation and corruption. If the sphere is subject to generation and corruption, it is the deity, may His name be sublime, who brought it into existence after its having been nonexistent. This is a first intelligible, for everything that exists after having been nonexistent must have of necessity someone who has brought [it] into existence—it being absurd that it should bring itself into existence. If, however, the sphere has not ceased and will not cease thus to be moved in a perpetual and eternal movement, it follows necessarily from the premises that have been set forth before that the mover that causes it to move in this eternal movement is not a body or a force in a body; it is in fact the deity, may His name be sublime. Thus it has become clear to you that the existence of the deity, may He be exalted—who is the necessary of existence that has no cause and in whose existence in respect to His essence there is no possibility—is proved by cogent and certain demonstrations, regardless of whether the world has come into being in time after having been nonexistent or whether it has not come into being in time after having been nonexistent. Similarly, demonstrations prove that He is one and not a body, as we have set forth before. For the demonstration that He is one and not a body is valid, regardless of whether the world has come into being in time after having been nonexistent or not—as we have made clear by means of the third philosophic method and when refuting the belief in His corporeality and when establishing His oneness by means of philosophic methods.

NOTES

1. Literally: in the four categories. I.e., those enumerated in the fourth premise.
2. Or: a window.
3. Literally: to him (or: to it). It is practically certain that the man who moved the stone is referred to in the Arabic pronominal suffix.
4. In this case the mover is supposed to be an immaterial entity.
5. The sphere being considered as the fifth body, Maimonides calls its mover, should that turn out to be a body, the sixth body.
6. This appears to be the probable meaning of the phrase. However, if one keeps to the letter of the text, it would seem that that which is at rest in the circumstances under discussion is "the mover" rather than "that which may be moved." There are certain considerations that seem to favor the latter interpretation.
7. In the singular in Arabic. In the context the Arabic word may mean the faculty of representation.
8. Namely, the opinion that regards the movement of the sphere as eternal.
9. The one posing four prima facie possible hypotheses regarding the nature of the mover of the sphere.
10. I.e., the second element entering into the makeup of the compound thing.
11. In this passage, Maimonides appears to be referring to one of Alexander of Aphrodisias' commentaries rather than to Aristotle himself.
12. Literally: And the matter is not free from three divisions.
13. Literally: pure.
14. *al-'illa wa'l-sabab*. These two terms are often synonymous, both of them meaning "cause." Sometimes, however, each may have a distinctive shade of meaning; in that case *sabab* tends to mean secondary cause.
15. In the sense of potentiality.
16. Namely, necessity of existence and the separately conceivable thing causing separation between the two hypothetical deities.
17. Assumed to exist ex hypothesi.
18. To be accomplished by the two deities whose existence is supposed.
19. I.e., the cause of the universe.

XIV

ODO RIGAUD

Odo Rigaud (Odo Rigaldus, Eudes of Rouen) was born near Paris around the beginning of the thirteenth century. He entered the Franciscan order (*ca.* 1236) and studied theology at the University of Paris (*ca.* 1240-45), where he held the Franciscan chair of theology after the deaths of Alexander of Hales and John of la Rochelle in 1245. Elected to the see of Rouen, he was consecrated bishop by Pope Innocent IV at Lyons, April 26, 1248. He was a favorite of Louis IX, king of France, and collaborated with him on a treaty with England (1258). His *Register of Visitations* gives an account of his episcopal activity from 1248 to 1269. He worked actively with St. Bonaventure for the reunion of the Greeks with the Roman Church at the Council of Lyons (1274). He died at Rouen, July 2, 1275.

During the first half of the thirteenth century the impact of the new Aristotelian literature seems to have revived interest among the avant-garde theologians as to how far systematic theology might be cast in the mold of a deductive science. As a bachelor of theology, Odo had heard Alexander of Hales and others at the Franciscan monastery at Paris discussing this problem. His own solution, given in this magisterial question held during his regency, reveals the influence of these earlier writers.

Following the pattern of an axiomatic science like Euclid's geometry, these theologians distinguished among the set of initial axioms those that were principles common to several or all sciences *(dignitates)* and those peculiar to the science in question *(suppositiones)*. Systematic theology, according to this conceptual model, has two types of axioms: (1) the generally accepted philosophical or rational truths considered to be "self-evident" to any thinking mind;

(2) the articles of faith, not evident to reason, but regarded by the believer to be certified by divine authority itself. These "articles" function, like the peculiar postulates of theology, as a "science." The systematic theologian then proceeds to deduce from these two sets of axioms, according to accepted rules of formal logic, a set of theorems or conclusions which constitute theology as a body of "demonstrated truths." Because it resembles in its formal structure Aristotle's ideal of *episteme* or *scientia* as outlined in the *Posterior analytics,* theology can be called a "science" in an extended sense of that term.

The present translation was made by A. B. Wolter especially for this volume.

Is Theology a Science?[1]

[ARGUMENTS FOR AND AGAINST THE THESIS]

The first point raised is whether theology is a science. It does not seem to be such for the following reasons:

1. Every science has some principles which are self-evident and do not require for their acceptance belief in anything beyond themselves. For "we know principles insofar as we know their terms." Once the meaning of "whole" and "part" is had, for example, we possess all we need to know this principle: "Every whole is greater than its part." Now it is through these principles that the others in the science in question derive their certitude. But the principles of theology do not beget belief of themselves nor are they points which come to mind of themselves. What is more, they require something from without, viz. the grace of faith. Therefore it is clear that theology is not a science.

2. Also, every science is about some subject, generally one whose parts and properties it considers, for, as the Philosopher says towards the end of Bk. I of the *Posterior analytics* [chap. 28]: "A single science is one whose domain is a single genus, whose parts and essential properties it considers." But since theology has to do with God who has no parts or properties, it is not a science.

3. Also the acceptance characteristic of faith is different from that of a science. But theology, considered according to the way it is taught in this life, has as its purpose to produce faith; therefore it does not aim at producing science. Hence theology is not a science. The minor of the argument is clear from that passage in St. John, chapter 20: "These things are written that you may believe."

4. Also every science has to do with what is universal and imperishable, as the Philosopher points out. But theology is in great part concerned with singular events and with what passes away, e.g. with historical events which are deeds concerned

with particulars. Therefore either theology is not a science or these things are not its concern. This second alternative however is clearly false.

5. Also every science involves the acceptance of something certain together with the recognition that it is certain, as is clear from the definition of "to know" *(scire)* in *Posterior analytics,* Bk. I [chap. 2]: "For we suppose ourselves to possess scientific knowledge of a thing when we know its cause and recognize it as the cause of the fact and know further that the fact could not be otherwise than it is." And Isidore also says that science has to do with an event perceived as certain. Since historical accounts are never certain and theology is concerned with such accounts, e.g. that Abraham begot Isaac, and the like, it is clear that theology is not a science.

6. Also every science is about things which the mind sees to be the case. Now historical events, although they may be believed, are never things the mind sees to be the case, and theology concerns things of this sort. The minor is clear from the words of Augustine who says in the *Book of 83 Questions*: "Some things are believed but never seen to be so. This is the case with the history of all human actions."

7. Also the acceptance of science contributes little or nothing to salvation, but the teaching of theology is of great value thereto, as is clear from *Romans* 1: "that believing you may have life." Therefore theology is not a science.

8. Also knowledge of the other sciences is not subjected in any way to the will. Willy-nilly a geometer believes that a triangle has three angles . . . etc. But since the acceptance of theological knowledge depends upon the will, theology is not a science. That it does so depend is clear from what Augustine says: "Other things a man can accept unwillingly, but he can only believe if he wills it."

9. Also Augustine says that science concerns the temporal, wisdom concerns the eternal. Since theology concerns the eternal, because it is about God and divine things, it is clear that one should call it not "science" but "wisdom."

On the other hand, both reason and authoritative sources prove theology to be a science. The proof from authorities are these:

a. Boethius in his work *On the Trinity* divides philosophy into three parts, namely into physics, mathematics, and metaphysics or theology, and he asserts that theology is a part of philosophy on a par with the other divisions. Now the other members of the division are sciences, consequently theology is also a science.

b. Hugh of St. Victor says: "All the natural arts serve the divine science." Therefore, not only is theology a science, but it is the noblest of them all.

c. In *Wisdom,* chapter 13, we read: "But all men are vain in whom there is no knowledge *(scientia)* of God." But this science seems to be nothing else but theology. Therefore theology seems to be a science.

d. *Wisdom,* chaps. 6 and 15, also speaks of the knowledge of God as "perfect understanding." If theology is knowledge of God, it is clear that theology is a science.

The proofs from reason are these:

e. Everything habitual which exists in the intellective part [of the soul] as a disposition is either a virtue or a science. Theology is such a habit. Since it is not a virtue, it is obvious it must be a science.

f. Also every acquired cognitive habit having certitude is a science. But theology is such an acquired form of habitual knowledge and it concerns something certain. Therefore it is a science. That it possesses certitude is clear from the following: What is seen in the light of grace is more certain and true than what is seen in the light of nature [i.e. of the natural power of the mind]. But theology is seen by the light of grace; other sciences by the light of reason. Therefore it is clear that theology possesses certitude.

g. What is known by divine inspiration is more true and certain than what is known by human reason. But theological knowledge comes by way of divine inspiration. Recall these texts: "All scripture is inspired by God" (2 *Tim.* 3:16); "But holy men of God spoke as they were moved by the Holy Spirit" (2 *Pet.* 1:21); and in verse 16, "We have the word of prophecy, surer still." But the other sciences, known through reason, possess certitude; therefore this is even more true of theology than of these others.

[THE BODY OF THE QUESTION]

I reply: To understand the previous discussion take note that there are two ways in which one can speak of science:

(a) properly and (b) in a more general way. In the proper sense, it is the name of a habit having certitude, which is within the scope of reason or the power of the intellect. As such it is the name of an acquired habit. In this sense, I admit theology is not a science. For if reason is not elevated and aided by the gift of faith, it is unable to give us this knowledge which transcends that of all the arts and sciences both by virtue of its subject matter (i.e. God, who transcends all things) and by reason of its technique; for theology does not advance through mere human arguments, but has reasons and principles of its own distinct from those of the other sciences. Now while these are evident by grace of the faith and are manifest to a soul illumined thereby, they are not at all evident to an unbeliever. Any infidel therefore can know metaphysics, because it proceeds by reasoning processes that fall within the scope of reason, but only a believer can know theology, for the reasons cited above.

But if science be understood broadly to be any kind of certain, intellectual knowledge, not a virtue (and here I say "intellectual" to distinguish it from sense knowledge; "certain" to differentiate it from opinions, which are never certain; and "not a virtue" to set it apart from faith [an infused virtue]), then in this special sense I grant that theology is a science. And herein lies the basis for those arguments proving theology to be a science. Understood in this fashion, science embraces both wisdom and science proper.

[REPLY TO THE INITIAL ARGUMENTS]

[To 1 and 3]

One way to answer the first objection, viz. that this science is not based on self-evident principles, obviously would be to concede it holds for a science in the proper sense only. Nevertheless, there is a better way to reply. Since there is no essential difference between postulates or principles of a given science, we can say that just as in other sciences we have (a) principles known to all, such as the axioms *(dignitates)*, (b) assumptions or postulates *(suppositiones sive petitiones)*, and also (c) conclusions, so too in theology. Here one must admit axioms manifest to all, e.g. "God is supremely good," "He must be loved by all," "He is supremely just," and such like; knowledge of these like that of principles is "written in our hearts"

[Rom. 2:15]. In addition there are postulates and these are the articles of faith. Finally, there are the conclusions that follow from these axioms and postulates.

Looking at these postulates, we see they resemble the postulates of the other sciences, and yet there is a difference between them. They are similar in that in theology the articles of faith are presupposed without proof, just as are the postulates of the other sciences. The difference, however, is this. In the other sciences, postulates like "Between two points only one straight line can be drawn," or "Unity is indivisible," and the like are evident to reason itself without any external help, whereas in theology, for acceptance of the postulates one needs in addition the gift of faith.

To the extent that theology accepts those axioms which are impressed on men's minds and does not have to go begging to other sciences for them, it is called wisdom, for it is, as it were, a knowledge of the highest causes. But to the extent that it draws conclusions from these principles, it is a science in an unqualified sense. But belief is also necessary, for knowledge of the postulates is accompanied by the acceptance of faith, and furthermore, so far as the conclusions go that are inferred from these postulates, we do not simply have science, but have faith because of these presuppositions.

And thus we see the solution not only to the first objection but also to the third, because the purpose of theology is not only to generate faith but also to produce knowledge or science. But faith comes first, and then science, as Isaiah points out: "Unless you shall have believed, you will not understand."

[To 2]

What must be said of the other objection is this. Certain forms are bound up with matter. Such are all the forms educed from the potentiality of matter, e.g. the fire form from what is potentially fire, the form of air from what is potentially air, and so on. Forms of this sort have their cause and their principles in the subject in which they are. They are known also through the principles of their subject. Other forms, however, are devoid of matter and they are not known through their cause or through the principles of their subject, but by a process of knowledge which moves from an awareness of its activity to a knowledge of the power behind it, and from a cognition of this power to knowledge of the substance having it.

What the Philosopher [Aristotle] says about a science considering parts and so on, therefore, is to be understood of forms bound up with matter. But God is not such a form, and hence the solution to the objection is clear.

Or one could say that his words are applicable to science in the proper sense of the term. But just as the name "science" can be given an extended sense, so also can the term "subject." Thus the name "subject" may be taken to hold for any autonomous subject; and the name "attribute," for any necessary predicate, whether it refers to a true accident or only to something resembling it.

[To 4]

As for the objection that singulars do not fall under a science, one answer given is that one speaks of science in two ways: either it refers to conclusions known from principles, and in this sense singular events do not fall under science; or science may be understood to mean principles known by way of the senses, and singulars do fall under science so understood. Historical events would fall under a science in this way to the extent that they make known moral truths. Thus the story of Abigail (1 *Kings* 25) makes it clear to us that "a mild answer calms wrath" (*Prov.* 15:1) and that of Nabal (1 *Kings* 25) that "a harsh word stirs up anger" (*Prov.* 15:1). Hence the solution to this objection is clear.

Another way of answering it is in terms of the various meanings of universal. One is universal by predication (e.g. "man"); another is universal in what it exemplifies (e.g. a figure held up for emulation); another is universal in its significance (e.g. the deeds of Abraham and Jacob); finally there is that which is universal in its causation (e.g. the sun, or God and Christ who are the universal cause of creation and reparation). Now in Sacred Scripture we find that which is universal in all of these senses. There are statements that are universal by predication, like *Matthew* 5:3: "Blessed are the poor in spirit, etc." or in the Old Testament: "If any male have not the flesh of his foreskin circumcised, etc." (*Gen.* 17:14). Although they are singular in themselves, the deeds of Abraham and Jacob and similar events are universal in what they exemplify, for "whatever things have been written have been written for our instruction." [*Rom.* 15:4]. Singular events according to an interior sense can signify many things, thus being universal in their significance. And there is also that which is universal in its causation, like Christ, of whom it can be said that although he is an individual person, as a cause he is universal. Obviously, then, historical events can fall under theology, where they are considered not merely in their literal sense but also according to that interior sense by reason of which they are invested with universality. But this is not the case with the other sciences.

There is a third way, however, of answering this objection, viz. that the situation is not the same in this science as in others, since the latter derive their certitude from human reason and human reason cannot be certain about singulars. That is why knowledge of singulars as such does not pertain to any other science. But this science derives its certitude from the light of faith and this light provides certitude about singular events as well. Hence the theologian is just as certain that Abraham begot Isaac as a geometer is that a triangle has three [sides]. That is why singular events can come under this science but not under others.

[To 5]

And from this the solution to the next objection is clear, viz. the objection that there is no certainty about singulars. But this must be declared to be false to the extent that singulars are considered in theology either because the light of faith provides certainty about them or because they derive certitude from the moral universal they illustrate, even though of themselves they would not be certain.

[To 6]

The solution to the next is also clear, since the objection can be understood as restricted to science taken in the proper sense. Or the objection must be understood to hold only for history in the literal sense, but not for historical events that serve as examples of moral truths. Or one could also say the historical elements in this case pertain to what is accepted on faith, and they follow from the acceptance of the theological postulates or articles of faith referred to above.

[To 7]

As for the objection that science has little or no value for virtue, it can be said that this statement must be understood of the purely speculative sciences. Theology however is not purely speculative, but is practical. One could also say that the philosopher understood this to hold for any knowledge whatsoever that does not lead to action. But this would not apply to theology, for though one might be a good preacher or theologian, if he does not wish to practice what he preaches, what he knows will profit him little or nothing.

[To 8]

To the objection that the knowledge in such a science [as theology] does not fall under the will, I grant this is true so far as the postulates of [the science] are concerned, as we have said, but it does not hold for the principles known naturally (i.e. the *dignitates*) or the conclusions that they entail. Consequently, the objection is not valid. A common conception of the mind, for example, would be "The Holy Spirit cannot lie." From this, it necessarily follows that whatever Moses said is true. And so the answer to this objection is clear.

[To 9]

As for the objection that theology ought not to be called science but wisdom, since science is concerned with the temporal but wisdom with the eternal, one must point out that theology is neither science nor wisdom in the sense that Augustine is speaking of, for he has in mind the gifts [of the Holy Spirit]. If theological knowledge be accompanied by an experience of internal grace, however, we can readily grant that it would be more proper to speak of it as wisdom than as a science. A distinction of the following sort ought to be introduced here. There is science as science, and knowledge of the liberal arts is this sort of thing. Then there is wisdom as science, and this is metaphysics or first philosophy, wherein there is no internal relish [such as that characteristic of the gift of the Holy Spirit]. There is also science as wisdom, and we find this in the Old Testament. Finally there is wisdom as wisdom, and this is in the New Testament. That theology is wisdom, then, one can readily grant, but this does not prevent it from being called a science in an extended sense of the term.

NOTES

1. Odo Rigaldus, *Quaestiones theologicae,* q. 1. Codex Vaticanus latinus 4263, fols. 43d-45c.

XV

ROGER BACON

Roger Bacon was born in England, probably between 1214 and 1220. He studied arts first at Oxford and then at Paris (*ca.* 1237). While serving as regent master at Paris he was among the first to lecture on the *Libri naturales* and the *Metaphysics* of Aristotle. Among his works dating from this period are his *Summa grammatica, Quaestiones* on Aristotle's *Physics* and *Metaphysics, Quaestiones* on the pseudo-Aristotelian *De plantis* and *Liber de causis,* and others now lost. These works are important in that they reveal one who was familiar with the recently discovered Aristotelian literature and Arabic philosophical sources. While presuming that he was closely following Aristotle, Bacon was in fact heavily influenced by the Neoplatonism of works such as the *Secret of Secrets,* and by Avicenna and Avicebron. Around 1247 he relinquished his teaching position at Paris and returned to Oxford, there to devote ten years to intensive scientific study, languages, and experimentation. Apparently during the latter part of this period he entered the Franciscan order, but failed to find there either the experimental equipment he deemed necessary or the recognition and freedom he desired for his work. Embittered and suffering from ill health, Bacon then worsened his situation by adopting certain views of extremist followers of Joachim of Fiore (a twelfth-century Cistercian mystic with an apocalytic interpretation of history), thus rendering himself suspect. As a consequence he was sent to Paris by his religious superiors, and restrictions were placed on his freedom to publicize his writings. However, his fortunes then changed for the better. His criticisms of the learning of his day and his proposal to revise the whole of human science so as better to place it at the disposal of theology had come to the attention of Pope Clement IV while he was still only a cardinal. Upon becoming Pope in 1265, he wrote to Bacon asking to see his writings on this subject, not realizing that the project was still in the planning stage. Moved to action by this request, Bacon succeeded in composing in a period of eighteen months his great encyclopedia, the *Opus maius*. This was followed shortly thereafter by his *Opus minor* and his *Opus tertium,* both completed before November, 1268. Bacon apparently returned to England and completed his *Communia mathematica, Communia naturalium, Compendium studii philosophiae,* and Greek and Hebrew grammars. However, his troubles had not ended. According to the *Chronicle of the Twenty-four Generals* (written in 1370), Jerome of Ascoli, Franciscan minister-general from 1274 until 1279, brought charges against his teachings because of "certain suspect novelties." Whatever the grounds for the charges, Bacon seems to have been imprisoned for a time, perhaps from 1277 to 1279. In any event, he was in the process of writing a *Compendium studii theologiae* when death came in 1292.

Bacon is well known for his independent spirit, his harsh criticism of contemporary thinkers, and his great emphasis on mathematics and experimental science. His chief work, the *Opus maius,* is divided into seven parts: the causes of error, philosophy as an aid to theology, the study of language, mathematics, optics, experimental science, and moral philosophy. In the first part, "Causes of Error" (see the following selections), he singles out four great obstacles hindering man in his pursuit of truth. Experimental science (any knowledge gained by experience, whether external or internal) is absolutely central to his proposed revision of human knowledge. (Cf. the second group of selections.) Finally, all other human sciences are to be subordinated to moral philosophy, fittingly described in the final part of his work. (Cf. the third selection.) This translation is by Robert B. Burke.

Opus Maius

[PART I: CAUSES OF ERROR (SELECTIONS)*]

Chapter I

A thorough consideration of knowledge consists of two things, perception of what is necessary to obtain it and then of the method of applying it to all matters that they may be directed by its means in the proper way. For by the light of knowledge the Church of God is governed, the commonwealth of the faithful is regulated, the conversion of unbelievers is secured, and those who persist in their malice can be held in check by the excellence of knowledge, so that they may be driven off from the borders of the Church in a better way than by the shedding of Christian blood. Now all matters requiring the guidance of knowledge are reduced to these four heads and no more. Therefore, I shall now try to present to your Holiness the subject of the attainment of this knowledge, not only relatively but absolutely, according to the tenor of my former letter, as best I can at the present time, in the form of a plea that will win your support until my fuller and more definite statement is completed. Since, moreover, the subjects in question are weighty and unusual, they stand in need of the grace and favor accorded to human frailty. For according to the Philosopher in the seventh book of the Metaphysics, those things which in themselves are susceptible of the most perfect cognition are for us objects of but imperfect apprehension. For truth veiled lies hidden in the deep and is placed in the abyss, as Seneca says in the seventh book of his De Beneficiis, and in the fourth of the Quaestiones Naturales; and Marcus Tullius

*From *The Opus Maius of Roger Bacon,* trans. R. B. Burke (Philadelphia: University of Pennsylvania Press, 1928), Vol. I, Part I, pp. 3-13, 19-23. Reprinted with the permission of the publisher.

says in the Hortensius that our entire intellect is obstructed by many difficulties, since it is related to those things which are most manifest in their own nature as is the eye of the night-owl or of the bat to the light of the sun, as the Philosopher declares in the second book of the Metaphysics; and as one deaf from his birth is related to the delight of harmony, as Avicenna says in the ninth book of the Metaphysics, wherefore in the investigation of truth the feebleness of our own intellect suffices for us, that we may to the best of our ability put extraneous causes and occasions of error at a farther remove from our weak power of sense perception.

Now there are four chief obstacles in grasping truth, which hinder every man, however learned, and scarcely allow any one to win a clear title to learning, namely, submission to faulty and unworthy authority, influence of custom, popular prejudice, and concealment of our own ignorance accompanied by an ostentatious display of our knowledge. Every man is entangled in these difficulties, every rank is beset. For people without distinction draw the same conclusion from three arguments, than which none could be worse, namely, for this the authority of our predecessors is adduced, this is the custom, this is the common belief; hence correct. But an opposite conclusion and a far better one should be drawn from the premises, as I shall abundantly show by authority, experience, and reason. Should, however, these three errors be refuted by the convincing force of reason, the fourth is always ready and on every one's lips for the excuse of his own ignorance, and although he has no knowledge worthy of the name, he may yet shamelessly magnify it, so that at least to the wretched satisfaction of his own folly he suppresses and evades the truth. Moreover, from these deadly banes come all the evils of the human race; for the most useful, the greatest, and most beautiful lessons of knowledge, as well as the secrets of all science and art, are unknown. But, still worse, men blinded in the fog of these four errors do not perceive their own ignorance, but with every precaution cloak and defend it so as not to find a remedy; and worst of all, although they are in the densest shadows of error, they think that they are in the full light of truth. For these reasons they reckon that truths most firmly established are at the extreme limits of falsehood, that our greatest blessings are of no moment, and our chief interests possess neither weight nor value. On the contrary, they proclaim what is most false, praise what is worst, extol what is most vile, blind to every gleam of wisdom and scorning what they can obtain with great ease. In the excess of their folly they expend their utmost efforts, consume much time, pour out large expenditures on matters of little or no use and of no merit in the judgment of a wise man. Hence it is necessary that the violence and banefulness of these four causes of all evils should be recognized in the beginning and rebuked and banished far from the consideration of science. For where these three bear sway, no reason influences, no right decides, no law binds, religion has no place, nature's mandate fails, the complexion of things is changed, their order is confounded, vice prevails, virtue is extinguished, falsehood reigns, truth is hissed off the scene. Therefore nothing is more necessary of consideration than the positive condemnation of those four errors through the chosen arguments of wise men which shall prove irrefutable. Inasmuch as the wise unite the first three together and condemn them, and since the fourth, owing to its exceptional folly, needs special treatment, I shall first attempt to show the banefulness of the three. But although authority be one of those, I am in no way speaking of that solid and sure authority, which either by God's judgment has been bestowed upon his Church, or which springs from the merit and dignity of an individual among the Saints, the perfect philosophers, and other men of science, who up to the limit of human utility are expert in the pursuit of science; but I am speaking of that authority, which without divine consent many in this world have unlawfully seized, not from the merit of their wisdom but from their presumption and desire of fame—an authority which the ignorant throng concedes to many to its own destruction by the just judgment of God. For according to Scripture "owing to the sins of the people frequently the hypocrite rules"; for I am speaking of the sophistical authorities of the irrational multitude, men who are authorities in an equivocal sense, even as the eye carved in stone or painted on canvas has the name but not the quality of an eye.

Chapter II

These three errors sacred Scripture reproves, sainted doctors condemn, canon law forbids, philosophy rebukes; but for reasons previously touched upon in regard to adducing philosophical principles, and since the judgments of philosophers in regard to these three are less widely known, I shall in the first instance adduce those judgments. Seneca indeed condemns all these three banes at once in the book of his Second Epistles near the end in a single statement. He says, "Among the reasons for our evils is the fact that we live according to examples, and are not regulated by reason but influenced by custom. That which if done by few we should not care to imitate, when many begin to do it, we do it also, influenced by numbers more than by higher motives, and an error when it has become general takes for us the place of truth." The Philosopher, in fact, through the whole course of his philosophy attacks unworthy authority and asserts in the second book of the Metaphysics that the chief sources of human error are custom and the influence of the masses. Seneca again in his book on the Happy Life says, "No man errs for himself alone, but he is the cause and author of another's error, and error transmitted from one to another tosses and drives us headlong, and we come to grief by the examples of other men." In his second book on Anger he says because of the evil of custom, "With difficulty are those vices lopped off which have grown up with us." Moreover in his book on Happiness of Life, in opposition to the common opinion he says, "Nothing involves us in greater evils than the fact that we regulate our lives by mere report, reckoning best that which has been so accepted by general consent, and we do not live according to reason but in accordance with our desire to copy others. Hence comes that heaping together of man tumbling over man. For in a great massacre of men, when the mob crowds upon itself, no one falls in such a way as not to drag his neighbor after him, and the first cause those that follow them to stumble into destruction. You may see this happening in every life." He likewise says in the same book, "The mob pits itself against reason in defence of its own bane"; and he adds, "Human affairs are not so well ordered that better counsels please the majority of us," and he continues, "A crowd is the worst of arguments." Marcus Tullius, also, in the third book of the Tusculan Disputations says, "When we have been handed over to school masters, we are not only imbued with divers errors, but truth yields to vanity and firmly established nature herself gives way to mere opinion." Also he says in the Lucullus, "Some complying with a friend or captivated by the mere discourse of some one to whom they have listened, form judgments about matters unknown to them, and driven as it were by stress of weather to some branch of study, no matter what, they cling to it as though to a rock. Many have chosen to remain in error and to defend the opinion to which they are sentimentally attached, rather than without obstinate prepossession to scrutinize that which they assert with the utmost positiveness." Because of the viciousness of custom he asks in the first book on the Divine Nature, "Is not the investigator of nature ashamed to seek testimony to the truth from minds steeped in custom?" Moreover in opposition to the notions of the mob he says in the introduction to the second book of Disputations, "Philosophy is content with few judges, shunning purposely the multitude to which it is an object of suspicion and hatred." In the same second book he says, "I think all things are the more praiseworthy if they occur without the knowledge of the public." But others attack these three errors separately. For in Adalardus' book on Questions about Nature the following query is put about weak authority: "What else is authority of this kind than a halter? Just as brute beasts are led with any kind of halter whithersoever one wishes, and do not perceive whither they are being led nor why; so not a few, captive and bound by beastlike credulity, mere authority leads off into danger." Moreover, in the book on the Eternity of the World he says, "The man who chooses one side of a question because of his love of custom cannot rightly discern the correct opinion." Averroës also at the end of his second book on the Physics says, "Custom is the chief cause hindering us from grasping many clear truths. Just as certain actions though harmful will become easy to the man accustomed to them, and for this reason he comes to believe that they are useful; similarly when one has become accustomed to believe false statements from childhood, the habit so formed will cause him to deny the truth, even as some men have become so used to eating poison that it has become to them a food." Averroës likewise maintains in his commentary on the second book of the Metaphysics that the contraries of the principles, provided they be of general repute, are more gladly received by the multitude and by those who follow the testimony of the majority, than are the fundamental principles themselves. And also Jerome in the introduction to the fifth book of his commentary on Jeremiah asserts that truth is contented with few supporters and is not dismayed by a host of foes. John Chrysostom in his commentary on Matthew says that those who have armed themselves with the multitude, have confessed themselves to be unprotected by truth.

Chapter III

THE EXPERIENCE OF THE INDIVIDUAL
DECIDES ANY MATTER WHICH HAS BEEN PROVED
BY AUTHORITIES WITH STILL GREATER CERTAINTY

For we experience in ourselves and in others that these three, involving as they often do evils, are still more frequently connected with the false. But if at any time they are united with the good and the true, the latter are almost always imperfect, and attain only a low rank in science. As a rule the daughter follows the example of her mother, the son the father's, the slave the master's, the porter the king's, the subordinate the superior's, the pupil the master's. Because it is a familiar trait of the sons of Adam to claim for themselves authority and to disseminate in the light their own standards. For all men, according to Aristotle in the fourth book of his Ethics, love their own works, as for example parents their children, poets their measures, and so on through the list. In fact, many have indulged in too great freedom in their writings, and have not hesitated even to insinuate to vicious and brutelike men the thought, Why do you not fill up your pages? Why do you not write even on the back of the sheet? These men are like a lame and blind shepherd with many sheep, which wandering through the by-paths of untruth they have neither the power nor the knowledge to recall to the more healthful pastures of science, and they are like birds desiring to fly without wings, assuming the office of a master before they have acquired the status of a good pupil. These men of necessity fall into so many errors, because lazy people, by comparing themselves with one another, come to reckon themselves lucky; just as when many competitors run a race, he whom despair of winning does not suffer to enter, no matter how precious the prize of victory appears in his eyes, nevertheless reckons himself lucky in comparison with the contestant who as he runs falls into an unseen pitfall. And thus we see with our very eyes that for one example of truth as well in science as in life there are more than a thousand examples of falsehood. For the world is full of examples of this kind, and one example of true perfection easily discovers ten thousand imperfect ones. In numbers nature has formed for us her own illustration of perfection and imperfection. A number is called perfect, the sum of whose aliquot parts exactly equals the number, but there is only one below ten, namely six; and one between ten and one hundred, namely 28; and one between one hundred and a thousand, namely 496; and one between a thousand and ten thousand, namely 8128; and so on. Would that this were the case among men, and it would be sufficient for mankind. But never has this been a fact either in life or science, nor will it be until the final destruction of sin, since not only is there a scarcity of those who are perfect in every virtue and science, but of those who have reached perfection in a single virtue or science. The first are and will be and have always been very few. For they are in fact perfect; since out of ten thousand men one is not found thus perfect either in his way of life or in the matter of wisdom. Would that of the second class of perfection there might be one in ten, and so on with the other classes, so that the perfection of numbers might be maintained in the case of human beings. But it is not so; nay, it is found to be quite the contrary. Similarly concerning custom we prove by experience in our own acts what has just been said with reference to types of individuals. Let any man you please consider his own life from his infancy, and he will find that in the majority of his acts it has been easier for him to reduce to habit what is false and evil. For, in what is good and true, repetition, such is our human frailty, is the mother of satiety, and the wretched man delights himself in the variety of things useful, according to the judgment of the authorities which I mentioned in the beginning; but he is, on the contrary, delighting in things evil and false and harmful to himself and to others. For in most of our actions, unless special grace and divine privilege intervene in the case of some perfect individuals, human corruption diligently persists in what is opposed to truth and salvation; the individual neither feels persistence in sin to be irksome, nor is prone to find vain things contemptible. But if a man from his youth should devote himself to truth in life and science, he in most of his activities persists in his imperfection and takes pleasure therein: perfection, in fact, more frequently saddens him, for it delights very few of us, and especially is this true in the rich fulness of the virtues and sciences; and for this reason youth seldom guards against error, and old age with the greatest difficulty climbs to perfection in anything. Of the mob the same statement holds good. For the great mass of mankind has always erred in regard to God's truth, and only the small body of Christians has received it; moreover, we know that most Christians are imperfect, a fact shown by the small number of saints. The same is true concerning philosophical doctrine; for the mass of mankind has always lacked the wisdom of philosophy. This is shown by the small number of philosophers. In fact, the rank and file of those devoting themselves to philosophy have always remained imperfect. For of famous philosophers Aristotle alone with his followers is stamped with the approval of all wise men, since he organized the branches of philosophy as far as was possible in his age; but nevertheless he did not reach the limit of wisdom, as will be clearly shown below.

Chapter IV

However little authority may be depended upon, it possesses, nevertheless, a name of honor, and habit is more strongly inducive to error than authority; but popular prejudice is more forceful than either of them. For authority merely entices, habit binds, popular opinion makes men obstinate and confirms them in their obstinacy. Habit is a second nature, as the Philosopher says in his book on Memory and Recollection, and in his book of Problems; and for this reason habit brings a greater force to bear than authority. Hence the Philosopher in the tenth book of his Ethics agrees with the sentiment of Jeremiah in regard to the Ethiopian's skin, saying that it is impossible or difficult for him who through habit has grown hardened in evil, to change for the better. Sallust also in his Jugurtha expresses the thought of Solomon when he says, "They spend their old age where they passed their youth." Popular sentiment in fact is far worse than other sentiments. For as Seneca says in the third book of his Declamations, "The multitude once stirred cannot preserve a due moderation." On this point John Chrysostom says in his commentary on Matthew, "They assembled to conquer by numbers him whom they were unable to overcome by their reason." We must consider carefully that the unenlightened throng is not only more energetic in its invitation to evil than the other two sources of error, but is more foolish and further removed from the pale of wisdom. For an example of perfection is drawn upon by an individual to form habit, but it suffices the throng not to sin. For in no rank of the Church is it required that the body at large should possess the perfection of the Church. For even among the religious a small number is fixed at the center of perfection, and the rest wander about on the circumference. Such is the case, as we clearly see, both in the ranks of the secular clergy and of the laity. For as with Moses so with Christ the common throng does not ascend the mountain. Nor in the transfiguration of Christ was the whole body of disciples taken with him, but only the three specially chosen; and when the multitude followed for two years Christ the teacher of perfection as he preached, it afterwards dismissed him, and finally cried out, Crucify him. For the common throng cannot continue anything that is perfect; would that it were avoiding error in life and in pursuit. We see that such is the case among the professors of philosophy as well as in the truth of our faith. For the wise have always been divided from the multitude, and they have veiled the secrets of wisdom not only from the world at large but also from the rank and file of those devoting themselves to philosophy. For this reason wise men of Greece meeting in the watches of the night devoted their leisure, apart from the multitude, to scientific collaboration, of which A. Gellius writes in his book of Attic Nights, the title indicating efforts of this kind made by learned men of Attica, that is Athenians, during the watches of the night in order to avoid the multitude. In this book he says that it is foolish to feed an ass lettuces when thistles suffice him. He is speaking of the multitude for whom rude, cheap, imperfect food of science is sufficient. Nor ought we to cast pearls before swine; for he lessens the majesty of nature who publishes broadcast her mysteries; nor do those matters remain secret of which the crowd is witness, as is shown in the book of Gems. Aristotle also says in his book of Secrets that he would break the celestial seal if he made public the secrets of nature. For this reason the wise although giving in their writings the roots of the mysteries of science have not given the branches, flowers, and fruits to the rank and file of philosophers. For they have either omitted these topics from their writings, or have veiled them in figurative language or in other ways, of which I need not speak at present. Hence according to the view of Aristotle in his book of Secrets, and of his master, Socrates, the secrets of the sciences are not written on the skins of goats and sheep so that they may be discovered by the multitude. For the wisest and most expert frequently find very great difficulty in the books of the ancients. When the Philosopher logically divides probability in his first book of Topics, he separates the multitude from the wise; for he says that that is probable which all men think, or the majority of men, or the wise; for under the term *all men* are included the multitude and the wise alike, therefore by the majority of men is meant the multitude; wherefore the insensate multitude has no partnership with the wise. This results not only from its own folly, but from the fact that in most cases it has a dull, weak head, prone to errors and productive of imperfection, at whose nod it is led in every circumstance, as I have noted in the preceding letter. Therefore, the ignorant multitude is never able to rise to the perfection of wisdom, for it is ignorant of the use of the things of greatest worth; and if by any chance it at length attains them, it turns all into evil, and accordingly by God's just judgment the paths of perfection are denied it; and it attains its greatest good when it is kept from sin. Its own name indicates all that has been said about it; for in all authors it is called the ignorant and insensate multitude. Now ignorance consists in error and imperfection, and therefore error and imperfection are native to the multitude, whose error is more frequent than its wish to perceive, however imperfectly, the truth. For many have been called but few chosen for the reception of the divine truth and of the philosophic as well. For the Philosopher says in the second book of Topics that we must think as the few, although we ought to talk as the many, considering the place and time; because to simulate at times the folly of the multitude is regarded as the highest wisdom, especially when it is in its mad mood. Hence from all these sources are inferred the evil and folly of these three causes of error, and their infinite harm to the human race. For this reason they are under suspicion in every case and not to be trusted. In an especial degree must popular prejudice be disregarded for the special reasons given, not but that at times these causes of error may hit upon the truth, but because as a rule they are involved in what is false; and very seldom do example and habit contain perfection; which moreover the multitude never attains, as I have explained before.

Chapter VIII

There is no remedy against these three evils unless with all courage we prefer strong authorities to weak ones, reason to custom, the opinions of the wise to popular prejudice; and let us not trust in the threefold argument, this has a precedent, or is the custom, or the general practice, therefore should be retained. For it is evident from what has been said before in accordance with the opinions of sacred writers and all men of science that the opposite conclusion far more logically follows from the same premises. Although the whole world be influenced by these causes of error, yet let us willingly consider what is opposed to common custom. For it is a great remedy against these evils, according to the statement of Averroës at the end of the second book of his Physics, that evil custom can be removed by the habit of considering what is opposed to it. For he bestows much labor on the opinion which is formed from habitually considering extraneous matters, confirming his conclusion by the result, and saying that for this reason popular opinion is held more firmly than the faith of those philosophizing, because the multitude is not accustomed to consider the opposite side of a question, while those philosophizing take many things into consideration. Therefore let not your Wisdom be surprised, nor your Authority consider it improper if I labor against popular custom and common precedents. For this is the only way of arriving at a consideration of truth and perfection.

Chapter IX

Not only indeed are there these general causes of evil in our vocation and in our life, but there is a fourth one worse than these three likewise common in every rank, and visibly dominating every individual. I have joined together the three causes already mentioned because the wise usually do so, and I have separated this fourth cause from the former ones on account of its especial harmfulness. For this is an extraordinary wild beast, devouring and destroying all reason, namely, the desire to appear wise, by which every man is influenced. For however little and worthless our knowledge we nevertheless extol it; we publish abroad much of which we are ignorant, where we can hide our ignorance, making a clever display that we may glory over nothing. Matters of which we are ignorant, where we cannot make a display of our knowledge, we slight, find fault with, abuse, and bring to naught, that we may not seem ignorant of any matter, glossing over our ignorance like a woman with her finery and meretricious coloring, a foul remedy. Hence we banish by this route from ourselves and from others what is most useful, important, full of every grace, and stable in its nature. This bane, moreover, in addition to its inherent harmfulness reaches the crowning point in its own baseness from the fact that it is the beginning and the source of the three causes of error already mentioned. For owing to excessive zeal in regard to our own feeling and the excusing of our ignorance there arises at once the presumption of weak authority, relying on which we extol what is ours and censure what is another's. Then since every man loves his own labors, we willingly form ours into habit. And since no man errs for himself alone, but delights in spreading abroad his madness among his neighbors, as Seneca says in the book of the Second Epistles, by our inventions we take possession of other men and give our inventions all the publicity possible. It is necessary, however, that these universal causes should be considered first, that error may be avoided and truth shine clear. For in spiritual disease the process is the same as in bodily disease; physicians learn the special and particular causes of a disease through symptoms; but the latter as well the former a knowledge of universal causes precedes, which the physician has to acquire from the processes of nature; since the Philosopher says in his book on Sense and the Sensible that where the principles of natural philosophy end the principles of medicine begin. Likewise accordingly in the cure of ignorance and error, that sane truth may be reached, before taking up the main point at issue the symptoms and particular causes must be shown; but before all universal causes are required without which neither symptoms nor particular causes show anything. For the pathway of learning from the universal to the particular is formed by nature for us, as the Philosopher says in the beginning of the Physics. For if we are ignorant of the universals we are ignorant of what follows the universals.

This fourth cause, moreover, exercised much evil influence of old, just as it is now found to be doing, a fact I make clear in the case of the theologians as well as in philosophy by experience and examples. For Moses, a most sincere man, received the wisdom of the law from God, against which Pharaoh and the Egyptians and the Hebrew people and all the nations murmured to such a degree that the chosen people of God was scarcely willing to receive this wisdom; and nevertheless the law prevailed against adversaries who neglected and hindered the wisdom they did not learn. In like manner Christ the Lord, proceeding with all guilelessness and without a shadow of deceit, and the Apostles, most sincere men, brought wisdom into the world, who met much opposition solely on account of ignorance of so great a novelty, and at length, although with the utmost difficulty, sacred truth was received. Then when sainted doctors wished to give fluent expositions of the divine law, and with the great force of the streams of wisdom to water the Church, they were reckoned for a long time heretics and inventors of falsehoods. For just as the prologues of the blessed Jerome to the Bible and his other works prove, he himself was called a corrupter of Scripture and a forger, and a sower of heresies, and in his own day was overwhelmed and unable to publish his works; but at length after his death the truth of his translation became manifest as well as his exposition, and were so widely circulated among all the churches, that no vestige of the ancient translation, that of the Seventy Interpreters, which the Church used formerly, can be found. So long as the most blessed Pope Gregory exercised his authority, his books were unassailed; but after his death famous men in the Church tried to have them burned, but they were preserved by a most gracious miracle of God and their wisdom has become manifest to the world along with their sweet truthfulness and devotion in the fullest measure. In like manner all the doctors of sacred Scripture encounter hindrance to the truth. For in refreshing men's zeal they have always met contradiction and hindrances, and yet truth gains strength and will do so until the day of Antichrist.

The same is true of philosophy. For Aristotle wished to complete the writings of earlier philosophers and to give new meaning to many things; and although a very wise man, he seemed to meet repulse and his wisdom to be under a cloud until almost our own times. For Avicenna was the first to recall to the full light the philosophy of Aristotle among the Arabs. For the rank and file of those engaged in philosophy were ignorant of Aristotle; for few attained even a slight knowledge of the philosophy of Aristotle before the time of Avicenna, a recent philosopher long after the time of Mahomet. Avicenna, moreover, the especial expounder and chief imitator of Aristotle, encountered many revolts on the part of others. For Averroës, a still greater man after these, as well as others, condemned Avicenna beyond measure; but in these times whatever Averroës says has received the approval of the wise, yet he, too, for a long time was neglected and rejected, and called in question by philosophers famous in their vocation, until gradually his wisdom has become clear and generally approved, although on some matters he has spoken less convincingly. For we know that in our own times objection had long been raised in Paris to the natural philosophy and metaphysic of Aristotle as set forth by Avicenna and Averroës, and through dense ignorance their books and those using them were excommunicated for quite long periods. Since the facts are as stated, and we today approve of the men we have mentioned as philosophers and sacred writers; and we know that every addition and increase in wisdom they have made are worthy of all favor, although in many other matters they have suffered a lessening of their authority, and in many matters they are superfluous, and in certain need correction, and in some explanation, it is clear to us that those who during their individual lives have hindered the evidences of truth and usefulness offered to them by the men mentioned above, have erred too far, and have been very harmful in this respect. But they have done this to extol their own wisdom and to palliate their ignorance. Therefore we ought to apply the same argument to our own case, so that when we reject and revile matters of which we are ignorant, we proclaim our action as a defense of our ignorance, and an exaltation of our scanty knowledge. Therefore let us permit works to be introduced rejoicing in the truth, since without doubt although with difficulty truth will prevail among wise men, until Antichrist and his precursors appear. For the goodness of God has ever been ready to increase the gift of wisdom through a succession of men and to change for the better their philosophic statements in the succession.

[PART VI: ON EXPERIMENTAL SCIENCE (SELECTIONS)]*

Chapter I

Having laid down fundamental principles of the wisdom of the Latins so far as they are found in language, mathematics, and optics, I now wish to unfold the principles of experimental science, since without experience nothing can be sufficiently known. For there are two modes of acquiring knowledge, namely, by reasoning and experience. Reasoning draws a conclusion and makes us grant the conclusion, but does not

Op. cit., Vol. II, Part VI, pp. 583-87.

make the conclusion certain, nor does it remove doubt so that the mind may rest on the intuition of truth, unless the mind discovers it by the path of experience; since many have the arguments relating to what can be known, but because they lack experience they neglect the arguments, and neither avoid what is harmful nor follow what is good. For if a man who has never seen fire should prove by adequate reasoning that fire burns and injures things and destroys them, his mind would not be satisfied thereby, nor would he avoid fire, until he placed his hand or some combustible substance in the fire, so that he might prove by experience that which reasoning taught. But when he has had actual experience of combustion his mind is made certain and rests in the full light of truth. Therefore reasoning does not suffice, but experience does.

This is also evident in mathematics, where proof is most convincing. But the mind of one who has the most convincing proof in regard to the equilateral triangle will never cleave to the conclusion without experience, nor will he heed it, but will disregard it until experience is offered him by the intersection of two circles, from either intersection of which two lines may be drawn to the extremities of the given line; but then the man accepts the conclusion without any question. Aristotle's statement, then, that proof is reasoning that causes us to know is to be understood with the proviso that the proof is accompanied by its appropriate experience, and is not to be understood of the bare proof. His statement also in the first book of the Metaphysics that those who understand the reason and the cause are wiser than those who have empiric knowledge of a fact, is spoken of such as know only the bare truth without the cause. But I am here speaking of the man who knows the reason and the cause through experience. These men are perfect in their wisdom, as Aristotle maintains in the sixth book of the Ethics, whose simple statements must be accepted as if they offered proof, as he states in the same place. . . .

But experience is of two kinds; one is gained through our external senses, and in this way we gain our experience of those things that are in the heavens by instruments made for this purpose, and of those things here below by means attested by our vision. Things that do not belong in our part of the world we know through other scientists who have had experience of them. As, for example, Aristotle on the authority of Alexander sent two thousand men through different parts of the world to gain experimental knowledge of all things that are on the surface of the earth, as Pliny bears witness in his Natural History. This experience is both human and philosophical, as far as man can act in accordance with the grace given him; but this experience does not suffice him, because it does not give full attestation in regard to things corporeal owing to its difficulty, and does not touch at all on things spiritual. It is necessary, therefore, that the intellect of man should be otherwise aided, and for this reason the holy patriarchs and prophets, who first gave sciences to the world, received illumination within and were not dependent on sense alone. The same is true of many believers since the time of Christ. For the grace of faith illuminates greatly, as also do divine inspirations, not only in things spiritual, but in things corporeal and in the sciences of philosophy; as Ptolemy states in the Centilogium, namely, that there are two roads by which we arrive at the knowledge of facts, one through the experience of philosophy, the other through divine inspiration, which is far the better way, as he says.

Moreover, there are seven stages of this internal knowledge, the first of which is reached through illuminations relating purely to the sciences. The second consists in the virtues. For the evil man is ignorant, as Aristotle says in the second book of the Ethics. Moreover, Algazel says in his Logic that the soul disfigured by sins is like a rusty mirror, in which the species of objects cannot be seen clearly; but the soul adorned with virtues is like a well-polished mirror, in which the forms of objects are clearly seen. For this reason true philosophers have labored more in morals for the honor of virtue, concluding in their own case that they cannot perceive the causes of things unless they have souls free from sins. Such is the statement of Augustine in regard to Socrates in the eighth book of the City of God, chapter III. Wherefore the Scripture says, "in a malevolent soul, etc." For it is not possible that the soul should rest in the light of truth while it is stained with sins, but like a parrot or magpie it will repeat the words of another which it has learned by long practice. The proof of this is that the beauty of truth known in its splendor attracts men to the love of it, but the proof of love is the display of a work of love. Therefore he who acts contrary to the truth must necessarily be ignorant of it, although he may know how to compose very elegant phrases, and quote the opinions of other people, like an animal that imitates the words of human beings, and like an ape that relies on the aid of men to perform its part, although it does not understand their reason. Virtue, therefore, clarifies the mind, so that a man comprehends more easily not only moral but scientific truths. I have proved this carefully in the case of many pure young men, who because of innocency of soul have attained greater proficiency than can be stated, when they have had sane advice in regard to their study. Of this number is the bearer of this present treatise, whose fundamental knowledge very few of the Latins have acquired. For since he is quite young, about twenty years of age, and very poor, nor has he been able to have teachers, nor has he spent one year in learning his great store of knowledge, nor is he a man of great genius nor of a very retentive memory, there can be no other cause except the grace of God, which owing to the purity of his soul has granted to him those things that it has as a rule refused to show to all other students. For as a spotless virgin he has departed from me, nor have I found in him any kind of mortal sin, although I have examined him carefully, and he has, therefore, a soul so bright and clear that with very little instruction he has learned more than can be estimated. And I have striven to aid in bringing it about that these two young men should be useful vessels in God's Church, to the end that they may reform by the grace of God the whole course of study of the Latins.

The third stage consists in the seven gifts of the Holy Spirit, which Isaiah enumerates. The fourth consists in the beatitudes, which the Lord defines in the Gospels. The fifth consists in the spiritual senses. The sixth consists in fruits, of which is the peace of God which passes all understanding. The seventh consists in raptures and their states according to the different ways in which people are caught up to see many things of which it is not lawful for a man to speak. And he who has had diligent training in these experiences or in several of them is able to assure himself and others not only in regard to things spiritual, but also in regard to all human sciences. Therefore since all the divisions of speculative philosophy proceed by arguments, which are either based on a point from authority or on the other points of argumentation except this division which I am now examining, we find necessary the science that is called experimental. I wish to explain it, as it is useful not only to philosophy, but to the knowledge of God, and for the direction of the whole world; just as in the preceding divisions I showed the relationship of the languages and sciences to their end, which is the divine wisdom by which all things are disposed.

[PART VII: MORAL PHILOSOPHY (SELECTION)]*

I have shown in what precedes that the knowledge of languages, mathematics, perspective, and experimental science are most useful and necessary in the pursuit of wisdom. Without these branches no one can advance as he should in wisdom, taken not only in an unrestricted sense, but also in relation to the Church of God and to the other three activities already described. I now purpose to disclose the principles of a fourth science that is better than all those previously mentioned and nobler. This science is preëminently active, that is, formative, and deals with our actions in this life and in the other. For all other sciences are called speculative. For although certain are active and formative, they are concerned with the actions of art and nature, not with morals, and they investigate the verities of things and of scientific activities which have reference to the speculative intellect and are not concerned with things pertaining to the active intellect, which is called active because it directs action, that is, good or evil action. Hence the term active is here taken in a restricted sense as applying to the actions of conduct, in accordance with which we are good or evil; although if we take the term active in a broad sense for all formative science, many other sciences are active. But this science is called in a self-explanatory way active because of the chief actions of man, which relate to virtues and vices, and to the felicity and misery of the other life.

This active science is called the moral science and the civil science, which instructs man as to his relations to God, and to his neighbor, and to himself, and proves these relations, and invites us to them and powerfully influences us thereto. For this science is concerned with the salvation of man to be perfected through virtue and felicity; and this science aspires to that salvation as far as philosophy can. From these general statements it is evident that this science is nobler than all the other branches of philosophy. For since it is the final inner purpose of human wisdom, and since the purpose is the noblest part in

*_Op. cit.,_ Vol. II, Part VII, pp. 635-40.

anything, this science is of necessity the noblest. Similarly this science alone or in chief measure is concerned with the same questions as theology; because theology considers only the five aforesaid, although in a different way, namely, in the faith of Christ. This science, moreover, contains a great deal of excellent testimony in regard to this same faith; and from afar surmises its principal articles to the great aid of the Christian faith, as what follows will make clear. But theology is the noblest of the sciences; therefore that science which is most closely related to it is nobler than the others. But that the very great utility of this science may be apparent, we must investigate its parts, to the end that we may draw what we wish from the parts and the whole.

Since, moreover, moral philosophy is the end of all branches of philosophy, the conclusions of the other sciences are the principles in it in accordance with the relationship of preceding sciences to those that follow; because the conclusions of preceding sciences are naturally assumed in those that follow. For this reason it is fitting that these conclusions in preceding sciences should be carefully proved and attested, so that they may be worthy of acceptance in the sciences that follow, as is evident from metaphysics. Therefore the principles of moral philosophy are attested in preceding sciences; and for this reason these principles should be drawn from the other sciences, not because they belong to these sciences, but because these sciences have prepared them for their mistress. Hence wherever they are found they are to be ascribed to moral philosophy, since in substance they relate to morals. And although they may be stated in other sciences, this is by grace of moral philosophy. Wherefore all such are to be considered in regard to moral philosophy and ascribed to it. Therefore if we wish to use them as they were intended to be used, they must be collected in moral science from all the other sciences. Nor is it strange if philosophers through the whole of speculative philosophy have diffused ethical principles, because they knew that these related to man's salvation; and therefore in all the sciences they have diffused beautiful thoughts, so that men might always be directed to the blessing of salvation, and that all might know that the other sciences are sought after only for the sake of that science which is the mistress of human wisdom. Therefore if I adduce from other places authorities other than those contained in books on morals, we should consider that these ought properly to be placed in this science. Nor can we deny that they have been written in books of this science, since in Latin we do not possess except in parts the philosophy of Aristotle, Avicenna, and Averroës, who are the principal authors in this subject. For just as theology perceives that truths bringing salvation belong to it, wherever it finds them, as I stated at the beginning and touched upon later, so also does moral philosophy claim as its right whatever it finds written elsewhere pertaining to it. This science is called moral science by Aristotle, and by others civil science, because it shows the rights of citizens and states. And since cities used to bear sway over countries when Rome ruled the world, this science is called civil from city [*civitas*], although it formulates the rights of kingdom and empire.

This science, moreover, in the first place teaches us to lay down the laws and obligations of life; in the second place it teaches that these are to be believed and approved, and that men are to be urged to act and live according to those laws. The first part falls under three heads; for first comes naturally man's duty to God and in respect to angelic beings; secondly, his duty to his neighbor; and thirdly, his duty to himself, just as the Scripture states. For in the first place in the books of Moses are the commands and laws in regard to God and divine worship. In the second place are those regarding a man's relationship to his neighbor in the same books and in those that follow. In the third place instruction is given in morals, as in the books of Solomon. Similarly in the New Testament these three alone are contained. For a man cannot assume other duties.

Not only on account of the first but of all that follows is it necessary that the principles of this science, by which the others are verified, should be set forth at the beginning. Certain of these principles are purely principles and are capable of being expressed only metaphysically. Others, although they are principles with respect to what follows, either are first conclusions of this science, or although they rejoice in some privilege of a principle, yet because of their very great difficulty, and because they meet with less contradiction, and because of their very great utility with regard to what follows, ought to be sufficiently demonstrated. Just as Aristotle in the beginning of his natural philosophy proves the first principle of that science, namely, that there is motion in opposition to those who maintained that there is only the one immovable. But we must note that metaphysics and moral philosophy are very closely allied; for each is concerned with God, the angels, life eternal, and many questions of this kind, although in different ways. For metaphysics through the common principles of all sciences investigates qualities metaphysically, and through the corporeal investigates the spiritual, and through the created discovers the Creator, and through the present life deals with the future life, and furnishes much introductory matter to moral philosophy. Metaphysics inquires into these subjects because of civil science, so that we have accordingly the right to unite this science with metaphysics, in order that the principles that must be explained in metaphysics may be assumed here, lest I should confound sciences differing from each other if I try to prove in this science what properly belongs to metaphysics.

I state, therefore, that God must exist just as this fact must be proved in metaphysics: second, that God's existence is naturally known to every man; and third, that God is of infinite power and of infinite goodness, and coupled with this that he is of infinite substance and essence, so that it follows that he is best, wisest, and most powerful. Fourth, that God is one in essence and not more than one. Fifth, that not only is God one in essence but triune in another way, which must in general be explained by the metaphysician, but here must be unfolded in special doctrinal form. Sixth, that he has created all things and rules in the realm of nature. Seventh, that besides corporeal things he has created spiritual substances which we call intelligences and angels; because intelligence is a term denoting a nature, but angel is a term denoting an office. This science inquires also how many there are, and what are the activities of these intelligences, in accordance with their relation to metaphysics, as far as it is possible for them to be known by human intelligence. Eighth, that besides angels he has made other spiritual substances which are the rational souls in men. Ninth, that he has made these immortal. Tenth, that the felicity of the other life is the highest good. Eleventh, that man is capable of this felicity. Twelfth, that God has the moral direction of the human race, just as he directs all else in the realm of nature. Thirteenth, that to those who live aright in accordance with God's direction God promises future felicity, just as Avicenna teaches in the tenth book of the Metaphysics, and that to those who live an evil life a horrible future unhappiness is due. Fourteenth, that worship is due to God with all reverence and devotion. Fifteenth, that just as a man's conduct toward God is regulated by the reverence required, so is his conduct toward his neighbor regulated by justice and peace, and his duty to himself by integrity of life. Sixteenth, that a man cannot by his own effort know how to please God with the worship required, nor how he should conduct himself as regards his neighbor and as regards himself, but he requires that the truth be revealed to him in these things. Seventeenth, that revelation must be made to one only; that this one must be the mediator of God and mankind, and the vicar of God on earth, to whom the whole human race is subject, and who must be believed without contradiction when it has been proved with certainty that he is such as has just been described; and he is the lawgiver and the high priest who in things temporal and spiritual has full power, as it were, a human God, as Avicenna says in the tenth book of the Metaphysics, whom it is lawful to adore after God.

By these principles metaphysics is united with moral philosophy, and approaches it as its final purpose. Avicenna thus beautifully joins them at the end of his Metaphysics. But the remaining principles belong to this science and are not to be explained in metaphysics, although Avicenna adds a number of them. But in the beginning of his book he gives as a reason for this the fact that he had not finished his Moral Philosophy and did not know whether he would complete it; and therefore he mingled with these principles many which properly belong to moral philosophy, as is evident to the inquirer. After these have been considered, the lawgiver at the beginning must take up the properties of God in particular, and of angels, and the felicity and misery of the other life, and the immortality of our bodies after the resurrection, and similar subjects to which the metaphysician could not aspire. For he is concerned in all these matters chiefly with the question as to existence; because it is his special function to make this question clear in regard to all matters, because he considers entity and being in their common properties. But other sciences take up the other questions involved in things; namely, what each one is, of what kind and size, and the like, in accordance with the ten categories. The moral philosopher, however, is not to explain all the secrets of God and of angels and of other questions; but he should explain those things that are needful for the multitude, and in which all men should agree, lest they fall into doubts and heresies, as Avicenna teaches in the Principles of Moral Philosophy.

I say, therefore, that moral philosophy in the first place explains the triune nature of God, a truth which the lawgiver holds through revelation more than through reason. But reason, the source from which philosophers have made many statements in regard to divine things in particular which transcend human reason and fall under revelation, has been touched upon already in the section on mathematics. For it was shown there how they could possess many noble truths regarding God, which were disclosed by a revelation made to them, as the apostle says, "For God revealed these things." But he revealed them rather to the patriarchs and prophets, who, it is agreed, had a revelation, and from whom the philosophers learned all things, as was clearly proved above. For the patriarchs and prophets handled divine things by the methods of theology or prophecy, but also by those of philosophy, because they discovered the whole of philosophy, as has been proved in the second part of this work. Moreover, the metaphysician was able to teach acceptably that God exists, and that he is naturally known, and that he is of infinite power, and that he is one, and that he is triune. But the mode in which the trinity exists he was not able to explain fully; and therefore this must be attested here. . . .

XVI

ST. BONAVENTURE

JOHN OF FIDANZA, known as St. Bonaventure, the "Seraphic Doctor," was born at Bagnorea near Viterbo in Tuscany around 1217. After becoming a master of arts in Paris, he joined the Franciscan order there (*ca.* 1243), taking the name *Bonaventura.* He began his study of theology under Alexander of Hales, the first Franciscan regent master at Paris. As a bachelor he lectured first on the Scriptures (1248) and then (1250-52) on the *Sentences* of Peter Lombard. His *Commentary on the Sentences* is regarded as perhaps the most perfect example of this form of medieval literature. Licensed by the chancellor of the university in 1253, he functioned as regent master of theology until 1257, when he was elected minister general or head of the Franciscan order. Due to the controversy between the secular masters and the mendicant friars, however, it was not until 1257 that he and Thomas Aquinas were formally received into the masters' guild. By that time Bonaventure had resigned his chair at the university to devote himself to the administration of the Franciscan order.

Though often absent on business for the order or the Church, Bonaventure continued to make Paris his general headquarters and retained his interest in academic affairs. He composed such works as the *Breviloquium* (a compendium of theology remarkable for its Christocentric orientation), *De reductione artium ad theologiam* (how all learning serves theology), and the *Itinerarium* or *Journey of the Mind to God.* All three reveal a striking gift for integrating and synthesizing the learning of the day. But the last two also served the practical purpose of silencing the anti-intellectuals among the friars, who claimed the academic life was incompatible with the ascetical aims of a follower of Francis of Assisi. More than anyone else, Bonaventure was largely responsible for the Franciscans being referred to in medieval times as "the teaching order," a title they shared solely with the Dominicans.

Various sermons he preached in Paris during his generalate, and especially the last two series of *Collationes,* or informal evening lectures given during Lent to students and faculty of the Paris house of studies, reflect his growing concern with the rationalistic cult of Aristotle and Averroës. This cult threatened the *raison d'être* of speculative theology and led to the condemnations of 1270.

In 1273 Bonaventure left Paris to become a cardinal bishop and to work with Pope Gregory X in organizing the second ecumenical council of Lyons. Here he played a major role in healing the rift between Greek and Latin Christendom. On July 15, 1274, shortly before the close of the council, Bonaventure died. He was buried solemnly in the presence of the Pope and delegates in the Franciscan church in Lyons.

For Bonaventure, as for all the scholastics of his day, it was Aristotle who provided the basic philosophic framework of speculation. But in consolidating the theological opposition to current "Averroistic rationalism" under the aegis of Augustine, Bonaventure brought about a renewed interest in Augustine's specific contributions to philosophy in such members of his "school" as Matthew of Aquasparta, Roger Marston, and John Peckham. Some of these Augustinian themes are reflected in the following selections translated by A. B. Wolter especially for this volume.

Is God's Existence a Truth That Cannot Be Doubted?[1]

There is a threefold way of showing that it is such a truth. The first is this: Every truth impressed upon all minds is a truth that cannot be questioned. The second is this: Any truth proclaimed by every creature is an indubitable truth. The third is this: Any truth is unquestionable if it is in itself most certain and evident.

[The First Way]

As to the first way, our procedure is to show both by authorities and by rational arguments that God's existence is something impressed upon every reasoning mind.

Damascene, in [*The Orthodox Faith*] Bk. I, chap. 3, says: "The knowledge of God's existence is implanted in us by nature."

Hugh [of St. Victor] speaks in a like vein: "God so tempered man's knowledge of himself that he can never be wholly ignorant that God is even as he can never fully comprehend what God is" [*On the Sacraments,* Bk. I, p. 3, chap. 1].

Boethius, likewise, declares: "A passionate desire for the true and the good has been implanted in the minds of men." [*On the Consolation of Philosophy,* III, 2]. A desire for what is true and good, however, presupposes a knowledge of the same. Consequently, impressed upon men's minds is both a knowledge of what is good and true as well as a passionate desire for what is most desirable. This good, however, is God. Therefore, etc.

Speaking of the Trinity, Augustine says in several places [Cf. e.g. *On the Trinity,* IX, chap. 2; XII, chap. 4; XIV, chap. 8] that its image [in the soul] consists in mind, knowledge, and love and that the soul is aware of this image in itself when it refers it to God. But if to be an image of God is something impressed by nature upon the soul, then the latter possesses a knowledge of God that has been implanted in it naturally. But the first thing knowable of God is that he is, therefore this is naturally implanted in the human mind.

The Philosopher [Aristotle], likewise, says that it would be incongruous if the most noble things we have would remain hidden from us [*Post. Analytics* II, chap. 19 99b 25]. Since God's existence is a most noble truth that is right there before us, it is incongruous that it should remain hidden from the human intellect.

Likewise, a desire for wisdom has been implanted in the minds of men, for the Philosopher says [*Metaphysics* I, chap. 1]: "All men by nature desire to know." But the most desirable wisdom is eternal. It is the desire for such, then, that is most deeply impressed upon the human mind. As we said before, however, there is no love for what is completely unknown. Consequently, some knowledge of this highest wisdom must be implanted in the human mind. But this means, first of all, knowing that God or Wisdom itself exists. Therefore, etc.

Likewise, the desire for happiness is so much a part of us that no one can doubt whether another wishes to be happy, as Augustine says in several places. Now happiness consists in the highest good, which is God. If then such a desire cannot exist without knowledge of some kind, knowledge that God or the highest good exists must needs be implanted in the very soul itself.

Likewise, the desire for peace is implanted in the very soul in such a way that it is sought even in what is opposed to it. Not even demons or the damned can be robbed of this desire as *The City of God,* Bk. XIX, [chap. 13], shows. But if a rational mind can find peace only in a being which is immutable and eternal, and desire presupposes an idea or knowledge, then knowledge of an immutable and eternal being is implanted in a rational spirit.

Likewise, impressed in the soul is a hatred of what is false. But hate is sparked by love. Consequently, even more strongly has a love for what is true been stamped upon it, especially for that [Truth] in whose likeness it was created. But if this be the First Truth then it follows of necessity that knowledge of the First Truth is impressed upon the rational mind. The fact that a hatred of the false is in truth implanted in the human mind is evident from this: no one wants to be deceived, as Augustine points out in his *Confessions,* Bk. X, [chap. 23].

In *The City of God*, Bk. XIV, [chap. 7], he goes on to show that hatred is caused by love, for no one hates anything unless he loves its opposite.

Likewise, self-knowledge is implanted in the human soul to this extent that of itself, the soul is both knowable and present to itself. But God is of himself both knowable and most intimately present to the soul. Consequently, a knowledge of God himself is implanted in one's very soul. You may object that there is no parity between the two cases, since the soul is proportionate to itself, whereas this proportionateness is lacking between God and the soul. This objection, however, does not hold water, for if proportionateness were a necessary prerequisite for knowledge, the soul would never arrive at any knowledge of God since it never becomes commensurate whether by nature, grace, or glory.

By these reasons, then, God's existence is shown to be something that the human mind cannot doubt, as it is naturally implanted in the mind. For one doubts only that of which he has no certain knowledge.

[The Second Way]

A second way of establishing this same conclusion is the following: Any truth which is proclaimed by every creature is one which cannot be questioned. That every creature indeed cries out that God exists is established from these ten self-evident postulates, given their antecedents.

If a being that is posterior exists, there is also a being which is prior, for nothing is posterior except by reason of something prior. If then there is a universe of posterior things, it is necessary that a First Being exists. If one must assume that priority and posteriority exist among creatures, then the realm of creatures implies and proclaims a first principle.

Also, if there is a being dependent on another, there is a being not dependent on another, for nothing can bring itself from nonexistence to existence. Therefore, a primary reason for bringing things into existence is required in the form of a First Being which is not brought into existence. If the being dependent upon another be called created, then, and that which is not so dependent be called the uncreated being, which is God, then all the differential attributes of being imply that God exists.

Also, if a contingent being exists a necessary being exists, since what is possible bespeaks an indifference to existence and nonexistence. But nothing can be indifferent to such unless it be by reason of something which is wholly determined to existence. If a necessary being, lacking all contingency, then is nothing other than God, and all else has something of contingency about it, then every difference of being implies that God exists.

Also, if there is relative being, there is absolute being, for what is relative can only terminate at what is absolute. But an absolute being dependent on nothing can only be something which has not received anything from another. But this is the First Being. All other beings, however, have something of dependence about them. Therefore, every difference of being necessarily implies that God exists.

Also, if there is being in an imperfect and qualified sense of the word, then there is being in an unqualified sense of the word. For what is being in a qualified sense can neither exist nor be understood unless it be understood by reference to what is perfect being, just as a privation cannot be understood save in reference to what is had. If, therefore, every created being is only in part being, and only the uncreated being is simply and perfectly such, then every difference of being necessarily implies that God exists.

Likewise, if something exists for the sake of another, then there is a being which exists for its own sake; otherwise nothing would be good. But a being which exists for its own sake can only be one than which nothing is better. This indeed is God himself. Therefore, since everything else is ordered to the latter, the whole realm of beings implies God so far as both existence and understanding are concerned.

Also, if there is being by participation, there is a being that is such of its essence. For we only speak of participation with reference to what is possessed essentially by some thing, since every thing accidentally such may be reduced to what is such essentially. Now every being other than the first, which is God, has being by participation. He alone has being by reason of his essence. Therefore, etc.

Likewise, if there is a potential being then there is a being that is actual, for no potency is reducible to act save by a being in act, nor would there be a potency if it were not reducible to act. If, then, a being which is pure act, possessing nothing that is only potential, is none other than God, then every other being implies necessarily that God exists.

Likewise, if there is composite being, there is a simple being, for what is composite does not have existence of itself. It is necessary then that it originate from what is simple. But a being which is most simple, lacking all composition whatsoever, is none other than the First Being: therefore, every other being implies God.

Likewise, if changeable being exists, then unchangeable being exists: for, according to what the Philosopher proves [in *Physics* VIII, chap. 5 and *Metaphysics* XI, chap. 7], motion is from a being at rest and for the sake of a being at rest. If a being wholly immutable, then, is none other than the First Being, which is God, and all else is created, and by that very fact, mutable, then God's existence is implied by any difference of being.

From these ten necessary and manifest postulates then, it follows that all the differences or divisions of being imply and proclaim that God exists. If every such truth, then, is a truth that cannot be doubted, God's existence must needs be an unquestionable truth.

[The Third Way]

The same conclusion is shown by a third way as follows: Every truth that is so certain that it cannot be thought not to be, is an indubitable truth. But God's existence is just such a truth. Therefore, etc. The first of these statements is self-evident; the second is shown in a variety of ways.

For Anselm declares in the *Proslogion,* chapter four: "I give thanks to thee, gracious Lord, because what I formerly believed by thy bounty, I now so understand by thy illumination that even if I were unwilling to believe that thou dost exist, I should be unable not to understand this to be true."

Likewise, Anselm proves this same point in the following way: God is that than which nothing greater can be thought of. But what is such that it cannot be conceived of as nonexistent is more true than something which can be so conceived. Therefore, if God is that than which nothing greater can be conceived, God cannot be conceived not to be.

Likewise, a being than which nothing greater can be conceived is of such a nature that it cannot be conceived unless it be in reality. For if it exists in thought only, then it is no longer a being, than which nothing greater can be conceived. Therefore, if such a being is thought to exist, it is necessary that such a being exist in reality as cannot be thought not to exist.

Likewise, says Anselm: "Thou alone art whatever it is better to be than not to be." But every unquestionable truth is better than every questionable truth. Therefore, unquestionable existence is to be ascribed to God rather than that which is questionable.

Augustine, likewise, says in the *Soliloquies* [I, chap. 8] that no truth can be seen except through the First Truth. But the truth by virtue of which all other truths are seen is that which is the most unquestionable truth of all. Therefore, not only is God's existence an unquestionable truth but one cannot conceive of any that is more so. Therefore, there is such a truth as cannot be conceived not to be.

He also proves this point [*ibid.* chap. 15] in this fashion: Whatever can be thought of can be stated. But one cannot say that God does not exist without saying at the same time that God exists. This is clear, because if no truth exists, then this is true: "No truth exists." And if this latter is true, then some truth exists. Now if some truth exists, the First Truth exists. Consequently, if it cannot be stated that God does not exist, neither can such be thought of.

Likewise, a truth is better known the more universal and prior it is. But that truth which states that a First Being exists is the first of all truths so far as both reality and our way of thinking about it are concerned. Therefore, it must be most certain and evident. But axiomatic truths, which are common property of the [human] mind are, by reason of their priority, so evident that they cannot be thought not to be. No intellect, then, can conceive the First Truth itself as nonexistent nor can it doubt about it.

Likewise, "there is no proposition more true than that in which the same thing is predicated of itself" [Boethius in *On Interpretation* II, chap. 4]. When I say "God exists," however, the existence predicated of him is wholly identical with God, for he is his very existence. No truth then is more evident or true than that in which existence is asserted of God. No one then can think it false or question it.

Likewise, no one can fail to know that "The best is best" is true; no one can think it is false. But that being which is most complete is the best. Everything that is most complete, however, is by that very fact something which actually exists. Therefore, if the best is best, the best exists. One can argue in a similar vein that if God is God, God exists. Now the antecedent is so true that it could not be conceived not to be. God's existence, then, is an indubitable truth.

[Objections to the Above]

Quite the contrary, however, God's existence is a truth one can question and he can be thought of as not existing.

[GOD CAN BE CONCEIVED NOT TO BE]

The following arguments show that God can be conceived not to be.

1. According to the Psalms (13:1) "The fool says in his heart, 'There is no God.' " "To say in one's heart," however, is to think. Hence, at least a fool can think of God as nonexistent.

2. Damascene, too, in [*The Orthodox Faith*], Bk. I, chap. 3, declares: "The pernicious malice of human nature has so prevailed that it leads some to such damnable and irrational depths of evil that they say: 'God does not exist'." Consequently, God can be conceived as nonexistent by evil men at least.

3. Likewise, as we read in the first epistle to the Corinthians, chap. 8 [v. 4]: "There is no such a thing as an idol." To conceive of God as an idol is the same as thinking he does not exist. God can be and at times is thought to be an idol. Therefore, one can think of God as nothing.

4. Likewise, one can think of anything that can mean something. But God's nonexistence can be meant, for example, by the proposition "God does not exist." Therefore, it is also possible to think this.

5. Objection, too, is taken to Augustine's argument that the proposition "No truth exists" implies that some truth exists. For if this proposition is true, then it has a contradictory. But no proposition entails or assumes its contradictory statement. On the contrary, it assumes it is not the case. It does not follow, therefore, from the fact that no truth exists that some truth exists.

6. Objection is also raised to Anselm's argument, where he proves that God exists from the fact that we have in mind a being greater than which nothing can be conceived. For on like grounds one might think that if someone were to conceive of an island greater than which nothing could be conceived, such an island would really exist. If such an argument is invalid, however, then so is Anselm's.

7. One can also question to what extent one can say that God cannot be conceived as not existing. If this means it cannot enter the mind, this is clearly false. If it means merely that in so thinking we think what is untrue, then on like grounds every necessary truth would be a truth of this kind.

[GOD'S EXISTENCE CAN BE QUESTIONED]

It is also shown that God's existence is a truth that can be questioned.

8. According to Richard of St. Victor: "Nothing is held with greater certainty than what we grasp by faith" [*On the Trinity* I, chap. 2] But a doubt can be entertained about what we hold by faith. A fortiori, then, we can doubt about any other known thing.

9. Things most hidden likewise admit of the greatest doubt. But God is most hidden, since he "dwells in light inaccessible" [I Tim. 6:16]. Consequently, one can doubt about him most of all. If we can doubt about other things, then a fortiori we can doubt about him.

10. Then too it is possible to doubt about things which are on a par with or inferior to the soul. But such things are more readily accessible to the soul than those above it. If God's existence is a truth which is above the human intellect, then, it seems that this especially can be doubted.

11. So far as God is concerned, for him to exist is for him to be just. But it is possible to doubt whether he is just. Consequently, one can doubt equally whether he is.

12. Then too, one strives in vain to prove what cannot be doubted. If no one can doubt the existence of God, then, he labors in vain who tries to prove this. If the saints and doctors then have not wasted their efforts by proving this, it follows that it is possible to have doubts about it.

13. Likewise, unless one knows what a whole is, he does not know this principle: "Every whole is greater than its part." Therefore, no one knows that God is, unless he knows what God is. If what God is can be doubted, then it can also be doubted whether he exists.

14. Then too, there would be no merit in believing that God exists, if this could not be subject to any doubt. But to believe that God exists is the starting point for all merit, for we read in the epistle to the Hebrews, chapter 11 [v. 6]: "For he who comes to God must believe that God exists, etc." If this falls within the sphere of merit, then it also falls within the sphere of the doubtful.

[Solution to the Question]

My answer is this. To understand what was said above, keep in mind that the indubitable is defined in terms of the inability to doubt. Our ability to doubt however stems from a twofold source. It arises either from the exercise of reason or from a defect of reason. The first says something about both the knower and the thing known whereas the second says something only about the knower. A truth which is questionable on the first count lacks evidence either in itself or with reference to the means of proof or as regards the mind which grasps it. Now the truth that God exists lacks evidence in none of these three ways.

For there is certain evidence so far as the knower is concerned, since a knowledge of this truth is congenital to the human mind insofar as the latter is an image [of the Trinity] and has implanted within it a natural desire, and hence a knowledge and likeness of that in whose image it was made and toward which it naturally tends, that it may be made happy.

There is also greater certainty as regards the reason establishing [the truth]. For all creatures, be they viewed from the vantage point of their perfectibility or their defects, cry out loud and strong that a God exists, whom they need because of their imperfection and from whom they receive their perfection. Consequently, in proportion to their greater or lesser perfection, some creatures cry loudly, others still louder, and others still shout the loudest of all that God exists.

This truth considered in itself is also most certain, for the very reason that it is a first and a most immediate truth, one in which not only is the cause of the predicate included in the subject, but one where the thing itself is wholly identical with both the being which is predicated and the subject of which it is predicated. Just as the union of what is most disparate is completely repugnant to our mind (for no intellect can conceive that some one thing is and is not at the same time), so too is it repugnant to our mind to divide what is wholly one and undivided. And therefore just as it is most evidently false that the same thing both be and not be, so too is it most evidently false that the same thing be that which in the highest measure exists and that which in no way exists. And so the truth that the first and highest being exists is most evident. And therefore, if indubitable is understood to mean that from which all doubt has been removed by a process of reasoning, God's existence is an unquestionable truth for whether the mind searches within, without or above itself, so long as it proceeds rationally, it knows certainly and unquestionably that God exists.

If we take the second meaning of indubitable, which excludes doubts arising from a defect of reason, we can grant that human deficiency makes it possible that some can doubt whether God exists. And in this respect there are three ways in which there may be a defect in the understanding of the knower accordingly as it involves an act of apprehending, an act of judging, or the process of fully analyzing. Doubt occurs in virtue of the act of apprehending if the meaning of the name God is not fully or correctly understood and one grasps only some of the essentials of what is meant. Thus the Gentiles regarded as God whatever was above man and could foresee something of the future. Therefore they believed idols to be gods and adored them as gods because they uttered some true predictions about what was to come. So far as the act of judgment is concerned, doubt may arise when the inference is based on partial knowledge. Thus the fool, failing to see how justice is manifested in the case of the wicked, infers there is no governance in the universe, and from this, that there is no first and supreme ruler, who is the all high and glorious God. Doubt can also arise in virtue of the act of analysis or resolution, if the carnal intellect does not know how to trace things back beyond what is evident from the senses as are bodily things. It was on this score that some thought that this visible sun, which holds a primary position among bodily creatures, was God, because they knew not how to trace things back to substances that are not corporeal or to first principles of things. And it is in this fashion that a doubt about the existence of God can arise in virtue of some defect of intellect itself in apprehending, judging, or analyzing fully what is involved. And someone whose mind is defective in this way can think that God does not exist because the significance of this name is not sufficiently or fully understood. But where there is an intellect which fully grasps the meaning of this name "God," not only is it unable to doubt that God exists, but it is not even able to conceive of him as nonexistent. Consequently, the reasons which prove this are to be admitted as valid.

[Reply to the Objections]

[To 1, 2 and 3] It is already clear how one should reply to the first objection based on the Psalms or Damascene. For it has to do with the kind of doubt that comes from a defect of

reason such as we find in a foolish mind which, by reason of a lack of insight or light, incompletely resolves what is involved or judges incorrectly or does not fully comprehend the meaning of this word "God." For the intellect itself has in itself in virtue of what is proper to its state sufficient light to repel this doubt and to extricate itself from its folly. Whence the foolish mind voluntarily rather than by constraint considers the matter in a deficient manner, so that the defect is on the part of the intellect itself and not because of any deficiency on the part of the thing known.

And this gives answer to the objection concerning the idol. For the Gentile thinks that God is an idol because his apprehension of what God is is deficient, since he does not consider him as the highest and best but merely as something which can do what man cannot. And that is why the error of deception and wavering of doubt can befall him. It is his own stubbornness that causes him to fall into error, so that he is without any excuse. But for all that, he is not completely deprived of the knowledge of God, for though in his perversity he desires to kneel to an idol, he has a natural instinct to worship God, against which he struggles when he throws himself into voluntary error.

[To 4] As for the objection that we can think of whatever we mean, it must be said that there are two ways in which we can think of a thing, namely by mere thought or by thought coupled with assent. So far as mere thought is concerned, what is false can be thought of as true and what is manifestly false can be thought of as manifestly true. But only what is either true or probable can be thought of by thought coupled with assent. Thought in the first sense is coextensive with speech, whereas thought in the second sense is more restricted. It is the latter that both Anselm and Augustine have in mind, and it is said of this kind of thought that God cannot be thought not to exist.

[To 5] As for the objection to Augustine's argument that a contradiction does not entail its contradictory, we must admit this is true so far as they are contradictories. But you must keep in mind that an affirmative proposition makes a double assertion: one in which the predicate is affirmed of the subject and the other in which the proposition is asserted to be true. By virtue of the first assertion an affirmative proposition is differentiated from a negative one, which denies the predicate of the subject. So far as the second assertion is concerned, how-

ever, affirmative and negative statements agree since they both assert something to be true. Contradiction is concerned not with the second type of assertion but with the first. For when it is stated that no truth exists, insofar as it negates the predicate of the subject this proposition does not imply its opposite, viz. that some truth exists. But to the extent that it asserts this to be true, it does entail that some truth exists. Nor should we be amazed at this, for just as every evil presupposes good, so too the false implies what is true. Consequently, this falsehood which states that no truth exists—since it deletes all truth by denying the predicate of the subject, yet assumes some truth by stating that it is true—includes both parts of a contradiction. Therefore, from the consideration of both aspects we can infer that it is false in itself and unintelligible to a mind that understands it aright. And it is this that Augustine desires to say.

[To 6] As for the objection about the island raised against Anselm's argument, one must insist that there is no parity here. For when I speak of a being than which nothing better or greater can be conceived, there is no repugnance between the subject and what is implied therein. Consequently, one can think of it as reasonable. But when I speak of an island than which nothing greater can be conceived, there is a repugnance between the subject and what is implied thereby. For island bespeaks an imperfect being, whereas the implication concerns a most perfect being. Since there is "opposition in what is added" [cf. Aristotle, *On Interpretation* II, chap. 2] therefore, the conception is irrational and in thinking it the intellect contradicts itself. It is not surprising then that we are unable to infer that what we are thinking of exists in reality. The case is quite different, however, with a being, or with God, where this opposition is lacking.

[To 7] From what has been said, the answer to the query, "How far are we unable to think of God's being as not being?" is clear. It is not a question of being unable to understand what the words signify or what is meant by the statement "God does not exist." It is only that God's being is something so evident in itself and so certain to the knower, that if he desires to consider it correctly, nothing can keep him from knowing the truth. For it is a most evident and immediate truth. There is no time or place or thing or thinker for whom it does not hold good. This is not so for other created truths.

[To 8] To the objection that we hold nothing to be more

certain than what we grasp by faith, one must say that while this holds good for the certitude with which we adhere to the truth, this is not the case with that certitude which is based on understanding, as is clearly apparent to one who considers the matter.

[To 9] As for the objection that this is a hidden truth and consequently most questionable, this must be pointed out. Although God be simple and uniform in himself, in one way he is hidden, in another manifest, as the Apostle hints in the first chapter of the epistle to the Romans: "What may be known about God is manifest to them." For some, to whom the Trinity of persons is not evident, find the trinity of attributes appropriated to them to be evident. And to some to whom the latter is not manifest, the unity of essence is evident. And the very Trinity of God is clear to one for whom the unity of essence is not evident. But what is first manifested about God is his very being and so far as this is concerned, he is not hidden but evident. This then is not questionable, but beyond doubt.

[To 10] As for the objection that the soul doubts about things beneath it or on a par with it, one must insist that this does not hold water. For while it is true that by nature God's being is above that of the soul, through knowledge he is within the soul and he is represented in the external world and every creature persuades us of this truth which is known and entailed by every truth.

[To 11] As for the objection that for God to exist and God to be just is the same, it must be declared that this does not follow. For while the two may be the same in themselves, this does not hold true of notions by which they are grasped or the effects in which they are mirrored. One can be evident, then, while the other is not.

[To 12] As for the objection that one labors in vain to prove what is unquestionable, it should be pointed out that this truth requires proof not because of any lack of evidence in itself, for it is already clear, but because on our part there may be something wrong about the way we are thinking about the matter. The arguments used in such a case, consequently, are more of the nature of an intellectual exercise than reasons which provide evidence of, or show forth the proven truth.

[To 13] As for the objection that unless one knows the terms he does not know principles, it must be conceded that this is true. But knowledge of some terms is hidden whereas that

of others is manifest. Furthermore, the knowledge one has of the meaning of a term may be more or less complete or most perfect. In these terms, the ability to know what God is perfectly and fully and in a comprehensive way is something proper to God alone. To know this clearly and perspicuously, however, is how the blessed [in heaven] possess this truth. But it may be known only in part and obscurely. And it is in this fashion that God is recognized to be the first and highest principle of all mundane things. This, considered in itself, is something that can be clear to all, for since anyone may know that he did not always exist, he knows that he had a beginning, and that the same is true of other things. And to the extent that this knowledge presents itself to all, and when grasped, it is known that God exists, to that extent this truth in itself is unquestionable for all.

[To 14] As for the objection that there is no merit in believing what cannot be doubted, this can be said: The reason belief in God is meritorious is not because of itself, but only inasmuch as it is the basis for an article of faith, such as God is triune, which rests upon it. For it is by reason of the latter that it can become a matter of merit, since if this alone were believed it would not produce merit. Now the Apostle speaks of this truth of God's existence insofar as it is the foundation for other truths one can believe. It is this basic truth that is implanted by nature in man lest, if the human mind were to know nothing of God in virtue of its own nature, it might excuse itself on the grounds of ignorance. And this is what Master Hugh says: "Therefore, from the beginning God wished to be neither completely hidden nor completely manifest to human consciousness, lest, were he fully manifest, faith would be without merit and there would be no room for a lack of faith since the latter would be convicted from the manifest, and faith in the hidden would not be exercised. But if he were entirely hidden, faith indeed would not be bolstered by knowledge and a lack of it would be excusable on the grounds of ignorance. Hence it was necessary that God should show himself obscurely, lest he remain completely unknown because he is completely hidden. And again it was necessary that having disclosed himself and having been recognized to some extent, he conceal himself lest he be wholly manifest. And this he did that man's mind might be stimulated by what was known and challenged by what was hidden" [Hugh of St. Victor, *On the Sacraments,* Bk. I, part 3, chap. 2].

Theory of Illumination[2]

[IS WHATEVER WE KNOW FOR CERTAIN KNOWN IN THE ETERNAL REASONS THEMSELVES?]

. . . I reply: . . . Take note that one can take the statement that whatever is known for certain is known in the light of eternal reasons in one of three ways. *One way* of understanding it is that the evidence from the eternal light is the entire and only reason why we know something for certain. Now this view is not the most correct one. If it were, there would be no knowledge of things except in the Word, and hence no difference between the knowledge in this life and that in heaven, or between knowledge of a thing in its own right and knowledge of it in the Word. Neither would the knowledge of science differ from that of wisdom, or the knowledge of nature differ from that of grace, or that of reason from that of revelation. But since all this is false, one ought not to hold this interpretation. But this view that nothing is known for certain save in the world of intelligibles and archetypes (a view which some have proposed and which was that of the early academicians) gives birth to the error pointed out by Augustine (*Against the Academics,* Bk. II), viz. since this world of intelligibles is hidden from men's minds, nothing at all can be known for sure—which is the view of the new academy. Consequently, whoever wishes to hold this first interpretation must also hold to their position and so fall into obvious error, for "a little mistake in the beginning makes for a big one in the end."

Another interpretation is that the influence of the eternal reason is all that is needed for certain knowledge, so that in knowing, the knower does not come in contact with the eternal reason itself but only with its influence. But this way of speaking does not do justice to St. Augustine, who argues expressly that in the case of certain knowledge, the mind is regulated not by something which it has, but by the immutable and eternal reasons which are above it in the eternal truth. Hence to say that when our mind knows, it does not get beyond the influence [i.e. the effect] of the uncreated light, is to say that Augustine was deceived, since his words cannot readily be twisted to support this interpretation. Now it would be exceedingly absurd to say such of that Doctor and Father [of the Church] who has the greatest authority among all the expositors of Sacred Scripture. Furthermore, the influence of this light would either be general (to the extent that God exercises it in all creatures) or something special (as is the case with the influence of grace). If it be general, then there is no more reason for calling God the giver of wisdom than for saying he makes the earth fertile. Neither are the grounds any greater for saying he gives knowledge than for saying he gives wealth. If it be something special as is the case with grace, then according to this interpretation all knowledge would be infused, and there would be no acquired or innate knowledge—all of which is absurd.

There is a *third interpretation,* then, midway as it were between the other two, viz. that for certain knowledge the eternal reason must function as a regulative and motivating factor along with created reason. And it is known by us in this life not in all its clarity, but in part by "contuition."

And Augustine insinuates as much in *On the Trinity,* Bk. XIV, chap. 14. "The sinner is reminded that he should turn to the Lord as to that light by which he was touched in some way even when he was turned away from him. For hence it is that even the godless think of eternity, and rightly condemn and rightly praise many things in the moral conduct of men." And he adds a little later that they do this through rules "written in the book of that light which is called Truth." That our minds somehow attain these rules and immutable reasons when they possess certain knowledge is something that both the nobility of knowledge and the dignity of the knower necessarily require.

The nobility of the knowledge does so, I say, because there can be no certain knowledge except where there is immutability on the side of what is knowable and infallibility on the part of the one who knows. Created truth, however, is not immutable in an unqualified sense, but only is so in a qualified one. Nor in virtue of itself is any created light wholly infallible. For as created, both proceed from nonexistence to existence. If then full knowledge requires a recourse to truth that is fully immutable and stable and to a light that is completely infallible, recourse must needs be had to transcendent art as to light and truth. Light, I say, which invests the knower with infallibility and what is knowable with immutability. Now since things have existence in the mind and an existence of their own as well as an existence in the eternal art, the truth they possess in the mind or on their own does not suffice to give the soul certain knowledge, since both are mutable, unless the soul is somehow in contact with these things as they are in the eternal art.

The dignity of the knower also requires this. For in the rational spirit there is a higher and lower part to reason. And just as the inferior part without the superior part does not suffice for a complete judgment of reason deliberating about what is to be done, so neither does it suffice for a complete judgment of reason as regards the basis for speculation [i.e. first principles and universals]. Now this superior part is that which is the image of God, and it is also that which inheres in the eternal reasons and which judges and defines with certitude what it defines by means of these reasons. And all this pertains to it insofar as it is an image of God.

For a creature is related to God as a footprint *[vestigium]*, as an image *[imago]* and as a likeness *[similitudo]*. Insofar as it is a footprint, it is compared to God as a principle; as an image, it is related to God as to its object; but as a likeness, it is united to God as to an infused gift. And therefore every creature that comes from God is a footprint; every one that knows God is an image; and each creature in whom God dwells, and only such, is a likeness. Corresponding to this triple degree of relatedness there is a threefold degree of divine cooperation.

In a work which proceeds from a creature as a footprint, God cooperates as a creative principle. In one which proceeds from the creature as a likeness, such as a work which is meritorious and pleasing to God, God cooperates by way of an infused gift. But in something which proceeds from the creature as an image, God cooperates in the role of moving reason *[ratio movens]*. Now, certain knowledge, which is the work of superior rather than inferior reason, is this sort of thing.

To the extent that certain knowledge pertains to the rational spirit insofar as the latter is an image of God, it is in such knowledge that it contacts the eternal reasons. But because it is not fully like to God so long as it remains in this life, it does not attain them clearly, fully, or distinctly. Still it attains them to a greater or lesser degree according to the degree of its likeness to God. But it always is in touch with them to some extent because the character of being an image is something inseparable from the soul. In the state of innocence where this image was not deformed by sin, and where the soul did not yet possess the divine likeness characteristic of the glorified state, it was in touch with them only partially, but not in a dark manner *[ex parte sed non in aenigmate];* in the state of fallen nature, however, the soul was deformed and the likeness to God gone so that it was in contact with these [eternal reasons] only partially and in a dark manner *[ex parte et in aenigmate]*. In the state of glory, however, where all deformity is erased and the soul attains its full likeness to God, it will be in touch with them in all their fullness and clarity.

But since it is not the soul as a whole that is an image, in addition to these reasons the soul is in touch with the likenesses of things abstracted from the fantasy. These are the proper and distinct reasons for knowing, and without them the light of the eternal reason is not of itself sufficient to produce knowledge so long as we are in this life, except perhaps where by a special revelation one transcends this state, as in the case of those raised to a state of ecstasy or in the revelations made to some of the prophets. One should grant, then, as the citations from Augustine expressly assert, that where all certain knowledge is concerned the knower is in touch with these reasons for knowing; but the manner is different for the wayfarer and the blessed, for the man of science and the man of wisdom, for the one prophesying and the one who understands things in the ordinary way. . . .

Theory of Seminal Reasons

ARE ALL THE FORMS INDUCED BY THE CREATOR OR BY A CREATED AGENT?[3]

. . . I reply: As for the case at hand, it should be pointed out that there are four theories about how the form is educed or comes to be.

[First View]

For some postulate a latency of form, like that proposed by Anaxagoras. And there are two ways in which this can be understood. [1] Either he assumed that these forms existed in matter as actualized, but that they did not reveal themselves externally, like a picture covered with a cloth. This interpretation is completely impossible, for it postulates the simultaneous existence of contraries in one and the same thing. [2] Another way of understanding the theory is this: the essences of the form are present in matter not merely latently but potentially, in such a way that matter has implanted within it from the very beginning all the forms in a germinal state (which is in accord both with philosophy and Sacred Scripture) and that these forms are brought to actuality by the action of some agent. But according to what the exegetes say, this theory was not understood in this latter way, but rather in the first way. For it was assumed that particular agents did not actualize, but merely uncovered [these forms].

[Second View]

The more modern philosophers held another view, according to which all the forms are from the Creator. And this theory can be understood in a twofold manner: [1] in the sense that God is the principal producing agent of everything that is brought into existence—and so understood, this view is true.

[2] Or it can be understood in the sense that God is the entire efficient cause and that particular agents do nothing more than adapt the matter, so that he is considered to produce other forms the way he does the rational soul. And it is in this latter way that these philosophers seem to understand this position. This interpretation, however, is impossible, because the particular agent induces either something or nothing. If nothing, then it does nothing. If it does induce something, then it seems that it produces some disposition. But how then is it able to produce now one, now another thing? This view therefore is not reasonable.

Another interpretation is that almost all the natural forms —at least those that are corporeal, such as the elementary forms and those of more complex substances—are in the potency of matter and are actualized by the action of particular agents. It is this opinion which the Philosopher seems to have held and which the doctors of philosophy and theology now commonly hold. But this view is given two interpretations.

[Third View]

For some say such forms are in matter by way of a receptive potency that is somehow also active or cooperative. For matter has both the possibility for receiving and an inclination to cooperate. But the form to be produced is also in the agent as the effective and originating principle, for every form by its very nature has the virtue of reproducing itself in kind. Hence the form is induced by an agent reproducing its own [form]. And they cite the case of a candle, where many are lighted by means of one; or the case of a single object producing many mirror images. For such forms, they say, do not have anything from which *[ex quo]* they are materially but only something [viz. an agent] from which *[ex quo]* they originate. And for this reason such forms are not said to be created or to come from nothing, for what is created in no way [pre]exists whereas a form produced in this way does in some way [pre]exist, both in virtue of the agent and of the matter.

[Fourth View]

The other interpretation is that forms are in the potency of matter not only as that in which *[in qua]* or somehow by which *[a qua]* but also as that from out of which *[ex qua]* [they arise]. And they say this not because it is the essence of matter to be that from which a thing is produced but because in matter itself there is something cocreated with it, from which the agent acting in the matter educes the form. Not, I say, that this something from which [the form is educed] is such that it becomes some part of the form to be produced, but it is rather that which can be and will become the form, even as a rosebud becomes a rose. And this view postulates that in matter are the verities *[veritates]* of all forms to be produced naturally. And when one is produced, the quiddity or essential verity does not appear as something wholly new; rather, what is new is the way it is arranged or set forth, so that what was there in potency has become actual. For act and potency do not differ because they refer to diverse quiddities, but because they refer to diverse ways in which the same thing can be, keeping in mind however that these ways do not represent accidental arrangements, but are something substantial. According to this view it is not such a great thing that a created agent has the ability to make something which exists in one way exist in another.

Of all the aforesaid interpretations, this last seems to be the most intelligible view and the one closest to the truth. And I believe this opinion should be held not only because reason persuades us to hold it but also because it is confirmed by the authority of St. Augustine in *Super Genesim ad litteram,* which the Master [of the *Sentences*] cites by way of proof, viz. that "what is produced by nature is produced in virtue of the seminal reasons." What these "seminal reasons" are we shall see later when we come to treat of them. According to this opinion then, a particular agent does educe and induce forms and produces natural things and the reasons adduced to establish this [viz. in the Pro and Contra of the question] are to be conceded. . . .

WAS WOMAN FORMED FROM THE RIB OF MAN ACCORDING TO A SEMINAL REASON?[4]

. . . Since the Master [Peter Lombard] says that some things happen because of causal reasons and some because of seminal reasons, there is a question here of how the two differ . . . for there seems to be no difference between them. . . .

I reply: To understand what was said above keep in mind the following: since the eminent doctor Augustine speaks ambiguously about seminal reasons in V and VI *Super Genesim ad litteram* and since it is especially to him we owe the use of these names [viz. causal and seminal reasons], it is not easy to distinguish properly between such words. For he himself speaks at times about the causal reasons being implanted and sometimes about how they are related to what is in the divine will. Still we can distinguish the following on the strength of the terms used.

Cause in general designates both an intrinsic and extrinsic principle as does causal reason, so far as the force of the word goes. A seed, however, is an intrinsic principle. And consequently causal reason covers both created and uncreated reasons; seminal reason, however, covers only created ones. So far as the force of the words go, one is general with respect to the other; insofar as they are paired off as distinct from one another, cause and causal reason designate an uncreated principle; seed and seminal reason, however, refer to a created principle. But cause and causal reason differ: cause indicates a productive principle whereas causal reason designates a rule directing that principle in its operation. Seed and seminal reason differ in similar fashion. But the rule for an uncreated agent is an ideal or exemplar form; seminal reasons, on the contrary, are natural forms.

From this it is clear that causal and primordial reasons are the same in reality and differ only mentally. For primordial reasons are so called because of a lack of any reasons prior to them; causal reasons are so called with reference to what follows from them. Also the first are called primordial insofar as they regard God as the first principle; causal are so called because they look to God as their ultimate end, who is as such the cause of causes.

Seminal and natural reasons likewise are really identical and differ only mentally. For a seed refers to such as that from which *[ex quo]*, nature, however, as that by which *[a quo]*; seminal reason is viewed as directing a power of nature so that from it something will come; natural reason, however, so that by it something will come. Or seminal reason looks to the incipient stage and internal power which moves and operates to produce the effect, whereas natural reason regards the similarity between the product and its producer and the customary way of acting. Hence it was appropriate to say of the magicians making serpents from rods that this was accomplished in accord with seminal reasons; but when serpents, as is their custom, beget serpents this is according to natural reasons, although it could rightly be said to occur according to either natural or seminal reasons.

When therefore it is asked whether some effect occurs according to causal or according to seminal reasons, one must reply that either this effect by God is such that a creature lacks all power to do it (as was the case with the world being made from nothing where no power was there on the part of the creature) or that the creature has only the power to obey (as obtained when many loaves of bread were multiplied from a single loaf which had only obediential potency). In both instances the effect occurs according to causal reasons God keeps in his will, since there is no demand for such on the part of the creature, but only that which arises because of the eternal disposition. But if the effect is such as to be in the power of nature and the latter has not merely the power to obey but also is able to produce the act, the effect is according to the seminal reasons. Such is clearly the case when man is generated from man or a tree from a tree. But note that this power of nature in regard to such effects can be either proximate and sufficient (as is the case with the semen which comes from the loins to generate a human body and which is rightly said to have in itself a seminal reason) or else it is remote and insufficient (as when it is said that a man is formed from food or bread, and the latter is said less properly to contain a seminal reason). For one does not speak of bread having the seminal reason of producing man save in an extremely broad sense of the term. What is thus remotely disposed as regards an effect, however, goes on to produce it by means which are either immediately or mediately ordered to the effect. If mediate, the effect can be said to be according to a seminal reason, as is the case if the bread is eaten and digested and converted into a humor, and afterwards in the loins is turned into semen and then into a man. If, on the other hand, it immediately goes on to produce its effect, as is the case where bread is immediately formed into the body of man, it is said to do this not according to seminal but according to causal reasons. For though there is some active power there that accounts for its becoming a body after many intermediate stages, it has only obediential potency as regards such a thing happening immediately.

When one asks then whether woman's body was in the rib seminally, one must answer No! if we understand seminal reason in its proper sense. If one takes it broadly, however, to mean any kind of active potency which exists in matter, then one may say a seminal reason was in the rib. Further, if one asks whether woman was made from the rib in accord with a seminal reason, the answer is No, because insofar as the way it was produced and the kind of body that was formed are concerned, apart from any additional factor the rib had this effect only in obediential potency. . . .

IS A SEMINAL REASON A UNIVERSAL OR A SINGULAR FORM?[5]

. . . I reply: . . . since there is sufficient agreement that a seminal reason is an active power implanted in matter and that this active power is the essence of the form, since from it the form comes to be by an operation of nature which does not produce anything from nothing, it is reasonable enough to assume that the seminal reason is the essence of the form to be produced and differs from the latter as being incomplete differs from being in act. But it is not so clear that the form or active potency which we call a seminal reason is universal. For there are various ways of talking about it accordingly as there are different views as to how the form is universal.

For some like to say that since the universals are not fictions, they exist really and in truth not only in the soul, but also in nature, and because everything in nature has a basis in matter, universal as well as singular forms exist in matter. And consequently, the difference between universal and singular forms is not that the former are abstracted from matter and the latter concretized in matter but they differ because one adds something to the other so that one is more, the other less complete. A sign of this is that when genera and species are put in an orderly arrangement the form of the species is most complete and most composed. But the form of the genus, by contrast to it, is a being in potency and it becomes more in act by adding a difference to it. And since the seminal reason is what one calls the form as incomplete, the advocates of this view say that a seminal reason is nothing else than a universal form.

Now this opinion is not to be taken lightly, for great men hold it and it seems to be in harmony with sense, reason, and authority. With authority because the Commentator [Averroës] himself says in chapter [8] of his commentary on [Book I of] the *Metaphysics* that matter receives singular forms through the mediation of universal forms. It accords with reason too, for since the singular is said to be a being in act, and matter a being in potency, and a universal form is to some extent a being in act and to some extent a being in potency, it would seem right and proper that matter comes to complete form by means of universal forms. It also is in accord with sense, because—as the Philosopher [Aristotle] likes to say (in the beginning of the *Physics*), our progress in knowledge is like the progress in nature in its operation. But in us the natural way is to proceed from the more to the less universal; therefore the same should be true of nature. . . .

Others, however, take the position that the universal is a form but not every form is properly speaking a universal. For there is the form of a part and the form of the whole, and the universal is not the form of the part but the form of the whole. For it is not *soul* that is said to be the universal with respect to an individual man, but rather it is *man* that is the universal. But they call that the form of the whole which indeed gives being to the whole, and this is the essence of the thing because it includes the whole being. This form is what the metaphysician considers. But the form of the part [i.e. the soul] is not properly speaking universal as it does not have being except reductively. Nevertheless it can be said in some sense to be universal at root, since it is indifferent with respect to many things which can come from it, even as a cause is said to be universal because it can do many things. And thus this active power which is in matter and which is called a seminal reason can also be said to be universal; not properly so called in the sense that the universal is considered by the metaphysician, but in the wider sense that it bespeaks a certain indifference in a principle, and as such it falls under the consideration of the philosopher of nature.

Now this position is held by many great men and the common way approves it more, and justly so, for it is in accord with reason, authority and sense. With reason, because the process of cognition and univocal predication requires the postulation of universal forms. If cognition is not complete unless the whole being of a thing is known, and if there is no cognition except through the form, then it is necessary to have some form which includes the whole being. But this is what we call the essence and this is a universal form, for as Avicenna says: "The essence is nothing else than the universal quiddity of a thing." Similarly, there is no true univocation unless some things really resemble one another by reason of a common form which is predicated of them essentially. But the form in virtue of which several things resemble one another cannot but be a universal form. On the other hand, a form which is predicated essentially of them cannot but be the form which includes the whole. Therefore the universal form is nothing else than the form of the whole, which since it was meant to be in many, as such is universal. It is particularized, however, not by the addition of an ulterior form but by being conjoined to matter, in which union matter makes the form its own and the form makes the matter its own, as was said above. And because this form is never separated from matter, it is never a universal form apart from a particular thing. But even though the one never exists without the other, it still differs from the other. For even though whiteness cannot exist without a body, it still differs from the body. Hence, inseparability does not always imply complete identity.

This viewpoint also is supported by authority. For the Philosopher says when I say "heaven," I speak of the form; when I say "this heaven," I speak of the matter. Boethius also says: "The species is the whole being of the individual"; consequently the universal form, which is the species, is the form of the whole, and it comprises the whole being and is the sufficient reason for knowing the substantial being of a thing.

Such a view is also in accord with sense, for the order and manner in which the species comes from the genus is different from that of the eduction of forms from matter. For the philosopher of nature says that matter first receives the elementary form and by its means it comes to the form of the mineral compound and by means of the latter to the organic form, for he looks to that potency of matter according to which it is progressively actualized by the operation of nature. But the metaphysician, who is concerned with the universal forms or essences by which singular things resemble one another, begins with the more universal and then goes to the less universal accordingly as there are more things that resemble one another according to the former than according to the latter. That in which there is the first point of resemblance is called the most general genus and that in which there is perfect resemblance is called the most special species. And that is why he says the species adds to the genus and this whole he discovers in the thing; he also says that the genus is simpler than the species and is found in more. And hence it is that in some respects the genus resembles God more than the species and in other respects the reverse is true. For God has together in himself all perfection—for the most noble contains the totality of what is noble—so that he is the most simple and wholly incapable of corruption; and he is also perfect and hence constituted in the fullest actuality. Creatures, to the extent that they can, resemble God partially. So far as simplicity and incorruptibility goes, the more universal resembles him more; but so far as actuality goes, the less universal resembles him more.

If one considers these two positions in general it is difficult to decide which is the more probable or likely. If one descends to particulars as regards the way nature operates, the viewpoints of the metaphysician and philosopher of nature diverge and there seems to be no way of reconciling them. Whiteness is defined one way, as was touched on above, but it is produced by nature in another way. It is defined by means of its genus, which is color, and color by the genus above it, and so on up to the supreme genus of its kind. But nature in producing it does not observe this order, for whiteness is produced in accord with the demands of the elementary qualities operating under the influence of light. Therefore the last-named view is the more intelligible and sensible and generally held.

Accepting this more general viewpoint then, one can reply to the question at issue as follows. A seminal reason is not a universal form if one takes this term properly to mean a thing which is able to be ordered as a genus. But if one understands by a universal form a form that exists in matter in an incomplete fashion and is indifferent with respect to a plurality of possible effects that can be produced, then a seminal reason can be called a universal form. . . .

NOTES

1. *Quaestiones disputatae de mysterio Trinitatis,* q. 1, art. 1, *Opera omnia,* tom, V (Quaracchi: 1891), 45-51.

2. *Quaestiones disputatae de scientia Christi,* q. 4, *Opera omnia,* tom. V (Quaracchi: 1891), 22-24.

3. *Commentaria in secundum librum Sententiarum,* d. 7, art. 1, *Opera omnia,* tom. II (Quaracchi: 1885), 197-99.

4. *Commentaria in secundum librum Sententiarum,* d. 18, art. 1, q. 2, *Opera omnia,* tom. II (Quaracchi: 1885), 436-37.

5. *Ibid.,* q. 3, 440-42.

XVII

ST. THOMAS AQUINAS

St. Thomas Aquinas was born at Roccasecca, Italy, in 1224/1225. He first studied at the Benedictine abbey of Monte Cassino and then moved on to Naples to continue his studies at the university there. He followed the liberal arts program at the university from 1239 until 1244, and while there was first introduced to Aristotelian philosophy and possibly also to Avicenna and/or Averroës. In 1244 he joined the Dominican order. In 1245 or 1246 he journeyed to Paris and eventually to Cologne, where he studied under Albert the Great from 1248 to 1252. There he entered the priesthood. In the fall of 1252 he returned to Paris to begin preparing for the doctorate in theology. He lectured there as bachelor in theology until 1256. At this time, however, the controversy between the secular masters at Paris and the mendicants (Franciscans and Dominicans) became acute. Various issues sharpened the conflict to such an extent that it was only after papal intervention that Aquinas was permitted to hold his inaugural lecture as master of theology in 1256. For some months thereafter both Thomas and Bonaventure lectured in their own colleges as masters, without their status being officially recognized by the university. It was only in August, 1257, that they were granted the full privileges of masters.

During this period Thomas had already produced some important works, including his commentary on the *Sentences* of Peter Lombard, the *De ente et essentia,* and the *De principiis naturae*. He continued to lecture as master of theology until 1259 and from 1256 to 1259 he prepared the *Disputed Questions on Truth,* some *Quodlibetal Questions,* and commentaries on the *De Trinitate* and the *De hebdomadibus* of Boethius. In 1259 he returned to the Roman province, and during his stay in Italy (until 1268) lectured in various Dominican priories, fulfilled other important functions for his order, undertook an intensive study of Aristotle, and wrote extensively. He continued to work on the *Summa contra gentiles,* which he had begun in Paris, and appears to have completed the *prima pars* of the *Summa theologiae.* Other works include the *Catena aurea, Exposition of Dionysius on the Divine Names,* and the *Disputed Questions on the Power of God.* His *Disputed Questions on Spiritual Creatures* and his *Commentary on Job* probably also date from this period.

In 1268 or 1269 he returned to Paris. Three great controversies demanded his attention during his stay there (1269-72): Certain conservative theologians in the Augustinian tradition were challenging the speculative theology recently developed by Albert and Thomas; a radical form of Aristotelianism, frequently known as Latin Averroism, had been developing in the arts faculty at Paris and, under the leadership of Siger of Brabant and Boetius of Dacia, presented a serious threat to Christian orthodoxy; the mendicants were again under attack from the seculars at Paris. Against the conservative theologians, Aquinas insists in his *De aeternitate mundi contra murmurantes* that human reason cannot prove the impossibility of an eternally created universe. The fact of creation in time can only be known through revelation. His *De unitate intellectus contra Averroistas* severely criticizes monopsychism, a central thesis of the radical Aristotelians. The concluding chapters of his *De perfectione vitae spiritualis* and his *Contra pestiferam doctrinam retrahentium pueros a religionis ingressu* are written in reply to attacks against the mendicants. Other important works composed during this period include a number of commentaries on Aristotle, some scriptural commentaries, major portions of the *Summa theologiae,* the *Disputed Questions on the Virtues, Quodlibetal Questions* I to VI and parts, at least, of the *Disputed Questions on Evil.*

In the spring of 1272 Thomas returned to Italy. Entrusted with forming a *studium generale* in Naples, he remained there until 1274. His writing activity continued until near the end of 1273. Early in 1274 he departed for Lyons to take part in a general council, but poor health interrupted his journey. He died at the Cistercian Abbey of Fossanuova in March, 1274.

The first and second selections are taken from the *De ente et essentia* and the *Summa theologiae* and are translated especially for this volume by A. B. Wolter. The third is from the *Disputed Questions on the Power of God* and is translated by L. Shapcote.

On the Composition of Essence and Existence in Created Substances[1]

What we still have to investigate is how there is an essence in separated substances [i.e. substances without matter] such as the soul, the intelligences, and the first cause.

Though all admit the first cause is simple, some attempt to introduce composition of matter and form into souls and the intelligences. Avicebron [Ibn Gabirol], the author of the *Fons Vitae,* seems to have sired this theory, but it runs counter to what philosophers generally say, since they refer to these substances as separated from matter and prove they lack such. Their strongest reason why is based upon the power of understanding such substances possess. For we see that forms are not actually intelligible, save as separated from matter and what goes with it. Neither are they produced as actual intelligibles except by virtue of an intelligent substance which receives them within itself and actuates them. Every intelligent substance then must be wholly immune to matter so that it neither has matter as part of itself nor is it impressed as a form upon matter in the way material forms are. Neither can one claim that it is not all, but only corporeal matter that impedes intelligibility. For if this were characteristic of corporeal matter alone, since matter is not called corporeal except to the extent that it is subject to corporeal form, then matter would have to derive its ability to impede intelligibility from the corporeal form. But this cannot be, because corporeal form itself, like all other forms, is actually intelligible when abstracted from matter.

Hence there is no composition of matter and form of any kind in the soul or an intelligence. On this score, then, essence cannot be said to be in them as it is in corporeal substances. But composition of form and existence is there. Consequently the comment in the ninth proposition of the *Book of Causes* states: "An intelligence is something having form and existence," where "form" means the quiddity or the simple nature itself.

It is plain to see how this is so. For whenever things are so related that one is the cause of another's existence, the cause can have existence without the other, but the converse is not true. Such a relation however holds for matter and form, because the form gives existence to the matter. And therefore it is impossible for the matter to exist without some form, though it is not impossible for some form to exist without matter since form as form does not depend on matter. But if some forms may be found which can exist only in matter, this occurs because of the gap between them and the first principle, which is act in a pure and primary sense. Those forms nearest the first principle then require no matter but are self-subsisting. For not every form needs matter, as was said, and the intelligences are forms of this sort. The essence or quiddity of these substances then does not have to be something other than the form itself. Hence the essence of a composite and a simple substance differ in that the essence of the former includes not merely form but matter whereas the essence of the simple substance comprises the form alone.

From this two further differences result. The first is that we can signify the essence of the composite substance in whole or in part. . . . Consequently the essence of a composite thing is not predicated in just any way of the composite. One cannot say, for example, that man is his quiddity. But the essence of a simple thing, which is its form, cannot be signified except as a whole because there is nothing there except the form itself to receive the form. And therefore in whatever way you take the essence of a simple substance, it is predicated of the substance. That is why Avicenna says: "The quiddity of what is simple is itself simple because there is nothing else to receive it."

The second difference is that since the essences of composite things are received into a limited amount of matter, they are multiplied insofar as that matter is divided. That is how some things specifically alike are numerically different. But since there is no matter to receive the essence of a simple substance, it cannot be multiplied in this fashion. Consequently it is impossible to find several individuals of the same species among such substances, but as Avicenna puts it: Here there are as many individuals as species.

Though such substances are mere forms devoid of matter,

they are not thereby so simple as to be pure act, but have an admixture of potentiality, as is clear from the following. Whatever does not pertain to the notion of an essence or quiddity is an extrinsic item and enters into composition with the essence, for no essence is intelligible in isolation from its parts. Now any essence or quiddity is understandable without anything being known about its existing. For I am able to know what a man or a phoenix is and still be ignorant of whether there is such a thing existing in the realm of nature. From this it is clear that "to be" is other than the essence or quiddity, unless perhaps there is something whose quiddity is its very existence. And there could only be one such, viz. that which is First, because nothing can be duplicated except (1) by adding some difference, in the way a generic nature is multiplied specifically or (2) by the form being received into distinct material, as the specific nature is multiplied in diverse individuals, or (3) because one is received by something and the other is not, e.g. if pure heat existed in isolation, it would be different from heat in things. Now if we assume there is something which is just "to be" or existence so that its existence is itself subsistent, this existence cannot receive any additional difference because it would not be just existence any more, but existence plus a certain form. Much less could matter be added to it, for it would then be a material rather than a subsistent existence. Hence there can be but one such thing, which is its existence. Consequently the existence of every other thing must be other than its quiddity, nature, or form. In intelligences then, their existence must be other than their form and therefore an intelligence has been referred to as "form and existence."

Now whatever pertains to anything is either caused by the principles of its nature, as man's ability to laugh, or it stems from some extrinsic principle, as the sun's luminosity in the atmosphere. But it cannot be that existence itself is caused by the form or quiddity as such—caused, I say, as by an efficient cause—for then something would be the cause of itself and something would produce itself in existence, which is impossible. Therefore everything whose existence is something other than its nature must derive its existence from another. And since everything existing through another is traced back to something existing of itself as its first cause, there must be some thing which is the cause or reason for the existence of all things and which is itself existence pure and simple. Otherwise there would be an infinite regress in causes, since everything which is not existence pure and simple has a cause of its existence, as has been said. It is clear then that an intelligence is form plus existence and that it has existence from the first being which is simply existence. And this is God, the first cause.

Now everything which receives something from another is in potency with respect to that, and what it receives is its act. The quiddity or form itself, then, which is the intelligence, must be in potency to the existence which it receives from God; and this existence is received as an act. Potency and act therefore are found in intelligences, but not matter and form except in an equivocal sense. Also "to suffer," "to receive," "to be a subject," and such like, which seem to be predicable of things in virtue of their matter, pertain equivocally to intellectual and corporeal substances as the Commentator [Averroës] says in his exposition on the third book of *On the Soul*.

And since the quiddity of the intelligence is the intelligence itself, as we have said, its essence or quiddity is its very self and its existence, received from God, is that by which it subsists in the realm of nature. That is why some say such substances are composed of a "that-by-which" *[quo est]* and a "that-which-is" *[quod est]* or, as Boethius puts it, of a "that-which-is" and existence *[esse]*.

And because intelligences are presumed to have both act and potency, it will not be difficult to find many intelligences which would be impossible if they contained no potentiality. Hence the Commentator declares in his exposition on the third book of *On the Soul* that if the nature of the possible intellect were not known, we could not discover a plurality of separate substances. It is by reason of their degree of potency and act that they are distinct, so that the higher intelligence which is closer to the first [being] has more actuality and less potentiality, and so too for the others. This gradation ends with the human soul, which is the lowest rung on the ladder of intellectual substances. Hence its possible intellect bears the same relation to intelligible forms as prime matter (the lowest grade of sensible existence) does to sensible forms, as the Commentator points out in the exposition on the third book of *On the Soul*. That also is why the Philosopher [Aristotle] compares it to a slate on which nothing is written. Because it has a greater measure of potentiality than other intelligible substances, the human soul is so close to material things that the material [component] is drawn to share in its existence, so that there is but a single existence in the one composite even though, as the soul's existence, it is not dependent on the body.

And after this form, which is the soul, other forms are to be found which are still more potential and closer to matter—so close that they cannot exist without matter. Among these also an order and a gradation obtain until we come to the first forms of the elements, which are the closest of all to matter. That is why they have no operation other than the dispositional ones towards active and passive qualities and the other things by which matter is disposed toward forms.

Does God Exist?[2]

[Pro and Con]

It seems that God does not exist:

[ARG. 1]

If one of two contraries were infinite, it would do away completely with the other. By "God," however, we mean something infinitely good. If God existed then, no evil could be found. But evil is encountered in the world. Consequently, God does not exist.

[ARG. 2]

Moreover, what a few sources can accomplish is not the work of many. Now it seems that everything in the world stems from sources other than God, since the products of nature have their source in nature; deliberate effects can be traced back to human reason or will as their source. There is no need then to assume a God exists.

On the other hand: in the book of Exodus God is represented as saying: *I am who am!*

[Reply to the Question]

Reply: It ought to be pointed out that there are five ways in which God can be proved to exist. Of these the first and most obvious is that based on change. For that some things change is certain and evident to the senses. But whatever is changed is changed by something else, for nothing can be altered unless it has a capacity or potentiality for the end result of the change. Now only some actual being can alter a thing. For to change is merely to bring something from a potential state to one of actuality. But only some being that is actual can bring something potential to actuality. For example, something actually hot like fire can transform a subject potentially hot like wood into something actually hot, and to that extent it changes or alters it. But it is impossible for the same subject to be simultaneously in a state both of potentiality and actuality with respect to the same property, though this could be so with respect to different properties. Thus something actually hot cannot be merely potentially so, but it may be potentially cold. It is quite impossible, then, that as regards the same property one and the same subject be at once both agent and recipient of the change or that it change itself. Anything in the process of change, therefore, must be altered by an agent other than itself, and this agent by still another. Infinite regress here is out of the question, for otherwise there would be nothing to initiate the change and hence nothing else would be altered. For secondary agents of change only function when moved by some primary mover, even as a stick moves nothing unless stirred by some hand. One is bound to arrive, then, at some first mover which is not moved or changed by any other, and this is what all understand by God.

The second way is based on the idea of an efficient cause. For in the sense-perceptible world we discover an order among efficient causes. It is never the case, in fact it is impossible, that anything should be its own efficient cause, since it would be prior to itself, which is impossible. Infinite regress in efficient causes is impossible since in all cases where efficient causes are concatenated, the first is the cause of the intermediary cause, and the intermediary (be it one or many) causes the last. If you eliminate a cause, however, you eliminate its effect. But if no cause is first, no intermediate or last cause will exist. If there were an infinite regress in efficient causes, however, there would be no first cause and thus no intermediate causes or ultimate effect, which is obviously false. It is necessary then to postulate some first efficient cause, which all call God.

A third way, based on the possible and necessary, runs as follows. We discover among things that for some it is possible for them to exist and also possible for them not to exist, for we find things that are first begotten and later perish and hence exist and then do not exist. That everything should be of this sort is not possible because what is possible to be nonexistent is at some time nonexistent. If all things were possible then, at some time nothing would exist. Were this true, nothing would be existing at present, because what is nonexistent begins to be only through something which already exists.

If therefore at any time nothing at all existed, then it would be impossible for anything to begin to exist and thus nothing would exist at present, which is clearly false. Hence not all beings are possible; there must be something in the realm of things that exists necessarily. Every necessary thing either has or has not an external cause of that necessity. Infinite regress in necessary things that are caused is not possible, just as it is out of the question with efficient causes, as has been explained. Therefore it is necessary to postulate something that is necessary on its own account and not by reason of some extrinsic cause, and this is the cause of the necessity of other things. And this everyone calls God.

The fourth way is based on the different degrees discovered among things, for we find some to be more good, others less so, some more true or noble, others less so, and also with other traits. But "more" or "less" express degrees of approximation to some superlative. For instance, the more something approaches what is hottest of all, the warmer it becomes. Something therefore is the truest and best and most noble of things and therefore it is most a being, for things which are the truest are also greatest as regards being, as [Aristotle] says in Bk. II of his *Metapyhsics*. Whatever is superior in any class is the cause of all the things which are in that class, just as fire, which is hottest of all, is the cause of whatever is hot, as we read in the same book. Therefore, there is some cause of existence and goodness and whatever other perfections are characteristic of things, and this we call God.

The fifth way is based on the fact that things are guided. For we see some things which lack knowledge, such as physical bodies, acting for some end. This is apparent from the fact that they always or generally act in the same fashion so as to attain the best result. Consequently it is clear they do this not by chance but by design. Those things which do not possess knowledge tend to an end only because they are directed by someone with knowledge and intelligence, even as an arrow aimed by an archer. There is some intelligent individual, consequently, who directs all natural things to their end. This we call God.

[Answer to the Initial Arguments]

To the first, one should reply the way Augustine does. "Since God is supremely good, he would not permit any evil at all in his works, unless he were so almighty and good as to bring good even from evil." It is a mark of God's infinite goodness then that he allows evil to exist and draws good from it.

To the second, the answer must be that since nature acts for a specific end under the direction of a superior agent, it is necessary that those things which occur by nature be traced back to God as their first cause. Similarly, whatever is done deliberately must also be traced back to some higher cause than human reason and will, because these are changeable and can cease to be and it is necessary that all things that can change or cease to be stem from some primary source which is immutable and necessary on its own account, as was explained.

NOTES

1. From *Le "De ente et essentia" de s. Thomas d'Aquin,* ed. by M.-D. Roland-Gosselin (2nd ed., Paris: J. Vrin, 1948), 29-37.

2. From *Summa theologiae,* I, q. 2, art. 3. (Various Latin editions were consulted, especially for difficult passages).

On the Power of God

[CAN THERE BE ANYTHING THAT IS NOT CREATED BY GOD?]*

The fifth point of inquiry is whether there can be anything that is not created by God. Seemingly this is possible.

1. Since the cause is more powerful than its effect, that which is possible to our intellect which takes its knowledge from things would seem yet more possible to nature. Now our intellect can understand a thing apart from understanding that it is from God, because its efficient cause is not part of a thing's nature, so that the thing can be understood without it. Much more therefore can there be a real thing that is not from God.

2. All things made by God are called his creatures. Now creation terminates at being: for the first of created things is being (*De Causis,* prop. iv). Since then the quiddity of a thing is in addition to its being, it would seem that the quiddity of a thing is not from God.

3. Every action terminates in an act, even as it proceeds from an act: because every agent acts in so far as it is in act, and every agent produces its like in nature. But primal matter is pure potentiality. Therefore the creative act cannot terminate therein: so that not all things are created by God.

On the contrary it is said (Rom. xi, 36): *From him and by him and in him are all things.*

I answer that the ancients in their investigations of nature proceeded in accordance with the order of human knowledge. Wherefore as human knowledge reaches the intellect by beginning with the senses, the early philosophers were intent on the domain of the senses, and thence by degrees reached the realm of the intellect. And seeing that accidental

*Reprinted with permission of the publishers from Thomas Aquinas, *On the Power of God,* (trans. L. Shapcote, London: Burns and Oates Ltd., 1932-34; reprinted Westminster, Md.: Newman Press, 1952). Question 3, article 5 (Book I, pp. 108-11).

forms are in themselves objects of sense, whereas substantial forms are not, the early philosophers said that all forms are accidental, and that matter alone is a substance. And because substance suffices to cause accidents that result from the substantial elements, the early philosophers held that there is no other cause besides matter, and that matter is the cause of whatever we observe in the sensible world: and consequently they were forced to state that matter itself has no cause, and to deny absolutely the existence of an efficient cause. The later philosophers, however, began to take some notice of substantial forms: yet they did not attain to the knowledge of universals, and they were wholly intent on the observation of special forms; and so they posited indeed certain active causes, not such as give being to things in their universality, but which transmute matter to this or that form: these causes they called intelligence, attraction and repulsion, which they held responsible for adhesion and separation. Wherefore according to them not all beings came from an efficient cause, and matter was in existence before any efficient cause came into action. Subsequent to these the philosophers as Plato, Aristotle and their disciples, attained to the study of universal being: and hence they alone posited a universal cause of things, from which all others came into being, as Augustine states (*De Civ. Dei* viii, 4). This is in agreement with the Catholic Faith; and may be proved by the three arguments that follow.

First, if in a number of things we find something that is common to all, we must conclude that this something was the effect of some one cause: for it is not possible that to each one by reason of itself this common something belong, since each one by itself is different from the others: and diversity of causes produces a diversity of effects. Seeing then that being is found to be common to all things, which are by themselves distinct from one another, it follows of necessity that they must come into being not by themselves, but by the action of some cause. Seemingly this is Plato's argument, since he required every multitude to be preceded by unity not only as regards number but also in reality. The second argument is that whenever something is found to be in several things by participation in various degrees, it must be derived by those in which it exists imperfectly from that one in which it exists most perfectly: because where there are positive degrees of a thing so that we ascribe it to this one more and to that one less, this is in reference to one thing to which they approach, one nearer than another: for if each one were of itself competent to have it, there would be no reason why one should have it more than another. Thus fire, which is the extreme of heat, is the cause of heat in all things hot. Now there is one being most perfect and most true: which follows from the fact that there is a mover altogether immovable and absolutely perfect, as philosophers have proved. Consequently all other less perfect beings must needs derive being therefrom. This is the argument of the Philosopher (*Metaph.* ii, 1).

The third argument is based on the principle that whatsoever is through another is to be reduced to that which is of itself. Wherefore if there were a *per se* heat, it would be the cause of all hot things, that have heat by way of participation. Now there is a being that is its own being: and this follows from the fact that there must needs be a being that is pure act and wherein there is no composition. Hence from that one being all other beings that are not their own being, but have being by participation, must needs proceed. This is the argument of Avicenna (*in Metaph.* viii, 6; ix, 4). Thus reason proves and faith holds that all things are created by God.

Reply to the First Objection. Although the first cause that is God does not enter into the essence of creatures, yet being which is in creatures cannot be understood except as derived from the divine being: even as a proper effect cannot be understood save as produced by its proper cause.

Reply to the Second Objection. From the very fact that being is ascribed to a quiddity, not only is the quiddity said to be but also to be created: since before it had being it was nothing, except perhaps in the intellect of the creator, where it is not a creature but the creating essence.

Reply to the Third Objection. This argument proves that primal matter is not created *per se:* but it does not follow that it is not created under a form: for it is thus that it has actual being.

[DOES GOD WORK IN OPERATIONS OF NATURE?]*

The seventh point of inquiry is whether God works in the operations of nature: and apparently the answer should be in the negative.

**Op. cit.,* question 3, article 7 (Book I, pp. 123-35).

1. Nature neither fails in necessary things nor abounds in the superfluous. Now the action of nature requires nothing more than an active force in the agent, and passivity in the recipient. Therefore there is no need for the divine power to operate in things.

2. It may be replied that the active force of nature depends in its operation on the operation of God. On the contrary as the operation of created nature depends on the divine operation, so the operation of an elemental body depends on the operation of a heavenly body: because the heavenly body stands in relation to the elemental body, as a first to a second cause. Now no one maintains that the heavenly body operates in every action of an elemental body. Therefore we must not say that God operates in every operation of nature.

3. If God operates in every operation of nature God's operation and nature's are either one and the same operation or they are distinct. They are not one and the same: since unity of operation proves unity of nature: wherefore as in Christ there are two natures, so also are there two operations: and it is clear that God's nature and man's are not the same. Nor can they be two distinct operations: because distinct operations cannot seemingly terminate in one and the same product, since movements and operations are diversified by their terms. Therefore it is altogether impossible that God operate in nature.

4. It will be replied that two operations can have the same term, if one is subordinate to the other. On the contrary, when several things are immediately related to some one thing, one is not subordinate to the other. Now both God and nature produce the natural effect immediately. Therefore of God's operation and nature's one is not subordinate to the other.

5. Whenever God fashions a nature, by that very fact he gives it all that belongs essentially to that nature: thus by the very fact that he makes a man he gives him a rational soul. Now strength is essentially a principle of action, since it is the perfection of power, and power is a principle of acting on another which is distinct (*Metaph.* v, 12). Therefore by implanting natural forces in things, he enabled them to perform their natural operations. Hence there is no need for him also to operate in nature.

6. It might be replied that natural forces like other beings cannot last unless they be upheld by the divine power. On the contrary, to operate on a thing is not the same as to operate

in it. Now the operation whereby God either produces or preserves the forces of nature, has its effect on those forces by producing or preserving them. Therefore this does not prove that God works in the operations of nature.

7. If God works in the operations of nature, it follows that by so doing he imparts something to the natural agent: since every agent by acting makes something to be actual. Either then this something suffices for nature to be able to operate by itself, or it does not suffice. If it suffices, then since God also gave nature its natural forces, for the same reason we may say that the natural forces were sufficient for nature to act: and there will be no further need for God to do anything towards nature's operation besides giving nature the natural forces. If on the other hand it does not suffice, he will need to do something more, and if this is not sufficient, more still and so on indefinitely, which is impossible: because one effect cannot depend on an infinite number of actions, for, since it is not possible to pass through an infinite number of things, it would never materialise. Therefore we must accept the alternative, namely that the forces of nature suffice for the action of nature without God operating therein.

8. Further, given a cause that acts of natural necessity, its action follows unless it be hindered accidentally, because nature is confined to one effect. If, then, the heat of fire acts of natural necessity, given heat, the action of heating follows, and there is no need of a higher power to work in the heat.

9. Things that are altogether disparate can be separate from each other. Now God's action and nature's are altogether disparate, since God acts by his will and nature by necessity. Therefore God's action can be separated from the action of nature, and consequently he need not operate in the action of nature.

10. A creature, considered as such, is like God inasmuch as it actually exists and acts: and in this respect it participates of the divine goodness. But this would not be so if its own forces were not sufficient for it to act. Therefore a creature is sufficiently equipped for action without God's operation therein.

11. Two angels cannot be in the same place, according to some, lest confusion of action should result: because an angel is where he operates. Now God is more distant from nature than one angel from another. Therefore God cannot operate in the same action with nature.

12. Moreover, it is written (Ecclus. xv, 14) that *God made man and left him in the hand of his own counsel.* But he would not have so left him, if he always operated in man's will. Therefore he does not operate in the operation of the will.

13. The will is master of its own action. But this would not be the case, if it were unable to act without God operating in it, for our will is not master of the divine operation. Therefore God does not operate in the operation of the will.

14. To be free is to be the cause of one's own action (*Metaph.* i, 2). Consequently that which cannot act without receiving the action of another cause is not free to act: now man's will is free to act. Therefore it can act without any other cause operating in it: and the same conclusion follows.

15. A first cause enters more into the effect than does a second cause. If, then, God operates in will and nature as a first in a second cause, it follows that the defects that occur in voluntary and natural actions are to be ascribed to God rather than to nature or will: and this is absurd.

16. Given a cause whose action suffices, it is superfluous to require the action of another cause. Now it is clear that if God operates in nature and will, his action is sufficient, since *God's works are perfect* (Deut. xxxii, 4). Therefore all action of nature and will would be superfluous. But nothing in nature is superfluous, and consequently neither nature nor will would do anything, and God alone would act. This, however, is absurd: therefore it is also absurd to state that God operates in nature and will.

On the contrary it is written (Isa. xxvi, 12): *Lord, thou hast wrought all our works in us.*

Moreover, even as art presupposes nature, so does nature presuppose God. Now nature operates in the operations of art: since art does not work without the concurrence of nature: thus fire softens the iron so as to render it malleable under the stroke of the smith. Therefore God also operates in the operation of nature.

Again, according to the Philosopher (*Phys.* ii, 2) man and the sun generate man. Now just as the generative act in man depends on the action of the sun, so and much more does the action of nature depend on the action of God. Therefore in every action of nature God operates also.

Further, nothing can act except what exists. Now nature cannot exist except through God's action, for it would fall into nothingness were it not preserved in being by the action of the divine power, as Augustine states *(Gen. ad lit.)*. Therefore nature cannot act unless God act also.

Again, God's power is in every natural thing, since he is in all things by his essence, his presence and his power. Now it cannot be admitted that God's power forasmuch as it is in things is not operative: and consequently it operates as being in nature. And it cannot be said to operate something besides what nature operates, since evidently there is but one operation. Therefore God works in every operation of nature.

I answer that we must admit without any qualification that God operates in the operations of nature and will. Some, however, through failing to understand this aright fell into error, and ascribed to God every operation of nature in the sense that nature does nothing at all by its own power. They were led to hold this opinion by various arguments. Thus according to Rabbi Moses [Maimonides] some of the sages in the Moorish books of law asserted that all these natural forms are accidents, and since an accident cannot pass from one subject to another, they deemed it impossible for a natural agent by its form to produce in any way a similar form in another subject, and consequently they said that fire does not heat but God creates heat in that which is made hot. And if it were objected to them, that a thing becomes hot whenever it is placed near the fire, unless some obstacle be in the way, which shows that fire is the *per se* cause of heat; they replied that God established the order to be observed according to which he would never cause heat except at the presence of fire: and that the fire itself would have no part in the action of heating. This opinion is manifestly opposed to the nature of sensation: for since the senses do not perceive unless they are acted upon by the sensible object—which is clearly true in regard to touch and the other senses except sight, since some maintain that this is effected by the visual organ projecting itself on to the object—it would follow that a man does not feel the fire's heat, if the action of the fire does not produce in the sensorial organ a likeness of the heat that is in the fire. In fact if this heat-species be produced in the organ by another agent, although the touch would sense the heat, it would not sense the heat of the fire, nor would it perceive that the fire is hot, and yet the sense judges this to be the case, and the senses do not err about their proper object.

It is also opposed to reason which convinces us that nothing in nature is void of purpose. Now unless natural things had an action of their own the forms and forces with which they are endowed would be to no purpose; thus if a knife does not cut, its sharpness is useless. It would also be useless to set fire to the coal, if God ignites the coal without fire.

It is also opposed to God's goodness which is self-communicative: the result being that things were made like God not only in being but also in acting.

The argument which they put forward is altogether frivolous. When we say that an accident does not pass from one subject to another, this refers to the same identical accident, and we do not deny that an accident subjected in a natural thing can produce an accident of like species in another subject: indeed this happens of necessity in every natural action. Moreover, they suppose that all forms are accidents, and this is not true: because then in natural things there would be no substantial being, the principle of which cannot be an accidental but only a substantial form. Moreover, this would make an end of generation and corruption: and many other absurdities would follow.

Avicebron *(Fons Vitae)* says that no corporeal substance acts, but that a spiritual energy penetrating all bodies acts in them, and that the measure of a body's activity is according to the measure of its purity and subtlety, whereby it is rendered amenable to the influence of a spiritual force. He supports his statement by three arguments. His first argument is that every agent after God requires subject-matter on which to act: and no corporeal agent has matter subject to it, wherefore seemingly it cannot act. His second argument is that quantity hinders action and movement: in proof of which he points out that a bulky body is slow of movement and heavy: wherefore a corporeal substance being inseparable from quantity cannot act. His third argument is that the corporeal substance is furthest removed from the first agent, which is purely active and nowise passive, while the intermediate substances are both active and passive: and therefore corporeal substances which come last, must needs be passive only and not active.

Now all this is manifestly fallacious in that he takes all corporeal substances as one single substance; and as though they differed from one another only in accidental and not in their substantial being. If the various corporeal substances be taken as substantially distinct, every one will not occupy the last place and the furthest removed from the first agent, but one will be higher than another and nearer to the first agent, so that one will be able to act on another. Again in the foregoing arguments the corporeal substance is considered only in respect of its matter and not in respect of its form, whereas it is composed of both. It is true that the corporeal substance belongs to the lowest grade of beings, and has no subject beneath it, but this is by reason of its matter, not of its form: because in respect of its form a corporeal substance has an inferior subject in any other substance whose matter has potentially that form which the corporeal substance in question has actually. Hence it follows that there is mutual action in corporeal substances, since in the matter of one there is potentially the form of another, and vice versa. And if this form does not suffice to act, for the same reason neither does the energy of a spiritual substance, which the corporeal substance must needs receive according to its mode.—Nor does quantity hinder movement and action, since nothing is moved but that which has quantity (*Phys.* vi, 10). Nor is it true that quantity causes weight. This is disproved in *De Coelo* iv, 2. In fact, quantity increases the speed of natural movement, thus a weighty body, the greater it is, the greater the velocity of its downward movement, and in like manner that of a light body in its movement upwards. And although quantity in itself is not a principle of action, no reason can be given why it should hinder action, seeing that rather is it the instrument of an active quality; except in so far as active forms in quantitative matter receive a certain limited being that is confined to that particular matter, so that their action does not extend to an extraneous matter. But though they receive individual being in matter, they retain their specific nature, by reason whereof they can produce their like in species, and yet are unable themselves to be in another subject. Hence we are to understand that God works in every natural thing not as though the natural thing were altogether inert, but because God works in both nature and will when they work. How this may be we must now explain.

It must be observed that one thing may be the cause of another's action in several ways. First, by giving it the power to act: thus it is said that the generator moves heavy and light bodies, inasmuch as it gives them the power from which that movement results. In this way God causes all the actions of nature, because he gave natural things the forces whereby they are able to act, not only as the generator gives power to heavy and light bodies yet does not preserve it, but also as upholding its very being, forasmuch as he is the cause of the power bestowed, not only like the generator in its becoming, but also in its being; and thus God may be said to be the cause of an action by both causing and upholding the natural power in its being. For secondly, the preserver of a power is said to cause the action; thus a remedy that preserves the sight is said to make a man see. But since nothing moves or acts of itself unless it be an unmoved mover; thirdly, a thing is said to cause another's action by moving it to act: whereby we do not mean that it causes or preserves the active power, but that it applies the power to action, even as a man causes the knife's cutting by the very fact that he applies the sharpness of the knife to cutting by moving it to cut. And since the lower nature in acting does not act except through being moved, because these lower bodies are both subject to and cause alteration: whereas the heavenly body causes alteration without being subject to it, and yet it does not cause movement unless it be itself moved, so that we must eventually trace its movement to God, it follows of necessity that God causes the action of every natural thing by moving and applying its power to action. Furthermore we find that the order of effects follows the order of causes, and this must needs be so on account of the likeness of the effect to its cause. Nor can the second cause by its own power have any influence on the effect of the first cause, although it is the instrument of the first cause in regard to that effect: because an instrument is in a manner the cause of the principal cause's effect, not by its own form or power, but in so far as it participates somewhat in the power of the principal cause through being moved thereby: thus the axe is the cause of the craftsman's handiwork not by its own form or power, but by the power of the craftsman who moves it so that it participates in his power. Hence, fourthly, one thing causes the action of another, as a principal agent causes the action of its instrument: and in this way again we must say that God causes every action of natural things. For the higher the cause the greater its scope and efficacity: and the more efficacious the cause, the more deeply does it penetrate into its effect, and the more remote the potentiality from which it brings that effect into act. Now in every natural thing we find that it is a being, a natural thing, and of this or that nature. The first is common to all beings, the second to all natural things, the third to all the members of a species, while a fourth, if we take accidents into account, is proper to this or that individual. Accordingly this or that individual thing cannot by its action produce another individual of the same species except as the instrument of that cause which includes in its scope the whole species and, besides, the whole being of the inferior creature. Wherefore no action in these lower bodies attains to the production of a species except through the power of the heavenly body, nor does anything produce being except by the power of God. For being is the most common first effect and more intimate than all other effects: wherefore it is an effect which it belongs to God alone to produce by his own power: and for this reason (*De Causis,* prop. ix) an intelligence does not give being, except the divine power be therein. Therefore God is the cause of every action, inasmuch as every agent is an instrument of the divine power operating.

If, then, we consider the subsistent agent, every particular agent is immediate to its effect: but if we consider the power whereby the action is done, then the power of the higher cause is more immediate to the effect than the power of the lower cause; since the power of the lower cause is not coupled with its effect save by the power of the higher cause: wherefore it is said in *De Causis* (prop. i) that the power of the first cause takes the first place in the production of the effect and enters more deeply therein. Accordingly the divine power must needs be present to every acting thing, even as the power of the heavenly body must needs be present to every acting elemental body. Yet there is a difference in that wherever the power of God is there is his essence; whereas the essence of the heavenly body is not wherever its power is: and again God is his own power, whereas the heavenly body is not its own power. Consequently we may say that God works in everything forasmuch as everything needs his power in order that it may act: whereas it cannot properly be said that the heaven always works in an elemental body, although the latter acts by its power. Therefore God is the cause of everything's action inasmuch as he gives everything the power to act, and preserves it in being and applies it to action, and inasmuch as by his power every other power acts. And if we add to this that God is his own power, and that he is in all things not as part of their essence but as upholding them in their being, we shall conclude that he acts in every agent immediately, without prejudice to the action of the will and of nature.

Reply to the First Objection. The active and passive powers of a natural thing suffice for action in their own order: yet the divine power is required for the reason given above.

Reply to the Second Objection. Although the action of the forces of nature may be said to depend on God in the same way as that of an elemental body depends on the heavenly body, the comparison does not apply in every respect.

Reply to the Third Objection. In that operation whereby God operates by moving nature, nature itself does not operate: and even the operation of nature is also the operation of the divine power, just as the operation of an instrument is effected by the power of the principal agent. Nor does this prevent nature and God from operating to the same effect, on account of the order between God and nature.

Reply to the Fourth Objection. Both God and nature operate immediately, although as already stated there is order between them of priority and posteriority.

Reply to the Fifth Objection. It belongs to the lower power to be a principle of operation in a certain way and in its own order, namely as instrument of a higher power: wherefore, apart from the latter it has no operation.

Reply to the Sixth Objection. God is the cause of nature's operation not only as upholding the forces of nature in their being, but in other ways also, as stated above.

Reply to the Seventh Objection. The natural forces implanted in natural things at their formation are in them by way of fixed and constant forms in nature. But that which God does in a natural thing to make it operate actually, is a mere intention, incomplete in being, as colours in the air and the power of the craftsman in his instrument. Hence even as art can give the axe its sharpness as a permanent form, but not the power of the art as a permanent form, unless it were endowed with intelligence, so it is possible for a natural thing to be given its own proper power as a permanent form within it, but not the power to act so as to cause being as the instrument of the first cause, unless it were given to be the universal principle of being. Nor could it be given to a natural power to cause its own movement, or to preserve its own being. Consequently just as it clearly cannot be given to the craftsman's instrument to work unless it be moved by him, so neither can it be given to a natural thing to operate without the divine operation.

Reply to the Eighth Objection. The natural necessity whereby heat acts is the result of the order of all the preceding causes: wherefore the power of the first cause is not excluded.

Reply to the Ninth Objection. Although nature and will are disparate in themselves, there is a certain order between them as regards their respective actions. For just as the action of nature precedes the act of our will, so that operations of art which proceed from the will presuppose the operation of nature: even so the will of God which is the origin of all natural movement precedes the operation of nature, so that its operation is presupposed in every operation of nature.

Reply to the Tenth Objection. The creature has a certain likeness to God by sharing in his goodness, in so far as it exists and acts, but not so that it can become equal to him through that likeness being perfected: wherefore as the imperfect needs the perfect, so the forces of nature in acting need the action of God.

Reply to the Eleventh Objection. One angel is less distant from another in the degree of nature than God from created nature; and yet in the order of cause and effect God and the creature come together, whereas two angels do not: wherefore God operates in nature, but one angel does not operate in another.

Reply to the Twelfth Objection. God is said to have left man in the hand of his counsel not as though he did not operate in the will: but because he gave man's will dominion over its act, so that it is not bound to this or that alternative: which dominion he did not bestow on nature since by its form it is confined to one determinate effect.

Reply to the Thirteenth Objection. The will is said to have dominion over its own act not to the exclusion of the first cause, but inasmuch as the first cause does not act in the will so as to determine it of necessity to one thing as it determines nature; wherefore the determination of the act remains in the power of the reason and will.

Reply to the Fourteenth Objection. Not every cause excludes liberty, but only that which compels: and it is not thus that God causes our operations.

Reply to the Fifteenth Objection. Forasmuch as the first cause has more influence in the effect than the second cause, whatever there is of perfection in the effect is to be referred chiefly to the first cause: while all defects must be referred to the second cause which does not act as efficaciously as the first cause.

Reply to the Sixteenth Objection. God acts perfectly as

first cause: but the operation of nature as second cause is also necessary. Nevertheless God can produce the natural effect even without nature: but he wishes to act by means of nature in order to preserve order in things.

[CAN GOD ENABLE A CREATURE TO KEEP ITSELF IN EXISTENCE BY ITSELF AND WITHOUT GOD'S ASSISTANCE?]*

The second point of inquiry is whether God can make a creature able of itself to keep itself in existence independently of God: and seemingly he can do so.

1. To create is more than to keep oneself in existence. Now a creature could have received the power to create according to the Master [Peter Lombard] (*Sent.* v, 4). Therefore it could have received the power to keep itself in existence.

2. The power of God over things surpasses the power of our intellect. Now our intellect can understand a creature apart from God. Much more therefore can God make a creature able of itself to keep itself in existence.

3. There is a creature made to God's image (Gen. i, 26). Now according to Hilary (*De Synod.*) an image is the undivided and united likeness of one thing adequately representing another: so that an image can be adequate to the thing of which it is the image. Seeing then that God needs no other to keep him in existence, it would seem that he could communicate this to a creature.

4. The more perfect the agent the more perfect an effect can it produce. Now natural agents can produce effects which are able to remain in existence without their causes. Therefore *a fortiori* God can do this.

On the contrary God can do nothing that is prejudicial to his own authority: and it would be prejudical to his dominion if anything could exist without his upholding it. Therefore God cannot do this.

I answer that God's omnipotence does not imply that he can make two contradictories true at the same time. Now the statement that God can produce a thing which does not need to be upheld by him involves a contradiction. For we have already proved that every effect depends on its cause in so far as it is its cause. Accordingly the statement that a thing needs not God

**Op. cit.*, question 5, article 2 (Book II, pp. 86-87).

to uphold its existence implies that it is not created by God: while the statement that such a thing is produced by God implies that it is created by him. Wherefore just as it would involve a contradiction to say that God produced a thing that was not created by him, even so it would involve a contradiction were one to say that God made a thing that did not need to be kept in existence by him. Wherefore God is equally unable to do either.

Reply to the First Objection. Since to create is to be the cause of something, and only that which has no cause needs not to be kept in existence by another, it is clear that not to need to be kept in existence by another is more than to create: even as to have no cause is more than to be a cause. Moreover it is not altogether true that the power of creating is communicable to a creature, seeing that it is the act of the first agent as we have shown above (Q. iii, A. 4).

Reply to the Second Objection. Although the intellect is able to understand a creature without understanding God, it cannot understand a creature not being kept in existence by God, since this involves a contradiction, as if one were to say that a creature is not created by God, as stated above (Q. iii, A. 5).

Reply to the Third Objection. Equality is essential to an image, not absolutely speaking but of a perfect image: such an image of God is not a creature but the Son of God; wherefore the argument proves nothing.

The *Reply to the Fourth Objection* may be gathered from what has been already said in the preceding answer.

[ARE THESE RELATIONS BETWEEN A CREATURE AND GOD REALLY IN CREATURES THEMSELVES?]*

The ninth point of inquiry is whether these relations between creatures and God are in creatures themselves: and it would seem that they are not.

1. There are certain relations which posit nothing real on either side; as Avicenna says (*Metaph.* iv, 10) of the relation between entity and non-entity. Now no relatives are further apart than God and the creature. Therefore this relation posits nothing real on our side.

2. We must not assert anything that leads to an indefinite

**Op. cit.,* question 7, article 9 (Book III, pp. 50-55).

process. Now if relation to God is something real in a creature, we shall have to go on indefinitely: since that relation will be a creature, if it be something real, and therefore will likewise bear a relation to God, and so on indefinitely. Therefore we must not assert that relation to God is something real in a creature.

3. Nothing has a relation except to one definite thing (*Metaph.* iv): thus *double* is not related to anything but *half;* and *father* is not related except to *son,* and so on. Therefore there must be correspondence between the things that are related and those to which they are related. Now God is simply one being. Therefore there can be no real relation in creatures to him.

4. The creature is related to God inasmuch as it proceeds from him. Now the creature proceeds from God as to its very substance. Therefore it is related to God by its substance and not by an additional relation.

5. A relation is a kind of mean between the related extremes. But there can be no real mean between God and the creature which is created by him immediately. Therefore relation to God is nothing real in the creature.

6. The Philosopher (*Metaph.* iv) says that if the reality of things depended on our opinion and perception, whatsoever we perceive would be real. Now it is clear that all creatures are dependent on the perception or knowledge of their Creator. Therefore all creatures are referred to God by their substance and not by an inherent relation.

7. It would seem that the more things are distant from one another the less are they related. Now there is a greater distance between the creature and God than between one creature and another. But seemingly the relation between one creature and another is nothing real: for since it is not a substance, it must be an accident and consequently must be in a subject, and therefore cannot be removed therefrom without the subject being changed: and yet we have asserted the contrary to be the case with relations. Therefore the creature's relation to God is nothing real.

8. Just as a created being is infinitely distant from non-being, so also is it infinitely distant from God. But there is no relation between created being and absolute non-being, according to Avicenna (*Metaph.* iv). Neither therefore is there a relation between created being and uncreated being.

On the contrary Augustine says (*De Trin.* v, 16): *It is*

evident that whatever begins to be predicated of God whereas it was not predicated of him before is said of him relatively: relatively, that is, not to an accident in God (as if something had accrued to him), but, without doubt, to an accident in the thing in relation to which God begins to be predicated. Now an accident is something real in its subject. Therefore relation to God is something in the creature.

Again, whatsoever is related to a thing through being changed is really related thereto. Now the creature is related to God through being changed. Therefore it is really related to God.

I answer that relation to God is something real in the creature. To make this clear we must observe that as the Commentator says (*Metaph.* xi, text. 19), seeing that of all the predicaments relation has the least stability, some have thought that it should be reckoned among the predicables because the predicaments *(prima intellecta)* have an objective reality and are the first things to be understood by the intellect: whereas the predicables *(secunda intellecta)* are certain 'intentions' consequent to our mode of understanding: inasmuch as by a second act the intellect reflects on itself, and knows both the fact that it understands and the manner of its understanding. According then to this view it would follow that relation has no objective reality, but exists only in the mind, even as the notion of genus or species and of 'second substances'. But this is impossible: because nothing is assigned to a predicament unless it has objective reality: since logical being is divided against the being that is divided by the ten predicaments (*Metaph.* v). Now if relation had no objective reality, it would not be placed among the predicaments. Moreover the perfection and goodness that are in things outside the mind are ascribed not only to something absolute and inherent to things but also to the order between one thing and another: thus the good of an army consists in the mutual ordering of its parts, to which good the Philosopher (*Metaph.* x) compares the good of the universe. Consequently there must be order in things themselves, and this order is a kind of relation. Wherefore there must be relations in things themselves, whereby one is ordered to another. Now one thing is ordered to another either as to quantity or as to active or passive power: for on these two counts alone can we find in a thing something whereby we compare it with another. For a thing is measured not only by its intrinsic quantity but also in reference to an extrinsic quantity. And again by its active power one thing acts on another, and by its passive power is acted on by another: while by its substance and quality a thing is ordered to itself alone and not to another, except accidentally: namely inasmuch as a quality, substantial form or matter is a kind of active or passive power, and forasmuch as one may ascribe to them a certain kind of quantity: thus one thing produces the same in substance; and one thing produces its like in quality; and number or multitude causes dissimilarity and diversity in the same things; and dissimilarity in that one thing is considered as being more or less so and so than another—thus one thing is said to be whiter than another. Hence the Philosopher (*Metaph.* v) in giving the species of relations, says that some are based on quantity and some on action and passion. Accordingly things that are ordered to something must be really related to it, and this relation must be some real thing in them. Now all creatures are ordered to God both as to their beginning and as to their end: since the order of the parts of the universe to one another results from the order of the whole universe to God: even as the mutual order of the parts of an army is on account of the order of the whole army to its commander (*Metaph.* xii). Therefore creatures are really related to God, and this relation is something real in the creature.

Reply to the First Objection. That between one creature and another there is a relation which posits nothing in either extreme is not due to the distance between them, but to the fact that certain relations are based not on any order in things, but on an order which is only in our intellect: but this does not apply to the order of creatures to God.

Reply to the Second Objection. The relations themselves are not related to something else by any further relation but by themselves because their very essence is relative. It is not the same with things whose essence is absolute, so that this does not lead to an indefinite process.

Reply to the Third Objection. The Philosopher concludes *(ibid.)* that if all things are related to the supreme good, the supreme good must be infinite by nature: and accordingly an infinite number of things can be related to that which is infinite by nature. Such is God, since the perfection of his essence is not confined to any genus, as we have stated above. For this reason an infinite number of creatures can be related to God.

Reply to the Fourth Objection. The creature is related to God by its essence as cause of that relation, and by that same relation, formally: thus a thing is said to be like in quality, causally; and by its likeness, formally: and for this reason the creature is said to be like God.

Reply to the Fifth Objection. When it is said that the creature proceeds from God immediately, we exclude an intermediate creative cause, but not the intermediate real relationship which arises naturally from the creature's production, even as equality results immediately from quantity: thus a real relation follows naturally the production of created substance.

Reply to the Sixth Objection. Creatures depend on God's knowledge as an effect depends on its cause, and not as though their very existence consisted in that knowledge, so that for a creature to exist would mean nothing else but that it is known by God. This was the view of those who contended that whatsoever is perceived is real, and that the reality of things depends on our thoughts and perception, so that to exist would be nothing but to be an object of perception or thought.

Reply to the Seventh Objection. The very relation that is nothing but the order between one creature and another may be considered as an accident, or as a relation. Considered as an accident it is something adhering to a subject; but not considered as a relation or order, for then it is mere towardness, something passing as it were from one thing to another and assisting that which is related. Accordingly a relation is something inherent, but not because it is a relation: thus action as action is considered as issuing from the agent; but, as an accident, is considered as inherent to the active subject. Wherefore nothing prevents such an accident from ceasing to exist without any change in its subject, because it is not essentially complete through its existence in its subject but through transition into something else: and if this be removed the essence of this accident is removed as regards the action, but remains as regards its cause: even so, if the matter be removed, the heating is removed, although the cause of heating remain.

Reply to the Eighth Objection. There is no order between created being and non-being, but there is between created and uncreated being, hence the comparison fails.

XVIII

SIGER OF BRABANT

ALTHOUGH LITTLE INFORMATION is available concerning the place and date of his birth, Siger's name indicates that he came from the duchy of Brabant. He was born probably around 1240 and he began to study liberal arts in Paris sometime between 1255 and 1260. He became master of arts between 1260 and 1265. In August, 1266, his name was cited by the papal legate, Simon of Brion, in connection with dissensions troubling the arts faculty. From his first years of teaching on that faculty, he had joined with others there in professing a radical version of Aristotelianism without regard for Christian orthodoxy. Called Latin Averroists by some and Radical or Heterodox Aristotelians by others, they encountered opposition from Bonaventure in conferences given in 1267 and 1268, from Thomas Aquinas in his *On the Unity of the Intellect Against the Averroists* (1270), and from Stephen Tempier, the bishop of Paris, in his condemnation of 1270. Siger's immediate reaction to this condemnation is unknown, but any calm introduced by the bishop's intervention was short-lived. Disturbances that broke out in the arts faculty in 1271-72 concerning the election of a rector were symptomatic of more profound divergences on the doctrinal level. Siger's party maintained its unreserved loyalty to philosophy and to Aristotle against the theologians and the orthodox members of the arts faculty. However, some modern interpreters hold that Siger himself began to modify his views in a more orthodox direction as he came to be influenced by Thomas Aquinas, while others reject this interpretation. In any event, on November 23, 1276, Siger of Brabant, Goswin of La Chappelle, and Bernier of Nivelles were cited by the inquisitor of France, Simon du Val, to appear before his tribunal. According to the text of the decree they had already departed from France. Siger seems to have appealed from the inquisitor's tribunal to the tribunal of the pontifical curia. Although he probably appeared before the tribunal of the curia and seems to have been absolved from the charge of heresy, he was detained there under some kind of surveillance. He died sometime before November 10, 1284, at Orvieto, where the curia was located under Pope Martin IV, stabbed by his secretary who had become demented. His works include some commentaries on Aristotle, different *opuscula* treating of questions in logic, metaphysics, physics, moral philosophy, and psychology, and some treatises that are now lost.

One of his most controverted theories had to do with the nature of the human intellect. His early discussion of the problem is strongly influenced by Averroës. There is one intellective soul for the human species, the last in the hierarchy of separated intelligences, which is itself composed of an agent and a possible (receptive) intellect. An individual man possesses neither a personal agent nor a personal possible intellect and therefore has no personal spiritual soul. Siger was sharply attacked for his theory by Thomas Aquinas in his *On the Unity of the Intellect* in 1270. According to the Italian philosopher, Agostino Nifo (d. *ca.* 1538 or 1545/6), Siger replied in a treatise now lost, *De intellectu,* wherein he continued to defend the separated character of the possible intellect but identified the agent intellect with God. This was followed by his important *De anima intellectiva* in 1272 or 1273 where, according to certain commentators, there is some mitigation of his denial of a personal intellective soul in man. The critical section appears in Chap. VII, translated for this volume by J. A. Arnold and J. F. Wippel. The propositions condemned by Stephen Tempier in 1270 have been added as an appendix to this chapter.

On the Intellective Soul

[CHAP. VII: WHETHER THE INTELLECTIVE SOUL IS MULTIPLIED IN ACCORD WITH THE MULTIPLICATION OF HUMAN BODIES][1]

As to the seventh point raised above, viz. whether the intellective soul is multiplied in accord with the multiplication of human bodies, it must be carefully considered insofar as such pertains to the philosopher and can be grasped by human reason and experience, by seeking the mind of the philosophers in this matter rather than the truth since we are proceeding philosophically. For it is certain according to that truth which cannot deceive that intellective souls are multiplied with the multiplication of human bodies. However, certain philosophers have thought otherwise.

According to philosophy, then: 1. A nature which is separated from matter in its being is not multiplied with the multiplication of matter. But according to the Philosopher the intellective soul enjoys being which is separated from matter, as we have already seen. Therefore, it should not be multiplied either with the multiplication of matter or with the multiplication of human bodies.

This reasoning is confirmed as follows. To differ in species, as man differs from ass, is to differ by reason of form. But to differ in number while belonging to the same species, as horse differs from horse, is to differ by reason of matter. For the form of horse is found in different parts of matter. Because of this it is asserted that what exists apart from any principle causing number or difference or multiplication lacks number, difference, and multiplication. But if the intellective soul enjoys being which is separated from matter then it exists apart from any principle that causes difference and number and multiplication of individuals within a species. Therefore, there do not seem to be many intellective souls within the same species.

2. No nature that subsists in itself and exists apart from matter and is thus individuated of itself can admit of numeri-

cally distinct individuals. But the intellective soul subsists in itself and exists apart from matter and is thus individuated of itself. Therefore it cannot admit of plurality of individuals within the same species.

Proof for the major: If it were of the essence of man to be this man or to be Socrates, just as there could not be many men each of whom would be Socrates or this man, neither could there be many men [at all]. Now if man subsisted in himself and apart from singulars, he would be individuated of his essence. Therefore every form that subsists in itself and has no materiality is individuated of its essence. And since nothing individuated can be common to many, no form enjoying being independently from matter can be common to many individuals. According to this reasoning, then, there is numerically only one intelligence in each species of intelligences separated from matter, a point on which all the philosophers have agreed. Wherefore, in holding that the ideas and species of material things are separated from matter, Plato posited only one individual per species.

For the minor, cf. chapter III above.

But someone might say that since there is an intellective soul in me God can make another like it and thus there will be more than one. To this it is to be replied that God cannot make that which is self-contradictory and repugnant. In like manner, God cannot produce many men, each of whom would be Socrates. For then he would make them to be many men and one man, many men and not many men, one man and not one man. But if the intellective soul is individuated of its essence and subsistent in itself and thus like Socrates, to make another intellective soul identical in species with one now existing would be to make it different from and the same as the first one. For in things separated from matter the individual is the species itself. Therefore, another individual within the species would be something contrary under that individual, which is impossible.

3. Something white can be divided into parts not because it is white but because it is quantified and continuous. But if there were something white that was neither quantified nor continuous, it would not be divisible into many white things. Nor would a separate and subsistent whiteness be divisible into many whitenesses. Just as that which is white is divisible into many white things because it is quantified and continuous, so too, if numerically distinct white things are actually found

within the same species this is because of the actual division of the quantified and continuous thing in which the whiteness is present. From this it is argued that a nature whose being is separated from the quantified and continuous in such fashion that it is neither quantified nor continuous nor exists in anything quantified or continuous is unable to admit of many individuals within the same species, because of the absence of a cause to multiply and render distinct the various individuals of that nature within that species. But the intellective soul exists apart from the quantified and continuous and is not itself quantified or continuous as the Philosopher [Aristotle] proves in *De anima* I. . . . Therefore, since the intellect exists apart from the quantified and continuous and is not itself quantified and continuous, it will not admit of many individuals within one species. For such plurality and multiplication arises by division of that which is continuous.

4. The Philosopher [Aristotle] says in *Metaphysics* XII, that if there were many individuals [heavens] of the same species there would be many first movers of the same species. And he notes that then the first mover would have matter because that which is one in species but many in number has matter. But if the intellect is impassible, and shares nothing in common with anything else, and is separated from the body and a potency without matter, as the Philosopher holds, then that same Philosopher would not be likely to think that it is one in species and many in number but rather that it is only one in number.

5. According to the mind of the Philosopher an infinity of men have already existed. But if intellective souls are multiplied with the multiplication of human bodies, the Philosopher would have to hold that souls are infinite in number, which does not seem to be the case. In the light of the above we must consider what kind of thing can be multiplied and predicated of numerically different members of the same species. And we must also determine how the various members of a species differ and in what respects.

Concerning the first point: It is to be noted that nothing that is singular and individuated can be multiplied into or predicated of many individuals within the same species. For then the singular and the universal would not differ. And since a subsistent form is numerically one and singular of its nature, it is clear that it cannot be multiplied into many individuals within the same species or predicated of them. That which is composed of form and determined matter as existing in this place or that is singular, like the entity named Socrates. Therefore, for the same reason Socrates can neither be multiplied into many nor predicated of them. Nor can the same material form as received in determined matter be multiplied into many or predicated of many. And in general, since everything that exists does so as a singular (granted that certain things may be understood or spoken of universally), no being viewed as it exists can be multiplied into many individuals within its species or predicated of them. Only a material form considered in the abstract or something composed of form and indetermined matter, as that which is signified by composite universals such as man or horse, can be multiplied into many within the same species and predicated of them.

Concerning the second point: It is to be said or understood that two individuals of the same species do not differ in form. As found in them form is not divided according to its substance. Of itself the matter of this individual is not divided from the matter of that individual. Rather one individual differs from another of the same species through this, that one possesses its form under determined dimensions or under a determined position as located here, while the other possesses the form of its species as located there. The form as found in the two individuals is not rendered other by diversity according to the form itself and its substance, for such diversity of form results in difference in species. Rather both individuals possess the one form, which is undivided as form. Nor should anyone wonder at us for saying that the form in each individual is one by that unity which follows upon its substance and yet that it is found here and elsewhere. When we understand a form to be one by the unity that follows upon its substance we do not have in mind something taken individually, but rather according to species, since a material form is not individuated of itself. It is not impossible for that which is one in species to be found in different individuals and to occupy different positions, thus being found here and elsewhere. . . . And just as form found in individuals is not divided as form either directly or by way of consequence, so too, neither is matter. It is not divided of itself, but is divided because quantified things are located here and elsewhere.

But there are weighty arguments according to which the intellective soul must be multiplied with the multiplication of human bodies, and authorities can also be cited for this view.

Thus Avicenna, Algazel, and Themistius maintain this. Themistius also holds that the agent intellect, taken as illuminating and as illuminated, is multiplied even though there is only one [supreme] illuminating intellect. All the more so does he mean that the possible intellect is multiplied.

Again, there are arguments for this view. If there were only one intellect for all men, when one knows then all would know. And one would not know while another did not. If to imagine is not the same as to understand, granted that the man who understands has phantasms, which the ignorant man lacks, this will not account for the fact that he knows more than the other. For the intellect in which actual understanding takes place is no more his than the ignorant man's, unless the position is changed.

For the sake of discussion someone might say that the one man knows and the other does not for this reason: that the act of intellection takes place by reason of one unique agent or one unique intellect operating in the man who knows, but not in the man who does not. Thus we described above how man understands or how the act of understanding may be attributed to man himself, namely, because the action of an agent united to matter is attributed to the whole composite. In the act of understanding the intellect unites itself to the one who knows and not to the one who does not know because it derives knowledge from the phantasms [of the knower]. Thus one man knows while another remains ignorant, not because the act of imagining on the part of one is greater than the act of understanding on the part of the other, nor because the intelligible species is found in the body of one rather than in the body of the other (for it exists apart), nor because they use different intellects in understanding (as the present position maintains), but because the act of understanding takes place by reason of the intellect, which is united to the body of one in operating but not to the body of the other.

But if someone should say this, then the argument may be developed in another way. Operations may be distinguished either by reason of the agent, or by reason of the time at which they occur. Thus if both you and I see the same object at the same time, the acts of sight are different [by reason of the agent]. If someone sees a white and a black object with one and the same eye, the acts of sight are different by reason of the object. If I see something white and then after some time see the same white object, the acts of sight differ by reason of time. Therefore, if two men understand the same intelligible object at the same time and if this takes place by means of one and the same intellect, this man's act of understanding will be the same as that man's act of understanding, which seems absurd.

Again, the Philosopher holds that the intellect is in potency to intelligible species and receptive of these species and is itself without species. But if there is only one intellect then it will always be filled with species and thus there will be no need for the agent intellect. Therefore, because of these difficulties and certain others, I acknowledge that I myself have been in doubt for quite some time both as to what should be held in the light of natural reason about this point and as to what the Philosopher thought about it. In such doubt one must hold fast to the faith, which surpasses all human reasoning.

APPENDIX TO CHAPTER XVIII

The Parisian Condemnations of 1270[2]

These are the errors which Stephen, Bishop of Paris, on the Wednesday following the feast of blessed Nicholas in the year of our Lord 1270 condemned and excommunicated along with all who shall have taught or asserted them knowingly.

The first article is: that the intellect of all men is numerically one and the same.

2. That this is false or inapt: Man understands.

3. That the will of man wills or chooses out of necessity.

4. That all that goes on here below falls under the necessitating influence of the celestial bodies.

5. That the world is eternal.

6. That there was never a first man.

7. That the soul, which is the form of man specifically as man, disintegrates with the corruption of the body.

8. That the soul in its state of separation after death does not suffer from corporeal fire.

9. That free will is not an active but a passive power and that it is moved in a necessary manner by the appetite.

10. That God does not know individual things.

11. That God does not know things other than himself.

12. That human actions are not governed by God's providence.

13. That God cannot endow a corruptible or mortal thing with the gift of immortality or incorruption.

NOTES

1. From P. Mandonnet, *Siger de Brabant et l'averroïsme latin au XIIIe siècle,* 2nd ed., 2 vols. *Les philosophes belges,* VI, VII (Louvain: Institut Supérieur, 1911-1908), Vol. 2, 164-69.

2. H. Denifle and A. Chatelain, *Chartularium Universitatis Parisiensis,* I (Paris, 1889), 486-87.

XIX

BOETIUS OF DACIA

ALTHOUGH HE is emerging as another leading representative of the movement in the arts faculty at Paris sometimes known as thirteenth-century Latin Averroism, relatively little is known concerning the life and career of Boetius. Although he is frequently referred to as Boetius of Sweden, recent research indicates that he probably came from Denmark. The dates of his birth and death are still unknown. He seems to have taught as a secular in the faculty of arts at Paris, where his name is linked with that of Siger of Brabant in the movement that resulted in the condemnation of 1277. There is some reason to believe that he later became a Dominican. It is no longer certain that he fled with Siger to the Papal court after the 1277 condemnation or that he was interned there.

Definitive exposition of his philosophical views is contingent upon the eventual publication of more of his works. Many of them were commentaries on Aristotle and, to judge from their titles, they seem to have ranged over the whole of philosophy. However, a number are still lost and very few have been edited. In fact, his very name had apparently disappeared from the history of philosophy until B. Hauréau rediscovered him in 1888. Further investigation suggested that his may have been an important role in the history of philosophy in Paris in the 1270s. The publication of his *De summo bono* (together with his *De sompniis*) by M. Grabmann and the more recent publication of his *De aeternitate mundi* (cf. Sajó in the bibliography) have confirmed this impression. In fact, the publication of the latter has elicited considerable discussion as to his views on faith and reason and their interrelationship. (Cf. Gauthier; Van Steenberghen; Gilson; Sassen; Sajó, 1954; Maurer; and Wilpert in the bibliography.) The prevailing opinion now seems to be that one does not find an explicit defense of the "double truth" theory in this work, contrary to some earlier interpretations. At the same time, however, one does find a number of the condemned propositions of 1277 more or less literally defended in this treatise.[1]

This work, as well as his *De summo bono,* have proven beyond doubt that Boetius was a thinker and writer of considerable stature. As regards the *De summo bono* itself, one finds there a masterly presentation of the life of philosophy as the pursuit of man's highest goal and the life of greatest happiness. It is clear from the text itself that Boetius is here describing the supreme good insofar as it is knowable by human reason. Nevertheless, at least one reference indicates his awareness of a higher kind of happiness, which man expects in the life to come, on the authority of faith. Boetius' unreserved praise for the life of philosophical contemplation has led some to conclude that this is a work of pure naturalism and absolute rationalism. Others, however, find nothing contrary to Christian belief in the treatise.[2]

It has been translated for this volume by J. F. Wippel.

NOTES

1. For a listing of the 219 propositions condemned by Stephen Tempier in 1277, cf. H. Denifle and A. Chatelain, *Chartularium Universitatis Parisiensis,* I (Paris, 1889), 543-61. For another listing in more systematic grouping, cf. P. Mandonnet, *Siger de Brabant et l'averroïsme latin au XIIIe siècle,* 2nd ed., vol. II (Louvain: Institut Supérieur, 1908), 175-91. For an English translation of the Mandonnet version cf. *Philosophy in the West. Readings in Ancient and Medieval Philosophy,* ed. J. Katz and R. H. Weingartner (New York: Harcourt, Brace & World, Inc., 1965), 532-42. For propositions which may have been directed against Boetius' *De aeternitate mundi,* cf. nos. 145, 9, 17, 18, and 90 in Denifle-Chatelain, corresponding to the following in the Mandonnet version: 6, 138, 215, 216, and 191.

2. Cf. E. Gilson, *History of Christian Philosophy in the Middle Ages* (New York: Random House, 1955), 399-402, for an analysis of this treatise and an indication of the possibility of diversity in interpreting it. It has also been noted that two of the propositions condemned in 1277 seem to refer to views defended by the *De summo bono.* Cf. nos. 40 and 154 in Denifle-Chatelain (nos. 1 and 2 in Mandonnet).

On the Supreme Good, or on the Life of the Philosopher[1]

Since in every kind of being there is a supreme possible good, and since man too is a certain species or kind of being, there must be a supreme possible good for man, not a good which is supreme in the absolute sense, but one that is supreme for man. The goods which are accessible to man are limited and do not extend to infinity. By means of reason we will seek to determine what the supreme good is which is accessible to man.

The supreme good for man should be his in terms of his highest power, and not according to the vegetative soul, which is also found in plants, nor according to the sensitive soul, which is also found in animals and from which their sensual pleasures arise. But man's highest power is his reason and intellect. For this is the supreme director of human life both in the order of speculation and in the order of action. Therefore, the supreme good attainable by man must be his by means of his intellect. Therefore, men who are so weighed down by sense pleasures that they lose intellectual goods should grieve. For they never attain their supreme good. It is insofar as they are given to the senses that they do not seek that which is the good of the intellect itself. Against these the Philosopher protests, saying: "Woe to you men who are numbered among beasts and who do not attend to that which is divine within you!"[2] He calls the intellect that which is divine in man. For if there is anything divine in man, it is right for it to be the intellect. Just as that which is best among all beings is divine, so also that which is best in man we call divine.

Moreover, one power of the human intellect is speculative and the other is practical. This is clear from this fact, that man theorizes concerning certain objects of which he is not the active cause, e.g., eternal things, and about others he acts under the direction of the intellect in choosing some fitting means whenever any human act is in question. From this, then, we know that these two intellectual powers are present in man. But the supreme good accessible to man in terms of the power of his speculative intellect is knowledge of what is true and delight in the same. For knowledge of what is true gives delight. An intelligible object gives delight to the one who knows it. And the more wondrous and noble the intelligible object and the greater the power of the apprehending intellect to perfectly comprehend, the greater the intellectual delight. One who has tasted such delight spurns every lesser pleasure, such as that of sense. The latter is, in truth, less, and is more base. And the man who chooses such pleasure is, because of that pleasure, more base than one who chooses the former.

It is because of this, because the object known gives delight to the one who knows, that the Philosopher [Aristotle] in Book XII of the *Metaphysics* maintains that the first intellect enjoys the most pleasurable life.[3] For since the first intellect is the most powerful in understanding and the object which it knows is the noblest, its essence itself—for what nobler object can the divine intellect have than the divine essence?—therefore, it has the life of greatest delight. No greater good can befall man in terms of his speculative intellect than knowledge of the universality of beings, which come from the first principle and, by means of this, knowledge of the first principle insofar as such is possible, and delight in it. Therefore, our conclusion above follows: that the supreme good accessible to man by means of his speculative intellect is knowledge of what is true in individual cases, and delight in the same.

Likewise, the supreme good accessible to man in terms of his practical intellect is the doing of good, and delight in the same. For what greater good can befall man in terms of his practical intellect than to choose the fitting means in human action and to delight therein?

For no man is just unless he takes delight in acts of justice. The same must be said of the acts of the other moral virtues. From what has been said one can evidently conclude that the supreme good open to man is to know the true, to do the good, and to delight in both.

And because the highest good possible for man is happiness, it follows that human happiness consists in knowing the true, doing the good, and taking delight in both. The military profession is prescribed in a state by the lawmaker for this reason, that when enemies have been expelled, citizens may devote themselves to intellectual virtues in contemplating the true, and to moral virtues in doing good, and thus live a happy life. For the happy life consists in these two. This then is a greater good, which man can receive from God and which God can give to man in this life. With reason does a man desire a long life who desires it for this, to become more perfect in this good. He who shares more perfectly in that happiness which reason tells us is possible for man in this life draws closer to that happiness which we expect in the life to come on the authority of faith. And since so great a good is possible for man, as has been said, it is right for all human action to be directed toward that good, so as to attain it. For just as all actions as regards a certain law are right and proper when they tend toward the end of the law, and better the more closely they approach the end of the law, while actions which are opposed to the end of the law or which are weak or indifferent without either being opposed to the end of the law or in accord with it, while all such actions sin against the law to a greater or lesser degree as is clear from what has been said, the same is true in man himself. All designs and deliberations, all actions and desires of man which tend to this supreme good which is accessible to man according to the above, these are right and proper. When man so acts, he acts in accord with nature. For he acts for the sake of the supreme good, to which he is ordered by nature. And when he so acts he is properly ordered. For then he is ordered to his best and his ultimate end. But all actions of man which are not ordered to this good, or which are not such as to render man stronger and better disposed for actions which are ordered to this good, all such actions in man are sin.

Wherefore the happy man never does anything except works of happiness, or works by means of which he becomes stronger and better fitted for works of happiness. Therefore, whether the happy man eats or sleeps or is awake, he lives in happiness so long as he does those things by means of which he is rendered more capable of the works of happiness. Therefore, all acts of man which are not directed to this supreme good of man which has been described, whether they are opposed to it or whether they are indifferent, all such acts constitute sin in man to a greater or lesser degree, as is clear. The cause of all such acts is inordinate desire. It is also the cause of all moral evil. Moreover, inordinate desire in man is the cause which most greatly prevents him from attaining that which is desired naturally. For all men naturally desire to know. But only the smallest number of men, sad to say, devote themselves to the pursuit of wisdom. Inordinate desire bars the others from such a good. Thus we find certain men pursuing a life of laziness, others detestable sense pleasures, and others giving themselves to the desire for riches. So it is that all today are prevented by inordinate desire from attaining to their supreme good, with the exception of a very small number of men, men who should be honored.

I say they are to be honored because they despise sense desire and pursue the delight of reason and intellectual desire, striving to know truth. Again I say they are to be honored because they live in accord with nature. All lower powers found in man are for the sake of the highest power. Thus the nutritive power is there for the sake of the sensitive. For the sensitive power is a perfection of an animated body, and an animated body cannot live without food. But it is the nutritive power which changes and assimilates food. Therefore, it follows that the nutritive power exists in man for the sake of the sensitive. And the sensitive power is for the sake of the intellective since, in us, intelligibles are derived from things imagined. Wherefore, we understand with greater difficulty things which of themselves cannot be imagined by us. But imagination presupposes the senses. The proof of this is that one who imagines is also affected on the level of sense. Wherefore, according to the Philosopher, imagination or *fantasia* is a movement arising from an actual exercise of sense.[4] [Just as all lower powers in man are for the sake of the higher,] so too all operations of man's lower powers are for the sake of the operations of his highest power, the intellect. And if, among the operations of the intellective power, there is one which is best and most perfect, all others naturally exist for its sake. When a man performs such an operation, he enjoys the highest state possible for man.

Such men are the philosophers, who spend their lives in the pursuit of wisdom. Wherefore, all powers found in the philosopher operate according to the natural order, the prior for the sake of the posterior, the lower for the sake of the higher and more perfect. But all other men, who live according to lower powers and choose their operations and the delights found in such operations, are not ordered in accord with nature. They sin against the natural order. For man to turn away from the natural order is sin in man. Because the philosopher does not turn away from this order, for this reason he does not sin against the natural order. Morally speaking, the philosopher is virtuous for three reasons. *First,* because he recognizes the baseness of action in which vice consists and the nobility of action in which virtue consists. Therefore, he can more easily choose the one and avoid the other and always act according to right reason. He who so acts never sins. But such is not true of the ignorant man. It is difficult for him to act rightly. *Secondly,* because he who has tasted a greater delight despises every lesser delight. But the philosopher has tasted intellectual delight in theoretical consideration of the value of beings. This delight is greater than that of sense. Therefore, he despises sense pleasures. But many sins and vices consist in excessive sense pleasure. *Thirdly,* because there is no sin in understanding and theorizing. There is no possibility of excess and of sin in the order of supreme goods. But the action of the philosopher is such a contemplation of truth. Therefore, it is easier for the philosopher to be virtuous than for another. So it is that the philosopher lives as man was born to live, and according to the natural order.

Since in him the lower powers and their operations are for the sake of the higher powers and their operations, and all taken together for the highest power and that highest action, which is contemplation of truth and delight in the same, above all, the first truth, the desire to know will never be satisfied until the uncreated being is known. As the Commentator says, all men naturally desire to know about the divine intellect.

Desire for any knowable object is a kind of desire for the first knowable object. This is the proof. The closer beings are to the first knowable being, the more we desire to know them and the more we delight in thinking of them.

Therefore, by studying the caused beings which are in the world and their natures and relationships to one another, the philosopher is led to consider the highest causes of things. For a knowledge of effects leads to a knowledge of the cause. And in noting that higher causes and their natures are such that they must have another cause, he is led to a knowledge of the first cause. And because there is pleasure in speculative knowledge, and all the more so the nobler the object known, the philosopher leads a life of very great pleasure. The philosopher also knows and observes that it is necessary for this cause to be its own cause of being, that is to say, not to have another cause. For if there were nothing in the universe which was not caused by another, then there would be nothing at all. He also notes that this cause must be eternal and unchangeable, always remaining the same. For if it were not eternal, then nothing whatsoever would be eternal. And again, since certain things in the world have begun to be, and since one being which begins to be cannot be a sufficient cause of another being which begins to be, as is evident, it clearly follows that all things in this world which begin to be must derive from an eternal cause. This cause is also unchangeable and always remains the same. For change is possible only in imperfect things. And if there is some most perfect being in the universe, it is right for this to be the first cause. The philosopher also notes that the entire being of the universe, with the exception of this first cause itself, must come from it and thus, that this first cause is the cause which produces beings and orders them to one another and maintains them in existence—certain ones in terms of their individual identity and without any kind of change (as the separated substances); certain ones according to their individual identity, but as subject to change (as the heavenly bodies); and certain ones in terms of their species alone (as those which are below the heavenly orbit, such as the lowest levels of beings). He also notes that just as all things derive from this first cause, so too, all things are ordered to it. For that being is the beginning of all things, the end of all things, and that through which all things are joined to their end, that being is the first being according to the philosophers and God the Blessed according to the holy men. Nevertheless, in this order there is great range. Those beings which are closest to the first principle are nobler and more perfect. Those which are farther removed from the first principle are lower and less perfect.

This first principle is to this world as the father of a family is to his household, as a commander to his army, and as the common good to the state. Just as the army is one because of the unity of its commander, and just as the good of the army is essentially in the commander and in others in terms of their relationship to him, so too, from the unity of this first principle derives the unity of the world, and the good of this world is essentially in this first principle and in other beings of this world, insofar as they participate in the first principle and are ordered to it. So it is that there is no good in any being in this world which is not a participation in the first principle.

Considering all these things, the philosopher is moved to wonder at this first principle and to love it. For we love that from which our goods derive, and we love that to the greatest degree from which our greatest goods derive.

Therefore, the philosopher, noting that all goods come to him from this first principle and are preserved for him insofar as they are preserved by this first principle, is moved to the greatest love for this first principle. This is in accord with right reason of nature and right reason of intellect. And since everyone takes delight in that which he loves and maximum delight in that which he loves to the maximum degree, and since the philosopher has the greatest love for this first principle, as has been indicated, it follows that the philosopher takes maximum delight in this first principle and in contemplating its goodness, and that this alone is right pleasure. This is the life of the philosopher. Whoever does not lead such a life does not live rightly. However, I call "philosopher" any man who lives according to the right order of nature and who has acquired the best and ultimate end of human life. And the first principle of whom we have spoken is the glorious and most high God, who is blessed forever and ever. Amen.

NOTES

1. M. Grabmann, "Die Opuscula De Summo Bono sive De Vita Philosophi und De Sompniis des Boetius von Dacien," *Mittelalterliches Geistesleben,* II (1936), 200-24. For the Latin text of the *De summo bono, ibid.,* 209-16.

2. Grabmann, 209, n. 18, notes that this statement cannot be found in the writings of Aristotle.

3. Cf. Aristotle, *Metaphysics* XII, 1072b, 24.

4. Cf. *De anima* III, 429a, 1.

XX

HENRY OF GHENT

Henry of Ghent was born in the first or second quarter of the thirteenth century at Ghent, or perhaps at Tournai. After a period of study at the Cathedral school at Tournai he pursued the arts program at the University of Paris, probably under William of Auvergne and Geoffrey of Bar. He became master of arts before 1270 and served as regent master of theology at Paris from 1276 until 1292. He died at Tournai in 1293. Although he was also canon of Tournai from 1267, archdeacon of Bruges in 1273, and archdeacon of Tournai in 1278, he was deeply involved in the life of the university throughout his period of regency. He served on the commission that drew up the propositions for the condemnation of 1277. In the controversy between seculars and mendicants in the 1280s he sided strongly with the seculars. Between 1276 and 1292 Henry conducted both ordinary and quodlibetal disputations. The former were published as his *Summa* and the latter constitute his fifteen *Quodlibetal Questions*. Although he also wrote on the *Metaphysics* and *Physics* of Aristotle, the *Summa* and the *Quodlibetal Questions* constitute his major contribution to theology. Because of the vast amount of philosophy contained therein, they are also major philosophical sources for students of late thirteenth-century philosophy.

After the condemnation of 1277, a number of theologians reacted against Thomism as well as against the radical Aristotelianism of Siger of Brabant and his party. The leading representative of this reaction among the secular theologians at Paris was Henry of Ghent. Heavily influenced by Avicenna as well as by the Neo-Augustinian tradition, his thought might be described as an Avicennian Augustinianism or, perhaps more accurately, as a Christian

Avicennism. Thus certain Avicennian themes, such as the theory of necessary emanation, were replaced by Christian correctives, here by the concept of creation. Writing against this Neoplatonic, Augustinian, and Avicennian background, Henry still retained a number of Aristotelian theses in his highly personal synthesis. His long and involved controversies with men such as Giles of Rome and Godfrey of Fontaines manifest his skill as a dialectician and his grasp of earlier philosophical views. Thus one finds an interesting survey of earlier arguments for the existence of God in the following selection, taken from his *Summa* (art. 22, q. 4) and translated for this volume by A. B. Wolter.

Can Creatures Be Used to Demonstrate God's Existence to Man?[1]

[ARGUMENTS FOR AND AGAINST THE THESIS]

The arguments that creatures cannot be used to demonstrate to man that God exists are these:

First: Any proposition known immediately and in a most self-evident way cannot be demonstrated by means of other things, because every demonstration makes use of something which is intermediate and better known. But "God exists" is such a proposition, since it predicates the same thing of itself, as is clear from what has been settled so far. Therefore, etc.

Second: In God, the "what-it-is" [or essence] and the "that-it-is" [or existence] are identical. But what God is cannot be demonstrated to man from creatures, as will be shown shortly. Therefore, etc.

Third: According to Book I of the *Posterior Analytics* [chap. 2 71b 17], a demonstration is "a syllogism productive of scientific knowledge." But that God exists is not something that can be known in this way, since it is one of the articles of faith, and "faith is . . . of things that are not seen", as the Apostle tells the Hebrews, chap. 11 [v. 20]. And Gregory declares: "Faith, for which human reason provides proof, has no merit."[2] Therefore, etc.

To the contrary is the Apostle to the *Romans,* chap. i: "For since the creation of the world his invisible attributes are clearly seen—his everlasting power also and divinity—being understood through the things that are made." Here the *Glossa*[3] adds: "God who by nature was invisible, fashioned a work which by its visibility would show forth its maker."

[THE BODY OF THE QUESTION]

In reply to this question it must be pointed out that those who assume that God's existence is completely self-evident would have to deny that God can be demonstrated to exist. But, as has been established earlier, this is not the case, for a great many are able to doubt God's existence. This is not because of any imperfection or uncertainty about God's existence itself, however, since from his being itself, this is most evident. It stems rather from the weakness of our intellect, unable as it is to intuit him as he is in himself. That it should draw its certainty, then, that God is from what it knows about creatures, thus demonstrating that God exists, is appropriate. As the *Glossa* points out: "That God, who by nature is invisible, might also be known from what is visible, he fashioned a work which by its visibility showed forth its maker, so that the uncertain might be known from what is certain, and that he might be believed to be the God of all"; this in view of what was said of this above.

A distinction is in order, however, as to what can be demonstrated. The nature of the thing itself may be such as to be simply demonstrable, or it may be demonstrable to us owing to the way our intellect is set up. With this distinction in mind the question is to be answered in this fashion. If one considers the nature of God in itself, then God's existence cannot be demonstrated to man, because there is no medium through which it could be known, for the simple reason that nothing intervenes between his existence and his essence, since they are completely identical as was indicated above. His existence, then, has nothing prior to, or more knowable than itself. Considered thus, God's existence seen face to face can be viewed immediately by man only in the future life, and when it is so seen, no longer will man be able to doubt the impossibility of God's being nonexistent. Neither will it be possible to conceive of him not being, but he will be the reason for demonstrating and knowing all else. That is why Avicenna says in Book VIII of his *Metaphysics:* "Because it is highest and most glorious, the First One has no definition and cannot be demonstrated by means of one, but he himself is the demonstration of every thing which exists."

But if we consider the way in which our intellect is set up, then indeed this can be demonstrated to it; not—I say—the existence God has in himself, but the "is" [esse] which is the sign of an affirmative judgment of the intellect, so that this statement asserting: "God is," is true. And this is what can be demonstrated to the intellect beginning with the creatures that are better known to it. Because they are essentially dependent upon God as their cause and source, creatures can be used to establish an irrefutable proof that he exists, as Augustine says in Series II, *Super Ioannem:* "Philosophers seek the creator through creatures because he can be found through creatures; and that especially is why the natures of creatures are to be investigated." And in his work *On True Religion* he says: "Not in vain or to no purpose ought one to view the beauty of the heavens and the order of the stars in virtue of which every kind of thing preserves its own proper nature and manner of being. In considering such, one should not indulge vain and perishable curiosity, but should take a step forward to what is immortal and endures forever," in order that from what we see, we may understand through a reasoning process those things which we do not see. For as the Apostle says, "since the creation of the world the invisible attributes of God are clearly seen through those things that are made" [Romans, I:20]. This is first demonstrated and secondly shown dialectically.

[I. Demonstrative Arguments]

All demonstrative proofs are to be reduced to one of two ways, that of causality and that of eminence. For, as Dionysius says in his work *On the Divine Names:* In any ordering of existing things if one abstracts from [what is imperfect and asserts what is perfect] in an eminent degree or [analyzes] any cause, one must of necessity be led back to that which is the highest of all. The method of removing [what is imperfect], however, does not help us to know that God exists. For it is the negative approach whereby we remove from God all creatural existence. But from even the greatest number of pure negations nothing affirmative can be inferred. Only by the ways of causality or eminence, then, if we begin with creatures, is it possible to know that God is. Of these two ways, that of causality is the more cogent.

[1. THE WAY OF CAUSALITY]

There is a threefold way of causality relating God to creatures which corresponds to the three ways in which he is their cause, namely as their efficient, formal, and final cause. And from each of the three arguments proving that God exists can be drawn.

[a. The Way of Efficiency]

Three arguments use the efficient cause as their basis. Of these the first and more manifest way is that which makes use of motion. The Philosopher [Aristotle] in the *Physics,* Book VIII [chap. 5] employs this way, proceeding in this fashion: We have the highest certitude based on the senses that some things are moved. To contradict this would be idiotic, since the senses attest to it. Everything moved, however, is moved by another. What he [Aristotle] says there is most effective in persuading one of this point. Now either there is an infinite progression, so that this is moved by that, and the latter by another, and so *ad infinitum,* or the process terminates with something unmoved by any other, and consequently, not moved at all. Were this not the case, then it would follow necessarily that nothing would move or be moved, since secondary movers move only in virtue of some primary motion. Since an infinite regress is impossible and yet it is clear that many things are moved, it is absolutely obvious that some first immovable mover must be postulated; and this is what we understand God to be. Therefore, etc.

A second argument drawn from the same way and which runs along similar lines is that based on what must be a necessary feature of that form of existence which is acquired by being moved, namely, that it is such that it can also not be. In Book I of *De coelo et mundo* [chap. 12] the Philosopher makes use of this way as follows: Since it is certain that things exist which can both be and not be and that nothing of this kind exists of itself (for the existence it actually has is from potency and nothing goes from potency to act save by virtue of something actually existing, because—as we have said in the previous argument—everything which is moved and transmuted is moved and transmuted by another), it is necessary then to postulate something else which cannot be nonexistent. For otherwise there would be an infinite regress, as is evident. Wherefore there must needs be such a thing as possesses existence necessarily and which is such that it has the cause of its necessity either from another or of itself. If from another then we have to ask again: Does this other have the cause of its necessity in still another or is it necessary of itself? Either there will be an infinite regress or we end up with something which has the cause of its necessity in itself. But since it is impossible to go on *ad infinitum,* what must be postulated is some necessary being which derives its necessity not from another but is such of itself. But, as the Commentator [Averroës] explains in the chapter on the necessary in the fifth book of the *Metaphysics,* this first cause of all things is what we call God. Therefore, etc.

The third argument, which pertains to the same way and proceeds in similar fashion, is that which makes use of the conditions of cause and caused. The former of itself has necessary existence and moves [other things]; the latter is moved and has its existence by reason of another. In Book II of the *Metaphysics* the Philosopher uses this way in proving there is an ultimate among efficient causes. What is certain and what we see before our very eyes in such sensible things as can begin to be and perish is that there is something whose existence is caused. Every such thing however must needs be caused and have its existence from another. For there is nothing which gives itself existence so that it would be its own cause, for then one and the same thing would be both prior and posterior to itself, which is impossible. Therefore, either there will be an infinite regress so that this is caused by that, and the latter by another, or else we shall end up with some first thing which is not caused by another. (Whether there be one or several such is not the issue here in the question about the being of God, but is a point that remains to be proved later in the question, namely, about his unicity.) It is impossible, however, to proceed *ad infinitum* where efficient causes are concerned since with all such, the first is the cause of the intermediate causes and the latter, whether one or several, are the cause of the last. If a cause ceases to exist, so too does its effect. Consequently, if there were not among efficient causes one which is first in the fullest sense of the term, neither would there be a last. It is necessary then to postulate some cause which is the first among all efficient causes and this we call God. Therefore, etc.

[b. The Way of Formal Causality]

The argument by way of formal causality is twofold, since the form is a principle both of being and being known. The one begins with the being things possess by reason of their form; the second is based upon the knowledge whose source is the form. Both proceed in the same manner as the argumentation of the previous way. The first is that for which Augustine searches in *On True Religion*. If there is one thing that we can be sure of, one thing which is there before our very eyes, it is the delightful beauty and decor possessed by every bodily nature, beginning with the very lowest of inanimate things, increasing with insensate organisms, becoming even greater in that which is sensate, and still greater in that nature endowed with reason which evaluates all the rest. For what judges is always of greater excellence than what is judged. Since in all this, beauty and agreeability is to be found, we are pleased. But since none of these possesses the ultimate in beauty, each suffers in comparison with what is better and is judged to possess so much beauty and to depart so much from perfect pulchritude. Now either there will be an infinite regress or we shall end up with something so beautiful and lovely that all else is judged by its beauty and decor and suffers in comparison. This immutable nature excelling every existing rational creature, since creatures are changeable, is undoubtedly what we call God. But since an infinite regress is impossible, we must needs postulate that there is a terminus which is God.

The second proof is that for which Augustine looks so long in his work *On Free Choice of the Will*, Book II [chaps. 3ff]. It is certain from our own experience that while we judge about the proper sensibles by reason of a particular sense, e.g. about colors by reason of sight, or about sounds by hearing, we are unable by these senses to determine what they have or do not have in common—for this latter we do by means of a kind of common internal sense. But even by this we cannot discern not only what they have in common but also what is proper to each. For we do this only in virtue of a higher power called reason. Since in all such, what judges is better and more noble than what is judged, it follows that there will be either an infinite regress or a termination in something so excellent that it is judged by none but is that in virtue of which all else is judged. But this immutable wisdom is without a doubt something above rational minds and above every mutable thing, since to pass judgment on what is mutable is the prerogative only of what is immutable. This immutable wisdom we call God. Since an infinite regress, however, is impossible, we are forced to postulate a termination in what can only be God.

[c. The Way of Final Causality]

So far as the way of final causality is concerned there is but one argument and it resembles the previous ones. The Philosopher [Aristotle] in Book II of the *Metaphysics* uses it in the following way. We see that one thing is ordered to another as to its end. The latter is ordered to something else as its end, and this is the case with all things (for what is *per se* and by nature the good of anything is its end and that for the sake of which it exists, as we read in Book III of the *Metaphysics*). This being so, either there will be an infinite regress or this hierarchy of ends will culminate in something ultimate, which is the good and end of all that precedes and has nothing beyond it as its good or end. But since this process cannot go on *ad infinitum,* as we said above, if no such thing exists, there will be nothing that comes to be for the sake of something, and thus the nature of the good will be destroyed and everything will occur by happenstance and without any purpose. It is necessary therefore to assume a terminal point in some ultimate good which is the end of all else. But this is just what we say God is, since he is the best of all beings. Therefore God exists.

[2. THE WAY OF EMINENCE]

After the way of causality, the more cogent way of proving God exists is that of eminence and it proceeds according to a twofold argumentation. One is along the lines of the formal cause argument of the first way, namely since all that is good and praiseworthy about a creature is still small and deficient, we trace it back to what is good and praiseworthy in a perfect and consummate sense, lest there be an infinite regress. Richard [of St. Victor] speaks of this in his work *On the Trinity*. What is most certain so that none can doubt it is that among such a variety of things there must be a highest, exceeded or excelled by nothing. This is the true entity and goodness, as it were, from which all else has its goodness and entity. And as Anselm puts it in the *Monologium,* chapter three, since there is no denying that some natures are better than others, reason persuades us that one of them is of such excellence that it neither has nor can have anything superior to it. And Augustine in *On Christian Doctrine,* Book I [chap. 7] says that those who by their intelligence go on to see what God is, prefer him to all other natures not only visible and bodily but also intelligible and spiritual—to all that is mutable. All certainly suffer in comparison with God's excellence. Neither can anyone be found who believes that God is excelled by anything. As is fitting, then, all agree that he is God whom they esteem above all things.

Another way of arguing by way of eminence proceeds by comparing what is to be approved of in creatures and the creator either simply or in terms of more or less. This is the argument Anselm uses in the beginning of the *Monologium*. Wherever we find something existing in varying degrees, there is something to be found which is simply such. Now among things we find both what is good and what is better, what is beautiful and what is more lovely, what delights and what is more delightful. Something is to be found then which is simply good, simply beautiful, simply delightful. In comparison to this, all else has only more or less. But where there is pure goodness as well as pure beauty, delightfulness, and so on, there is God. Hence God exists.

The Philosopher in the *Metaphysics*, Book IV, uses a similar argument against those who insist that every opinion is only an estimate and there is nothing scientifically certain. For they still say that estimates differ from one another by reason of their greater or lesser degree of truth. The Commentator [Averroës] develops the argument even more clearly than the text as follows: If anything is to have more of the truth and less of falsity, then something must be simply true and in reference to this other things are said to be more or less true. For what has more of the truth and less of falsity, since it is an admixture of contraries, must have something above it which is more true. But if this other is not simply true but has an element of falsity in it, then it too has something greater above it. Now there is either an infinite regress or a termination in what is true without qualification. The latter is that which is the truest of all and is the cause of the truth of whatever is below it, as we read in the *Metaphysics*, Book II, where the Commentator says that this is the proper cause of all things and is God. Therefore, etc.

[II. Probable Arguments]

Fragmentary and probable arguments are also used to

argue the same point. These however are reducible to the above demonstrative proofs in the way that every probable reason is reducible to one that is necessary. Such an argument by way of efficient causality is that of Richard in his work *On the Trinity* [PL 196, col. 893ff]. He presupposes two self-evident divisions. The first is that whatever is or can be thought of either exists eternally or begins to be in time. The second is that whatever exists has its existence of itself or by reason of another. These being presupposed, he argues in terms of a fourfold division. Every being either exists eternally and of itself or neither eternally nor of itself, or in one of two intermediary ways: viz. either eternally and not of itself, or of itself but not eternally. It is this last alternative that he rules out first as being wholly impossible, for whatever does not exist eternally begins to be according to the first division proposed. Hence it has its existence from another and not of itself, according to the second division proposed. Then, using the second and third members of his fourfold classification, he argues to the existence of the first in this fashion. If something does not exist of itself, whether it exists eternally (as the third member says) or not (as the second says), it must needs have its existence from another (according to the second division proposed). There is then the question of whether this other exists by reason of some further thing. Either we admit an infinite regress, which is impossible, or we shall come to something which does not have its existence from another. This then will be something which is both eternal and of itself and this we call God. Therefore, etc.

Damascene argues in the same way in Book I [of *The Orthodox Faith*] thus: Everything which is or can be thought of is creatable or not. If creatable, then it is variable and has gone from nonexistence to being. But this is not in virtue of some other creatable, lest there be an infinite series of questions about this other from which it proceeded to be. Therefore, it is by reason of something uncreatable. This however is what we assume God to be. Therefore, etc.

The same form of argument with a slightly different subject matter is this. All that is or can be, is either a cause or caused or both. Everything caused, however, has existence from a cause other than itself since nothing causes itself to be. Either there will be an infinite regress or there will be some cause which is not itself caused and this is what we call God. Hence, God exists.

In chapter three of Book I, Damascene argues to the same conclusion using the notion of conservation. Everything composed that can be dissolved into something simple and indissoluble is conserved in existence, since of itself it will fall into nothingness. Every mundane thing is of this sort. Therefore, etc.

Some argue to the same conclusion from the governance of the world by way of final causality in this fashion. All natural things act for the sake of an end according to the Philosopher in Book II of the *Physics*. But they do so without any knowledge of it, for they possess no knowledge. However, what lacks knowledge is not directed toward a definite end unless it be guided by one who knows of it, even as the arrow is aimed by the archer. There is then some knower by whom all natural things are governed in regard to their end and this is what we assume God to be. Therefore, etc.

Anselm in the *Monologium* and Augustine in *On True Religion, Soliloquies,* and *On Free Choice of the Will* reach the same conclusion on the basis of the nature of truth as follows: Truth cannot be nonexistent, but is eternal and immutable, as is argued persuasively in the aforesaid works frequently and prolixly. But eternal truth is nothing else but God. Therefore it is necessary that God exist. This argument proceeds by the way of final causality. And so it becomes irrefutably clear that if we assume that any being exists, we must postulate that God exists.

[REPLY TO THE ARGUMENTS AT THE BEGINNING]

Against the first argument (that every demonstration proceeds by way of some prior and better known middle term), it must be said that this is true either simply or so far as we are concerned. Now while there is no medium for proving God exists which is prior or better known purely and simply, there is nevertheless one which is such so far as we are concerned, as has been said. For just as we may doubt about God's existence by grasping something with our mind which is the divine essence confusedly signified by the name, so too can we be convinced of his existence by means of a creature which is known to us. But this is something which has to do with the mind's knowledge and is not in the nature of things themselves.

To the second argument, that in God the "what-it-is" [or

essence] is the same as the "that-it-is" [or existence], while it must be admitted that this is true of the being [esse] by which he subsists in himself, it is not true of the "is" [esse] which signifies an affirmation of the intellect. Therefore, even though the former "that-it-is" cannot be known if the "what-it-is" is not known, as shall be made clear later on, the latter can be, as has been asserted above and will be brought up again later.

As for the third, viz. that since the existence of God is an article of faith, it is not demonstrable, this must be pointed out. Of the things that can be believed, some are simply such, those which are a matter of belief for all since they simply exceed natural reason's powers of investigation, e.g., that God is triune. This kind of truth is in no way demonstrable from creatures, although we may find certain features about creatures with which such a truth fits in and which can be used to lead the mind to believe such a truth more firmly. But it is only through the light of faith and God revealing it that we believe such a truth and it is by the merit of faith that what we at first believed, we come to understand by reason of a light infused from above. The reason, then, that probable arguments should be adduced is to clarify such a truth and not to convince those who are opposed to it, for there are no reasons in the nature of things that can do such, since the notion of the Trinity is not something which can be revealed in creatures, a point we shall take up later. The type of truth which can be believed by some, however, is of a different kind. It does not completely transcend the understanding of natural reason. Such is the truth that God exists or that there is but one God. For those who have not a mature mind, such truths cannot be proved from what they know of creatures, but are matters of pure belief. For others, however, who are of a more subtle mind, such truths are probable, and for these individuals such truths are to some extent knowable and to some extent a matter of belief, viz. insofar as any arguments drawn from creatures do not prove them to a man in this life with the same clarity as he hopes to have about them through vision in the life to come. In such as these faith and scientific knowledge (or understanding) stand side by side, as we said before. As for what is added from Gregory (viz. that faith would be without merit, and so on) one should reply that there is one type of reason which serves as a prelude to faith by proving what must be believed and causing faith. This holds, however, only for such truths as are matters of belief for some but not for all. But in such a case there is no merit, if a truth of this kind is held only because of what is known by reason. But if by reason we come to have faith in other things that are to be believed, or if it follows upon faith, reason does not destroy merit. That is why philosophers who come to have faith believe meritoriously many things about God which they knew before or know afterwards by reason. That is why Augustine says in *On the Trinity,* Book VIII, chap. 9: "Faith helps us in our knowledge and love of God, not as though he were completely unknown or unloved, but in such a way that he may be known more clearly and loved more steadfastly." A reason of this kind rather augments than destroys merit.

NOTES

1. *Summa quaestionum ordinariarum,* art. 22. q. 4 (Paris, 1520 ed., photo-reprint St. Bonaventure, N. Y.: Franciscan Institute, 1953) I, fol. 132v-134r.

2. St. Gregory the Great, *XL Homiliarum in Evangelia,* liber II, hom. 26 (PL 76, 1197).

3. The reference is to Peter Lombard's collection of glosses (*Magna Glossatura*). Cf. Peter Lombard, *Collectanea in omnes D. Pauli Apostoli epistolas* (PL 191, 1326). Peter has taken this citation from pseudo-Ambrose (PL 17, 57).

XXI

JOHN DUNS SCOTUS

JOHN DUNS SCOTUS, known as the Subtle Doctor, was born in Scotland no later than 1266, probably at the Duns estate on the outskirts of the present town of Duns in Berwickshire. His uncle, Elias Duns, vicar general of the Scottish Franciscans, invested him in the habit of the order at an early age. He was ordained priest at Northampton, March 17, 1291 by Oliver Sutton, Bishop of Lincoln. Though he spent some time at Cambridge, Oxford and Paris were the principal scenes of his intellectual activity. He seems to have completed by 1301 the thirteen-year training program required for a master of theology at Oxford, and he had, by then, been at work for at least a year revising for publication his lectures on the *Sentences* of Peter Lombard, the *Opus oxoniense* or *Ordinatio*. Only the long list of trained bachelors like himself awaiting their turn to occupy the Franciscan chair of theology there prevented him from incepting as a master at Oxford.

When the turn came for the English province to provide a talented candidate for the Franciscan chair of theology at Paris, Scotus was sent, to begin lecturing once more on the *Sentences* in the fall of 1302. Except for brief banishment, along with other students who refused to support Philip the Fair in his quarrel with Pope Boniface over taxation of Church property to support the French armies, Scotus continued these lectures (known as the *Reportata Parisiensia*) until the spring of 1305, when he became regent master. The single set of *Quodlibetal questions* suggest that his regency at Paris may not have been longer than a year. The common custom of rotating the more brilliant lectors among various study houses of the order may have been responsible for his being sent elsewhere to teach. We know he was functioning as a lector in

Cologne in February, 1308. He died there the following November 8 and was buried in the Franciscan church, where his remains are still venerated.

The following selections are from his earliest extant lectures, presumably given at Oxford and antedating his *Ordinatio*. The translation is by A. B. Wolter.

On the Existence of God*

[QUESTION ONE: DOES AN INFINITE BEING EXIST?]

1. The first question raised in connection with the second distinction is this: "In the realm of beings is there some being which is actually infinite?"

[Pro et Contra]

It would seem not, for:

[Arg. I] If one of two contraries were actually infinite, it would be incompatible with anything other than itself. But good and evil are contraries. Hence, if some good were actually infinite, nothing would be actually evil, which is false.

2. In answer to this some say that the evil in the universe is not a true contrary to God or the infinite good, because he has no true contrary. But this is no solution, for whether the contrariety be formal or only virtual between two things, if one of the two be infinite, it will tolerate nothing contrary either to itself or to its effect. If the sun, for instance, possessed infinite heat either formally or virtually, nothing would be cold. Consequently, if some good were actually infinite either virtually or formally, then throughout the universe evil, as the contrary of some good, would be simply non-existent.

3. [Arg. II] An infinite body would not allow another body to coexist; therefore an infinite spirit will not allow another spirit to coexist. The antecedent is evident from Bk. IV of the *Physics*.[1]

The consequence is thus proved: just as two bodies cannot coexist in one place because of their opposed dimensions,

*From *John Duns Scotus: A Treatise on God as First Principle,* ed. and trans. by Allan B. Wolter, pp. 157-89.

so neither does it seem possible for two spirits because their actualizations are opposed.

4. Another proof of the same consequence is this: If another body could coexist with an infinite body, then there would be something larger than an infinite body. It would seem then that if another spirit existed in addition to the infinite, there would be something virtually greater than the infinite.

5. [Arg. III] Furthermore, whatever is here and nowhere else is limited in its whereabouts; what exists now but not then is of limited time; and what acts by this action and no other is limited in action, and so on. But whatever exists is a "this" in such a way that it is no other; therefore it is finite, whatever it be.

6. [Arg. IV] Furthermore, if some power were infinite, it would cause movement instantaneously, as Bk. VIII of the *Physics* proves.[2] Motion, therefore, would occur instantaneously, which is impossible.

7. *To the contrary:*

In Bk. VIII of the *Physics*,[3] the Philosopher [Aristotle] says that the first mover is infinite. And therefore his power does not reside in any magnitude—not in an infinite magnitude, because there is no such thing, nor in a finite magnitude, because something of greater magnitude would have a greater power. But this argument is not valid unless it be understood of something that is infinite in power, because a body, like the sun, would be infinite in duration.

[QUESTION TWO: IS IT SELF-EVIDENT THAT AN INFINITE BEING EXISTS?]

8. This poses the further question: Is the existence of something infinite, such as God's existence, a fact that is self-evident?

[Pro et Contra]

The arguments that it is are these:

[Arg. I] Damascene says in the first chapter:[4] "The knowledge that God exists is implanted in everyone." Such knowledge, however, is self-evident, as is clear from Bk. II of the *Metaphysics*,[5] where first principles, which are like the [proverbial] door, are presented as something self-evident.

9. [Arg. II] Furthermore, the existence of a thing is self-evident if it is impossible to think of anything greater than it. For if one were to grant the opposite of the predicate, it would destroy the subject; because if the thing in question did not exist one could think of something greater, viz. its existence, which is greater than its nonexistence. And this seems to be Anselm's argument in chapter two of the *Proslogion*.[6]

10. [Arg. III] That truth exists is self-evident; therefore etc. Proof of the antecedent: Whatever follows from its own denial is self-evident. But truth is such, because if you affirm that truth exists, then it is true that you affirm this and hence truth exists; if you may deny that truth exists, then it would be true that truth does not exist. And therefore some truth still exists.

11. [Arg. IV] Furthermore, those propositions are self-evident which derive their necessity from that fact that their terms have at least that qualified existence that comes from being in the mind. All the more then is that proposition self-evident which owes its necessity to the being of the thing and terms in an unqualified sense. But "God exists" is such a proposition. Proof of the antecedent: Suppose that neither a whole nor its part existed. The very fact that these terms in the mind are related the way they are, guarantees "Every whole is greater than its part" to be a necessary truth. In such a case, however, the terms would have only a qualified existence in the mind.

12. *To the contrary:*

No mind can deny what is self-evident; but God's existence can be denied for "The fool says in his heart, 'There is no God' " [Psalms 13, 1].

[I. Reply to the Second Question]

13. We must answer this second question first. To solve it, we must understand first of all what is meant by a self-evident proposition. Then it will be clear if "God exists" (or some other proposition in which "existence" is predicated of something belonging to God, such as "An infinite being exists") is self-evident.

14. To understand the meaning of "self-evident proposition," know that when a proposition is said to be such, the

word "self" does not rule out every cause whatsoever, because it does not exclude knowledge of the terms. For no proposition is self-evident unless there is knowledge of its terms. What is excluded is any cause or reason which is not essentially included in the concepts of the terms of the self-evident proposition. Hence, that proposition is self-evident which does not need to borrow knowledge elsewhere, but draws the evidence of its own truth from the knowledge of its terms and has the sole source of its certitude within itself.

15. But the name, now, is one term and the concept associated with it is another, the difference between them being that of a name and its definition. Proof: In a demonstration, the definition of one of the extremes serves as a middle term, the remaining term in the premises being the same as in the conclusion. The extreme differs from the middle term as the defined differs from the definition. If the term and concept of the thing defined were the same as that of the definition, then the most cogent form of demonstration would involve a begging of the question. What is more, it would have but two terms. Consequently, the concept of the definition is different from that of the thing defined in so far as the latter is expressed by the name which is defined.

16. Furthermore, Bk. I of the *Physics*[7] says that much the same thing happens in the relation of names to their definitions as does in the relation of the whole to its parts. The thing defined is known even before its definition is discovered by an analysis of the parts it has. Wherefore, in so far as the concept of the definition is expressed by the name of the thing defined, it is something confused and is known before [the definition]. But it is expressed more distinctly by the name of the definition, which distinguishes the several parts of the defined. Hence the concept associated with the name of the thing defined is other than that of the definition.

17. From this it follows that a proposition is not self-evident if our only knowledge of it stems from a definition of its terms. For, inasmuch as only that proposition is self-evident which is evident from a knowledge of its terms, and the definition and the name are different terms, it follows that a proposition whose evidence stems exclusively from the definition of its terms, is not self-evident, since it borrows its evidence from something beyond itself and it can be a conclusion with reference to some other proposition.

18. Likewise, if a proposition whose evidence stemmed

from the definition of its terms were self-evident, then every proposition would be self-evident that is in the first mode of *per se* predication, such as "Man is an animal, and a body" and so on, up to "substance." Consequently, knowledge of the definition is not enough to make a proposition self-evident.

19. Therefore that proposition only is self-evident which draws its evidence solely from the knowledge of its terms and does not borrow it from the evidence for other concepts.

20. From this we see there is no point or purpose in distinguishing propositions which are self-evident by their nature from those which are self-evident to us; or among the latter, those which are self-evident to the wise from those which are self-evident to the foolish; or those which are self-evident of the first order from those which are self-evident of the second order. For a proposition is not called self-evident because it happens to be in a particular mind, but because its terms are by their nature apt to cause self-evident knowledge in any intellect which conceives them as self-evident in themselves. And therefore nothing is self-evident which can be demonstrated to any intellect. Nevertheless, grades do exist among self-evident propositions according to their value or lack of it. Thus, "It is impossible for the same thing to both be and not be" is of more value than this: "Every whole is greater than its part," etc.

21. Secondly, turning now to the question at issue, I say this: Suppose one means by the name "God" something which we do not conceive perfectly–such as "this divine essence" where the latter term is grasped as self-evident, as would be the case, for instance, if God, seeing himself, were to impose this name "God" upon his essence. Then one might ask whether "God exists" or "This essence exists" would be self-evident. I say that they would be, because the terms in this case are such that they are able to make such a proposition evident to anyone who grasped the terms of the proposition perfectly, and "self-evident" could not be more aptly applied than to this essence.

22. But suppose you ask whether existence is predicated of any concept which we have of God's essence, so that such a proposition would be self-evident wherein existence is predicated of such a concept, as when we say for example that "The infinite exists." To this I say: No! For nothing which can be the conclusion of a demonstration is self-evident from the

knowledge of its terms. But every proposition predicating existence of any concept we have of God is just such, viz. the conclusion of a demonstration. Proof: Anything which pertains to a more comprehensive but less extensive concept according to the first mode of *per se* predication, can also be shown to pertain *per se* to a broader concept by using the more comprehensive concept as a middle term. For instance, if some attribute pertains primarily to "triangle," it can be demonstrated to be an attribute of "figure" by means of "triangle." Every concept that we use to conceive of God, however, is less comprehensive than "this essence." Therefore, by using as middle term "this essence" to which existence primarily pertains, one could demonstrate existence of every concept that we use to conceive of God. Consequently, no proposition such as "An infinite being exists" is self-evident from a knowledge of its terms but it borrows its evidence from something else, and hence is not self-evident.—The major of this argument, however, can be asserted in an even more universal form, viz. whatever pertains to something primarily, does not pertain to another except in virtue of that nature to which it belongs primarily. But "existence" belongs primarily to "this divine nature." Therefore it is not ascribed [primarily] to some property [of this essence], neither does it pertain to any other [divine attribute] except in virtue of the nature of [the divine] essence. Therefore, no proposition in which existence is predicated of some property of this [divine] essence which we conceive is primarily true, but it is true only by reason of some other truth, and consequently it is not a primary or self-evident proposition.

23. Furthermore, if a proposition is self-evident, then any intellect which conceives its terms, will by that very fact know that the proposition is true. But this is not the case with such a proposition as "God exists"—where by God is meant not this essence which we conceive, but some concept which we have about this essence—or "God is infinite" or "An infinite being exists." Therefore, it is not self-evident. The major is evident. The minor is established as follows. Everyone who assents to any proposition either because of faith or belief or because it is demonstrated, grasps the meaning of the terms. But we assent to this: "God exists" either because of faith or because of a demonstration. Therefore, the meaning of the terms are known prior to faith or demonstration. But this

apprehending of the terms does not make us assent to the proposition, otherwise we should not know it only by faith or demonstration.

24. What is more, there is a third argument. To understand it, you must keep in mind first of all that some concepts are *simply simple* and others are not. That concept is simply simple which is not reduced to some prior or simpler concept, nor is it fully resolved into more than one concept. Such are the concepts of being, and of the ultimate differences. But a concept that is not simply simple is one which, though it be simply grasped, i.e. nothing is affirmed or denied about it, is nevertheless resolved into more than one concept of which the one can be conceived without the other. Such is the concept of the species which can be resolved into a genus and a difference. Consequently, even though a concept be simple in the sense that nothing is affirmed or denied, one must distinguish further whether it is simply simple or not in the aforesaid sense. From this it is clear how one should understand or explain the statement of the Philosopher in Bk. IX of the *Metaphysics*[8] where we read that so far as simple concepts are concerned the deception characteristic of what is composite is absent. It is not a question here of an affirmation or negation of anything, for one can err by asserting something of a simple concept just as one can say something true or false of a composite concept. What he has in mind is that "the definition of the composite is a long rigmarole,"[9] in which many concepts are lumped together and error can arise concerning their conjunction. Sometimes the combination may even include contradictory elements as is the case with "dead man" [i.e. a man without a soul] or "irrational man" [where man is defined as a rational animal]. But such is not the case where simple notions are concerned, for here either one grasps the whole or he grasps nothing.

25. Keeping this explanation in mind, I argue as follows: No proposition about a concept which is not simply simple will be self-evident, unless it also be self-evident that the components of such a concept go together, as I shall prove. Every proper concept that we have of God, however, is not simply simple and consequently, nothing is self-evident of such a concept unless we know that the parts of such a concept essentially go together. But, as I shall prove shortly, it is not self-evident that this is the case. As a consequence, no proposition in which anything is asserted of any concept we have of God

will be self-evident, e.g. "God exists" or "An infinite God exists."

26. Proof of the major: no notion is true *of* anything unless it first be true in itself. For if it is false in itself, it will not be true of anything. This is clear from Bk. V of the *Metaphysics* in the chapter "About the False,"[10] where the Philosopher intends to say that the false in itself includes a contradiction, whereas what is false of something is that which is not false of everything whatsoever, as is the case with the false in itself. Consequently, it is necessary that one must first know that a thing is true in itself before one can know that it is true of something. But if one does not grasp that the parts of a concept that is not simply simple go together, he does not conceive something that is true in itself and hence does not conceive it as being in something or as true of something. Nothing therefore is self-evidently known about a concept which is not simply simple unless one first recognizes that the parts of this concept go together.

27. The other proposition assumed in the argument is also true, viz. that every concept which we have of God is not simply simple, because every such concept I have of God has to do with what is common to me and to him, as will become clear later.[11]

28. The other assumption is true too, viz. that it is not self-evident that the parts of the concept we use to think of God go together, because it can be demonstrated that one part goes with the other, as is the case, for example, when we demonstrate "God is infinite" or "God exists" (where by "God" we mean what we conceive God to be).

29. From this it is clear that they are incorrect who claim such propositions as "God exists," "A necessary being exists," or "What is operating is in act" are self-evidently known on the grounds that the opposite of the predicate is inconsistent with the subject, and therefore the proposition is self-evident.

I say that they are not self-evident, because whenever you use a concept that is not simply simple as the subject you must have self-evident knowledge that the parts go together, which is not the case with "A necessary being exists" and "What is operating is in act," for it is not self-evident that something necessary exists, but this can be demonstrated. That is why the Heracliteans were wont to deny "necessary being" and assert that all is in continuous motion. It is the same with "What is operating is in act," because it is not self-evident that there is actually anything which is operating. Hence it does not follow from the fact that the opposite of the predicate is inconsistent with the subject that the proposition in question is necessary. Indeed, it may even be that such a proposition is false, as is the case with "An irrational man is an animal": for this is inconsistent: "No animal exists, yet an irrational man exists." It is the same with the proposition: "Something greater than God exists," which is false, even though the opposite of the predicate is inconsistent with the subject.

30. If you insist that the predicate is already posited in the subject in the proposition like "A necessary being exists" or "What is operating is in act" and consequently they are self-evident, I reply that this does not follow, because it is not self-evidently known that the notions which are presumed to be present in the subject can actually go together.

31. To this it is objected on logical grounds that if the opposite of the predicate of some proposition is inconsistent with the subject, then from the existence of the subject follows the existence of the predicate. For example, in the proposition "Man is an animal," the opposite of animal is inconsistent with man; therefore this follows: "If a man exists, an animal exists." Hence, if in the proposition "An irrational man is an animal," the opposite of the predicate is inconsistent with the subject, then this would follow: "An irrational man exists, therefore an animal exists." Hence the medium used to infer this, viz. "An irrational man is an animal," is true. Therefore, if the opposite of the predicate is inconsistent with the subject, the proposition will be true and necessary.

To this I say: the inference does not follow, because those extremes must be united for which the inference holds. But in this: "An irrational man exists, therefore an animal exists," the consequence holds solely because of "man" and not because of "irrational," and therefore it is by virtue of "Man is an animal" that it holds. Consequently, the following is not an inference: "An irrational man exists, therefore a man exists," because "irrational" adds nothing to the inference, and to go from one thing to the same thing is not an inference; neither then is this: "A necessary being exists, therefore it exists."

32. And so it is clear, then, first of all what a self-evident proposition is, seeing that it is one which draws its evidence from the concepts of its terms and from nothing else, whatever be the intellect which conceives those terms. For this follows what was said above [cf. 14-20].

33. It is also clear in what way "God exists" is self-evident and in what way it is not. For if we mean by God "this divine essence" which we do not conceive, it is a self-evident truth; but if we mean by God, that which we first conceive God to be in such universal terms as "first principle" and "infinite" and many such like, then the truth is not self-evidently known, as has already been shown.

[II. To the Arguments at the Beginning of the Second Question (par. 8-11)]

34. [To Arg. I] As for the first reason, based on Damascene's statement that the knowledge of God is implanted in all, I say that in the same place he says that "no one knows God except by revelation" so that it is necessary to gloss his statement. Therefore it can be said that the cognition of God is implanted in everybody, not in particular but in universal terms and according to common notions which are most appropriately applied to God, and therefore by way of appropriation it is said that the knowledge of him is implanted in all. Hence "being" and "act," etc. are most appropriately applied to God. Or one could say that the knowledge of God is implanted in everyone by reason of their knowledge of creatures, from which they come to know God. But even for him the knowledge of God is not self-evident.

35. [To Arg. II] As for the other, where it is argued that according to Anselm the existence of a thing is self-evident, if it is impossible to think of anything greater, I reply that such is not the case. Hence Anselm's intention there is not to show that the existence of God is self-evident, but that it is true. And he makes two syllogisms, of which the first is: "Something is greater than anything which does not exist; but nothing is greater than the highest; therefore the highest is not non-being." There is another syllogism: "What is not a non-being, exists; but the highest is not a non-being, therefore the highest exists."

36. [To Arg. III] As for the other reason, where it is claimed: "That truth exists is self-evident," I say for one thing the argument fallaciously affirms the consequent, since it proceeds from truth in general to this "Truth" which is God. For another, I say that it is not self-evident that "truth exists." And when it is argued that "If truth does not exist, it is true that truth does not exist," I say that the consequence does not fol-

low, because there is no truth except fundamentally in things and formally in the intellect. But if nothing is true, then nothing exists and consequently in nothing is there truth. Hence, it doesn't follow that if truth does not exist, therefore this dictum "Truth does not exist" is true.

37. [To Arg. IV] As for the next argument, when it is claimed that the proposition "God exists" has terms which are purely necessary, whereas this is not the case with "Every whole is greater than a part thereof" I say that the necessity of the proposition is not a necessity characteristic of real things, but it consists of the evidence for the proposition which is in the mind because the terms are there. "God exists," however, has a necessity and an evidence that stems from reality, but the other proposition has the greater evidence in the mind, once its terms are known, and consequently it is self-evident, whereas the other is not.

[III. Reply to the First Question]

38. In answer to the first question one must say this. Some properties of the infinite being have reference to creatures and from the existence of their referents, the existence of these properties can be inferred. From this it follows that the proper way to know the existence of God and his infinity is by way of such divine properties as have reference to creatures.

[A. GOD'S EXISTENCE DEMONSTRATED FROM PROPERTIES WHICH REFER TO CREATURES]

39. Now there are two properties of God which have reference to creatures, one is eminence in goodness, the other is causality. Eminence is not subdivided further, but causality is. According to some,[12] its divisions are: exemplar, efficient and final cause. Such say that the exemplar cause gives a thing its essential being. But I say here (and later on in more detail[13]) that the exemplar cause is not to be numbered alongside of the efficient cause, for it is only as a concomitant factor of an efficient cause that the exemplar in the mind of the artisan gives any being to a thing. And if [the exemplar in view of its effect] can be considered as a formal cause, then it would pertain to eminence rather than to causality, for the more excellent being contains virtually the forms of other things and contains them

unitively. Hence in God there are these three: eminence, efficiency and finality.

[1. The Argument from Efficiency]

40. Now efficiency can be considered either as a metaphysical or as a physical property. The metaphysical property is more extensive than the physical for "to give existence to another" is of broader scope than "to give existence by way of movement or change." And even if all existence were given in the latter fashion, the notion of the one is still not that of the other.

It is not efficiency as a physical attribute, however, but efficiency as the metaphysician considers it that provides a more effective way of proving God's existence, for there are more attributes in metaphysics than in physics whereby the existence of God can be established. It can be shown, for example, from "composition and simplicity," from "act and potency," from "one and many," from those features which are properties of being. Wherefore, if you find one extreme of the disjunction imperfectly realized in a creature, you conclude that the alternate, the perfect extreme exists in God.

Averroës, therefore, in attacking Avicenna at the end of Bk. I of the *Physics,*[14] is incorrect when he claims that to prove that God exists is the job of the physicist alone, because this can be established only by way of motion, and in no other way —as if metaphysics began with a conclusion which was not evident in itself, but needed to be proved in physics (For Averroës asserts this falsehood at the end of the first book of the *Physics*). In point of fact, however, [God's existence] can be shown more truly and in a greater variety of ways by means of those metaphysical attributes which characterize being. The proof lies in this that the first efficient cause imparts not merely this fluid existence [called motion] but existence in an unqualified sense, which is still more perfect and widespread. Now the existence of a primacy in the higher class does not follow logically from the existence of a primary in a lower [or more specific] class, unless that member is the most noble. For example, this does not follow: "The most noble donkey exists, therefore the most noble animal exists." Consequently, from the property of being the most noble being, one can argue better to a primacy among beings than from the primacy characteristic of a prime mover.

41. Hence, we omit the physical argument by which a prime mover is shown to exist and, using the efficiency characteristic of beings, we argue that among beings there is one which is a first efficient cause. And this is Richard's argument in Bk. I, chapter eight *On the Trinity*.[15]

Some being is not eternal, and therefore it does not exist of itself, neither is it caused by nothing, because nothing produces itself. Hence, it is from some other being. The latter either gives existence in virtue of something other than itself or not. And its existence, too, it either gets from another or not. If neither be true—i.e., if it neither imparts existence in virtue of another nor receives its own existence from another—then this is the first efficient cause, for such is the meaning of the term. But if either of the above alternatives holds [viz. if it receives existence, or imparts it to others only in virtue of another], then I inquire about the latter as I did before. One cannot go on his way *ad infinitum*. Hence, we end up with some first efficient cause, which neither imparts existence in virtue of another nor receives its own existence from another.

42. Objections, however, are raised against this argument. To begin with, it seems to beg the question, for it assumes that there is an order and a first among causes. But if no efficient cause is first, then both the order and the terminus in such causes would have to be denied.

43. Furthermore, inasmuch as the argument begins with a contingent premise, it does not seem to be a demonstration. For a demonstration proceeds from necessary premises, and everything exists contingently which owes its existence to God. Consequently, with reference to God this statement is contingent: "Some being is non-eternal," because from it this statement follows: "Some non-eternal being exists," and this latter is contingent.

44. Furthermore, since there is no demonstration of the reasoned fact, neither does there seem to be any demonstration of the simple fact.[16] For, whenever some conclusion is established by a demonstration of the latter type, one can always set up a converse demonstration of the reasoned fact (from cause to effect). But from the existence of the first cause, the existence of other things cannot be inferred by a demonstration of the reasoned fact; therefore, neither is the converse relation demonstrable as a simple fact.

45. To solve these objections, then, know this to begin

with. Incidental [*per accidens*] causes are not the same as causes that are ordered to one another incidentally, just as essential [*per se*] causes are not the same as causes essentially ordered to one another. For when I speak of essential [i.e. *per se*] and incidental [i.e. *per accidens*] causes, I express a one to one relationship, viz. between a cause and its effect. But when causes are said to be incidentally or essentially ordered, two causes are being considered with reference to a single effect, so that we have a two to one relationship. Now causes are essentially ordered if one is ordered to the other so that [together] they cause a third thing, the effect. But causes are incidentally ordered if one is not ordered to the other in the very act of causing the effect. This would be the case with father and grandfather with regard to the son.

46. Secondly, it follows from this that essentially ordered causes differ from incidentally ordered causes in a threefold way:

The first difference is this: one cause depends essentially upon the other in order to produce an effect, which is not the case with causes that are ordered to a single effect only incidentally. Wherefore, the single causality of one of the incidentally ordered causes suffices to produce the single effect, whereas the causality of only one of the essentially ordered causes does not suffice.

47. From this, the second difference follows, viz. where essentially ordered causes are concerned, their causality differs in kind and they are not related to their effect in the same way. But the causality of all the incidentally ordered causes is of the same kind, since they can be referred immediately to the same effect.

48. From this, too, the third difference arises, viz. that the causalities of all of the essentially ordered causes concur simultaneously to produce the effect. For what is needed to cause an effect is that all its necessary causes concur. But all the essentially ordered causes are necessary causes. Therefore, all such must actually concur to bring about the effect. But this is not required where incidentally ordered causes are concerned, because each of itself possesses perfect causality as regards its effect, and they are of one kind so far as their immediate effect is concerned.

49. With these things presupposed, then, what remains to be shown is that the proof for a first cause does not involve a

begging of the question. Therefore, I first prove that there is such a first where essentially ordered causes are concerned. I do this:

First, by the argument of the Philosopher, Bk. II of the *Metaphysics*[17] (and that of Avicenna, too, Bk. VIII, chapter one)[18] which seems to be this: All causes intermediate between the first and the last, cause by virtue of the first, so that their causality is derived from the first. As the Philosopher points out there, it is not derived from the last but from the first, for if "to cause" pertains to any of them, a fortiori it will pertain to the first. Now the minor of his argument seems to be this: "If the series of causes is infinite then all are intermediate causes." Consequently they all cause in virtue of some first cause, so that it is necessary to assume a first among efficient causes.

50. But you may object: When you say in the minor, "Every cause in an infinite series is an intermediate cause," either you mean by intermediate such causes as lie between a first and a last in the series, and so assume that there is a first, or else you mean it in a purely negative sense [i.e. as being neither the first nor last], in which case there are four terms, and again the conclusion does not follow.

51. I say, therefore, that the statement first assumed by the Philosopher is not the major in the argument, but is antecedent thereto. The argument, consequently, goes in this way. Every intermediary cause having a first and a last, derives its causality from the first. Hence the causality of the intermediary causes comes from the first. But if there were an infinity of such causes, they would all be intermediary. Hence, their causality is derived from some first. But if they are infinite, then there is no first. Hence, there is and there is not a first cause!

Proof of the aforesaid consequence:

All causes in anyway intermediate, be they positively or negatively so, are caused. Therefore, the whole concatenation of intermediary causes is caused. Hence, it is caused by something which is outside the concatenated series. Hence, there is a first.

52. What is more, the causalities of all the essential causes must concur simultaneously to produce their effect, as was pointed out above. But an infinity of things cannot so concur to produce one thing, hence there is not an infinity of such causes and therefore a first cause does exist.

53. Furthermore, a cause which is prior as regards the

causation has a more perfect causality, and the more it is prior, the more perfect its causality. Hence, a cause with infinite priority would have an infinite causality. But if there were an infinite regress in essentially ordered causes, then there is a cause with infinite priority. To assume an infinite regress, then, is to grant a cause whose causality is infinite. But surely a cause which exercises infinite causality when it causes, does not depend upon anything else, and as such it would be the first. Therefore, etc.

54. Furthermore, to be able to produce something is not a property which of itself entails imperfection. But whatever is of such like is able to exist in something without imperfection. And thus there must be an efficient cause in which it can exist in this way, which is impossible if the cause does not produce its effect independently, and this means it is the first efficient cause. Therefore, etc.

55. Likewise, if one assumes an infinity of incidentally ordered causes, it still follows that there is a first in essentially ordered causes, for those causes which are incidentally ordered are in individuals of the same species. Then [one argues] as follows: No deformity is perpetual, unless it is brought about by a perpetual cause—outside this coordination—which perpetuates this deformity. Proof: Nothing that is part of this concatenation can be the cause of the whole of this perpetuated deformity, because in such incidentally ordered [causes], one is the cause of one only. Therefore, it is necessary to postulate —beyond this deformed concatenation—some first essential cause which perpetuates it. The deformation, then, is due to the deformed cause, but the continual uniformity of this deformity will be due to a cause outside this concatenation. And thus, if there is a process in incidentally ordered causes, there will still be a terminal point in some first essential cause upon which all the incidentally ordered causes depend.

In this way we avoid begging the question as regards a terminus and order of essential causes.

56. Now for the second objection raised against the aforesaid argument, viz. that it proceeds from something contingent, scil. "Something other than God exists." The philosophers would say that this is something necessary because of the essential order that holds between the cause and what it produces.

But I say, first, that even though it be contingent with reference to God, it is nevertheless most evident, so that anyone who would deny the existence of some being which is not eternal needs senses and punishment.[19] And therefore, from what is contingent in this way we can establish something necessary, for from the contingent something necessary follows, but not vice versa.

57. Also, I say that although things other than God are actually contingent as regards their actual existence, this is not true with regard to potential existence. Wherefore, those things which are said to be contingent with reference to actual existence are necessary with respect to potential existence. Thus, though "Man exists" is contingent, "It is possible for man to exist" is necessary, because it does not include a contradiction as regards existence. For, for something other than God to be possible, then, is necessary. Being is divided into what must exist and what can but need not be. And just as necessity is of the very essence or constitution of what must be, so possibility is of the very essence of what can but need not be. Therefore, let the former argument be couched in terms of possible being and the proposition will become necessary. Thus: It is possible that something other than God exist which neither exists of itself (for then it would not be possible being) nor exists by reason of nothing. Therefore, it can exist by reason of another. Either this other can both exist and act in virtue of itself and not in virtue of another, or it cannot do so. If it can, then it can be the first cause, and if it can exist, it does exist—as was proved above. If it cannot [both be and act independently of every other thing] and there is no infinite regress, then at some point we end up [with a first cause].

58. To the other objection (viz. that whenever an argument proceeds by way of a demonstration of simple fact, a converse demonstration of the reasoned fact can be constructed), one must say that such is not always true, because when we argue from the effect to the existence of a cause our argument may merely prove that the latter is a necessary condition rather than a sufficient reason for the effect. But it is only when the argument from effect to cause establishes [in addition] that the latter is a sufficient reason that the above principle [of converse demonstration] holds good.

59. And so we show from efficiency, to begin with, that something which is first exists, for—as we have made clear—something exists which makes all possible things possible. But that which makes all possibles possible cannot fail to exist of

itself, for otherwise it would be from nothing. Therefore, it must needs be actually self-existent. And so our thesis is proved.

[2. The Argument from Finality]

60. That something first exists is established secondly from finality. Something is suited by its very nature to be an end. Hence it so functions either in virtue of itself or in virtue of another. If the first be the case, we have something which is first; if it functions as an end only in virtue of another then this other is suited by its very nature to be an end, and since there is no infinite regress, we arrive at some end which is first. This is the argument of the Philosopher in *Metaphysics,* Bk. II[20] and Bk XII[21] about the most perfect good, and it is also the argument of Augustine in *On the Trinity,* Bk. VIII, chapter three:[22] "Consider this good and that good, abstract from the 'this' and the 'that,' and consider, if you can, simply the good itself, and thus you will see God, who is not good by reason of some other good but is the goodness of all that is good."

[3. The Argument from Eminent Perfection]

61. The third way is that of eminence. Some good is exceeded in perfection, or is able to be exceeded if you prefer to argue from possibility. Therefore, there is something which exceeds or is able to exceed something else in perfection. The latter either is or is not able to be exceeded or is actually exceeded in perfection by something else. If it is not, then it is first in the order of eminence, if it is not first and there is no regress *ad infinitum,* then we argue the same as before.

62. And so we show that something is first in three ways, first in the order of efficiency, first in the order of eminence and first in the order of ends.

And this triple "first" is one and the same because the first efficient cause is fully actualized, while the most eminent is the best of things. But what is fully actualized is also the best, with no mixture of evil or potentiality. Then too, the first efficient cause does not act for the sake of anything other than itself, for if it did, this other would be better than it. Consequently, it is the ultimate end, and hence first in the order of ends. The same thing, then, enjoys [a triple primacy].

63. Before establishing that some being is infinite, we

prove God is his own knowledge, for if his knowledge were not his nature but something accidental to it, then as the first efficient cause of everything, he would produce his knowledge. But God acts with knowledge; hence he would have to know about this knowledge beforehand. About this prior knowledge we inquire as before. Either there will be an infinite regress before something is known—and then nothing will be known—[or we admit finally that God is his own knowledge].

[B. PROOF OF THE INFINITY OF GOD]

64. I turn now from these things to the thesis to be proved and declare that this most eminent being, which is both the ultimate and as well as the first efficient cause, is infinite.

65. The first proof of this makes use of the notion of efficiency as employed by the Philosopher in Bk. VIII of the *Physics*[23] where he argues that, inasmuch as the first mover moves for an infinite time, it follows that he has infinite power.

66. Of course you may object to this argument on two grounds: first, the antecedent as a matter of fact is not true, since motion will not continue forever.

67. Furthermore, the inference itself seems to be invalid, since, according to the mind of the Philosopher, a body like the sun, though its power is finite, will continue to move things for an infinite time—and as a matter of fact, it could move things for an infinite period.

68. For these reasons, some reword the argument in this fashion. Where a cause produces its effects in virtue of itself alone, it has in its power at once all the effects which are produced in succession, for such an agent cannot receive power to act from anything other than itself, and hence it holds within its power at one and the same time all the effects it will eventually produce. The first efficient cause acts in virtue of itself and hence holds in its power at one and the same time all the effects which are successively produced, and these are potentially infinite. But this is to have infinite power. Now this is not, they say, the case with the sun, since it acts in virtue of something other than itself, and consequently it does not hold in its power at one and the same time all of the effects it will eventually produce.

69. Also, were the first mover to move for an infinite period of time, it could produce eventually an infinity of things, because with each movement it could produce something and

this by reason of itself alone. But to possess in itself an ability to produce an infinity of things is to possess infinite power.

70. These reasons, however, are not conclusive because an effect does not become more perfect because it continues to exist for more than a moment. Whiteness which lasts for a hundred years, for instance, is not more perfect than whiteness which lasts for a day. In like manner, a cause does not become more perfect because it produces its effect repeatedly instead of once. The same strength that enables something to move once a day, will enable it to move for an infinite period of time. All that is established, consequently, is the eternity of the cause, but from this one cannot infer its infinity.

71. Furthermore, to produce several individuals of the same species successively is not a matter of any greater perfection than to produce one individual at one time. Something hot [like the sun], for example, does not become more perfect by making several things hot over a period of time than it was when making one thing hot. But this infinity of things which are produced by means of motion concerns things which are only individually, and not specifically, distinct. Consequently, its production implies no greater perfection [in the cause] than does the production of a single individual.

72. Still one must say that the argument of the Philosopher is valid, for even though the antecedent is false if it is understood of what is actually the case, the antecedent is true if you take it of what could be the case, without adverting to whether it is or not. For if the first mover could move for an infinite period of time and it does not derive this power from anything other than itself, then it possesses such power of itself. And from this follows the further conclusion that it is of infinite power, so that the inference is valid. The proof lies in this. Whenever numerical plurality in one extreme requires a greater perfection in the other extreme, where the plurality of the one is infinite, the perfection of the other is infinite. For example, if to carry ten objects requires more strength than to carry one, then to carry an infinite number requires infinite strength. To produce several things at one time, however, requires more power than to produce but one; therefore, to produce an infinity requires infinite power. But the first mover, so far as it itself is concerned, could produce an infinity at one time, as I shall prove. Therefore, in itself it will be of infinite power.—Proof of the assumption: It is clear that the first efficient cause has power as a remote cause to cause an infinity at

once, if such an infinity were able to be produced. But if the proximate causes by which things are produced successively all existed at the same time as the remote first cause, they could produce an infinity at once. Since the power of the first efficient cause, however, includes all the formal powers of the intermediary causes which are potentially infinite, and it possesses all of the causalities of all intermediary causes in an even more perfect way than if they were actualized, as will be proved, it follows that the first efficient cause, so far as it itself is concerned, has power to produce an actual infinity. Proof of the assumption: It is clear that the first cause possesses the causality of the proximate cause more perfectly than the latter, because this latter has its causality only in virtue of the first cause. Similarly, the second cause possesses the causality of the third cause more perfectly than the latter, since the third cause receives its causality from the second, and so on down to the lowest cause. Consequently, the first cause possesses more perfectly the causalities of the intermediary causes, from first to last, than they do themselves.

73. Another proof of the implication is this. It is not that the causality of the production is more perfect that the second cause is needed to work with the first cause. (Proof: if it were for the sake of a more perfect causality that several causes are needed to produce a given effect, then the effect produced by the lot would be more perfect than the effect produced by one cause; now it is the effect furthest removed [from the first cause] that needs all the causes, whereas the nearest effect needs only the first cause. But since the more remote effect is less perfect than the proximate effect, it follows that it is not because of any weakness in its causality that the first cause requires the cooperation of a second cause.) Hence, if the first cause could produce an actual infinity of effects provided only that all of the infinitely numerous intermediary causes were actualized, then it follows that so far as the first cause itself is concerned, it could produce an infinity, and consequently, it will be infinitely powerful.

74. That is why the philosophers wished to say that the reason a second cause was needed to cooperate with the first cause was not because of any deficiency as regards causality, but it was to explain how an imperfect effect could be produced. For they thought that it was only through the intervention of some intermediary cause that an imperfect effect could be produced by a perfect first cause.

75. Using this way of efficiency, some add as a further proof of our thesis that inasmuch as the first being is able to create, it must have infinite power. They show that this follows because there is an infinite distance between contradictories which nothing short of an infinite power can bridge. Hence, since to create is to make something from nothing, it follows that if the first efficient cause can create, its power is infinite.

76. This argument, however, has no force.

First, it assumes that there is a creation—which is something we take on faith—and consequently, it is not a demonstration.

Secondly, between contradictories there is the least of all "distance," for no matter how little something departs from the one extreme, it immediately comes under the other. Hence there is the least latitude or distance here, although virtually speaking the distance between contradictories is greatest because this minimal distance between them establishes the "distance" and opposition between all other extremes.

77. What is more, the argument has another defect inasmuch as distance can be understood to be infinite in two ways. Either the distance in itself is infinite in the sense that it lacks limits as would be the case if one has an endless line, or the distance is infinite by reason of one of the extremes. We speak of a creature being infinitely distant from God, for instance. This is only because the one extreme is infinite. And even if we assumed the existence of the most perfect creature possible, between such a creature and God there would still be an infinite distance in the second sense. And it is in just this sense that "distance" between something and nothing or between affirmation and negation is to be understood. Consequently, negation is no more distant from affirmation than is the affirmation itself, and therefore whatever is able to make the affirmation is able to bridge the distance. Consequently, the argument is not conclusive.

78. The second main argument for infinity stems from divine knowledge. As was said above, whenever numerical plurality implies the presence of greater perfection, then an infinite number implies the presence of infinite perfection. Knowledge whereby several things are known distinctly is more perfect than knowledge whereby only one such is known, as I shall prove. Hence, knowledge of an actual infinity requires infinite perfection. Now the first intelligent and efficient cause with a single intellection knows an infinity of things actually

and distinctly, as I shall show. Therefore, it is actually of infinite perfection.

79. Proof of the first assumption: To know each object distinctly requires some perfection, hence to know several objects in this way is something more perfect. If then there is a single intellection which actually contains the knowledge of them all, it will be of greater perfection than would be the knowledge of only one.

Proof of the second assumption, that God's knowledge has to do with an actual infinity, like an infinity of figures and numbers: Wherever you have a potential infinity, if all its members were to exist at the same time, you would have an actual infinity. This is clear if you consider the consequences of any alternate hypothesis. Consider the intelligibles which we know by thinking of one after another. They are potentially infinite and they are all actually known by God, because he knows whatever can be. Hence, he knows an actual infinity.

80. The third argument for infinity is drawn from the fact that the divine essence itself serves as the [principle or] reason why God knows. For just as knowledge wherein several things are grasped distinctly is more perfect than that wherein but one is known, so also is the principle for knowing several things more perfect than is a principle for knowing only one of them. And an essence which represents several things distinctly will be more perfect than one which represents but one. But the divine essence represents an infinity of things distinctly, and consequently, its power of representation is infinite. Therefore the [essence itself] is infinite.

81. What is more, the reason this is so lies not merely in the ability of [the essence] to make all things known distinctly but because it produces a clear vision of a thing like a stone.[24] If something is the precise effect of some cause, and nevertheless something else can produce the same effect in even more perfect fashion, the proper cause cannot add anything to the perfection of the latter. If something be the precise cause of *a* for instance, and if *b* causes the same effect even more perfectly, then it is impossible that *a* should add anything to *b*. For were there any perfection to be added, it would be because *b* lacked some perfection needed to produce the effect in question, since it is precisely this effect that *a's* power is adequate to achieve. Any object, however, by its very nature is fitted to be the precise and proper cause of an [intuition or] vision of itself. It is impossible, then, that such a vision be achieved in an even more

perfect manner unless it be by reason of something to which nothing in the way of perfection could be added. But such a vision is had even more perfectly by reason of the divine essence, so that neither a stone, nor any other essence, could add anything to the perfection of the divine essence. But anything of this kind is infinite. Therefore, etc.

82. The fourth argument for infinity is derived from the fact that God is an end. Our will can love a good that exceeds that of any finite good. This we know, first, because our intellect can know such a good, and also because our will is inclined to seek an infinite good, for it delights in evoking such an act of love, which would not be the case if it were not inclined to do so. If the ultimate end were not an infinite good, however, the will would not be inclined towards, nor seek, an infinite good. Proof: It is incompatible with the very notion of an ultimate end that there be any good greater than it, as we have shown [Cf. par. 60]. For then it could either exist of itself, or in virtue of another, neither of which can be assumed to be the case. If the ultimate end, then, were finite and not infinite, it would be impossible for any good to be infinite. And if this were so, the will could neither love the infinite nor be inclined towards it, because it has no inclination towards the opposite of its object.

83. The fifth argument for infinity is based on the eminence [of God]. Anything to which infinity is not repugnant, is not simply perfect unless it is infinite. For instance, if the tenth degree of some perfection is not repugnant to a certain thing, then it is not simply perfect unless it possesses the tenth degree. But to being *qua* being infinity is not repugnant, as will be proved. Therefore, the most eminent and most perfect being will be infinite.

84. Proof of the assumption: If "infinite" were repugnant to "being," then the repugnance would either be formal, like "man" and "not-man," or virtual, like "man" and "not-risible." The first is not the case, for formal repugnance stems from the meaning of the terms. But as Avicenna teaches in Bk. I of the *Metaphysics*,[25] the meaning and notion of "being" cannot be made any clearer. The concept of "infinite" is also clear, because the infinite is that which cannot be surpassed. But there is no contradiction between these notions, for there is no contradiction that something be a being and that it cannot be surpassed. Neither is there any virtual repugnance, for the primary attributes of "being" such as "true," and "good" and such like, are most evidently characteristic of being. But

this is not the case with "infinite," for "being" does not of itself include "infinite" as a coextensive attribute. Consequently, "being is infinite" is not a primary truth unless you add in disjunction its opposite [viz. "being is either infinite or finite"].

85. Also since an amount of power is of greater perfection than an amount of mass, and since infinity is not repugnant to the latter, then neither is it opposed to the former.

86. Another proof of the same point is this. Any faculty naturally perceives any lack of harmony in its object, and it will not naturally put up with it or be content with it. If then "infinite" were something that contradicted "being," our mind would be naturally repelled by "infinite being" as something which includes a contradiction. But this is false, for our mind rather than finding any contradiction discovers its rest therein.

[IV. To the Arguments at the Beginning of the First Question (par. 1-6)]

87. Consider the first argument, where it is said that if one of the contraries were infinite, it would be incompatible with anything other than itself. It must be admitted that this would be true if we were dealing with an agent that was necessitated by its nature to act, as is clear from the case cited about the sun. It is not true, however, if that which is either virtually or formally contrary turns out to be an agent which is not necessitated in this way. Hence, if God acted by a necessity of his nature, it would not be possible for evil to occur, for it is virtually contrary to himself and formally contrary to what he causes, viz. the good of the universe.

88. You may object that the philosophers assumed that God and the first good acted out of necessity in their nature, and still they admitted that evil could occur in the world.

To this I reply that they could not save the fact that evil occurs contingently or that anything occurs contingently, on the assumption that God acts by a necessity of his nature. For if God produced the first effect in such a way, since the latter could only in turn produce something in virtue of the first [being] by which it was produced, it follows that this next effect is also produced by a necessity of nature, and so on down [through the hierarchy of celestial causes] to the fact of my sitting now, which would also need to be produced by a necessity of nature.

89. Still the philosophers could maintain that evil occurred in the world by a necessity of nature, since they claimed that God moved one series of causes which terminated in the eduction of the form and another series which brought about the superabundance of matter. That the body of an animal is an organism results from the first series, whereas that it has too many members is a consequence of the second. And so it happens that the animal turns out to be a freak. Yet this does not happen contingently, because if the one cause acts necessarily, so the other impedes its action necessarily. There is no alternative good, however, to evil of this kind, for it was a matter of necessity that these other causes impede the action since they are the stronger.

90. But you may say that although the Philosopher assumed that a heavenly body was necessarily produced by God, he still held that such a body, like the sun, had different movements, and according to its proximity or distance from us it could cause events contingently, and in consequence, some things do occur contingently.

I claim this does not follow. For while he could admit that even though God acts of necessity by reason of the way explained above, it could be that something does not exist forever, and to that extent, has contingent existence. But he could not consistently hold that the thing occurred contingently [i.e. that it need not have occurred at the time it did] as the reason above proves [Cf. par. 88].

91. [To Arg. II] The second main argument should be answered by denying the validity of the inference. And as for the proof wherein it is claimed that just as two bodies cannot coexist in one place because of their opposed dimensions, so neither can two spirits because of their opposed actualizations, it should be pointed out that there is no parallel between the two. The reason this holds in regard to bodies is that one body fills a place to the full extent that place can be filled. Similarly, the reason two opposed forms cannot coexist in matter is that matter is perfected by one to the extent of its capacity. But beings are not so proportioned that one being takes up all the room so that there cannot be more than one.

92. As for the other proof of the inference, I say again that there is no parallel. If one assumed that another body coexisted with an infinite body, there would be an opposition viz. that there would be something both infinite and finite. But if a finite spirit is assumed to coexist with an infinite spirit

such an opposition does not follow, because when the finite spirit is present with the infinite, there is no one thing which results that is of greater perfection than is the infinite spirit itself, for the latter's perfection stems from itself whereas the other's is derived from another.

93. [To Arg. III] As for the other argument, we must point out that it does not follow. Neither is the manner of arguing valid except for what is finite. It is not valid as regards the infinite, as for example, when it is assumed that whereabouts is infinite and a body is infinite. For then it does not follow "This body is in this place in such a way that it is in no other, therefore it is finite as to its whereabouts." Or, "Motion is at this time so that it is not at another, therefore it is finite in time" does not follow either according to the view of the Philosopher, who assumed that motion was perpetual. And so too it does not hold for what they try to prove, viz. "God is just this essence in such a way that he is no other, therefore he is finite." What does indeed follow is that he is not numerically infinite, but it does not follow that he is not intensively infinite.

94. [To Arg. IV] As for the next, we must insist that the Philosopher did not say that if an infinite power were to move things, it would do so in an instant. What he intended to prove there was that infinite power does not reside in any magnitude, because if it did it would move things instantaneously. And the reason is this: an infinite power, if it were to move things according to the utmost of its power and by a necessity of nature, would move them instantaneously (Proof: if it were to move things only over a period of time, then some other finite power could be increased to a point where it could move an equal amount in an equal period of time, and thus the two powers, each doing the utmost it could do, would be equal). If an infinite power were to reside in some body, however, it would be a power to move, since it is clear enough from the context that the Philosopher there is speaking about a power which is divided up according to the divisions of a body so that the greater power resides in what is larger and in any part thereof it is only there in part. And what is more, since a body can be divided and can differ as to the position of its parts, it is the whole that is needed to produce movement. And consequently [if it were infinite] it would move things and do so instantaneously [which is a contradiction]. Now although we too postulate an infinite power, we do not claim

that it moves things to the utmost of its ability. Hence it does not follow that it moves things in an instant. What does indeed follow is that it could act instantaneously and could transfer a body from one place to another in an instant, but this is not to "move" in the proper meaning of the word. Neither would there be any motion in such a case.

95. The Philosopher, you may object, claimed the first mover acted of necessity and to the utmost of its ability, and he proves it to be of infinite power. Still it does not follow that it moves instantaneously, for he admits that the heavens move in time.—I say that if the Philosopher were to postulate that the first mover acts necessarily, he cannot also assume that anything is moved immediately; motion can only occur through the intervention of some finite cause. With this Averroes agrees in Bk. XII of the *Metaphysics*,[26] where he says that the heavens have a double motor cause, one which exists apart and guarantees the perpetuity of the movement, and another which is captivated by the former. But it is only the combination of the two that allows for temporal movement.

NOTES

1. Cf. Aristotle, *Physic.* III, c. 5 (204b 19-22).
2. *Ibid.*, VIII, c. 10 (266a 24-266b 6).
3. *Ibid.*, (266a 10-24).
4. *De fide orthodoxa*, c. 1 (ed. Buytaert, Franciscan Institute Publ. Text series No. 8, p. 12; PG 94, col. 790).
5. Aristotle, *Metaphysica* II, c. 1 (993b 4-5).
6. Anselm, *Proslogion*, c. 2 (PL 158, 227-28).
7. Aristotle, *Physic.* I, c. 1 (184a 26-184b 3).
8. Aristotle, *Metaphy.* IX, c. 10 (1051b 25-28, 13-15).
9. *Ibid.*, VIII, c. 3 (1043b 23-32).
10. *Ibid.*, V, c. 29 (1024b 31-32).
11. The reference is to the first question of distinction 3 where he shows that every simple concept that applies to God is univocally predicable of God and some creature and every concept which applies exclusively to God is composite and is constructed by affirming, denying and interrelating conceptual elements that are simple and univocally predicable of creatures. Confer A. Wolter, *Duns Scotus: Philosophical Writings* (Edinburgh: Nelson and Sons, 1962). 19-28.
12. Henry of Ghent, *Summa quaestionum ordinariarum*, art. 22, q. 4 vol. I (Parisiis, 1520), fol. 132M.
13. *Lectura oxoniensis* I, dist. 26, n. 19.
14. Averroës, *Physica* I, com. 83 (*Commentaria in Aristotelis opera*, Venetiis, 1483).

15. Richard of St. Victor, *De Trinitate* 1, c. 8 (PL 196, col. 894).

16. See Aristotle, *Prior Analytics* I, c. 13 (78a 22-78b 34) for the distinction between a demonstration of the reasoned fact and of the simple fact. The former roughly corresponds to an a priori demonstration, e.g. from cause to effect; the latter gives no cause or prior reason why such a fact occurs but only why we know the fact to be the case.

17. Aristotle, *Metaphys.* II, c. 2 (994a 11-13).

18. Avicenna, *Opera* (Venetiis, 1508), fol. 97rb-va.

19. See Aristotle, *Topica* I, c. 9 (105a 4-5).

20. Aristotle, *Metaphys.* II, c. 2 (994b 9-13).

21. *Ibid.*, XII, c. 10 (1075a 11-23).

22. Augustine, *De Trinitate,* VIII, c. 3 (PL 42, col. 949).

23. Aristotle, *Phys.* VIII, c. 10 (266a 10-267b 26).

24. Scotus is saying that God has intuitive rather than abstract knowledge of all things; the latter abstracts from the existence or non-existence of the thing in question so that on the basis of such abstract knowledge one could not say whether the thing exists or doesn't exist. But "clear vision" or intuitive knowledge is a simple awareness not only of what the creature is but also of its existential condition (i.e. of its existence, if it does exist, or its nonexistence if it does not exist). Man is also capable of some degree of intuitive knowledge, for example, of his own states of mind or internal actions such as doubting, thinking, willing, etc. In such a case, the mind and the thing known intuitively interact to produce the knowledge in question. In abstract knowledge, some intelligible species (containing only certain information about the object) substitutes for the object. Scotus is arguing that in God, knowledge of creatures is something he possesses by reason of his nature or essence and that since this knowledge is already most perfect or intuitive, any action on the part of the object, were such possible, would add nothing to the perfection of God's knowledge.

25. Avicenna, *Metaphys.* I, c. 6 (*Opera,* fol. 72rb).

26. Averroës, *Metaphys.* XII, com. 41.

XXII

AGENT INTELLECT

THE FOLLOWING TREATISE appears to date from the early fourteenth century. It has been edited and thoroughly studied by M. Grabmann in his *Mittelalterliche Deutung und Umbildung der aristotelischen Lehre vom νοῦς ποιητικός nach einer Zusammenstellung im Cod. B III 22 der Universitätsbibliothek Basel* (Munich: Verlag der Bayerischen Akademie der Wissenschaften, 1936). Cf. pp. 85-102 for the Latin text and pp. 7-52 for a German paraphrase with added comments.

Because the author remains unknown, our notes will at times refer to him as the "anonymous author" and at other times will simply refer to the Basel manuscript, meaning the relatively small part of that manuscript containing this work and edited by Grabmann (fol. 182va-183vb). Grabmann's investigations indicate that this treatise is to be dated some time between 1308 and 1323. He suggests that the author was a theologian and a member of the Dominican order (p. 5).

The discussion begins with a theological question: Does beatitude consist in an act of the agent intellect, if one grants that it consists in an act of the intellect? The author then enters into a long discussion as to the nature of the agent intellect, thus lending great historical and philosophical interest to the work. He catalogues a series of classical and contemporary opinions as to the nature and function of the agent intellect. The variety of theories considered suggests that at this time certain questions raised by Aristotle's discussion of the same, above all in *De anima* III, 5, were still very much at issue. Among those who did defend the need for an agent intellect, disagreement arose as to whether there is only one for all mankind (be it God or some lower intelligence), or whether there is an individual agent intellect for every particular human being. The relationship between the agent and possible intellect was also a point of disagreement. Before our author can return to the theological question, he finds it necessary to determine whether or not the agent intellect itself can actually be said to understand or to know. If the text is an interesting illustration of the variety of opinion found among the scholastics who philosophized, it is also an instance of the usage of philosophy by a scholastic theologian.

In the final analysis, the author finds the views of "Brother Thomas" more to his liking both as regards the nature and function of the agent intellect (the philosophical question) and as regards its possible role in beatitude (the theological question). Nevertheless Grabmann's words of caution should also be noted: "If in this solution, in opposition to the view of Dietrich of Freiberg, the teaching of St. Thomas is favored and accepted, this can only be understood in the sense that this solution is in the line of and consequent upon Thomistic philosophy. Aquinas himself never dealt *ex professo* either with the question of the priority between the agent and the possible intellect or with the question as to whether beatitude resides in one or the other" (p. 52).

The treatise has been translated by J. F. Wippel especially for this volume.

Beatitude and the Agent Intellect

Whether beatitude consists in [an act] of the agent intellect, it being granted that it consists in [an act] of the intellect: Reply: First it must be determined how the agent intellect is present in us. This is to indicate what is meant by the agent intellect as to its quiddity. Secondly, the question itself must be answered. As regards the first point there are sixteen opinions.

[1. Plato]

The first theory is that of Plato, who denies that there is an agent intellect. This is because he defended ideas which are intelligible of themselves. If such were true, an agent intellect to make things potentially intelligible actually intelligible would not be necessary for the abstraction of ideas. Just as prime matter is to sensible forms, so is the possible intellect to intelligible forms. But prime matter does not receive the forms of sensible things simply by means of the action of some separated substance, but rather by the action of a form of the same kind, that is to say, a form which is in matter. For like is produced by like. Wherefore, this flesh is generated by a form which is found in this flesh and in these bones, according to *Metaphysics* VII.[1] Since, therefore, the possible intellect is not a separated substance according to Alexander [of Aphrodisias], neither is the agent intellect. Thus the agent intellect would not seem to be needed. However, Aristotle undermined the foundation for this view in *Metaphysics* VII[2] and in many other passages where he rejected the ideas.

[2. The View of Certain Theologians]

The second theory is held by certain theologians and maintains that the agent intellect is the universal intellect, the creator of all things, and God Himself. They ground this view on the authority of the Philosopher [Aristotle], who says that the agent intellect is that which makes all things.[3] But to make all things is the act of the first cause. Therefore, the agent intellect is nothing other than the first cause. Again, all things are understood by the light of the agent intellect. But all things are understood by the power of the first cause. Therefore, etc.

However, this view will not stand. For the action of the first cause does not rule out the actions of second causes. God is the first cause and the agent intellect is a second cause. Therefore, etc. Again, God has not bound his will to creatures, as the Mutakallims[4] seem to say, according to Averroës in *Metaphysics* XI. However, such would be the case if this theory were correct. Therefore, etc.

The theory in question seems to agree with Avicebron's position in the *Fons Vitae,*[5] to the effect that no body is an agent. Rather a spiritual substance passing through bodies produces those actions which seem to be performed by the bodies themselves. And because God is present to each and every thing by his essence, his presence, and his power, it seems that the actions in question can be attributed to God. However, this position contradicts a higher truth. As God is to them [bodily creatures] in the order of being, so is he to them in the order of action and in the order of intellection. For just as he is being of himself, so does he know of himself. And just as he is a cause of being, so is he a cause of intellection. For all things were made through him, according to John, I. But according to the first mode he does not exclude the action of second causes. Otherwise individual agents would not act. Therefore, neither does he do so in the second way. Therefore, in addition to that universal intellect, which is the light that enlightens every man, an agent intellect is required.

The arguments presented by the theologians for their theory do not apply. *In reply to the first.* That God makes all things is true without qualification. According to John, I, all things have been made through him. However, the agent intellect does not make things without qualification. Rather it makes things potentially intelligible actually intelligible. *In reply to the second.* All things are understood by the power of the agent intellect as a proximate and immediate cause. But all things are understood by the power of the first cause as a remote and universal cause.

[3. Alexander of Aphrodisias]

The third theory is that of Alexander, who maintains that the agent intellect is a separated substance and that it is always in act. When the habitual intellect has been perfected in us, the agent intellect becomes a form of our intellect. And before this happens, as a result of its influence on the possible intellect, man becomes an actual knower. He [Alexander] posits the possible intellect in human nature in order to prepare for receiving the influence of the agent intellect. This view is faulty both as regards the agent intellect and as regards the possible intellect.

It evidently falls short as regards the possible intellect, since a corporeal organ is not required for intellection. For Aristotle says that the possible intellect is an unmixed principle which is not joined to a body.[6] Therefore, the act of intellection is independent from the body. But a preparation [for receiving the influence of the agent intellect] which follows upon the mixing of the elements depends on the body. Therefore, such a preparation which follows upon a mixture of the elements cannot be a principle of intellection. But the possible intellect is that whereby we understand all things, as is stated in *De anima* III.[7] Therefore the possible intellect itself is not such a preparation.

This theory also falls short as regards the agent intellect. In every nature there must be an active principle, sufficient for the work of that nature. This is clear in the case of the soul. One of its operations consists in the particular act of nutrition. Therefore it has an active principle for that action, that is to say, the nutritive power. Another consists in a passion, such as that of a sense [viz., perception]. Again, there is a principle for this in the soul, namely the sensitive power. But among all lower agents, man is more perfectly an agent, he whose proper and natural act is to understand. Therefore, man has his own principles for this act. But this action cannot be completed without passion and action. The intellect is acted upon by the intelligible object (passion). For every reception is a passion. At the same time, the intellect makes potential intelligibles actually intelligible (action). Therefore man possesses both [an active and a passive principle] as his own. The intellect which is acted upon is the possible intellect. That which produces actual intelligibles is the agent intellect.

Therefore, neither the agent intellect nor the possible intellect is a separated substance.

[4. Avicenna]

The fourth theory is that of Avicenna. He holds that the agent intellect is a separated substance, and that we know by means of an outflow of intelligible forms from it. In order to understand this it should be noted that Avicenna held that the forms of sensible things preexist in an immaterial way in the intelligences. Here he differs from Plato, who maintained that the forms of sensible things exist in themselves outside the divine mind and free from matter. As Aristotle represents his theory, he called these forms ideas. Moreover, Avicenna holds that the forms of sensible things derive from the first intelligence in due order until one arrives at the last intelligence which he calls the agent intellect. According to his thinking, the intelligible species of sensible things flow into our souls. But on account of forgetfulness, which the soul undergoes because of the body, it is prevented from turning to the agent intellect and receiving this influx of intelligible species. This impediment is overcome by study and by examination. From which it follows, according to Avicenna, that our proper activity in acquiring knowledge is only a kind of preparation in a recipient for receiving a form or receiving knowledge, and the removal of obstacles which impede the reception of species. According to him, once this has taken place, the agent intellect, itself a separated substance, infuses the intelligible species into our intellect.

This position can be countered and rejected in the same way as that of Alexander. In addition to this, the union of soul and body would not be natural. It [the union] cannot be set up for the sake of the soul, since it produces forgetfulness in the soul. Nor can it be for the sake of the body, since form does not exist for matter nor the the higher for the sake of the lower, but precisely the opposite, according to *Physics* II.[8]

[5. Averroës]

The fifth theory is that of Averroës. He maintains that the agent intellect is a separated substance and in this agrees with the above-mentioned theories.[9] But as regards its manner of union with us, he says that the agent intellect is related to theoretical intelligibles as form is to matter. Since, therefore, theoretical intelligibles are joined to us by means of phantasms, it is also necessary for the agent intellect to be joined and united to us. For it is, as it were, the form of the theoretical intelligibles. But theoretical intelligibles may be found in three degrees. At certain times they are only potentially present to us. At other times, some are actually present and some are potentially present. On other occasions, all are actually present. In the first case the agent intellect is only potentially joined to us. In the second, it is present to us partly in act, partly in potency. In the third case, that is, when all the theoretical intelligibles are actually present in us, then the agent intellect is perfectly united with us as a form. And then we understand perfectly by means of it.

This position considered in itself is not valid. It is to be rejected like the opinion of Alexander, with which it agrees in holding that the agent intellect is a separated substance. Again, its way of uniting the agent intellect with us will not stand. For according to this view the agent intellect is united to us by means of species which have become actually present to the intellect. But species which are actually present to us are joined to us by means of phantasms, as he holds, which themselves are related to the agent intellect as colors to light and to the possible intellect as colors to sight. But neither the act of sight, to see, nor the act of the sun, to illuminate, neither can be attributed to a colored object such as wood, in which there is color. Therefore, in the same way, according to Averroës neither the act of the possible intellect, to understand, nor the act of the agent intellect, to render potential intelligibles actually intelligible, neither can be attributed to man.

[6. The First View of Themistius]

The sixth theory is attributed to Themistius, to the effect that both the agent intellect and the possible intellect are multiplied according to the number of individual men. In this it differs from the above views. It also maintains that the agent intellect always understands, and in this it agrees with the above theories.

As regards the second point, this theory is to be rejected. If the agent intellect which is joined to us always understands, then the possible intellect becomes useless. But there is nothing useless in nature, according to *De caelo et mundo,* I.[10] Perhaps someone will reply that the possible intellect is found in the soul for this reason, to receive its perfection from the body. This will not suffice. It is not fitting to postulate a twofold mode of intellection in the soul with respect to one and the same object, even though it may not be superfluous to posit both a natural and supernatural mode, as in the angel with respect to God. Such, however, would follow from this theory. For we would understand the same things by means of the agent intellect and the possible intellect. Again, if the agent intellect itself understands, then we would always understand by means of it. But we are not conscious of this. This too seems to be unfitting because, according to the Philosopher in the *Posterior Analytics,* it is not fitting to posit the noblest habits within ourselves and then to maintain that they are unknown to us.[11] Therefore, it is even more unfitting to maintain that acts are unknown to us. Thirdly, such an act [of a continually understanding agent intellect] is completely unknown to us.

[7. The Second View of Themistius]

The seventh theory, like the previous one, is also held by Themistius. He maintains that the agent intellect is the habit of principles, basing himself on Aristotle's statement in *De anima* III,[12] to the effect that the agent intellect is like a habit, and again, that it is like art. But art is a habit of our intellect. So too, therefore, is the agent intellect.

However, this does not hold. It is by the power of the agent intellect that all intelligible objects are known to us, since it is by means of the agent intellect that, whereas they were potentially intelligible, they become actually intelligible. But we do not know all things by means of the habit of first principles, but rather conclusions. Therefore, the agent intellect is not a habit.

Again, the agent intellect does not presuppose any previous act of intellection. But the habit of principles does presuppose a knowledge of terms. For we know principles only insofar as we know the terms. Therefore, the agent intellect is not the habit of principles. Nor does his citation from the Philosopher apply, to wit, that the agent intellect is a habit. The Philosopher did not mean that the agent intellect is that kind of habit which belongs to the first species of quality, as those understand who say that it is the habit of principles. The habit of principles is derived from the senses, as is clear from

Posterior Analytics II.[13] Therefore, the habit of principles must result from the action of the agent intellect, to which it pertains to render actually intelligible the phantasms which were only potentially intelligible. Thus, when Aristotle says that the agent intellect is a habit, he uses the term "habit" insofar as it is distinguished from "principle" and from "potency." In this sense every form and every act can be called a habit, according to the Philosopher's statement in the *De generatione:* When habits, i.e., forms, are present in matter, the change ceases.[14] This is also clear from the Philosopher's way of speaking, because he himself says that it [the agent intellect] is a habit in the way light is a habit.

As to the second statement, that the agent intellect is like art, it is to be noted that art can be compared to the artist's mind. From this standpoint the agent intellect is not like art. In another way, however, art can be compared to the artefacts themselves, which are investigated by means of art. Taken in this sense, the agent intellect is like art. For just as it belongs to art to introduce form into matter, so does it belong to the agent intellect to prepare the phantasms so that they may move the possible intellect.

[8. John Philoponus (Johannes Grammaticus)]

The eighth theory is that of John the Grammarian. He maintains that both the agent intellect and the possible intellect constitute something real within the soul. But as to whether they are both found as something real in one and the same soul, he replies in the negative. They are rather found in distinct souls. Thus the intellect of a teacher is described as agent intellect in relationship to his pupil. But when related to the teacher himself, then it is called the possible intellect. Wherefore, in *De anima* II[15] it is stated that he who is a potential knower learns and receives knowledge from one who actually knows. For nothing can reduce itself from potency to act. You might note that knowledge is acquired not only by teaching but also by discovering. Wherefore, at times one moves from the state of potential knower to actual knower by his own activity, by discovering. One might reply that the possible intellect always receives its universal principles from others so that, being an actual knower in this sense, it can then move itself to act according to Albert's position.

This view [that of John the Grammarian] is not valid.

For neither the same motion nor the same mode is to be attributed to that which is generated by nature and that which arises by art. Fire generates fire in the order of nature by reducing matter from potency to act as regards its form. But the teacher produces knowledge in the student by way of art. Among the arts there are certain ones in which an effect is never produced except by means of some extrinsic agent. Thus a house is produced by a builder, since there is no active moving principle in wood and stones, but only a passive one. But there is another kind of art which produces its effect not by acting as a principal cause, but rather by serving as an aid, as is true of medicine. For man is also healed by nature. Therefore, the art of teaching is like art of the second type rather than the first, since one must admit some active principle within the learner not only as to second intelligibles but also as to universal principles. Teaching does not cause them, since they are naturally known, according to the Commentator [Averroës] in *Metapyhics* II.[16] But the teacher's intellect aids and assists. Therefore just as it is said that man is healed, so is it said that man acquires knowledge by discovery and by teaching.

[9. Henry of Ghent]

The ninth theory is that of Henry of Ghent, to the effect that the agent intellect is not really distinct from the soul [i.e., from the substance of the soul]. He maintains that the soul is a principle which elicits its operations actively and of itself, without depending on powers which would be really distinct from it absolutely speaking, but only under a certain respect.[17]

This theory is to be rejected because, according to the Commentator in *De anima* III,[18] the intellect is to intelligible forms just as matter is to sensible forms. But matter does not receive real forms unless a really distinct agent introduces them. Therefore, in like fashion, the agent intellect, being that by means of which forms are received in the possible intellect, is really distinct both from the possible intellect and from the soul. Moreover, if powers are distinguished because of their different relationships, it will follow that neither the agent intellect nor the possible intellect is a single power. For the agent intellect has one relationship to the phantasms and another to the possible intellect. Therefore the agent intellect will not be a single power. Likewise, the possible intellect enjoys one relationship to principles and another to conclusions. Therefore, in the same way, it will not be a single power.

[10. Godfrey of Fontaines]

The tenth theory is that of Godfrey, who holds that the agent intellect is really identical with the memory but distinct from the possible intellect. He argues that the agent intellect and memory are the same because that which is attributed to the agent intellect is also attributed to memory. Thus it pertains to the memory to preserve species. But this also pertains to the agent intellect, whose function it is to make all things.

This theory will not stand. Insofar as memory is taken as a part of the image [of God in the soul] it does not signify anything really distinct from the possible intellect. Rather it is really the possible intellect itself insofar as the latter receives and preserves intelligible species. For according to *De anima* III,[19] the soul is the "place of the species," although not the whole soul but the intellect. There memory is likened to the sense memory whose function it is to preserve sensible species. Wherefore, just as the possible intellect is really distinct from the agent intellect, so too, the agent intellect is distinct from memory.

In reply to his argument, the agent intellect and memory preserve species in different ways. The agent intellect preserves them virtually and by way of efficient causality. For it is that to which it pertains to make all things. But it pertains to memory to preserve species as their subject, since it is the "place of the species."

[11. James of Viterbo]

The eleventh theory is that of James of Viterbo. He maintains that the agent intellect is really one and the same power as the possible intellect. He argues as follows. Just as the will remains one and the same even though it is mover and moved and active and passive with respect to itself, so too, while remaining one and the same, the intellect is both active and passive. But the possible intellect is passive. Therefore the possible intellect and the agent intellect are one and the same.

This theory will not stand. For the Philosopher proves in *De anima* III[20] that the agent intellect is separable and free from being acted upon and unmixed from this, that the agent is nobler than the patient, and the principle [originating force] is nobler than the matter [that it forms]. These characteristics were established as regards the possible intellect. From this it follows that they apply with greater force to the agent intellect. But this proof would amount to nothing if these powers were really one and the same. For one would prove the same thing by means of the same thing about the same thing. Therefore, etc.

Nor does the analogy with the will hold. Granted that the will moves itself to act once the object is present, and once it has been actualized, granted that it moves itself to the means ordered to the end, nonetheless, the will is not an active cause with respect to its object. On the contrary, the good presented to the will by the intellect actually moves the will. Therefore, when the will moves itself, it does not reduce its objects from potency to act, whereas the agent intellect does make that which is potentially intelligible actually intelligible.

[12. Durandus]

The twelth theory is that of Durandus, who maintains that there is no need to posit an agent intellect. Powers become known through their acts. Therefore, if an agent intellect is to be posited, this will be because of its activity with respect to the phantasms. Such activity will involve either impressing something on the phantasms or abstracting from them. But neither type of activity is present, as can be shown in detail. An impressed power would itself be corporeal since that which is received in a body is itself corporeal. Such would be of no value as regards intellection. Nor can it act on the phantasms by abstracting. For then it will either know the abstraction or it will not. If it does not know it, then it will act by chance and luck. If it does know the abstraction, then an act of understanding on the part of the possible intellect will not be needed. This, however, is false. The major is evident, since the operation manifests the form.

This view is false and is also contrary to the mind of the Philosopher. His statements about the agent intellect suffice to establish the opposite. As regards the argument offered:

In reply to the minor, to the effect that the agent intellect cannot impress anything on the phantasm because it would then be corporeal, it is to be noted that a power can be taken as corporeal in three ways: (1) as corporeal both in its subject and in its effect (cf. the power present in fire, i.e., heat); (2) as corporeal in its effect but not in its subject (cf. the power present in forms); (3) as corporeal in its subject but not in its effect, as is true of the power introduced into the phantasms by the agent intellect.

In reply to the second part of the minor: When he says that it [the agent intellect] either knows [the abstraction or does not know it] I reply that it does not. Nor does it abstract by chance, since it does this according to nature. Therefore, etc.

[13. Anonymous]

The thirteenth theory holds that the possible intellect is always present within the soul but that the agent intellect, which perfects the possible intellect, comes from without. Thus the possible intellect is more natural [to the soul] than the agent intellect. The view of some, that the possible intellect is a certain power arising from the soul itself while the agent intellect is a kind of light coming from an exterior principle, seems to reduce to this same theory. Wherefore the agent intellect is like the light found in the moon, not as coming from the moon, but as from the sun.

Against these one may argue as follows. To a proper passive principle there must correspond a proper active principle in the order of nature. But according to their view, the agent intellect and the possible intellect are related as active and passive. Therefore, if one is found within the nature of the soul as natural [to it], the same must hold for the other. Again, the agent intellect appears to be more natural to the soul than the possible intellect, since action manifests the form. But the action of the agent intellect is natural and it always acts naturally, whether we will it or not. This is not true of the activity of the possible intellect. For we understand when we will to do so. Therefore the possible intellect does not appear to be more natural to the soul than the agent intellect, but rather the contrary seems to be true. Again, the agent intellect is either a natural or a supernatural power. If the first, then it arises from the soul with the other powers and together with the nature of the soul itself, just as heat arises in fire and together with fire. Therefore, it does not come to the soul from without. If the second is the case [if the agent intellect is a supernatural power], then, since the agent intellect is a kind of light, it will follow that whatever we understand we understand in virtue of a supernatural light.

[14. The First Theory of Magister Theodericus (Dietrich of Freiberg)]

The fourteenth theory is that of Magister Theodericus [Dietrich of Freiberg], to the effect that the agent intellect is to be identified with a hidden [and unconscious] intellection. He maintains that, according to Augustine, our intellection is divided into an actual concealed and unconscious intellection, and an unconcealed intellection. In proof he appeals to blessed Augustine, *De trinitate* XIV, chap. 7: "We learn from this that in the hidden recesses of the mind there is a certain knowledge of certain things, and that when we think of them, they then proceed, as it were, to the center and are placed, so to speak, more clearly in the sight of the mind. . . ."[21] In a second passage in *De trinitate* XV, chap. 26 of the large or chap. 63 of the small text, Augustine writes: "But that is a more profound depth of our memory, where we also find those contents which we think of for the first time, and where the inner word is begotten which does not belong to the language of any nation, as it were, knowledge of knowledge, vision of vision, and understanding of understanding, for the understanding, which appears in thought, comes from the understanding which already existed in the memory but was latent there. . . ."[22] On the basis of these passages it is maintained that there is a certain concealed kind of intellection within us.

However, considered in itself, this view will not stand. For this concealedness either rises from the side of the object so that the concealed intellection will be hidden to all, or else it arises from the side of the knowing subject so that it remains hidden to the knower that he does know such an object. The first alternative cannot be true. For each and every thing is manifest insofar as it is known. But an intelligible concealed object is actually known to all. For that which is grasped by intellection is known. Therefore this concealedness does not arise from the side of the object. Nor will the second alternative stand. To say that man actually knows something but that he never does nor can advert to it is senseless. And just as an action concerning a vacuum is itself vacuous, so too is this [concealed intellection] itself concealed and unknown.

Again, insofar as something is more actually and more perfectly known, to that extent it is more manifest to the one who knows. But according to the defenders of this position this [hidden] kind of knowledge is most perfect, since it is knowledge by its essence and is never interrupted. Therefore, etc.

Again, according to the Philosopher it is impossible for us to possess the noblest habits and for them to be unknown to us.[23] Therefore, with even less reason could the noblest acts remain unknown to us. But intellection is the noblest act. Therefore, it is not possible for there to be an actual but concealed intellection within ourselves. Nor does the argument of certain ones hold, that this act remains unknown to us because of the likeness it bears to unconcealed intellection, just as an act of gratuitous [supernatural] love remains hidden because of its likeness to an act of natural love.[24] This analogy does not apply. According to Dietrich these acts [concealed intellection and unconcealed intellection] are very different. The one is intellection by its very essence and the other is intellection by means of species. The one is continuous while the other admits of interruption. The one depends on phantasms while the other does not.

Secondly, I will show that this position is not according to the mind of Augustine. Augustine does not call this hidden intellection an actual hidden intellection, but rather an habitual hidden intellection. To return to the first text cited above, "We learn from this . . . ," Augustine's point here is clear from the example which he cites shortly before. In determining how one skilled in both music and geometry may be said to know music, he says that such a person loves and remembers it even when he does not think of it.[25] It is clear that this knowledge is only habitual and not actual, as they would have it.

Again, even if there were such a concealed and unconscious intellection according to Augustine, it still could not be identified with the Philosopher's agent intellect. For according to the Commentator in *De anima* III, if there were separated universals such as Plato's ideas, Aristotle would have no need for an agent intellect.[26] Augustine, however steeped in the philosophy of Plato as he was, no more posited an agent intellect than did Plato himself.

I will also show that even if one grants that the agent intellect is posited in order to preserve the notion of an image [of God in the soul], nonetheless, their theory does not safeguard that image. *Proof:* The production of a word is necessary for an image. But actual and unconcealed [manifest] knowledge is necessary for the production of a word since, according to Augustine, a word is "knowledge together with love." Therefore, if the agent intellect is identified with this concealed knowledge, no word will be produced by it. Then it will not suffice to safeguard the notion of an image.

[15. The Second Theory of Magister Theodericus (Dietrich of Freiberg)]

Since we have seen that such an actual concealed intellection is purely fictitious, another theory held by the same thinker must now be examined. He maintains that the agent intellect as found in us is a substance and that it is an intellect through its essence.

To prove the first point [that the agent intellect within us is a substance] he offers the following arguments.

1. That is truly a substance in which an image of the Trinity is truly and properly found. But such is the agent intellect. Ergo, etc. In proof of the major it is argued that an image bespeaks conformity according to consubstantiality of nature. Conformity in the accidental order does not constitute an image. In the case of quantity it [conformity] is simply equality. In the case of quality it is likeness.

2. An image is a certain conformity of the soul to God both as regards the unity of essence and the trinity of persons. But it is impossible to find in any accident unity of essence and within that same unity distinction according to active and passive origin. Therefore, the same conclusion follows as from the first argument.

3. According to Augustine, *De trinitate* IX, chap. 6, no accident can pass beyond its subject. But the mind loves other things by means of that love whereby it loves itself. And it knows other things by means of that [same knowledge] whereby it knows itself. Therefore, the same conclusion follows, [that the agent intellect is a substance].

To prove the second point, that the agent intellect is an intellect through its essence, he argues that such is true first, because it knows itself through its essence, and secondly, because it knows all other things. As to the first point, it is argued that every intellect through its essence also knows itself through its essence. But the agent intellect is of this type. Therefore, etc. In proof of the minor it is argued that that which is of a given kind through its essence in the concrete order is also such through its essence in the order of formal abstraction. For example, just as man is man through his essence, so is he essentially man through humanity. Therefore, just as the agent intellect is an intellect through its essence, so is it an intellect through intellectuality. As humanity is in man, so too, intellectuality in its own way is a formal principle with respect to the essence [of the intellect]. But this is nothing else than for the intellect to turn toward itself intellectually and to know itself through its essence.

Again, the agent intellect is separated and free from admixture and from parts and from any kind of extraneous nature. Therefore, that which operates is its very essence and its operation is through its essence.

The first point [that the agent intellect is a substance] is to be rejected. If the agent intellect is a substance, it is either a separated substance, or else it is a substance which is either the soul itself or the nobler part of the substance of the soul. But the agent intellect cannot be a separated substance, for then one would return to the ancient theories already refuted above. Nor can it be a substance which is the soul itself. For then the substance of the soul would be an intellect through its essence and there would be no reason for its union with the body. Nor can it be the nobler part of the substance of the soul, since the essence of the soul is completely simple. This is also clear from the Philosopher's statement in *De anima* III, that the agent intellect is a habit and that it is a light.[27] The term "habit" is not used here to indicate something which subsists in itself. And the light is a participated light. Therefore, the agent intellect is not a substance.[28] Again, according to the Philosopher, neither the agent intellect nor the possible intellect is present to the soul as a part in a whole. Nor can any substance exercise an influence on the essence of the soul save God alone. Therefore both the agent and the possible intellects are in the soul as proper accidents in a subject.

In reply to the first argument, it is to be noted that our image [the image of God in the soul] falls far short of the uncreated "image" [prototype]. In fact, the difference is far greater than the similarity. There is, to be sure, a similarity in terms of the unity of essence and the distinction of supposits in the divine and of powers in creatures, both as to their origin and their equality. For whatever one power can do, so can another. Thus, that which can be recalled by the memory can be willed by the will and understood by the intellect. In these and in certain like respects there is similarity. There is diversity, however, in that there [in the divine] the supposits are substances, whereas [in the soul] the powers are accidents. The supposits subsist, while the powers inhere. Again, there each supposit is a principal source of action while here [in the soul] one power acts by means of another. There are many other differences.

Or again it may be noted that that in which the image is present as in the subject of a power is itself a substance. And it is such with respect to the unity of essence, i.e., with respect to the essence of the soul. But that in which it [the image] is present as in its proximate rather than its first subject as regards the threeness of persons is not the substance but rather the powers or the acts of these powers.

In reply to the second argument, it is to be said that in the uncreated image there is unity of essence and within that same essence there is distinction [of persons] by reason of origin. But for the created image it is enough to have unity of essence together with distinction of realities belonging to the same essence by way of powers and properties, among which origin and ordering to one another are included. Note, too, on this point that some maintain that the agent intellect does not belong to the image, since, as they see it, its operation does not treat of eternals but only of material things, that is, of phantasms. Others hold that the agent intellect does not belong to the image as a special power distinguished from all others, but rather as something common to all the powers. For the agent intellect acts upon that which the memory recalls and the will wills and the possible intellect understands.

In reply to the third argument, it is to be noted that if no accident can go beyond its subject in the order of being, it can do so in the order of action. Thus heat goes beyond its subject by warming other objects. In like fashion the will and the intellect do not go beyond their subject, the essence of the soul, in the order of being. But they do so in the order of action, by understanding and willing other objects.

The second point, that the agent intellect is an intellect through its essence and that it knows all things through its essence and always knows them, this too must be rejected. For the ultimate reason for the union of soul and body is the perfection of the soul or of the [human] composite, but not the perfection of the body. But if the soul could know itself and other things through its essence without phantasms, there would be no reason for its union with the body. For the bodily senses would not be required for it to know. But this is false. Therefore, the view that it always knows through itself and without phantasms is also false.

Again, the forms of things are like numbers, according to Metaphysics VIII.[29] But the more closely a number approaches unity, the simpler is that number. Therefore, in like manner the more closely a form approaches to God the simpler is that form. And the greater its degree of simplicity, the more perfect is the form. Angels more closely approach the first being and therefore they are simpler, enjoy greater nobility, and are more perfect. Nonetheless, they do not know themselves and other things through their essence alone, as is clear from the statement in the *Liber de causis,* that every intelligence is filled with forms. Therefore, etc.

Again, Aristotle notes in *Physics* I that all of our knowledge begins with the senses.[30] And in the *Posterior Analytics* I he notes that when one sense is lacking, the knowledge that derives from that sense will also be lacking. Such would not be the case if the intellect could know itself and other things through its essence.

In reply to his [Dietrich's] first argument, it is to be noted that the assertion that the agent intellect is an intellect through its essence may be understood in four different ways. First, it may be taken to mean the agent intellect exists of its essence so that its essence is its reason for existing, and insofar as it exists no further qualification need be added to the expression "It is." Such would be false, since God alone exists of his essence. All other things exist by participation, as is indicated in *De anima* II: "All things participate in the divine being."[31] Secondly, it may be understood to mean that it is an intellect of its essence, that is to say, the [agent] intellect is an intellect through its essence. This can be taken in two ways. It may mean that the intellect understands through its essence. In this sense the statement is false. Or it may mean that the intellect makes things that are not actually intelligible actually intelligible through its essence. Taken in this sense it would be an intellect through its essence virtually but not formally. So understood it is correct to say that it is an intellect through its essence. Fourthly, to be an intellect through its essence may be taken to mean that through its essence the intellect either knows all things or at least knows some. Taken in this sense the statement is false. For then the intellect would both exist through its essence and understand through its essence. It should be noted that in this expression "to be an intellect through its essence" the preposition[32] "through" *[per]* designates nothing [else than] the intellect's very being when taken in the first way. According to the second and third usages, it refers to the intellect's operation. According to the fourth, it refers both to its being and its operation.

In reply to [Dietrich's] second argument it is to be said that the agent intellect is not separated without qualification from every other nature so as to be found in no [subject] as a potency or an act. Again, it is not an intellect through its essence by formal and essential predication. It is rather said to be an intellect because of its effect, since it makes potential intelligibles actually intelligible. Wherefore, granted that the agent intellect is an agent through its essence, yet it is not an intellect through its essence. It neither understands nor exists through its essence, since it exists by way of participation.

[16. The Theory of Brother Thomas (Aquinas)]

The sixteenth is that of Brother Thomas. He maintains that the agent intellect is something found in the soul itself and that it is really distinct from the possible intellect. According to the Philosopher in *De anima* III, in all of nature [two factors are found, one which serves as matter] and one which serves as the cause and the productive principle, which latter, by making, is related to the former as art to matter.[33] From this it follows that just as these two differences are found in all of nature, so must they be found in the soul. But in the soul they are the agent intellect and the possible intellect. Therefore, etc. But art is really different from matter. Therefore, the agent intellect, which he compares to art and the productive principle, is really distinct from the possible intellect, which he compares to matter. Moreover, nothing operates except by means of a power which is formally present within it. Wherefore, according to *De anima* II, that whereby we live and sense is form and act.[34] But the activity of both, that is, of the agent and the possible intellect, is found in the soul itself and properly belongs to man. Therefore, etc.

[17. Resolution of the Question]

The original question must now be answered: Whether beatitude consists in [an act] of the agent intellect. There are two points of view regarding this question. Certain ones such as Magister Theodericus [Dietrich] reply in the affirmative. They present the following arguments.

1. Beatitude immediately pertains to that which is highest in us. But this is the agent intellect because it is an intellect through its essence, because it is an agent, and because it is always in act.

2. Man exists for the sake of his activity and above all for the sake of his most perfect activity. For, according to the Philosopher in *De caelo et mundo* II, each and everything exists for the sake of its highest activity.[35] Our highest activity is intellectual and is the act of the agent intellect, since it is an intellect through its essence. The possible intellect is only a kind of participated intellectuality.

3. The agent is superior to the patient.

4. That which bespeaks unqualified perfection should be found in the cause not only virtually but also in the formal sense, just as light is formally in the sun while heat and certain other things are only virtually present there. Intellection bespeaks unqualified perfection. Therefore, it is formally present in the intellect and in the noblest manner. Therefore, beatitude consists in an act of the agent intellect.

5. An agent contains its act virtually. But a power *[virtus]* is found in a given subject according to its proper mode. Therefore, in this case it is found according to an intellectual mode. Hence the agent intellect itself understands.

[CRITICISM OF THE ARGUMENTS]

In reply to the first argument it is to be noted that the statement [that the agent intellect is that which is highest in man] is true insofar as it is viewed as an agent, but not in the absolute sense. For it is an agent not in that it understands, but in that it renders potential intelligibles actually intelligible. As to the possibility of describing it as an intellect through its essence, cf. above [under the fifteenth theory]. To say that it is always in act is not true as regards the act of understanding but rather as regards making things intelligible.

In reply to the [fourth][36] argument: Intellection is virtually present in the agent intellect according to its proper mode, i.e., it both has as its function and actually does render potential intelligibles actually intelligible. Wherefore, they are not virtually present in it as in that which understands but rather as in that which renders things intelligible.

In reply to the [fifth][37] argument it is to be said that the statement [that an agent contains its act virtually] is true of a cause in the absolute sense both as regards being and as regards action. Nor does the fact that it [the agent intellect] is called an intellect prove their point. For even the formative power in the soul is sometimes called "soul" by the philosophers since it virtually contains in itself all of the differences and powers of the [various] members.

As regards the original question, Brother Thomas holds another view. He maintains that beatitude does not consist in an act of the agent intellect. He argues as follows. Beatitude does not reside in that which is not noblest in us, but rather in that which is noblest. But the possible intellect is nobler than the agent intellect. This may be shown from the side of the act and from the side of the object.

First, it is clear from the standpoint of the act. It pertains to the agent intellect to make potential intelligibles actually intelligible and to abstract and illumine the phantasms, or, according to some, to separate them. But it pertains to the possible intellect to understand that which has been separated and abstracted. Therefore, the agent intellect exists [and acts] for the sake of the possible intellect. If the possible intellect had actual intelligibles as its object, as Plato maintained, then there would be no need for an agent intellect. Therefore, the agent intellect is for the sake of the possible intellect. Again, it is a nobler thing merely to know that which has been separated and abstracted rather than to separate and abstract.

Secondly, it is clear from the standpoint of the object. Corporeal phantasms still subjected to material conditions constitute the object of the agent intellect. But the object of the possible intellect is the quiddity insofar as it is purified and separated from such conditions. Therefore, etc. Wherefore just as a higher technician takes something from a lower one for his own purposes (as the seaman receives a ship already prepared for his use by the shipbuilder and the shipbuilder produces a ship fitted for use by the superior technician), so too, the same is true of the agent intellect in relationship to the possible intellect. Therefore, beatitude does not consist in an act of the agent intellect.

NOTES

1. Aristotle, *Metaphysics* VII, 8 (1034a 5).
2. *Metaphysics* VII, 14.
3. Aristotle, *De anima* III, 5 (430a 15).
4. The terms "mutakallimūn" and "Mutakallims" have been used with reference to the school of Muslim theology known by Thomas Aquinas and by others in the thirteenth century, such as our anonymous author, as the *loquentes in lege Maurorum*. Cf. Gilson, *History of Christian Philosophy in the Middle Ages* (New York: Random House, 1955), pp. 182-83; Majid Fakhry, *Islamic Occasionalism and Its Critique by Averroës and Aquinas* (London: George Allen & Unwin Ltd., 1958), pp. 25ff. Note the role of Maimonides and Averroës in making their views known to the Latin West of the thirteenth century. For a general treatment of Muslim theology cf. L. Gardet-M.-M. Anawati, *Introduction à la Théologie Musulmane* (Paris: J. Vrin, 1948).
5. *Avencebrolis Fons vitae. Ex arabico in latinum translatus ab Iohanne Hispano et Dominico Gundissalino,* ed. Cl. Baeumker, *Beiträge zur Geschichte der Philosophie des Mittelalters, I,* 2-4 (1892-95), 41, 177.
6. *De anima* III, 5 (430a 18).
7. *Ibid.,* 430a 15.
8. Aristotle, *Physics* II, 8 (199a 31).
9. Cf. the theories of Alexander and Avicenna.
10. Aristotle, *De caelo* I, 4 (271a 33).
11. ________, *Posterior Analytics,* II, 19 (99b 25ff).
12. *De anima* III, 5 (430a 15).
13. *Posterior Analytics,* II, 19 (100a 4ff).
14. *De generatione et corruptione* I, 7 (324b 18).
15. *De anima* II, 5 (417b 12).
16. Averroës, *In Metaph.* II, 2 (*Aristotelis Stagiritae libri omnes cum Averrois Cordubensis variis in eosdem commentariis,* Vol. VIII (Venice, 1552), 17v.
17. Central to this theory is the denial of any real distinction between the soul and its powers. Powers are distinguished from the soul only in a relative sense, insofar as they are viewed in relationship to distinct objects.
18. Averroës, *In De anima* III, 1 (*loc. cit.,* Vol. VI) 160v.
19. *De anima* III, 4 (429a 27).
20. *De anima* III, 5 (430a 18).
21. Cf. St. Augustine, *The Trinity,* tr. Stephen McKenna, C.SS.R., *The Fathers of the Church,* Vol. 45 (Washington: The Catholic University of America Press, 1963), 423.
22. *Op. cit.,* 507. However, note that the text in question appears

in chap. 21 rather than the chap. 26 of the "large" or the chap. 63 of the "small" text cited by the author of the Basel Ms.

23. Cf. note 11 above.

24. The Latin *intelligere patiens* seems to be a typographical error for *intelligere patens*. Cf. Grabmann, *op. cit.*, p. 95 (*intelligere patiens*) but compare with Grabmann, p. 38 (*intelligere patens*).

25. The Basel Ms. reading "even though he is not thinking of *geometry* itself" (italics added) seems to betray Augustine's thought here (p. 96). Augustine's point is that one may be said to remember, know, and love an art in which he is skilled even though he does not *think of it* here and now. For an English translation, cf. Saint Augustine, *The Trinity, op. cit.*, p. 423: "But we say most rightly: 'This man, whom you behold in a discussion about geometry, is also an accomplished musician, for he remembers his art, understands it, and loves it; but although he knows it and loves it, he is not thinking about it now, since he is thinking about geometry which he is now discussing.' "

26. Averroës, *In De anima* III, 3 (*loc. cit.* Vol. VI), 170r.

27. *De anima* III, 5 (430a 15).

28. Following the interpretation given by Grabmann in his German version (*op. cit.*, p. 41), we have changed the Latin text "Ergo non est intellectus per essentiam" to read "the agent intellect is not a substance." For this is the point at issue here, to prove that the agent intellect is not a substance. Further on the author takes up the other point, to prove that the agent intellect is not an intellect through its essence.

29. *Metaphysics* VIII, 3 (1043b 34).

30. *Physics* I, 1.

31. *De anima* II, 4 (415a 29). Aristotle's statement is somewhat qualified by the context. His point is that since no perishable living thing can partake in what is eternal and divine in the fullest sense by uninterrupted possession, it does so insofar as its particular nature will allow, by producing another like itself, i.e., by reproduction.

32. Read "praepositio" rather than "propositio" as found in the Latin text on p. 99. Cf. Grabmann, *op cit.*, p. 43. We have inserted *aliud quam* into the Latin text for the sake of meaning: "per primo modo denotat nihil (?) [aliud quam] ipsum esse. . . ." (p. 99).

33. *De anima* III, 5 (430a 10-13).

34. *De anima* II, 2 (414a 12).

35. *De caelo* II, 12 (292b 4ff).

36. Apparently the author feels that his refutation of the first argument also contains a reply to the second and third arguments. His "ad secundum" is really a reply to argument four and his "ad tertium" is his reply to argument five.

37. Cf. note 36 above.

XXIII

WILLIAM OCKHAM

William Ockham was probably born around 1280 in the village of Ockham, on the outskirts of present-day London. After his entry into the Franciscan order, he took up studies leading to the mastership in theology at Oxford (*ca.* 1307-20). His title of "Venerable Inceptor" suggests he did not function there as regent master after his inception and inaugural lecture, probably because Lutterell, an over-zealous Thomist and chancellor of the University, challenged his teachings. Though the Bishop of Lincoln, at the request of the university itself, deposed Lutterell in 1322 and the king refused to allow him to leave the country, he eventually obtained permission to visit the papal court in Avignon, where he brought accusations against Ockham. In 1324, Pope John XXII summoned Ockham to Avignon and appointed a commission to examine his teachings. Though the investigations dragged on for the best part of two years, and two lists of articles, often blatantly misrepresenting Ockham's position, were drawn up by the commission, the Pope was obviously dissatisfied and no official condemnation was ever issued.

Meanwhile, Ockham became involved in the question of evangelical poverty when he was ordered to study the matter by the Franciscan general, Michael of Cesena, who had been detained at Avignon because of his open opposition to the papal decision on the matter. Because of statements of Pope John that seemed to be inconsistent with earlier papal documents, Ockham sided with his superior against the Pope. Further complicating the picture was John's personal view, retracted on his deathbed, that the beatific vision, because of the radical dependence of the soul upon the sense faculties, could not be bestowed on man prior to the general resurrection of the body. In studying the works of earlier canonists, Ockham had discovered the view that even a pope acting as a private individual can put himself outside the communion of the Church since he is not *ex officio* immune to all sin, and in particular to a sin against faith. If he personally holds a position officially declared heretical by the Church, and when this is called to his attention he continues openly to hold it, he has automatically severed his connection as a member of the Church and can no longer be considered pope. Ockham obviously had convinced himself that Pope John had done just that. When John convoked a general chapter of the Franciscan order for the purposes of electing a new general, it is not surprising that Michael fled Avignon, together with Ockham and two other friars. At Pisa they met Louis, the Bavarian, who was returning to Munich from Rome, where he had installed an anti-pope and had been crowned Emperor by him.

Though the friars were excommunicated by the pope and the Franciscan order for apostasy, they continued to live in Munich under the protection of Emperor Louis. It was during this period that Ockham composed his "political works." Michael died in 1342 with the seal of the order still in his possession. The theory that Ockham returned the seal after the death of Louis the Bavarian in 1347, sought reconciliation with the Church, and may even have signed a formula of submission, is questionable. Consequently there seems to be no solid reason to challenge the inscription on his tomb in the Franciscan church at Munich which gave the date of his death as August 10, 1347. In 1802, when the church was demolished, Ockham's remains along with those of Michael were removed to some as yet undiscovered location.

It is perhaps worth remarking that none of Ockham's philosophical or theological doctrines were ever officially condemned by the Church, and even his political views on Church-state relations are generally recognized by contemporary Catholic scholars as being in advance of his time. At any rate, his nonpolitical writings were enormously influential in shaping and giving impetus to the empirical trend, which reached its peak in the late Middle Ages.

Ockham has frequently been misrepresented as holding that the possibility or impossibility of an event is something that has its roots in an arbitrary decision of God. The following question, translated by A. B. Wolter especially for this volume, is his *ex professo* treatment of the subject.

On Possibility and God[1]

My question is this: Is the inability to perform the impossible a characteristic of God that is prior [by nature] to the impossible's inability to be made by God?

[Arguments for and Against the Thesis]

It seems that God's inability to perform the impossible is the prior characteristic for the following reason. That God can make what is possible is prior to the possible's capacity to be made by God. In the same vein then God's inability to make the impossible should be prior to the impossible's inability to be made by God. The antecedent is evident from the fact that everything that pertains to God is prior to anything that pertains to a creature, and consequently also to anything that the creature gets from God. Therefore, since the ability to make the possible is a divine characteristic, this should pertain to God in some prior fashion than that the impossibility of being made by God should be a characteristic of a thing other than God.

To the contrary: Nothing that suggests any lack of perfection can be a primary attribute of God.

[The View of Henry of Ghent][2]

One answer to the problem is this. Any attribute of God which signifies something that is not perfection purely and simply is not as such a primary attribute of God. But since something of this sort is attributed to a creature by virtue of its relationship to God, it is also attributed to God. Of such sort are those [divine] names which express God's relations to creatures and which are therefore predicated of God because creatures bear this relationship to him. For example, God is said to be a "Lord" because since time began he has had a "servant." And therefore "power over creatures" is an action-predicate ascribed to God because the creature in itself is a potential recipient of such action from its creator.

The additional point is made, however, that both the possible action on God's part and the recipient possibility of the creature can be viewed either subjectively or objectively. If God's power is viewed in terms of its subject, then it is prior to the potentiality of the creature, no matter how you look at the latter. The reason is that power so considered is a perfection purely and simply. Considered from the standpoint of its object, however, God's power is not such a perfection and therefore one can ascribe it to God only because the creature possesses a recipient capacity as regards God. Therefore it is said that absolutely speaking, this passive capacity is something a creature has only because God has the power to act. Consider these four relationships to what is possible, namely the two ways of viewing God's power to act (i.e. one which views this power as God's attribute, the other which sees it as a feature of the creature) and the two ways of viewing the recipient capacity of a creature (viz. as an attribute of the creature itself and as something which it has received from God). Now the following order obtains. God's power to act considered in itself is that from which the creature derives its recipient capacity considered in itself. A concomitant of this capacity is its relationship to God in virtue of which God in turn is said to have power with reference to the creature.

Against this view we can use his [Henry's] own counter-argument.[3] For he claims elsewhere that we don't say, "It is impossible for God to do something because it is impossible for the thing in question to be done." Rather we assert the reverse, viz., "It is impossible for God to do this, therefore it is impossible for this to be done." Similarly one argues affirmatively that "Because it is possible for God to do this, therefore it is possible for this to be done" and not the reverse, viz., "It is possible for this to be done, therefore God can do it." This argument clearly gives God's power as regards creatures priority over the creature's recipient capacity as regards God and by implication it also gives God's inability to do the impossible priority over the impossible's inability to be done by God. And from this it is clear he would have to say that not everything which relates to creatures is ascribed to God because the creature is related to him, but rather the converse. Such relative attributes are ascribed to creatures because other relative attributes are ascribed to God.

Also, there is no more reason for ascribing to God some relationship to a creature on the grounds that the creature bears a relationship to him than there is for attributing something to a created cause on the grounds that its effect bears a relationship to such a cause. The minor is evident because according to him, when a created cause has a real relation, it follows that the cause is first altered in some real fashion before the effect is produced. It doesn't do to object that the parallel between God and the created cause breaks down since God bears only a logical and not a real relation [to the creature], whereas a cause is really related [to its effect]. For the impossibility of one real relation arising from another is no greater than for one logical relationship to arise from another. Hence the impossibility of a created cause acquiring a relationship because of a relationship in the effect is no greater than in the case of God, for God receives less in the way of both real and logical entities from a creature than does a created cause from its effect.

Similarly, if from one real aspect there does not arise a second corresponding real aspect, by the same token one logical relationship does not arise from another corresponding logical relation. But the relationship of a creature to God is a logical relationship, for there is certainly not something real involved, since what does not exist is not referred really. Therefore from this relationship a logical relationship of God to creatures does not arise.

Furthermore, against [Henry's] other point that God's power to act is prior to the creature's recipient capacity and that the former is a pure perfection, one can argue thus. No matter how you view it, one simply can't have an ability to do something apart from all reference to the something in question. Therefore this power to act is a power to act in regard to something. But this something is not God because God doesn't cause God, neither does God act upon God. Therefore this something is a creature. Hence God's ability to act no matter how you look at it involves a reference to the creature. Consequently, even as a primary attribute of God this power to act has reference to a creature. According to him [Henry], then, it would not be a perfection purely and simply.

A confirmatory argument: He says that just as the recipient capacity has two aspects, so also there are two aspects to the power to act, one of which refers this ability to God. Now I ask: Just how is this relationship [i.e. power to act] referred to God? Either he is its foundation or he is the term [i.e. object over which the power is exercised]. If God is the foundation, then the relationship has another term and this can only be the creature; therefore this relationship has its term in a creature and consequently cannot be a primary attribute of God nor can it be a perfection purely and simply. If God is the term of the relationship, then since a thing is said to be able to act with reference to some recipient which is passive or submissive with respect to the action, it would follow that God would be passive, which is impossible. And so it is quite clear that this view contains inconsistencies.

[The View of Duns Scotus][4]

Another view is that the primary reason something is impossible is not to be found in God [but in the thing itself] which is simply impossible because it is inconsistent that what it is should happen. The explanation is this. Included in the simply impossible are incompatible elements which are such in virtue of their intelligible content or essential meanings. But viewed in terms of their originative source, these incompatibles flow from the same fountainhead as do these essential meanings. And hence the following logical order obtains. (1) In the first logical moment[5] the divine intellect produces a thing in that kind of existence it has as an intelligible object.[6] (2) In the second logical moment, the latter has possibility [i.e. can be actually realized] precisely by reason of what it is. Now just as God by his intellect produces the possible in its mode of being as a possible, so does he give this mode of being to each of the incompatible elements that make up an impossible. And these possibles produced [by the divine intellect] are mutually incompatible in virtue of what they are, so that they cannot exist together in one thing and from two such no third thing can be formed. Now this incompatibility which they possess precisely in virtue of what they are, they owe—in terms of its origins—to the divine intellect which produced them as possible modes of being. From the incompatibility of its elements the incompatibility of the figment as a whole follows. And from this it follows that it is impossible for any agent whatsoever to make it. And here the whole sequence ends. It does not end up with denying some kind of possibility to God.

Now some of [Scotus'] statements can be contested. First of all it does not seem proper to speak of the divine intellect "producing" the creature in a kind of intelligible existence. If all that a thing acquires through an action is a way of specifying or naming it in terms of an extrinsic frame of reference, whereas it gets nothing in the way of being or existence as such, then the thing in question is not "produced" through such an act. But a creature receives nothing as such from the fact it is known by God; it is just that one may denominate it with reference to something extrinsic to itself. It is the same as with the object of a created intellect which is not "produced" by being known, but has merely acquired a new name in terms of an extrinsic frame of reference. Consequently, the creature is not produced in intelligible being or existence.

Furthermore, were a creature produced in such a way, it would be precisely because it is known or because it was nothing before being produced, or because it was not intelligible before this. It is not because of the first, for then the divine essence would be produced in intelligible existence when it is known and then anyone knowing God would produce God in intelligible being. It is not because of the second reason, since a creature is still nothing even after it is known. Neither is it on account of the third, since it is not the case that the divine essence was intelligible prior to its self-knowledge.

Furthermore, according to him, nothing is produced in this kind of intelligible existence unless something is also produced in real existence. But when the creature is produced by the divine intellect, it is produced only in existence as an intelligible, and hence something else has to be produced in real existence. But nothing can be, as is clear inductively.

Furthermore, take what he says about a thing being produced in intelligible existence in the first logical moment and having existence as a possible in the second logical moment. To the contrary: I'll concede [for the purpose of argument] the first logical moment in which the intellect precedes the intelligible being of the creature. But I ask: At this moment is the creature possible or not possible? If it is possible, then it is possible before it is produced in intelligible being. If it is not possible, then it is repugnant that the creature exist.

Furthermore, he says the sequence ends with the impossibility of any agent making it and not with some corresponding relationship in God. To the contrary: For every relationship of the possible creature to God there is a corresponding relationship in God to the creature as a possible mode of being. In the same way, to the negation of such a relationship there will be a corresponding negative relationship in God to the impossible; hence the sequence does not end with the latter. If one objects that in God there is no relationship correlative to the relationship of the possible creature to God, one can counter that either this relationship of the creature as a possible is real or it is logical. It is not real because it has no real foundation. Hence it is a logical relation which arises in virtue of the intellectual act of considering the creature with reference to God according to him [Scotus]. But the mind can just as well consider God with reference to the creature as the reverse; therefore, etc.

[Ockham's Own Opinion]

Therefore I answer the question in a different way. As a general rule to every related thing, if it be properly designated, there corresponds some correlative, and where the correlative terms are related as cause and effect, or as "ability to act" and "the capacity to be acted upon," the correlatives are by nature simultaneous. Because they are such and each entails the other, one is no more the cause of the other than vice versa.

Since father and son are simultaneous by nature in the way the Philosopher speaks of simultaneity of nature in the chapter on "relation" in the *Categoriae,*[7] it follows that the son is not more a son than the father is a father, nor is the reverse true. Neither is it more the case that the son is because the father is, than it is that the father is because the son is. Neither is it more the case that *the son has a father because the father has a son* than it is that *the father has a son because the son has a father*. And when the mutual entailment holds precisely because of the nature of the correlatives, it is universally true that one proposition is no more the cause of the other than vice versa.

And when one asks whether the inability of doing the impossible is something God has prior to the impossible's inability to be made by God, I say that the inability to do the impossible is not something that God has prior to the impossible's inability to be done by God. Neither is the impossible's inability to be made by God prior to God's inability to do the impossible.

And in the same fashion I say of the affirmative form: the ability to do the possible or to create a creature is not something God has prior to the creature's ability to be made by God but they are simultaneous by nature in the same way that "to be able to make" and "to be able to be made" are simultaneous by nature, according to the Philosopher; that is to say, "Something can make" does not come before "Something can be made," neither is the reverse true.

Suppose one says that whatever a creature has, it has from God, therefore "to be possible" is something which belongs to it that is from God. "To be able to make something" is not something God gets from anything else, but has of himself, and whatever pertains to a thing of itself, pertains to it before anything it has by reason of something other than itself. Hence "to be able to make something" is something which pertains to God before "the ability to be made" pertains to the creature, and they are therefore not simultaneous. To this one should counter that whatever a creature has that is real, viz. as some inherent quality, it has from God as from its originative source. But not everything which pertains to it by way of predication does it have from God in this way, except in the same way one can speak of God having from God such predicates [as may be affirmed of him]. Because such predications when they are actually and really made, then they are from God.[8] And hence "to be possible" is something a creature has of itself, but it is not a real something inhering in the creature [like a real accident]. But the creature is truly possible of itself in the same way that man of himself is not an ass. Therefore arguments like the above do not hold except for those things which pertain to it in reality, in the way that a whole has its parts and its accidents. It is not a proper mode of speech to say that possible existence pertains to a creature, but to speak properly one ought to say that the creature is possible, not because anything pertains to it, but because it can exist in the real world.

[Reply to the Argument at the Beginning]

To the initial argument, I say that God is not able to make before a creature is able to be made. Indeed a creature's ability to be made has the same priority with God's being able to make it.

NOTES

1. William Ockham, *Ordinatio* (*Sent.* I). dist. 43, ed. A. B. Wolter in *Franziskanische Studien* 32 (1950), 92-96.

2. Henry of Ghent, *Quodlibet* 6. q. 3 (Paris, 1518 ed., photoreprint Louvain: Bibliothèque S. J., 1961), fol. 220-21.

3. *Quodlibet* 8, q. 3. fol. 304.

4. Duns Scotus, *Ordinatio I,* dist. 43, *Opera omnia,* VI (Civitas Vaticana: typis polyglottis Vaticanis, 1963), 359-61.

5. Literally, an *instans naturae*. Though Scotus does not admit any temporal sequence or priority among those attributes God has from all eternity, he does believe one can distinguish a certain order of nature (i.e. a certain logical priority) among these attributes or properties in virtue of what they are. Knowledge of a creature's possibility does not logically entail a decision to create, but God's decision to create (made from all eternity) does entail knowledge of its possibility. If B entails A, but not vice versa, A is said to be prior by nature to B even when there is no temporal precedence. As one may number various moments of time to create a framework for discussing a temporal order of events, so Scotus distinguished various *instantia naturae* or "logical moments" to show the logical sequence of such nonmutual entailments.

6. Literally, "produces it *in esse intelligibili.*" Like Meinong, Scotus distinguished between thinking or knowing and the "intelligible content" of the knowledge or thought. He speaks of the latter as having a "diminutive kind of existence." Since the intelligible content of any creature is limited, Scotus argued it would be derogatory to the infinite perfection of God's mind to make it in any way dependent upon the finite intelligibility of the creature. Like an artist who first gives his "creation" existence in his mind, God does not know the possible because it has some logically prior intelligibility, but he invests it with intelligibility by knowing it.

7. Aristotle, *Categoriae,* chap. 7 (7b-15).

8. According to Aristotle, when a man makes an affirmation or mental judgment, a real or physical concomitant change takes place in the soul or mind. It acquires a new accidental entity which falls in the category of "quality." This new reality, Ockham points out, may be said to come from God as the first cause of all things created.

XXIV

NICHOLAS OF CUSA

NICHOLAS OF CUSA (also known as Nicholas Krebs and as Nicholas Cusanus) was born at Kues (Cusa) on the Moselle in 1401. After early studies with the Brothers of the Common Life in Deventer, Holland, he studied philosophy at Heidelberg, canon law at Padua, and theology at Cologne. He received the doctorate in canon law in 1423, and seems to have taught for a few years at Cologne after 1425. He then took an active part in the Council of Basel, where his prestige was considerably enhanced by the publication of his *De concordantia catholica,* in which he defended the superiority of a general council over the pope. However, as time went on, he changed his position, having concluded that only the papacy could insure unity for the Church. In 1437-38 he served as a member of a papal commission sent to Constantinople to negotiate with the Greek Church about plans for eventual reunion with Rome. He had become a priest between 1436 and 1440 and was made a Cardinal in 1448 and Bishop of Brixen in 1450. After zealously fulfilling a mission as papal legate to Germany from December, 1450, until March, 1452, Nicholas took possession of his diocese. Although the years after 1457 were clouded by a bitter conflict with Duke Sigmund of Austria and Nicholas found it necessary to flee from his diocese, he continued to perform important missions for the Church. He died in 1464.

This active career in ecclesiastical activities notwithstanding, Nicholas managed to do a considerable amount of writing, ranging over the areas of political theory, religion, science, philosophy, and theology. Among works of philosophical interest, particular mention should be made of his *De docta ignorantia* and his *De coniecturis.*

He had come into contact with the theories of Ockham and the terminists at Heidelberg, with Averroism at Padua, and apparently with some form of Thomism and some followers of Albert at Cologne. Troubled by the controversies of the various schools of the time and not finding any hope of reconciliation in Aristotelian dialectics, he preferred to turn to the Neoplatonic Christian tradition.

The following selection is taken from the *De docta ignorantia* (Book. II, chaps. 2, 3) and is translated by Germain Heron.

On Learned Ignorance

THE BEING OF A CREATURE COMES IN A MYSTERIOUS WAY FROM THE BEING OF THE MAXIMUM*

From the foregoing lessons in sacred ignorance we have learned that God alone is 'a se,' that in Him 'a se,' 'in se', 'per se', and 'ad se' are all one, that He is, in other words, the Absolute; we learned, too, that necessarily every essence is indebted to Him for whatever existence it possesses. Otherwise, how could a being that is not 'a se' exist, if it did not receive its existence from the Eternal Being? As jealousy has no place in God, He cannot give a reduced form of being as such, so that the corruptibility, divisibility, imperfection, diversity, plurality, and other things of this kind, which are found in creatures that come from Him, are not attributable to Him, the Maximum, who is eternal, indivisible, most perfect, simple, one; nor have such things any positive cause. We have already shown that the infinite line is infinite straightness and as infinite straightness it is the cause of all linear being; the curve, on the other hand, qua line is from the infinite, qua curve it is not; in fact, curvature is a consequence of finiteness: a curve is a curve because it is not infinite; it would cease, in other words, to be a curve if it were infinite. So also is it with things: that they have being in a reduced form, that they are diverse and distinct and have other similar marks of imperfection are not effects of any cause; they are the consequences of their nature which cannot be other than finite. Therefore, what is attributable to God is the fact that a creature has unity, separate existence and is in harmony with the universe; and the greater its unity, the greater its resemblance to God; but it is an effect of its contingent nature —not attributable to God or any positive cause—that its unity

*Reprinted with permission of the publisher from Nicolas Cusanus, *Of Learned Ignorance*, trans. G. Heron, (London: Routledge and Kegan Paul Ltd., 1954). Book II, Chap. 2, pp. 71-75.

is in a plurality, its individual existence amidst confusion and its harmony amidst discordancy.

Is it possible, then, for anyone to understand the being of a creature by considering at once the absolute necessity which produced it, and the contingency which is for it an indispensable condition of existence? A creature is not God, nor is it nothing; it is, as it were, posterior to God and prior to nothing, or it stands between God and nothing, according to one of the sages: God is the opposite of nothing with being as the intermediary. And yet it cannot be a compound of being and non-being. It seems, therefore, that it is neither being, for it is derived from being, nor non-being, for it is prior to nothing, nor a compound of these; and in considering these separately or conjointly, our intellect, which is unable to reconcile contradictories, does not comprehend the being of a creature, though it knows that every creature has its being from the Maximum. As being ab alio, it is unintelligible, since the being from whom it comes is incomprehensible—just as the being of an accident is not intelligible; as long as its subject of inhesion is not understood. The creature, qua creature, therefore, cannot be called one, since it is derived from unity; it cannot be said to be more than one, since it owes its being to unity; nor can it be at once one and more than one. In virtue of its nature its unity lies in a plurality. What we have said here ought equally to be applied, it seems, to simplicity and composition and the other contradictories.

Since the creature is created by the being of the Maximum, and since in the Maximum there is no difference between being, doing and creating, then it seems that it is one and the same thing to say that God creates as to say that God is all things. If, then, creation means that God is all things, how can the creature be conceived as other than eternal, when the being of God is eternal, or better, eternity itself? No one doubts its eternity in-so-far as the creature itself is the being of God; in-so-far, therefore, as it is temporal it is not from God, for He is eternal. How reconcile a creature's being at once temporal and eternal? Necessarily the creature's existence was possible from eternity in the Being; yet it was not possible for it to exist prior to time, for before time there was no 'before'; consequently it has always been when it was possible for it to be.

How is it possible, then, for anyone to understand how God is the form of being without being involved in creation? A composite can be formed only by beings between which there is some proportion; the infinite line and the finite curve, therefore, are unable to form a composite whole, for it is evident to all that between the infinite and the finite there is no possible proportion. How, then, can the intellect grasp that the curved line has its being from the infinite straight line, which, though not its informing form, is its cause and raison d'être? The curve cannot share the essence of the infinite line by taking part of it, since it is an infinite and indivisible essence; nor can it share it as matter shares the form, as Socrates and Plato, for example, share the human form; nor as parts share in the whole, as, for example, the universe shared by its parts; nor does it share it as several mirrors may be said to share in different ways the same face; for a mirror is a mirror before it receives the image of the face, whereas a creature is nothing if it is not 'ab esse': 'ab esse' is its very definition.

A creature is not a positively distinct reality that receives the image of the infinite form; it is merely the image and nothing more, and in different creatures we see accidentally different images of that form. Since that is so, how is it possible for us to understand that the various creatures share in different ways the one infinite form? It is as if a work of art were to have no other being than that of dependence, and of total dependence on the idea of the artist, from whom it would receive its being and by whose power it would be conserved in being; or it is like the image of the face in the mirror, provided we suppose that the mirror in itself and of itself is nothing before or after the reflection.

We are also unable to understand how God can manifest Himself to us through visible creation. He is not like our intellect, which is only known to Him and us; which, before coming to think, had no form, but proceeds, when thinking, to take the form of colour, sound, or something else from the images in the memory; then, after taking on another form of signs, words or letters, it manifests itself to others. God does not manifest Himself in that way. Whether His purpose in creating the world was to manifest His goodness, as pious people believe, or whether, as the Infinite Necessity, He created it to do His Will and have creatures who would be obliged to obey Him, who would fear Him and who would be judged by Him, it is clear whatever His purpose may have been, that He does not assume another form, since He is the form of all forms; and it is likewise clear that He does not manifest Himself in positive signs, for these signs, if they existed, would naturally in their turn demand others in which to exist, and so on to infinity.

Who can understand how all things, whilst different from one another by reason of their finite nature, are an image of that unique infinite form? God, so to speak, is incidentally brought to view in a creature, in the same way as a substance, so to speak, is incidentally presented to us by an accident and a man incidentally reproduced in a woman. Only in a finite fashion is the infinite form received. Every creature is, as it were, 'God-created' or 'finite-infinity', with the result that no creature's existence could be better than it is. It is as if the Creator had said 'Let it be produced', and, because God, who is eternity itself, could not be brought into being, that was made which could most resemble God. The inference from this is that every creature, as such, is perfect, though by comparison with others it may seem imperfect. God in His infinite goodness gives being to all in the way in which each can receive it. With Him there is no jealousy; He communicates being without distinction; and, since all receive being in accord with the demands of their contingent nature, every creature rests content in its own perfection, which God has freely bestowed upon it. None desires the greater perfection of any other; each loves by preference that perfection which God has given it and strives to develop and preserve it intact.

IN A MYSTERIOUS WAY THE MAXIMUM ENVELOPS AND DEVELOPS ALL THINGS*

The first part of this work contains all that can be said or thought about truth in-so-far as it is subject to investigation. All that is in agreement with what we said there of the first truth is necessarily true; all that conflicts with it is false. There it was shown that, above all others, there must be one sole Maximum, which is at once all things and in which even the minimum and maximum are identified. As unity unites all, the Maximum, which is infinite unity, must envelop all; and it is not simply the maximum as unity, which comprises every number, but it is the Maximum because it envelops all things. Just as in number, which is a development of unity, only unity is to

**Op. cit.*, chap. 3, pp. 75-79.

be found, so in all things which exist only the Maximum is to be found.

Quantity is a development of unity, and here unity is called a point, since there is nothing but a point to be found in quantity; just as there is nothing to be found in a line, no matter where you may divide it, but a point, so there is nothing in a surface or a solid but a point. There is one point, not more; and that one point is infinite unity itself, for infinite unity, whilst it contains within itself the line and quantity, is the point which is their term, perfection and entirety; and its first development is the line, in which there is nothing to be found but the point.

In the same way rest is unity, in which all movement is contained; for on close examination movement is seen to be rest drawn out in an orderly series. Movement, therefore, is the first development of rest. In like manner all time is comprised in the present or 'now'. The past was present, the future shall be present, so that time is only a methodical arrangement of the present. The past and the future, in consequence, are the development of the present; the present comprises all present times, and present times are a regular and orderly development of it; only the present is to be found in them: The present, therefore, in which all times are included, is one: it is unity itself. So, too, is diversity contained in identity, inequality in equality, divisions or distinctions in simplicity. There is not an all-inclusive maximum of substances, another of quality or quantity, and so on; there is one sole Maximum which embraces all things—the maximum, which is also the minimum, and in which the inclusion of diversity in identity is not a contradiction. Just as unity precedes distinction, so the point, which is perfection, precedes magnitude, for that which is perfect is prior to all that is imperfect: rest is prior to movement, identity to diversity, equality to inequality, and so on for all that is convertible with unity. Unity is convertible with eternity, for there cannot be more than one Eternal. God, therefore, envelops all in the sense that all is found in Him; He is the development of all in the sense that He is found in all.

To make this clear let us take an example. Number, which is a development of unity, presupposes an act of reason. Reason is a faculty of the soul, and it is because animals have no soul that they cannot count. Number, then, is accounted for by our mind, which distinguishes the many individuals that share a common nature; and similarly the plurality of things is accounted for by God's mind, in which by reason of its all-embracing unity, the multiplicity of things exists without plurality. Things cannot share in precisely the same way the equality of being. Plurality, which in Him is unity, has arisen from the fact that in His eternity He has understood one thing existing in one way, another in another way. It is unity that gives to plurality or number the only being it has. Without unity number would be impossible, for plurality can only be explained as a development of unity; unity, therefore, exists in plurality. How all is in one and one in all is above our understanding. Knowing, as we do, that God's understanding is His being and that His being is infinite unity, how could any of us understand that God's mind is the origin of the plurality of things?

If—continuing with our example of number—we consider that number is the mind's measurement of a multitude by a unit common to all, it would seem as though God, who is the unit, were multiplied in things, since His understanding is His being; and yet we know that any multiplication of that unit, which is the infinite maximum unity, is impossible. How, then, is plurality conceivable without a multiplication of the unit from which it has its being? or how are we to understand multiplicity in unity, if there is no multiplication? In one species, it may be said, there is a plurality of individuals and in one genus a plurality of species; but there is this difference that apart from the individuals the genus or species has no existence outside the abstracting intellect.

God's being, which is unity, is not abstracted by the mind from things, nor is it united to or immersed in things; it is, therefore, beyond anyone to understand how the plurality of things is a development of the unity which is God. If we consider things without Him, they are as number without unity: nothing; if we consider Him without things, He exists and the things do not; if we consider Him as He is in things, we are regarding things as something else in which He exists—an error which we pointed out in the last chapter, where we saw that the being of a thing is from the Being, God, and cannot, therefore, be 'other' in the sense of being totally different; if we consider a thing such as it is in God, then it is God and Unity.

All that remains for us to assert is that the plurality of things is due to the fact that God is in nothing. Take away God from the creature and you are left with nothing; take away the substance from a composite being, the accidents also disappear and nothing remains. Is it possible for the human mind to grasp this? The accident ceases to exist when the substance is removed, and its ceasing to exist in that instance is due to the fact that to inhere is of the nature of an accident and that its subsistence is the subsistence of the substance. Yet it cannot be said that an accident is nothing, for while it inheres in its substance it confers something on it, e.g. it is by quanity that a substance is quantified. This does not apply here, since the creature does not inhere in God in that manner. An accident gives something to a substance, the creature contributes nothing to God; in fact, an accident gives so much to a substance that, although the accident has its being from the substance, the substance cannot exist without any accident; but this can in no way apply to God.

The creature comes from God, yet it cannot, in consequence of that, add anything to Him who is the Maximum. How are we going to be able to form an idea of creature as such? If the creature as such is really nothing and has not even as much entity as an accident, how are we to accept as explanation of the development of the plurality of things the fact that God is in nothing, since nothing cannot be predicated of any entity? If you say: 'all theology is circular; God's will is the omnipotent cause, and He is His will and His omnipotence', you are thereby necessarily admitting that you are completely ignorant of how it comes about that God in His unity embraces all, whilst His unity is developed in plurality; you are simply admitting that you are conscious of your ignorance of the method even though you may know the fact that God's unity embraces all: all in God is God, all things come from His unity and in all things He is what they are, like truth in an image. It is as if a face were reproduced in its own image. With the multiplication of the image we get distant and close reproductions of the face. (I do not mean distance in space but a gradual distance from the true face, since without that multiplication would be impossible.) In the many different images of that face one face would appear in many, different ways, but it would be an appearance that the senses would be incapable of recognizing and the mind of understanding.

BIBLIOGRAPHY

Note: Abbreviations Used in Bibliography

ADHL *Archives d'Histoire Doctrinale et Littéraire du Moyen Age*

Beiträge *Beiträge zur Geschichte der Philosophie (und Theologie) des Mittelalters*

PL J. P. Migne, *Patrologiae cursus completus. Series prima in qua prodeunt Patres, Doctores Scriptoresque Ecclesiae Latinae* (Paris: 1844 ff.)

RTAM *Recherches de Théologie Ancienne et Médiévale*

I. GENERAL HISTORIES OF THE PHILOSOPHY OF THE MEDIEVAL PERIOD

A. H. Armstrong, ed., *The Cambridge History of Later Greek and Early Medieval Philosophy* (Cambridge, 1967): Part V, "Marius Victorinus and Augustine," R. A. Markus; Part VI, "The Greek Christian Platonist Tradition . . . ," I. P. Sheldon-Williams; Part VII, "Western Christian Thought from Boethius to Anselm," by H. Liebeschütz; Part VIII, "Early Islamic Philosophy," R. Walzer. T. J. de Boer, *The History of Philosophy in Islam* (London, 1903; repr. 1961). P. Böhner and E. Gilson, *Christliche Philosophie von ihren Anfängen bis Nikolaus von Cues,* 3rd ed. (Paderborn, 1954). F. Copleston, *A History of Philosophy, II: Medieval Philosophy, Augustine to Scotus* (Westminster, Md., 1950); III: *Ockham to Suarez* (Westminster, Md., 1953). M. De Wulf, *Histoire de la philosophie médiévale*, 6th ed., 3 vols. (Louvain, 1934, 1936, 1947). A. Forest, F. Van Steenberghen, M. de Gandillac, "Le XIIIe siècle," in *Le mouvement doctrinal du XIe au XIVe siècle, 2nd ed.* (Paris, 1956), 193-348. E. Gilson, *La philosophie au moyen âge des origines patristiques à la fin du XIVe siècle,* 2nd ed. (Paris, 1952); *History of Christian Philosophy in the Middle Ages* (New York, 1955), indispensable, with copious notes. M. Grabmann, *Die Geschichte der scholastischen Methode,* 2 vols. (Freiburg, 1909-11; repr. Basel/Stuttgart, 1961). I. Husik, *A History of Mediaeval Jewish Philosophy* (Philadelphia, 1944). D. Knowles, *The Evolution of Medieval Thought* (London, 1962). G. Leff, *Medieval Thought: St. Augustine to Ockham* (London, 1958). A. Maurer, *Medieval Philosophy* (New York, 1962). J. Pieper, *Scholasticism: Personalities and Problems of Medieval Philosophy* (New York, 1960). F. J. Roensch, *Early Thomis-*

tic School (Dubuque, 1964), studies important figures in the early history of Thomism; see esp. Bibliography, 318-37. F. Ueberweg, *Grundriss der Geschichte der Philosophie,* vol. 2, *Die patristische und scholastische Philosophie,* 11th ed., B. Geyer (Berlin, 1928; repr. Basel/Stuttgart, 1961). F. Van Steenberghen, *Aristotle in the West* (Louvain, 1955); *Histoire de la philosophie. Période chrétienne* (Louvain, 1964); *The Philosophical Movement in the Thirteenth Century* (Edinburgh, 1955); *La Philosophie au XIIIe Siècle* (Louvain, 1966), excellent study of events leading to the crisis of "heterodox Aristotelianism" at Paris at time of Siger of Brabant. P. Vignaux, *Philosophy in the Middle Ages: An Introduction* (New York, 1959).

II. STUDIES OF SPECIAL PROBLEMS AND TOPICS

J. Collins, ed., *Readings in Ancient and Medieval Philosophy* (Westminster, Md., 1960), studies of some major thinkers in the ancient and medieval periods. A. C. Crombie, *Medieval and Early Modern Science,* 2 vols. (Cambridge, Mass., 1959), esp. vol. 1, pp. 249-54 for further bibliography on medieval translation movement into Latin. J. de Ghellinck, *l'Essor de la littérature latine au XIIe siècle* II (Paris, 1946), 15-42 on translations from Arabic and Greek into Latin. E. Gilson, *Being and Some Philosophers,* 2nd ed. (Toronto, 1952); *Reason and Revelation in the Middle Ages* (New York, 1938); *The Spirit of Mediaeval Philosophy* (London, 1936; repr. 1950), important discussion of Christian elements in medieval philosophy. M. Grabmann, *Mittelalterliche Deutung und Umbildung der aristotelischen Lehre vom* νοῦς ποιητικός *nach einer Zusammenstellung im Cod. B III 22 der Universitätsbibliothek Basel. Untersuchung und Textausgabe* (Munich, 1936), study of various medieval theories of the agent intellect. C. H. Haskins, *The Rise of Universities* (New York, 1923; repr. 1940, paperback ed., 1957). R. Klibansky, *The Continuity of the Platonic Tradition during the Middle Ages. Outline of a Corpus Platonicum Medii Aevi* (London, 1939). O. Lottin, *Psychologie et morale aux XIIe et XIIIe siècles,* 6 vols. (Gembloux 1942-60). H. Rashdall, *The Universities of Europe in the Middle Ages,* new ed. by F. M. Powicke and A. B. Emden, 3 vols. (Oxford, 1936). C. Vollert, L. Kendzierski, P. Byrne, *St. Thomas Aquinas, Siger of Brabant, St. Bonaventure, On the Eternity of the World* (Milwaukee, 1964), translations and helpful introductions.

III. GENERAL COLLECTIONS IN ENGLISH TRANSLATION

E. R. Fairweather, *A Scholastic Miscellany: Anselm to Ockham* (Philadelphia, 1956). A. Hyman and J. J. Walsh, *Philosophy in the Middle Ages: Christian, Islamic, and Jewish Traditions* (New York, 1967). J. Katz and R. Weingartner, eds., *Philosophy in the West. Readings in Ancient and Medieval Philosophy,* with new trans. by J. Wellmuth and J. Wilkinson (New York, 1965). R. McKeon, *Selections from Medieval Philosophers,* 2 vols. (New York, 1929-30). H. Shapiro, ed., *Medieval Philosophy. Selected Readings from Augustine to Buridan* (New York, 1964).

IV. SPECIFIC PHILOSOPHERS

St. Augustine

WORKS: The most complete edition is still that of the Benedictines of St. Maur (1679-1700), repr. by J. P. Migne, PL 32-47, but it is gradually being replaced by modern critical editions, especially in two series still incomplete: *Corpus Scriptorum Ecclesiasticorum Latinorum* (Vienna, 1866-) and *Corpus Christianorum, Series Latina* (Turnhout, 1953-). In the latter, many sermons unknown to the Maurists have begun to appear. TRANSLATIONS: *The Works of Aurelius Augustine,* 15 vols., M. Dods, ed. (Edinburgh, 1872-76). *A Select Library of the Nicene and Post-Nicene Fathers of the Christian Church,* ed. P. Schaff, Vols. I-VIII (New York, 1886 ff.). *Ancient Christian Writers,* ed. J. Quasten *et al.* (Westminster, Md., 1946-). *The Fathers of the Church,* ed. R. J. Deferrari *et al.* (Washington, 1947-). *The Library of Christian Classics* (London/Philadelphia) contains: *Augustine: Earlier Writings,* ed. J. H. S. Burleigh, VI (1953); *Augustine: Confessions and Enchiridion,* ed. A. C. Outler, VII (1955); *Augustine: Later Works,* ed. J. Burnaby, VIII (1955). For fuller bibliography cf. E. Nebreda, *Bibliographia Augustiniana* (Rome, 1928). T. Van Bavel, *Répertoire bibliographique de saint Augustin 1950-60* (The Hague, 1963) evaluates thousands of recent works on Augustine. For particular studies of Augustine cf. P. Alfaric, *L'Evolution intellectuelle de saint Augustin* (Paris, 1918), a much-discussed defense of the theory that at the time of his baptism Augustine was more of a Neoplatonist than a Christian; N. H. Baynes, *The Political Ideas of St. Augustine's De Civitate Dei* (London, 1936); G. Bonner, *St. Augustine of Hippo; Life and Controversies* (Philadelphia, 1963), good as guide to his career and literary production; V. J. Bourke, *The Essential Augustine* (New York, 1964) with details on where the various works of Augustine occur in series and which are available in English translations; C. Boyer,*Christianisme et néo-Platonisme dans la formation de saint Augustin* (Paris, 1920, rev. ed. Rome, 1953), important contribution to the discussion concerning the Platonism and Christianity of Augustine; *L'Idée de vérité dans la philosophie de saint Augustin* (Paris, 1921), a rather Thomistic interpretation of Augustine's theory of illumination; E. Gilson, *The Christian Philosophy of St. Augustine* (New York, 1960), one of the finest introductions to Augustine's philosophy; J. Hessen, *Augustins Metaphysik der Erkenntnis* (Leiden, 1960), interesting if not generally accepted interpretation of Augustine's theory of illumination; J. M. Le Blond, *Les conversions de saint Augustin* (Paris, 1950); F. Cayré, *La contemplation augustinienne* (Bruges, 1954), good on Augustine's theology of the spiritual life; P. Courcelle, *Recherches sur les "Confessions" de saint Augustin* (Paris, 1950); J. Guitton, *Le temps et l'éternité chez Plotin et saint Augustin,* 2nd ed. (Paris, 1955); H. I. Marrou, *Saint Augustin et la fin de la culture antique,* 4th ed. (Paris, 1958); F. van der Meer, *Augustine the Bishop* (New York, 1961), detailed study of his later life; J. J. O'Meara, *The Young Augustine* (London, 1954), important account of his development and of events leading up to his conversion; E. Portalié, *Dictionnaire de Théologie Catholique* I.2:2268-2472, tr. R. J. Bastian as *A Guide to the Thought of St. Augustine* (Chicago, 1960), valuable as an introduction.

Boethius.

WORKS: PL 63 and 64, uncritical edition. For particular editions cf. *Anicii Manlii Severini Boethii In Isagogen Porphyrii Commenta,* G. Schepss and S. Brandt (Vienna, 1906); *De Consolatione Philosophiae,* ed. A. Fortescue (London, 1925), another Latin version ed. by G. Weinberger, *Corpus Scriptorum Ecclesiasticorum Latinorum* 67 (Vienna, 1934), another by L. Bieler, *Corpus Christianorum Series Latina* 94 (Turnhout, 1957); English translation and Latin text of the *Consolation* and the *Theological Tractates* in H. F. Stewart, E. K. Rand, *Boethius . . . ,* (Cambridge, Mass., 1918; repr. 1962). STUDIES: H. M. Barret, *Boethius: Some Aspects of His Times and Work* (Cambridge, 1940). H. Brosch, *Der Seinsbegriff bei Boethius* (Innsbruck, 1931). J. Collins, "Progress and Problems in the Reassessment of Boethius," *The Modern Schoolman,* 23 (1945) 1-23, survey of nineteenth- and twentieth-century research on Boethius. C. Fay, "Boethius' Theory of Goodness and Being," *Readings in Ancient and Medieval Philosophy,* ed. J. Collins (Westminster, Md., 1960), 164-72, for a discussion of the *De hebdomadibus.* H. R. Patch, *The Tradition of Boethius. A Study of His Importance in Medieval Culture* (New York, 1935). G. Schrimpf, *Die Axiomenschrift des Boethius (De Hebdomadibus) als philosophisches Lehrbuch des Mittelalters* (Leiden, 1966), an interesting analysis of the *De hebdomadibus* and a study of later medieval commentaries on it.

Fridugis

WORKS: The text of *De nihilo et tenebris* found in PL 105: 751-56 is defective. A critical edition by E. Dümmler can be found in *Monumenta Germaniae Historica, Epistolae Karolini Aevi,* t. II (Berlin, 1895), 552-55. J. A. Endres, "Fredegisus und Candidus," in *Philosophisches Jahrbuch,* 19 (1906) 439-50, contains some biographical background. His philosophical views are inferred largely from a letter of Agobard, Archbishop of Lyons, *Contra objectiones Fredegisi* in PL 104: 159-74 and *Monumenta Germaniae Historica, Epistolae Karolini Aevi,* t. III (Berlin, 1898) 210-21.

John Scotus Eriugena

WORKS: PL 122. The missing part of the commentary on Pseudo-Dionysius' *De caelesti hierarchia* has been edited by H. F. Dondaine, AHDL 25-26 (1950-51), 245-302. Also cf. C. E. Lutz, *Johannis Scotti Annotationes in Marcianum* (Cambridge, Mass., 1939). STUDIES: H. Bett, *Johannes Scotus Erigena: A Study in Mediaeval Philosophy* (Cambridge, 1925). M. Cappuyns, *Jean Scot Erigène. Sa vie, son oeuvre, sa pensée* (Louvain/Paris, 1933), indispensable. M. Dal Pra, *Scoto Eriugena ed il neoplatonismo medievale* (Milan, 1941).

St. Peter Damian

WORKS: PL 144-45. *S. Pier Damiani: De divina omnipotentia e altri opuscoli,* ed. P. Brezzi, B. Nardi (Florence, 1943), containing *De divina omnipotentia, De sancta simplicitate scientiae inflanti anteponenda, De perfectione monachorum, De vera felicitate ac sapientia.* For translations, cf. *St. Peter Damian: Selected Writings on the Spiritual Life,* tr. P. McNulty (London, 1959). STUDIES: O. J. Blum, *St. Peter Damian: His Teaching on the Spiritual Life* (Washington, 1947). F. Dressler, *Petrus Damiani Leben und Werk* (Rome, 1954). J. Gonsette, *Pierre Damien et la culture profane* (Louvain, 1956). J. Leclercq, *Saint Pierre Damien: ermite et homme d'église* (Rome, 1960).

St. Anselm

WORKS: *S. Anselmi Cantuariensis Archiepiscopi Opera Omnia,* F. S. Schmitt, ed., 6 vols. (Edinburgh, 1946-61), critical ed. The Gabriel Gerberon ed. (Paris, 1675) repr. in PL 158-59 is generally reliable. English translations: *Saint Anselm: Basic Writings (Proslogium, Monologium, Gaunilon's: On Behalf of the Fool, Cur Deus Homo)* tr. S. W. Deane, intro. C. Hartshorne, 2nd ed. (La Salle, Ill., 1962); tr. of *Proslogion* and *Why God Became Man* in E. Fairweather, *A Scholastic Miscellany: Anselm to Ockham* (London/Philadelphia, 1956); *St. Anselm's 'Proslogion,' With 'A Reply on Behalf of the Fool' by Gaunilo and 'The Author's Reply to Gaunilo,'* tr. with intro. and commentary by M. J. Charlesworth (Oxford, 1965); *Truth, Freedom, and Evil: Three Philosophical Dialogues by Anselm of Canterbury,* ed. and tr. J. Hopkins and H. Richardson (New York, 1967). STUDIES: R. W. Church, *Saint Anselm* (London, 1870). A. Daniels, "Quellenbeiträge und Untersuchungen zur Geschichte der Gottesbeweise im dreizehnten Jahrundert mit besonderer Berücktsichtigung des Arguments im Proslogion des hl. Anselm," *Beiträge,* 8 (Münster, 1909), on the reaction of medieval thinkers to Anselm's ontological argument. C. Hartshorne, *Anselm's Discovery: A Re-examination of the Ontological Proof for God's Existence* (La Salle, Ill., 1965). Desmond P. Henry, *The De Grammatico of St. Anselm: The Theory of Paronymy* (Notre Dame, 1964), cf. pp. 23-78 for text and translation of the *De Grammatico; The Logic of Saint Anselm* (Oxford, 1967). J. McIntyre, *St. Anselm and His Critics: A Re-interpretation of the Cur Deus Homo* (Edinburgh, 1954). A. Plantinga, ed., *The Ontological Argument from St. Anselm to Contemporary Philosophers,* intro. R. Taylor (New York, 1965). R. W. Southern, *Saint Anselm and His Biographer* (Cambridge, 1963).

Honorius of Autun

WORKS: *Opera Omnia,* PL 172. The *Philosophia Mundi* (PL 172:39-102) belongs to William of Conches; Honorius' *Cognitio vitae* is among the works of Augustine (PL 40:1003-32). STUDIES: E. Amann, "Honorius Augustodunensis," *Dictionnaire de Théologie Catholique* 7.1:139-158. J. A. Endres, *Honorius Augustodunensis* (Kempten/München, 1906). E. M. Sanford, "Honorius, *Presbyter* and *Scholasticus,*" *Speculum,* 23 (1948) 397-425.

Peter Abelard

WORKS: PL 178 is indispensable but should be supplemented and corrected with help of later editions. *Ouvrages inédits d'Abélard,* ed. V. Cousin (Paris, 1836). *Petri Abaelardi Opera,* ed. V. Cousin *et al.,* 2 vols. (Paris,

1849, 1859). *Peter Abaelards philosophische Schriften,* ed. B. Geyer in *Beiträge* 21, nos. 1-4 (Münster, 1919-33), including *Logica "Ingredientibus"* (commentaries on Porphyry's *Isagoge* and Aristotle's *Categories* and *De Interpretatione*) and *Logica "Nostrorum petitioni sociorum"* (second commentary on Porphyry). *Peter Abaelards Theologia "Summi Boni,"* ed. H. Ostlender in *Beiträge,* 35, nos. 2-3 (1939), tr. J. R. McCallum as *Abailard's Christian Theology* (London, 1948). *Petrus Abaelardus, Dialectica,* ed. L. M. De Rijk (Assen, 1956). *Pietro Abelardo Scritti Filosofici,* ed. M. Dal Pra (Rome/Milan, 1954). TRANSLATIONS AND STUDIES: E. Gilson, *Héloïse and Abélard* (Chicago, 1951). J. R. McCallum, *Abailard's Ethics,* tr. of the *Scito Teipsum* and intro. by trans. (Oxford, 1935). J. T. Muckle, *The Story of Abelard's Adversities, A Translation with Notes of the Historia Calamitatum* (Toronto, 1954). J. G. Sikes, *Peter Abailard* (Cambridge, 1932), life.

Peter Lombard

WORKS: *Petri Lombardi Libri IV Sententiarium,* 2 vols., 2nd ed. (Quaracchi, 1916), new ed. in preparation. STUDIES: P. Delhaye, *Pierre Lombard, sa vie, ses oeuvres, sa morale* (Paris, 1961). J. de Ghellinck, "Pierre Lombard," *Dictionnaire de Théologie Catholique* 12.2:1941-2019. *Miscellanea Lombardiana* (Novara, 1957), many interesting articles. The Review *Pier Lombardo* (Novara, founded 1953 but now defunct), many interesting articles.

Richard of St. Victor

WORKS: *Opera Omnia,* PL 196. *Liber exceptionum* PL 177:193-284, also ed. J. Chatillon (Paris, 1958). *Sermones centum,* PL 177:901-1210, attributed together with *Liber exceptionum* to Hugh of St. Victor in PL. *De Trinitate,* ed. J. Ribaillier (Paris, 1958), ed. and Fr. tr. G. Salet (Paris, 1959). STUDIES: G. Dumeige, *Richard de Saint-Victor et l'idée Chrétienne de l'amour* (Paris, 1952), cf. bibliography 171-85. A. M. Ethier, *Le "De Trinitate" de Richard de Saint-Victor* (Paris, 1939). C. Ottaviano, *Riccardo di S. Vittore, la vita, le opere, il pensiero* (Rome, 1933).

Avicenna

WORKS: *Avicennae perhypatetici philosophi ac medicorum facile primi opera in lucem redacta . . . ,* (Venice, 1508; repr. Frankfurt am Main, 1961), for medieval Latin version of those parts of the *Shifā'* available in Latin translation for thirteenth century. *Die Metaphysik Avicennas,* tr. M. Horten (Halle, 1907), German tr. of the *Metaphysics* of the *Shifā'*. A. J. Arberry, *Avicenna on Theology* (London, 1951), pp. 9-24 for translation of his autobiography as dictated to and completed by his pupil and secretary Juzjānī. *La Métaphysique du Shifā',* tr. G. C. Anawati (Montreal, 1952), Fr. tr. of the *Metaphysics* of the *Shifā'*. *Avicenna's Psychology,* tr. of *Kitāb al-najāt,* Bk. II, chap. 6, F. Rahman (London, 1952). GENERAL BIBLIOGRAPHIES: G. C. Anawati, *Essai de bibliographie avicennienne* (Cairo, 1950), section 4 for works about Avicenna in languages other than Arabic. S. Naficy, *Bibliographie des principaux travaux euro-*

péens sur Avicenne (Teheran, 1953). STUDIES: S. M. Afnan, *Avicenna, His Life and Works* (London, 1958). L. Gardet, *La pensée religieuse d'Avicenne (Ibn Sīnā)* (Paris, 1951), important. A. M. Goichon, *La distinction de l'essence et de l'existence d'après Ibn Sīnā (Avicenne)* (Paris, 1937) with helpful bibliography, 504-20; *La philosophie d'Avicenne et son influence en Europe médiévale*, 2nd ed. (Paris, 1951). S. H. Nasr, *An Introduction to Islamic Cosmological Doctrines* (Cambridge, Mass., 1964), 175-274 on Avicenna.

Averroës

WORKS: *Aristotelis opera cum Averrois commentariis* (Venice, 1562-1574; repr. Frankfurt am Main, 1962), Latin translations of Aristotle with commentaries of Averroës. A new edition is being prepared by the Mediaeval Academy of America. TRANSLATIONS: *Tahāfut al-Tahāfut (The Incoherence of the Incoherence)*, tr. S. van den Bergh, 2 vols. (London, 1954). *Averroës On the Harmony of Religion and Philosophy*, tr. G. F. Hourani (London, 1961). *Averroës' Commentary on Plato's Republic*, ed. and tr. E. I. J. Rosenthal (Cambridge, 1966). STUDIES: L. Gauthier, *Ibn Rochd (Averroès)* (Paris, 1948), good general survey of his life, works, thought. S. Munk, *Mélanges de philosophie juive et arabe* (Paris, 1859; repr. 1955) cf. 418-58 for Averroës, dated but still valuable. G. Quadri, *La Philosophie arabe dans l'Europe médiévale* (Paris, 1960), 198-340 for Averroës. E. Renan, *Averroès et l'averroïsme. Essai historique*, 4th ed. (Paris, 1882).

Moses Maimonides

WORKS: *The Guide of the Perplexed*, tr., intro., notes by S. Pines (Chicago, 1963) with introductory essay by L. Strauss, best English translation. For an important series of articles cf. H. A. Wolfson, "Maimonides and Halevi," *The Jewish Quarterly Review*, N.S., 2 (1911-12), 297-337; "Maimonides on the Internal Senses," *Ibid.*, 25 (1934-35), 441-67; "Note on Maimonides' Classification of the Sciences," *Ibid.*, 26 (1935-36), 369-77; "Hallevi and Maimonides on Design, Chance, and Necessity," *Proceedings of the American Academy for Jewish Research* 11 (1941), 105-63; "The Platonic, Aristotelian, and Stoic Theories of Creation in Hallevi and Maimonides," in I. Epstein, E. Levine, C. Roth, eds., *Essays in Honor of the Rev. Dr. J. H. Hertz* (London, 1942), 427-42; "Maimonides on Negative Attributes," in A. Marx and others, eds., *Louis Ginzberg Jubilee Volume* (New York, 1945), 411-46. Z. Diesendruck, "Die Teleologie bei Maimonides," *Hebrew Union College Annual*, 5 (1928), 415-534.

Odo Rigaud

TRANSLATION: *The Register of Eudes of Rouen*, tr. S. M. Brown, ed., with intro., notes, and appendix by J. F. O'Sullivan (New York and London, 1964). STUDIES: P. Andrieu-Guitrancourt, *L'Archevêque Eudes Rigaud et la vie de l'Eglise au XIIIe siècle, d'après le "Regestrum Visitationum"* (Paris, 1938). K. F. Lynch, "The Alleged Fourth Book on the Sentences of Odo Rigaud and Related Documents," *Franciscan Studies*, 9 (1949), 87-145.

R. Ménindès, "Eudes Rigaud, Frère Mineur," *Revue d'Histoire Franciscaine,* 8 (1931), 157-178.

Roger Bacon

WORKS: *Fr. Rogeri Bacon Opera Quaedam Hactenus Inedita,* J. S. Brewer, ed. (London, 1859) contains *Opus Tertium, Opus Minus, Compendium Studii Philosophiae,* and *Epistola de secretis operibus artis et naturae, et de nullitate magiae.* Cf. P. Duhem, *Un fragment inédit de l'Opus tertium de R. Bacon* (Quaracchi, 1909) and A. G. Little, *Part of the Opus Tertium of Roger Bacon* (Aberdeen, 1912) for supplements to the *Opus Tertium.* Cf. also *Opus Maius,* ed. by J. H. Bridges, 3 vols. (Oxford, 1897-1900; repr. Frankfurt am Main, 1964) and F. Delorme and E. Massa, *Rogeri Baconis Moralis Philosophia* (Zurich, 1953) for complete text of Part VII, which is incomplete in Bridges. For other works cf. R. Steele (with individual volumes by F. M. Delorme, A. G. Little, and E. Withington), *Opera hactenus inedita Fratris Rogeri Baconis,* 16 fascicles (Oxford, 1905-40); H. Rashdall, *Fratris Rogeri Bacon Compendium Studii Theologiae* (Aberdeen, 1911). TRANSLATIONS: T. L. Davis, *Roger Bacon's Letter Concerning the Marvelous Power of Art and Nature and Concerning the Nullity of Magic* (Easton, 1923). *The Opus Majus of Roger Bacon,* tr. R. B. Burke, 2 vols. (Philadelphia, 1928; repr. New York, 1962). STUDIES: A. C. Crombie, *Robert Grosseteste and the Origins of Experimental Science 1100-1700* (Oxford, 1953), 139-62. T. Crowley, *Roger Bacon, the Problem of the Soul in His Philosophical Commentaries* (Louvain and Dublin, 1950), good on hylemorphism. S. C. Easton, *Roger Bacon and His Search for a Universal Science* (New York, 1952), with extensive bibliography. A. G. Little, ed., *Roger Bacon Essays Contributed by Various Writers on the Occasion of the Commemoration of the Seventh Centenary of His Birth* (Oxford, 1914), discussion of his life and works in the Introduction.

St. Bonaventure

WORKS: *S. Bonaventurae Opera Omnia,* 10 vols. (Quaracchi, 1882-1902). Second redaction of *Collationes in Hexaëmeron,* ed. F. Delorme (Quaracchi, 1934). TRANSLATIONS: *Saint Bonaventure's De Reductione Artium ad Theologiam,* commentary, intro., and tr. E. T. Healy (St. Bonaventure, N. Y., 1935). *Saint Bonaventure's Itinerarium mentis in Deum. With an Introduction, Translation and Commentary* by P. Boehner (St. Bonaventure, N. Y. 1956), the best among many translations of this work. *The Works of Bonaventure,* tr. J. de Vinck (Paterson, N. J., 1960-). GENERAL BIBLIOGRAPHIES: E. Gilson, *History of Christian Philosophy . . . ,* 685-86. Ueberweg-Geyer, *Grundriss der Geschichte der Philosophie, II: Die Patristische und Scholastische Philosophie,* 11th ed. repr. (Basel, 1961), 735-38. *Bibliographia Franciscana* XI- (Rome, 1965-) for studies after 1953. STUDIES: E. Bettoni, *St. Bonaventure* (Notre Dame, 1964). J. G. Bougerol, *Introduction to the Works of Bonaventure* (Patterson, 1964), quite helpful. B. A. Gendreau, "The Quest for Certainty in St. Bonaventure," *Franciscan Studies,* 21 (1961), 104-227. E. Gilson, *La philosophie de saint Bonaventure* (Paris, 1924; 2nd ed. Paris, 1943; English tr. of 1st ed., London, 1938), highly important, but should be reassessed in light of more recent studies, such as those by Bougerol, Gendreau, Robert, Roch. R. P. Prentice, *The Psychology of Love According to St. Bonaventure* (St. Bonaventure, N. Y. 1951), a comparison of Bonaventure and M. Scheler. P. Robert, "St. Bonaventure, Defender of Christian Wisdom," *Franciscan Studies,* N.S. 3 (1943), 159-79; "Le problème de la philosophie bonaventurienne," *Laval théologique et philosophique,* 6 (1950), 145-63, *ibid.* 7 (1951), 9-58. R. J. Roch, "The Philosophy of St. Bonaventure. A Controversy," *Franciscan Studies,* 19 (1959), 209-26. A. Schaefer, "The Position and Function of Man in the Created World According to St. Bonaventure," *Franciscan Studies,* 21 (1960), 261-316 and 22 (1961), 233-82.

St. Thomas Aquinas

WORKS: *Opera Omnia,* 25 vols. (Parma, 1852-73; repr. New York, 1948-50), noncritical but almost complete. *Opera Omnia,* 34 vols. (Paris, 1871-80), noncritical but almost complete. Leonine edition, *S. Thomae Aquinatis, Opera Omnia* (Rome, 1882-). For a complete list of Thomas' works with their editions and chronology, cf. I. T. Eschmann, "A Catalogue of St. Thomas's Works: Bibliographical Notes," in E. Gilson, *The Christian Philosophy of St. Thomas Aquinas* (New York, 1956), 381-439. No attempt will be made here to list all the works that have been published individually. For an accessible list of the many available in English translation cf. V. J. Bourke, "St. Thomas Aquinas," *The Encyclopedia of Philosophy,* 8 (New York, 1967), 114-16. GENERAL BIBLIOGRAPHIES: V. J. Bourke, *Thomistic Bibliography,* 1920-1940 (St. Louis, 1945). P. Mandonnet and J. Destrez, *Bibliographie thomiste* (Le Saulchoir, 1921) rev. ed. M. D. Chenu (Paris, 1960). P. Wyser, *Thomas von Aquin* and *Der Thomismus,* fascicles 13-14 and 15-16 of *Bibliographische Einführungen in das Studium der Philosophie* (Bern, 1950-51). STUDIES: V. J. Bourke, *Aquinas' Search for Wisdom* (Milwaukee, 1965), excellent. M. D. Chenu, *Toward Understanding St. Thomas* (Chicago, 1964), masterly introduction to his works. F. C. Copleston, *Aquinas* (Baltimore, 1955). C. Fabro, *La nozione metafisica di partecipazione secondo S. Tommaso d'Aquino,* 2nd ed. (Turin, 1950); *Participation et causalité selon S. Thomas d'Aquin* (Louvain, 1961), major contributions to a growing recognition of importance of participation in Thomas' metaphysics. J. de Finance, *Etre et agir dans la philosophie de saint Thomas,* 2nd ed. (Rome, 1960). R. Garrigou-Lagrange, *Reality: A Synthesis of Thomistic Thought* (St. Louis, 1950). L. B. Geiger, *La participation dans la philosophie de saint Thomas* (Paris, 1942), another major contribution to rediscovery of role of participation in Aquinas. E. Gilson, *The Christian Philosophy of St. Thomas Aquinas* (New York, 1956). M. Grabmann, *Die Werke des hl. Thomas von Aquin,* 3rd ed. (Münster, 1949), classic study of chronology and authenticity of works of Aquinas. R. J. Henle, *St. Thomas and Platonism* (The Hague, 1956). G. P. Klubertanz, *St. Thomas Aquinas on Analogy* (Chicago, 1960). T. Litt, *Les corps célestes dans l'univers de saint Thomas d'Aquin* (Louvain, 1963), shows influence of medieval "physical" theory on certain metaphysical positions in Aquinas. J. Maritain, *Art and Scholasticism* (London, 1930). B. Montagnes, *La doctrine de l'analogie de l'être d'après saint Thomas d'Aquin* (Louvain, 1963), one of the finest treatments of analogy. A. Walz, *Saint Thomas d'Aquin,* French adaptation by P. Novarina (Louvain, 1962), excellent biography.

Siger of Brabant

WORKS: Of the works generally admitted to be authentic, the following have been edited and published: *Quaestiones logicales,* ed. P. Mandonnet, *Siger de Brabant et l'averroïsme latin au XIIIe siècle,* 2nd ed., 2 vols. (Louvain, 1911-1908) II, 55-61. *Quaestio utrum haec sit vera: homo est animal, nullo homine existente, ibid.,* 65-70. *Impossibilia, ibid.,* 73-94. *Quaestiones naturales, ibid.,* 97-107. *Tractatus de anima intellectiva, ibid.,* 145-71. *Questiones morales* and another set of *Questiones naturales,* both ed. F. Stegmüller, "Neugefundene Quaestionen des Siger von Brabant," RTAM, 3 (1931), 172-82. *Quaestio de aeternitate mundi,* ed. W. J. Dwyer in *L'Opuscule de Siger de Brabant "De aeternitate mundi"* (Louvain, 1937). *Siger de Brabant. Questions sur la Métaphysique,* ed. C. A. Graiff (Louvain, 1948). *De necessitate et contingentia causarum,* ed. J. J. Duin, *La doctrine de la providence dans les écrits de Siger de Brabant* (Louvain, 1954), 14-50. TRANSLATIONS: *On the Necessity and Contingency of Causes,* tr. by J. P. Mullally and W. Quinn in H. Shapiro, *Medieval Philosophy* (New York, 1964), 414-38. *Question on the Eternity of the World (De Aeternitate Mundi),* tr. L. H. Kendzierski in *St. Thomas Aquinas, Siger of Brabant, St. Bonaventure On the Eternity of the World* (Milwaukee, 1964), 84-95. STUDIES: In addition to the important studies by Mandonnet and Duin cited above, cf. L. Kendzierski, "Eternal Matter and Form in Siger of Brabant," *The Modern Schoolman,* 32 (1955), 223-41; A. Maurer, "*Esse* and *Essentia* in the Metaphysics of Siger of Brabant," *Mediaeval Studies,* 8 (1946), 68-86; F. Van Steenberghen, *Les oeuvres et la doctrine de Siger de Brabant* (Brussels, 1938); *Siger de Brabant d'après ses oeuvres inédites,* 2 vols. (Louvain, 1931-42); *Aristotle in the West* (Louvain, 1955), chaps. 7, 8; "Nouvelles recherches sur Siger de Brabant et son école," *Revue Philosophique de Louvain,* 54 (1956), 130-47; for his most recent thought on Siger cf. *La philosophie au XIIIe siècle* (Louvain, 1966), 357-456.

Boetius of Dacia

WORKS: M. Grabmann, "Die Opuscula De Summo Bono sive De Vita Philosophi und De Sompniis des Boetius von Dacien," AHDL 6 (1931), 287-317, repr. with some additions to the introduction in *Mittelalterliches Geistesleben,* 2 (1936), 200-24. G. Sajó *Un traité récemment découvert de Boèce de Dacie De mundi aeternitate. Texte inédit avec une introduction critique, avec en appendice un texte inédit de Siger de Brabant Super VI° Metaphysicae* (Budapest, 1954). Cf. in particular his *Introduction critique,* 13-37, 49-79. *Boetii de Dacia. Tractatus de aeternitate mundi,* ed. G. Sajó (Berlin, 1964), critical text. STUDIES: R. A. Gauthier, *Bulletin Thomiste,* 9 (1954-56), 926-32. E. Gilson, "Boèce de Dacie et la double vérité," AHDL 21 (1955), 81-99. M. Grabmann, *Neu aufgefundene Werke des Siger von Brabant und Boetius von Dacien* (Munich, 1924). S. S. Jensen, "On the National Origins of the Philosopher Boetius de Dacia," *Classica et Mediaevalia,* 24 (1963), 232-41. A. Maurer, "Boetius of Dacia and the Double Truth," *Mediaeval Studies,* 17 (1955), 233-39. G. Sajó, "Boetius de Dacia und seine philosophische Bedeutung," *Miscellanea Mediaevalia,* 2 (1963), 454-63, good on recent research on Boetius. F. Sassen, "Boethius van Dacie en de theorie van de dubbele waarheid," *Studia Catholica,* 30 (1955), 262-73. F. Van Steenberghen, *La philosophie au XIII*[e] *siècle* (Louvain, 1966), 402-12. P. Wilpert, "Boethius von Dacien—Die Autonomie des Philosophen," *Miscellanea Mediaevalia,* 3 (1964), 135-52.

Henry of Ghent

WORKS: *Quodlibeta,* 2 vols. (Paris, 1518; repr. Louvain, 1961). *Summa quaestionum ordinariarum,* 2 vols. (Paris, 1520; repr. St. Bonaventure, N. Y., 1953). STUDIES: *J. Gómez Caffarena, Ser participado y ser subsistente en la metafisica de Enrique de Gante* (Rome, 1958). J. Paulus, *Henri de Gand. Essai sur les tendances de sa métaphysique* (Paris, 1938), the classic on Henry.

John Duns Scotus

WORKS: *Opera Omnia,* L. Wadding ed., 12 vols. (Lyons, 1639), repr. with Vivès ed., 26 vols. (Paris, 1891-95), most of authentic and some spurious works contained therein; critical ed. C. Balić (Vatican City, 1950-). TRANSLATIONS: *The De Primo Principio of John Duns Scotus,* ed. and tr. E. Roche (St. Bonaventure, N. Y., 1949). Also ed. and tr. A. B. Wolter, *John Duns Scotus: A Treatise on God as First Principle* (Chicago, 1966). Also by Wolter, *Duns Scotus: Philosophical writings* (Edinburgh and London, 1962) with Latin text and English trans., paperback ed. (Library of Liberal Arts, 1964) without Latin text. GENERAL BIBLIOGRAPHIES: O. Schäfer, *Bibliographia de vita, operibus et doctrina Johannis Duns Scoti doctoris subtilis ac mariani, saec. XIX-XX* (Rome, 1955), best bibliography to date. Cf. also *Johannes Duns Scotus* in *Bibliographische Einführungen in das Studium der Philosophie,* 22 (Bern, 1953); *Bibliographia Franciscana* XI- (1965-), for works appearing since 1954. STUDIES: In addition to the treatments in the histories of philosophy by Copleston, Böhner-Gilson, Maurer, and Weinberg, cf. S. Day, *Intuitive Cognition: A Key to the Significance of the Later Scholastics* (St. Bonaventure, N. Y., 1947), theory of knowledge; R. Effler, *John Duns Scotus and the Principle "Omne Quod Movetur ab Alio Movetur"* (St. Bonaventure, N. Y., 1962), theory of motion and the will; E. Gilson, *Jean Duns Scot. Introduction à ses positions fondamentales* (Paris, 1952); M. J. Grajewski, *The Formal Distinction of Duns Scotus* (Washington, 1944); W. Hoeres, *Der Wille als reine Vollkommenheit nach Duns Scotus* (Munich, 1962); J. K. Ryan, B. M. Bonansea, eds., *John Duns Scotus, 1265-1965* in *Studies in Philosophy and the History of Philosophy* III, (Washington, 1965); P. Vier, *Evidence and its Function According to John Duns Scotus* (St. Bonaventure, N. Y., 1951), theory of knowledge; A. B. Wolter, *The Transcendentals and their Function in the Metaphysics of Duns Scotus* (St. Bonaventure, N. Y., 1946).

William Ockham

WORKS: *Quodlibeta Septem* (Paris, 1487; Strasbourg, 1491; repr. Louvain, 1962). *Summa Logicae* (Paris, 1488; Bologna, 1498; Venice, 1508, 1522, 1591; Oxford, 1665), mod. ed. P. Boehner, *Pars Prima* and *Pars IIa et Tertiae Prima* (St. Bonaventure, N. Y., 1951-54), his main logical work. *Super IV Libros Sententiarum . . . Quaestiones* (Lyons, 1495), readily available in *Opera plurima* (Lyons, 1494-96; repr. 1962), vols. 3 and 4; critical ed. G. Gál, S. Brown, *et alii* (St. Bonaventure, N. Y., 1967-). *Summulae in Libros Physicorum* (or *Philosophia Naturalis*) (Venice, 1506; Rome, 1637; repub. London, 1963). *Guillelmi de Ockham Opera Politica,* vol. 1, J. G. Sikes, ed. (Manchester, 1940) vols. 2, 3, H. S. Offler, ed. (Manchester, 1963, 1956). *Tractatus de Praedestinatione et de Praescientia Dei et de Futuris Contingentibus,* ed. P. Boehner (St. Bonaventure, N. Y., 1945). *Ockham: Philosophical Writings,* ed. and tr. P. Boehner (Edinburgh, 1957), with Latin text and English translation, paperback ed. without Latin text (Library of Liberal Arts, 1964). *Expositio in Librum Porphyrii De Praedicabilibus,* ed. E. A. Moody (St. Bonaventure, N. Y., 1965). STUDIES: L. Baudry, *Guillaume d'Occam I: L'Homme et les oeuvres* (Paris, 1950), important. P. Boehner, *Collected Articles on Ockham,* ed. E. M. Buytaert (St. Bonaventure, N. Y., 1958). E. A. Moody, *The Logic of William of Ockham* (New York, 1935). H. Shapiro, *Motion, Time, and Place According to William Ockham* (St. Bonaventure, N. Y., 1957). D. Webering, *Theory of Demonstration According to William Ockham* (St. Bonaventure, N. Y., 1953).

Nicholas of Cusa

WORKS: *Opera* (Paris, 1514). *Opera* (Basel, 1565). *Nicolai de Cusa Opera Omnia,* 14 vols. (Leipzig, 1932-). *De Pace Fidei,* ed. R. Klibansky and H. Bascour (London, 1956). TRANSLATIONS: *Of Learned Ignorance,* tr. G. Heron (London, 1954). *Unity and Reform: Selected Writings of Nicholas De Cusa,* ed. J. P. Dolan (Notre Dame, 1962). STUDIES: H. Bett, *Nicholas of Cusa* (London, 1932). M. P. de Gandillac, *La philosophie de Nicholas de Cues* (Paris, 1941). J. Koch, *Nikolaus von Cues und seine Umwelt* (Heidelberg, 1948). P. E. Sigmund, *Nicholas of Cusa and Medieval Political Thought* (Cambridge, Mass., 1963). K. H. Volkmann-Schluck, *Nicolaus Cusanus* (Frankfurt am Main, 1957).

Cf. *The Encyclopedia of Philosophy,* 8 vols. (New York, 1967) and the *New Catholic Encyclopedia,* 15 vols. (New York, 1967) for articles on most of the individual thinkers whose selections appear in this volume.

INDEX